# OUR QUEEN

Robert Hardman is one of Britain's best-known observers of the monarchy. He has covered royal life for more than twenty years, both as a Fleet Street royal correspondent and as the writer of several internationally acclaimed royal documentaries. He interviewed the Prince of Wales for his famous BBC One birthday film *Charles at 60*, and toured Windsor with Prince Philip for the much-loved BBC One series, *The Queen's Castle*. He is the writer of both the series and the book, *Monarchy: The Royal Family At Work*, which has been screened worldwide. He writes for the *Daily Mail*.

## Praise for OUR QUEEN

'A superb portrait of the Queen as she enters her Diamond Jubilee year.'
Andrew Roberts, *Sunday Telegraph* (Books of the Year)

'Written in an informed and stylish way, *Our Queen* is easily the best royal book in years.'
Richard Kay, *Daily Mail* (Books of the Year)

'Hardman knows his subject intimately and has used enviable access to produce a richly detailed and thoughtful account.'
*Daily Telegraph*

700039444337

'Simply magnificent. This gripping, fascinating and authoritative tour de force – covering the Queen herself, the power and the celebrity of Britain's royalty with equal panache – gleams with a unique combination of insider anecdotes, deep knowledge, personal experience and superb storytelling by Britain's outstanding royal observer.'
Simon Sebag Montefiore, author of *Jerusalem*


'This book abounds with insights. Yet its real value lies in the sheer quality of the writing and the consistently sound judgement that Hardman brings in teasing out the true character of one of the world's most exemplary human beings.'
*Mail on Sunday*


'Hardman is the best chronicler of the monarchy writing in the British press today, superbly well informed, witty and wise.'
William Shawcross, *Evening Standard*


'Hardman has been granted interviews of a kind that few others have, and his book will be a valuable quarry for anyone writing about the monarchy.'
*Literary Review*

'*Our Queen* depicts the quiet revolution that has occured at the Palace. *Our Queen* is becoming the new management manual in Downing Street and Whitehall. Hardman's access has been remarkable. He explains how cleaners now use the monarch's swimming pool while she entertains prime ministers next door, and the Duke of Edinburgh shares the same gravy as the chauffeur.'
Alice Thomson, *The Times*

'With wit and panache, Hardman unveils a prismatic portrait of a thoroughly moden monarch.'
*Publishers Weekly*

'Hardman's book abounds in picturesque detail about what goes on behind the scenes in royal establishments.'
Philip Ziegler, *Spectator*

'Robert Hardman offers a convincing tour of the British monarchy as an institution, apeing the vantage point of the fly-on-the-wall documentary.'
*Economist*

Also available by Robert Hardman

*Monarchy: The Royal Family at Work* (Ebury)

# OUR QUEEN

## ROBERT HARDMAN

arrow books

Published by Arrow Books 2012

2 4 6 8 10 9 7 5 3

Copyright © Robert Hardman 2011

Robert Hardman has asserted his right under the Copyright, Designs
and Patents Act 1988 to be identified as the author of this work

This book is a work of non-fiction.

This book is sold subject to the condition that it shall not,
by way of trade or otherwise, be lent, resold, hired out,
or otherwise circulated without the publisher's prior
consent in any form of binding or cover other than that
in which it is published and without a similar condition,
including this condition, being imposed on the
subsequent purchaser

First published in Great Britain in 2011 by Hutchinson

Arrow Books
Random House, 20 Vauxhall Bridge Road,
London SW1V 2SA

www.rbooks.co.uk

Addresses for companies within The Random House Group Limited can be found at:
www.randomhouse.co.uk/offices.htm

The Random House Group Limited Reg. No. 954009

A CIP catalogue record for this book
is available from the British Library

ISBN 9780099551157

The Random House Group Limited supports The Forest Stewardship Council (FSC®),
the leading international forest certification organisation. Our books carrying the FSC label
are printed on FSC® certified paper. FSC is the only forest certification scheme endorsed
by the leading environmental organisations, including Greenpeace. Our paper procurement
policy can be at www.randomhouse.co.uk/environment

Typeset in Ehrhardt MT by Palimpsest Book Production Limited, Falkirk, Stirlingshire

Printed and bound by CPI Group (UK) Ltd, Croydon, CR0 4YY

# FOR MY WIFE, DIANA

# Acknowledgements

In producing a comprehensive portrait of the most enduring international public figure of the last sixty years, it has been essential to have a good view. From the outset, I have enjoyed privileged access not only to events, royal engagements and some of the daily routines of Palace life but also to every level of every department of the Royal Household. For that, I am most grateful to Her Majesty The Queen.

I would particularly like to thank His Royal Highness The Duke of Cambridge for granting me his first author's interview and His Royal Highness The Duke of York for his thoughts and insights.

Despite this extraordinary opportunity, this is not an authorised publication. I have had an entirely free hand with my research. I have asked my own questions, made my own observations and drawn my own conclusions. But I am particularly indebted to Samantha Cohen, Assistant Private Secretary to The Queen, and Ailsa Anderson, her successor as Press Secretary, for their help and forbearance in response to my persistent requests for interviews and access during the last two years. This book would be much thinner without them, if indeed it had been written at all.

All the departments of the Royal Household and their staff have been generous with their time. My thanks go to the Earl Peel, Sir Christopher Geidt, Edward Young, Doug King, Sir Alan Reid, Air Vice-Marshal Sir David Walker, Lieutenant Colonel Andrew Ford and Jonathan Marsden and their respective teams at Buckingham Palace, along with Sir Michael Peat and his staff at Clarence House.

Those who work for the Sovereign are, understandably, wary of discussing their jobs and experiences with strangers bearing notebooks. Some of those to whom I have spoken had never previously given any sort of interview about their work. Some had been grilled by me before but were good enough to talk to me all over again. They are all named in these pages and I am very grateful to them all.

Arranging all this has been a substantial logistical undertaking. My thanks go to Dr Ed Perkins, Colette Saunders, David Pogson, Meryl Keeling, Jen Stebbing, Zaki Cooper and Marnie Gaffney at Buckingham

Palace; to Dame Anne Griffiths in the Duke of Edinburgh's Office; to Paddy Harverson and Patrick Harrison at Clarence House; to Miguel Head and Nick Loughran at St James's Palace; to Frances Dunkels and Emma Shaw at the Royal Collection; to Dr Lucy Worsley at Historic Royal Palaces; to Marcus O'Lone and Helen Walch at the Sandringham Estate.

I am also very grateful to so many former members of the Royal Household who have helped me in so many ways, in some cases over many years. They include the Earl of Airlie, Lord Fellowes, Lord Janvrin, Sir William Heseltine, Sir Malcom Ross, Sir Miles Hunt-Davis, Dr Mary Francis, Elizabeth Buchanan, Ron Allison, Charles Anson and Stuart Neil.

No study of any constitutional monarch would be complete without recourse to that monarch's Prime Ministers. I wish to thank David Cameron, Tony Blair and Sir John Major for their insights and their time. The Queen has been served by more than 150 Prime Ministers across all her realms during her reign. I have met several of them during my twenty years of reporting on royalty. But I would like to thank, in particular, John Key, Prime Minister of New Zealand, and Malcolm Fraser, former Prime Minister of Australia, for their time in relation to this book.

I am also indebted to the Foreign Secretary, William Hague, and his predecessors, Jack Straw, Sir Malcolm Rifkind and Lord Hurd for the accumulated wisdom of their many years in the royal orbit, whether in one of the Great Offices of State or other ministerial positions.

Among the Queen's many representatives, I am particularly grateful to Lord Shuttleworth, Chairman of the Association of Lord-Lieutenants, William Tucker, Lord-Lieutenant of Derbyshire and David Briggs, Lord-Lieutenant of Cheshire, along with their respective staff. Overseas, I am grateful to Eric Jenkinson, High Commissioner to Trinidad and Tobago, Dr Noël Guckian, Ambassador to Oman, Dominic Jermey, Ambassador to the United Arab Emirates, Julian King, Ambassador to Ireland, and all their respective teams. The Queen's many roles have taken me in many directions. For their help in studying the Head of the Commonwealth, I thank His Excellency Mohamed Nasheed, President of the Maldives, Kamalesh Sharma, the Commonwealth Secretary-General, and Dr Danny Sriskandarajah, Director of the Royal Commonwealth Society.

My thanks go to Dr Rowan Willams, the Archbishop of Canterbury, and Nigel McCulloch, the Bishop of Manchester and Lord High Almoner, for talking to me about the Supreme Governor of the Church of England.

Men and women of every rank and age from across the Services have helped me to understand that crucial bond which they all share with the Head of the Armed Forces and the Royal Family. It is always a pleasure to talk to them.

There are many people who have helped this book to take shape in all sorts of ways. What they all have in common is that they have seen some merit in my endeavours and have gone out of their way to help. I am grateful to them all. Some prefer to remain anonymous. Others include Alastair Bruce of Crionaich, Edward Llewellyn, Catherine Fall, Ciaran Ward, Arabella Warburton, Vanessa Burgess, Sir Sydney Chapman, Sir Michael Willcocks, Alexander Galloway, William Chapman, James North, Elizabeth Scudder, Sir Antony Jay, Edward Mirzoeff, Marie Papworth, Sir Simon Dawbarn, Wesley Kerr, Peter Wilkinson, Daniel Sleat, Harriet Hewitson, Hugo Hardman, Victoria Zawoda, Sophie Douglas-Bate, Tamsin Bruce-Gardyne, Alice Beck, Lucinda Lambourne, James Bethell, Didy Grahame, Sir Michael and Lady Parker, Lesley Hamilton, John Phillips, Dr Stephen Spurr, Duncan Jeffery, Alan Duncan MP, Kate Hoey MP, Bob Honey, Robin Roberts, Don and Cathryn Kelshall, and James Dolan.

I have been extremely fortunate to draw on the advice, support and expertise of some our most eminent historians and biographers. Simon Sebag Montefiore, Andrew Roberts, William Shawcross and Kenneth Rose have all been kind and wise in equal measure. I am also grateful to Dr Amanda Foreman, Frances Osborne, Dr Jane Connors and Derek Ingram for their help. Wherever I have drawn on the scholarship of others, I hope that the credit is clear and unambiguous. And to my Fleet Street colleagues, to the photographic fraternity and the television crews, I say thank you for your camaraderie along the way.

At Hutchinson, I owe a very great deal to my editor, Paul Sidey, for his unfailing enthusiasm and wisdom, and I also thank Paulette Hearn, Charlotte Bush, Jocasta Hamilton, Philippa Cotton, Emma Mitchell, Eleanor Wheeler and Amelia Harvell. I am also most grateful to Selina Walker at Arrow. From the very start of this project, I have been indebted to my unflappable agent Charles Walker, at United Agents, and to his assistant Katy Jones. A considerable part of this book, of course, owes nothing to my words and everything to the superb photography of my old friend and former Fleet Street colleague Ian Jones. Bravo to him.

These pages have been written in many places and many countries. But I am particularly grateful to my mother-in-law, Marion Cowley, my parents, Richard and Dinah Hardman, and Santa Sebag Montefiore for providing somewhere quiet to concentrate as the deadlines have loomed. No one, though, has been more supportive, despite all the lost weekends and truncated holidays, than my darling wife, Diana. This book is dedicated to her.

# Introduction

*'It's amazing that she didn't crack'*

When the world comes to look back on the early twenty-first century, two events in Britain – just weeks apart – will be lodged in the collective memory. One will be the 2012 London Olympics, a spectacular fortnight of international sporting endeavour. The other will be a celebration of a woman who has become so firmly established on the world stage that, in the words of one Commonwealth leader, she is no longer seen as merely British or, indeed, as merely human. She is the living incarnation of a set of values and a period of history. In Britain, she is Tower Bridge and a red double-decker bus on two legs, not to mention Big Ben, afternoon tea, village fêtes and sheep-flecked hills in the pouring rain. In the wider world, she is the newsreel figure who just has carried on going into digital high definition. More than one hundred nations – that's more than half the countries on earth – did not even exist in their present form when she was crowned. While her presence is taken entirely for granted at home, to millions of people around the planet she represents continuity on a scale bordering on the incomprehensible.

'She's incredible,' says Prince William, Duke of Cambridge, during a poignant and thoughtful first interview on someone he describes as 'my grandmother first – and then she's the Queen'. No one, surely, is better placed to imagine what it must have been like to succeed to the throne, as the Queen did, at twenty-five. Sitting in his office in St James's Palace a few days before his own twenty-ninth birthday, the Prince ponders the enormity of her task: 'Back then, there was a very different attitude to women. Being a young lady at twenty-five – and stepping in to a job which many men thought they could probably do better – it must have been very daunting. And I think there was extra pressure for her to perform.' He remains in awe of the way she managed it: 'You see the pictures of her and she looks so incredibly natural in the role. She's calm, she's poised, she's elegant, she's graceful and she's all the things she needs to be at twenty-five. And you think how loads of twenty-five-year-olds – myself, my brother and lots of people included – didn't have anything like that. And we didn't have that extra pressure put on us at that age. It's amazing that she didn't crack. She just carried on and kept going. And that's the thing about her. You present a challenge in front of her and she'll climb it. And I think that to be doing that for sixty years – it's incredible.'

Only one other monarch has marked sixty years on the throne. Queen Victoria's Diamond Jubilee, however, was a celebration of imperial might featuring a rare and somewhat valedictory appearance by a reclusive Britannia figure. The Queen Empress was too lame to make it up the steps into St Paul's Cathedral for her own service of thanksgiving. The clergy processed outside to her carriage instead. After sixty years of Queen Elizabeth II, the mood is entirely different. There is no triumphalism. Instead, the dominant emotion is one of pride in those quiet virtues of service, duty, stability. And the Monarch herself has no trouble with steps of any sort, whether they lead up to cathedrals or aircraft. In 2010, her list of engagements actually rose by almost 20 per cent. The schedule for 2011 – including the wedding of Prince William and Catherine Middleton, the momentous inaugural state visit to the Republic of Ireland and the state visit by President Barack Obama of the United States all within days of each other – would prove busier still.

A jubilee, by definition, is a retrospective occasion. It is an invitation for everyone to view today's world through a sepia-tinted lens. 'If you compare life now, everything is incomparably better today than when the Queen came to the throne,' says former Prime Minister Sir John Major. 'I hope that will be a theme throughout the celebrations.'

But in looking backwards, we run the risk of ignoring the most remarkable aspect of this reign – namely the monarchy today. Historians and psychiatrists talk about 'Queen Victoria syndrome', a capacity to shield oneself away from reality and live in the past. Queen Elizabeth II syndrome is the exact opposite.

The more I have followed the monarchy professionally over two decades, the more I have seen it running counter to all conventional wisdom about family businesses and ancient institutions. This operation has emphatically not become more set in its ways as the management grows older. It has actually changed more in the last twenty-five years than in the previous one hundred and twenty-five. At times through necessity, at times through choice, it has adapted and repositioned itself again and again while the rest of us have barely noticed. 'The great challenge of this organisation is management of change,' says the Duke of York. 'And that's where the Queen has been so successful. This institution, under her leadership and guidance, has been able to change in a way and at a pace which reflects what is required by society.' The Queen herself is an extraordinary double act – the never changing, ever changing Monarch who happens to be the oldest in history, entering her jubilee year at the age of eighty-five. Yet no one thinks of her as a little old lady in a black dress harrumphing that she is not amused.

We see Queen Victoria in Highland seclusion and set in aspic. We see Queen Elizabeth II walking dogs or watching a dancing display somewhere in the South Seas. She is a 'now' person, not a 'then' person.

That is why this book is not a life story but, instead, a portrait of our Queen today. It is not a chronology but a study of a thoroughly modern monarch. There have been many excellent biographies of the Queen, notably those by Sarah Bradford, Robert Lacey, Elizabeth Longford and Ben Pimlott. In recent years, the picture has also been enhanced by superb biographies of Queen Elizabeth The Queen Mother by William Shawcross and Hugo Vickers. Equally, Jonathan Dimbleby has produced the definitive work on the Prince of Wales while Basil Boothroyd, Tim Heald and Gyles Brandreth have all captured the oceanic contribution of the Duke of Edinburgh to both royal and public life. The volume of work devoted to the tragically short life and times of Diana, Princess of Wales, is a library in itself.

Naturally, I have explored the past to put the present in context and have unearthed old files and fresh material from throughout the Queen's six decades on the throne. But what follows is a contemporary inside view of one of the most respected public figures in the modern world. The Queen has never granted an interview and, I dare say, never will. At some point, many years from now and in another reign, an official biographer will be granted access to the diary she writes dutifully every night. Until then, her thoughts will remain, for the most part, off-limits.

But I have been granted special access to those who really know her and those who work – and have worked – with her. I have spoken to members of the Royal Family, prime ministers, private secretaries, prelates, pages, footmen and friends. I have been able to follow her around the world, around the country and around her own palace at close quarters. The jubilee may be an occasion for all of us to look back over the last sixty years but the star turn will prefer to keep looking ahead. She accepts that her anniversary is a big deal for some. The Lord Chamberlain's Office has already declared an amnesty on tat. 'Normally, we don't allow people to stick the Queen's arms on things like mugs,' says Deputy Comptroller Jonathan Spencer. 'But for the jubilee, we are giving them a free-for-all and saying, "Go for it."' Even so, she will be mildly bemused and faintly embarrassed by all the fuss. History is important to her but the present is rather *more* important.

One day, in the midst of my research, I followed the Queen to a service in Westminster Abbey, the royal holy of holies – crowning place, marrying place, funeral place of sovereigns for almost a millennium. Several months later, billions would tune in to watch Prince William marry Catherine Middleton here inside Edward the Confessor's mighty foundation. At the end of this particular service, the Queen was taken to a side chapel to meet a team of experts beginning a £200,000 renovation of the most sacred royal relic of the lot, St Edward's Chair. It is also called the Coronation Chair although it is otherwise known, simply, as *The* Throne. It has sat in the Abbey for seven hundred years and has been used at every coronation since the fourteenth century. Scotland's sacred Stone of Scone slots in beneath it. The Queen was sitting on this battered oak seat, six feet tall and etched with centuries-old graffiti, when she was crowned Monarch herself. What was striking about this moment, though, was the Queen's reaction. She might have been viewing a moderately interesting new traffic control centre in the West Midlands. She listened politely to a short explanation about the restoration work. Then she admitted that, despite visiting the Abbey countless times throughout her reign, she had not actually seen the chair since 1953. It was nice to see it in one piece, she said, but time was pressing. And, with that, she was off. She then moved next door to the Abbey's education centre where she spent twice as long watching children from a local primary school learning how to draw a Tudor rose.

# I

# *Her Achievement*

*'She's really determined to finish everything she started'*

Judging by the internal memos, it's surprising that the Queen was able to see her audience – or indeed breathe. This was to be her finest hour, a gathering of the mightiest in the land to salute the all-conquering heroine of the seven seas. Less than a year after her Coronation, the dizzyingly glamorous young Sovereign and her consort were to be welcomed home from what, to this day, remains the greatest royal tour of all time.

So there was to be no holding back on the vital ingredients as the Lord Mayor of London and his court started planning the grandest post-war feast the capital had seen. No less than £174 – more than 10 per cent of the entire food budget – was to be spent on tobacco. There were to be individual mixed boxes of cigars (two sizes) and cigarettes (both Turkish and Virginia) for each of the 401 Mansion House guests, plus red leather match cases and extra supplies of Punch cigars and Fribourg & Treyer cigarettes just in case anyone ran out. And why not? The Prime Minister, Sir Winston Churchill, would expect nothing less.

The bill for musical entertainment, on the other hand, was not to stretch beyond £50 (only £11 more than the budget for 'white gloves'). Fortunately, the Band of the Royal Artillery was happy to oblige for £47. The well-nourished members of the food-tasting committee were eventually able to agree on a menu and the invitations were finally dispatched. And thus began an ill-concealed scramble for the hottest ticket since the Coronation itself.

On 2 June 1953, Westminster Abbey had staged the first global television spectacular in history as the Queen was crowned. Five months later, she departed on a journey which would take her all the way around the world. Her purpose was to greet and be greeted by the newly rebranded 'Commonwealth', even if most people still insisted on calling it 'the Empire'. To celebrate her return in May 1954, the City of London would stage this official state luncheon. As plans for the royal homecoming were being drawn up in the capital, the tour had reached its zenith in

Australia. That country had never seen a sovereign in the flesh before. The adoration and adulation were astonishing, even by the standards of Coronation-era Britain. On one Sydney evening, more than a quarter of a million people turned out just to watch the Queen return from the theatre. When the Lord Mayor of Sydney held a banquet, there were two thousand casualties on the streets at what became known as 'sardine corners'. The entire rail network was shut down when thousands spilled on to the tracks to wave at the royal train.

According to Australia's Dr Jane Connors, who has studied the social and cultural impact of the tour in depth, even the most remote parts of Australia experienced mayhem. The dairy town of Lismore saw the first traffic jam in its history. More than 30,000 people squeezed into the town of Casino (population: 8,000) to welcome the Queen, including the injured passengers from an overturned bus who refused to seek hospital treatment until the royal couple had left. Despite heavy flooding, remote communities tackled mudslides and swollen rivers to see their sovereign. Mr and Mrs Allingham of Southwick, both aged seventy-five, spent three days on horseback, swimming across several creeks en route, to cheer the Queen in Townsville. A million people lined the road into Melbourne from Essendon Aerodrome. More than five hundred were hurt, one critically, when a stand collapsed in Cairns. The *Melbourne Age* found a group of Aboriginal children who had collected enough dingo scalps to pay for a two-thousand-mile round trip by bus.

The British press decided enough was enough. 'GO EASY,' demanded a *Daily Mirror* headline. 'YOU MAY HARM THE QUEEN'. But as the Queen headed for home via the Indian Ocean and Malta, where she joined the stylish new Royal Yacht *Britannia*, the excitement in Britain was reaching similar levels. Documents in the City archives show that the Lord Mayor was batting off requests thick and fast. One City councilman lobbied the organising committee to find a seat for the American preacher Billy Graham (he was informed that there was already a surfeit of 'Ecclesiastical representatives').

Churchill himself elected to join *Britannia* off the Isle of Wight on the eve of a triumphal journey up the Thames. When the Queen caught him nodding off during the after-dinner film, she urged him to go to bed. 'Now we have you home,' he replied, 'I shall sleep very well.' A day later, he was standing at the Queen's side as the Royal Yacht sailed beneath Tower Bridge, to the cheers of a city *en fête*. To this day, she likes to recall his running commentary on the approach as he proclaimed the Thames not as 'a muddy old river' but as 'the silver thread that runs through British history'.

Ahead of the great luncheon, the Queen travelled in state through the capital. At Temple Bar, the historic gateway to the City itself, there was a formal welcome from the Lord Mayor and his panoply of fur-hooded, velvet-robed, cocked-hatted, sword-bearing sheriffs, aldermen and remembrancers – almost everyone, in fact, bar Dick Whittington and his cat. Shortly afterwards, the Prime Minister and his Cabinet, the leaders of the Church, the judiciary, the Forces, the Civil Service, the City and 'the Learned Institutions' were assembled in morning dress at the Mansion House to welcome the Queen plus her husband, mother, sister and cousins to lunch. A suitably colourful menu (by the austere standards of the day) had been prepared in honour of such an exotic tour. 'Avocado pear and shrimps' was to be followed by 'Scotch Salmon Hollandaise', 'Spring Chicken St George' and 'Strawberry Melba', accompanied by Australian wines and a 1945 Krug champagne (plus 'cold luncheon' for staff and 'beer and sandwiches in the Gaoler's Room' for the BBC).

Through the plumes of post-prandial smoke, the Lord Mayor, Sir Noël Bowater Bt MC, summed up the tour as follows: 'As an achievement of inspired conception and brilliant execution,' he told the Queen, 'it will ever remain a glittering jewel in the casket of a nation's memory.'*

The Queen's equally colourful response captures the energy and sense of purpose of those early years of the reign. 'Mount Cook soaring above the snows of the Southern Alps of New Zealand is but remotely related to the scorched rocks of Aden,' she declared. 'Yet, in these lands, their peoples hold strongly to certain common principles which all of them believe to be vital. In all of them, the idea of a parliamentary, democratic form of government is accepted and respected . . . part of the ultimate heritage of every one of my people.' Even in the midst of all this euphoria, though, she readily acknowledged that there was no point in maintaining a monarchy simply for the sake of it. 'The structure and framework of constitutional monarchy could easily stand as an archaic and meaningless survival,' she went on. 'But wherever we have been, we have received visible and audible proof that it is real and living in the hearts of the people.'

Tens of thousands were waiting outside the Mansion House, demanding her appearance on the balcony. The same crowds which had cheered her carriage all the way through London to the luncheon cheered her all

---

* The Lord Mayor's speech was restrained compared to Churchill's Address of Welcome in the Commons two days earlier: 'The gleaming episode of the Queen's journey among her peoples, their joy in welcoming her . . . constitutes an event which stands forth without an equal in our records, and casts a light – clear, calm, gay and benignant upon the whole human scene.'

the way back to the Palace. Were there no bounds to the heart-soaring brilliance of this new Elizabethan age? Who could possibly dispute Cecil Rhodes's axiom that to be English was to have 'won first prize in the lottery of life'? The whole world, it seemed, was in love with the twenty-eight-year-old Gloriana. As Churchill put it: 'Even Envy wore a friendly smile.'

Nearly sixty years later, the Queen is on her way back to London's ancient financial district. But today's crowd is no more than a hundred-strong. Most are just passers-by who have noticed a small cluster of television cameras. A celebrity must be imminent. But which one? All are delighted to discover that it's the Queen, yet a little surprised at the absence of fuss. But that is how the Queen likes it these days. And today she does *not* want to meet the great and the good. Just the good. As the capital's financial district continues to recover from the self-inflicted wounds of economic meltdown, the Queen is coming to salute those who do not move money around but simply keep the Square Mile going – the Tube staff, the police, the caterers and so on. She will not meet a banker all day. And there will be no cocked hats and swords at Temple Bar, either. Her car will just drive straight past.

She starts with the Royal National Lifeboat Institution's Tower Station, the busiest in Britain. The small floating base below Waterloo Bridge has had three thousand 'call-outs' and saved 183 lives in the last eight years. Today, it is low in the water, weighed down with all the staff, the fund-raisers and the top brass who have descended from elsewhere. No one wants to miss the R in RNLI.

A Palace press officer informs the media that the Queen will be wearing a Stewart Parvin red rusted tweed coat and a Rachel Trevor-Morgan hat. It's raining when she arrives. She has no umbrella but does not appear to mind. She meets the duty crew and watches video footage of a disturbed man jumping off Westminster Bridge three months earlier. She shudders as he lands in the water but the crew have him out again within seconds.

As she makes her way around, it is clear that what interests her most is not the mechanics of lifesaving but the voluntary dimension to the entire operation. She talks to Roger Cohen, fifty-four, who commutes from Sussex to do shifts here every few weeks. Gary Pittaway, forty-four, mans a lifeboat when he is not doing his day job with the Metropolitan Police. The Queen learns that one of her own officials, Major General Keith Cima, Governor of the Tower of London no less, is also a volunteer here. He may be a major general at the Tower but down here he is expected to make the tea like everyone else. He is not here today. It is later explained that he has ample opportunity to meet the Queen in his other life and is letting others take his place on this occasion.

It's a warts-and-all tour. The Queen is even shown the changing rooms. She stands in the rain for a photograph but there's so little space that the photographer has to climb into a boat and move offshore in order to squeeze everyone inside the shot. 'Thanks very much,' she says almost jauntily and heads off to Aldgate Tube station. There she meets the staff who handle six million commuters a year. Some were on duty the July day a suicide bomber killed seven people here in 2005. They present her with a Tube sign for a non-existent station called 'Buckingham Palace'.

And so to lunch. It could scarcely be a more different affair from that sunny fiesta of quasi-imperial effusion in 1954. Back then, the Lord Mayor wore robes over his velvet Court suit. Today's Lord Mayor, Nick Anstee, is in a lounge suit with only a small chain of office to denote his position. Some City grandees are said to be miffed that they have not been invited to a royal lunch attended by bus drivers and secretaries. There will be no Mansion House silverware or portraits, either. The lunch is on the thirty-ninth floor, the top tier of one of the City's most modern buildings, the glass-fronted 'Gherkin'. At the very top, there is a final flight of stairs up to pre-lunch drinks on the observation deck where a hundred guests are sipping champagne. It's one of the best views in London but no one is admiring the scenery. All eyes are on the stairwell. A hush descends as the top of that Rachel Trevor-Morgan hat rises into view.

A lunch of salmon terrine, loin of lamb and bread and butter pudding is being cooked by young chefs from the Hoxton Apprentice, a restaurant which turns the long-term unemployed into catering professionals. Until recently, many of these cooks had no skills and no prospects. Head chef Leon Seraphin, twenty-nine, had been homeless when Hoxton turned his world around. He ended up working at White's Club where he served both Prince William and David Cameron – 'nice chap, salads only' – before returning to Hoxton. He cannot wait to get home and tell his family that he has cooked for the Sovereign. Upstairs, Hoxton's founder, Gordon da Silva, chats to the Queen and is astonished when she mentions that two of his apprentices have worked at the Palace. He knew that – but didn't expect that she would.

At lunch, the Queen sits at a round table of ten who include two train drivers and an administrative assistant from Tower Bridge. In 1954, the Queen dined on a raised platform. Today she is on 'Table 3'. She has the head of London Underground on her right and the Lord Mayor on her left. He delivers a short speech at the end in which he thanks the Queen and praises the 'indispensable' work of the City's service

workers. There is no smoking, no port and no brandy. There is no band
or entertainment, for that matter, and no one is wearing white gloves
either. The Queen thanks the cooking team and leaves for her next
engagement at Tower Bridge. In 1954, it raised its two one-thousand-ton
arms to their full height as HMY *Britannia* sailed through with the
Queen and Churchill on board. Today, staff have already been told not
to open the bridge in her honour. She has seen it all before, thanks very
much, and does not want to disrupt the traffic. As she leaves the Gherkin,
she is greeted by the first decent crowd of the day. Word has spread
among City workers that the Queen is having lunch in their midst.
Several hundred are waiting to see her leave and, in the finest traditions
of the City, they all get a bonus – because the Queen leaves twice. The
Lord Mayor sees her safely into her State Bentley, the four-ton flagship
of the royal fleet. And then nothing happens. The car will not start.
There is an awkward pause that must seem a toe-curling eternity for
the Lord Mayor and the Queen's chauffeur. And then she gets out of the
car. With certain heads of state, there would be panic stations, much
yelling into electronic cuffs, a public inquiry and high-level redundan-
cies. But the Queen seems to be rather amused. 'So much for new
technology,' she says in mock despair to the Lord Mayor and cheerfully
climbs into the 'back-up', a police Range Rover. And off she goes in a
convoy of two cars and one police outrider – the sort of modest motorcade which might be laid on for, say, a middle-ranking trade minister
from the European Union.

What is she thinking as she hitches a ride in a borrowed car through
the City? A stranger comparing the bugle-parping newsreel coverage of
1954's royal progress through the Square Mile with today's modest events
would conclude that the monarchy had endured a catastrophic decline
during the intervening decades. From global adulation to a conked-out
car? What a comedown for a sovereign who could once precipitate the
greatest voluntary assembly of people ever seen in whichever country she
chose to set foot.

There will, though, be no complaints from the Queen today. Nor will
there by any grumbles from her family or her advisers. She has led her
country for so long – far longer than any Western leader since her great-
great-grandmother – that she knows that it is not a numbers game. She
is well aware that loyalty and affection are not solely measured by the
depth of a crowd or the viscosity of a formal welcome.

Fifties Britain was another world. As the figurehead of a nation in
desperate need of revitalisation and reassurance after an exhausting battle
for survival, she could hardly fail in those early days. The true mark of

her success is that, six decades later, she remains, by a considerable margin, the most popular figure in British public life.

It has not been a simple case of good fortune or of reacting to events as they unfold. There has been a game plan running through this entire reign. And it is one which continues to serve the Queen well according to the second in line to the throne (or, as he puts it, 'the young bloke coming through').

'She's so dedicated and really determined to finish everything she started,' says Prince William. 'She'll want to hand over knowing she's done everything she possibly could to help and that she's got no regrets and no unfinished business; that she's done everything she can for the country and that she's not let anyone down – she minds an awful lot about that.'

Having inherited an Edwardian (some would say Victorian) institution in 1952, she has not merely kept it going. She has put it through the most vigorous reforms of modern times. She has managed to remain simultaneously regal, popular, inclusive and relevant in a twenty-first-century world. She sits at the head of a hereditary institution often associated with rigid tradition. Its critics might even call it an anachronistic pantomime. Yet that same institution is busier and more dynamic than ever, with more going on around the Queen the older she becomes. It's not merely about developing a royal presence on Facebook or Twitter. Internal records show that, between 2005 and 2010, the amount of hospitality at Buckingham Palace actually rose by 50 per cent. Shortly after her eighty-fifth birthday in 2011, the Queen was presiding over three of the most exciting but demanding royal events of the twenty-first century within the space of a remarkable month – Prince William's wedding, that state visit to Ireland and only the second state visit to Britain by an American president.

'Ireland was fantastic,' recalls Prince William. 'We all wanted it to go smoothly because it was such a big deal.' Even on honeymoon in the Seychelles, the new Duke of Cambridge – and new Colonel of the Irish Guards – was tracking events in Dublin closely. 'I was keeping a careful watch on the internet, hearing the odd snippet and seeing the photographs. I know a lot of Irish people and so many of them were so excited about the visit that I knew it would go well.'

The wedding would turn out to be one of the most watched events in global television history, a cracking blend of state pageantry and family occasion which would produce an eternal collage of classic moments – from the balcony kiss to the Aston Martin departure to a jubilant off-duty verger filmed cartwheeling down the Abbey aisle.

It was widely interpreted as a 'shot in the arm' for the monarchy, an event which would somehow lead the institution towards the 'modern world'. In fact, the monarchy needed no such introduction. Behind the scenes, it had long since undergone a broader internal revolution, including a shift in management culture away from the gentleman amateur to unisex professionalism. The result is a Royal Household which has changed from top to bottom.

Not only are a third of senior staff now women but the chambermaid of yesteryear (now a 'housekeeping assistant') is sometimes a he, can also double up as a footman and is more likely than not to have a degree. One recent housekeeping assistant arrived with a 2:1 in physics from Prince William's old university, St Andrews. Among the current crop of footmen is a graduate in aeronautical engineering from one of Britain's top universities. 'You probably have enough expertise in here to assemble a nuclear bomb,' observes one member of the Household, surveying the staff serving at a Palace reception. Indeed, by any set of modern diversity criteria, the Royal Household can now compete easily with most of corporate Britain.

The Duke of York is quick to point out that this accelerated pace of royal change has been driven by external factors. 'That's a function of society, not necessarily a function of the Palace,' says the Queen's second son and fourth in line to the throne. 'Fifty years ago it was not remotely possible or sensible to fly to the United States or the Middle East and come back in a day. And the great advantage was it took time for communication to happen, which allowed thinking time. Now, people communicate instantaneously.' But having spent ten years as the Special Representative for UK Trade and Investment (a post he has now relinquished), he has observed plenty of change management in practice. And the Duke acknowledges that the monarchy is going to have to adapt even more rapidly in the future. 'That need to restructure or to change is more frequent because of the change of pace of life.'

History has known no monarch like the Queen. She has travelled farther and met more foreign leaders than all her predecessors put together. If one works on the basis that she has met 150 new people every day of her adult life (a low estimate since she can do the same in one walkabout and three hundred people at a single reception), then the Queen has personally met almost four million people – the entire population of New Zealand, say. Since presenting her first decoration in 1952, she has personally held six hundred investitures at which almost 100,000 individuals have received an honour, a chat and a handshake.*

* The very first medal she presented during her reign was the Victoria Cross, awarded to Private William Speakman of the King's Own Scottish Borderers. He fought off repeated enemy assaults with grenades, stones and even empty bottles during the Korean War.

The history of the British Monarchy can be said to fall very roughly into four phases. From the ancient Britons to James II, monarchs ruled largely as they pleased (with a few cack-handed exceptions, notably Charles I). There followed 150 years of constitutional adjustment. The balance of power shifted from the monarchy to Parliament while England and Scotland merged to make Great Britain and then, with Ireland, to create the United Kingdom. Then came the third phase – the age of Empire – from Victoria to George VI. Britain and its monarchy had never enjoyed such prosperity and influence, controlling or administering a quarter of the earth's surface and population. With huge industrial advances, however, came industrial warfare. It was the age of global conflicts. There were revolutions abroad and political upheavals at home, not least universal suffrage and Irish independence. At the very moment that Britain was adjusting to a lesser role in the new world order, with its Empire evolving into the new Commonwealth, George VI died. Thus began the fourth phase of monarchy – the post-imperial media age. And only one sovereign has been through it.

The Queen has not had to lead her country through all-out war, as her father did, but she has had to come to terms with two fundamental changes. No British monarch has seen more of a demographic shift on their watch. Nor has any previous royal generation been monitored by twenty-four-hour television and an omnipresent mass media.

When the Queen came to the throne, Britain was a monocultural nation. Between 1945 and 1958, the country underwent its greatest religious revival since the mid-nineteenth century, clothed in its now forgotten 'Sunday best'. Following half a century of immigration from the Commonwealth and elsewhere, nearly five million Britons – 8 per cent of the population – are from non-white backgrounds (and the number of people attending a Church of England service in any given week is now down to around one million). This transformation into a multicultural nation has overlapped precisely with the reign of the Queen. And she has not simply observed this seismic social change. She has unquestionably been part of the process. As Dr Rowan Williams, the Archbishop of Canterbury, points out, her role has been critical: 'She's demonstrated the possibility of stability in rapidly changing circumstances. It's a "Don't panic" message.'

The Commonwealth, which numbered eight countries when the Queen came to the throne, now numbers fifty-four independent nations. Many are former colonies built on slavery and exploitation. And yet they not only enjoy active membership of this old imperial club: despite being fiercely independent nations, they have also chosen to retain the Queen as their head of state. To many strands of modern thinking, it seems bizarre that the formerly oppressed should embrace the former oppressor so warmly. That, undoubtedly, is due in no small part to the Queen herself. No monarch has engaged with so many different faiths or visited so many different places of worship. Yet, the Queen has (quietly) been one of the most diligent Supreme Governors in the Church of England's modern history. There is no contradiction in any of this. It is her devotion to the Commonwealth which endears her to so many minority communities in Britain. And it is her devotion to the Church of England which endears her to so many of Britain's minority faiths as they, like her, deal with an increasingly secular world. She is, thus, emblematic of both Old Britain and New Britain. Might historians perhaps one day look back on this as her greatest achievement?

Or might they argue that it has been her ability to steer the monarchy through the turbulence generated by the modern media? At the start of the reign, public support was a given. Buckingham Palace could operate a semi-Trappist press office with a 'no comment' default mode because the function and role of the monarchy was accepted and seldom questioned. Huge changes in public and media attitudes to authority have changed all that. The subsequent transformation in royal public relations has eclipsed anything seen in any previous reign. That public support now has to be justified and seen to be earned. Some historians, among them Ben Pimlott and Sarah Bradford, have dated this change of mindset back to 1969, the year of the first modern royal documentary. It could, equally, be argued that the monarchy learned this lesson at the time of the Abdication. Regardless, it is well understood today. 'Whether you call it deference or respect, it has to be found. It doesn't come solely from position,' says Lord Peel, the current Lord Chamberlain and the most senior official in today's Royal Household. 'You have an advantage if you have the position of Monarch or Prince of Wales. But you have to carry out your role in a way that people respect. It doesn't just happen. It has to be earned.'

No British politician – not even Churchill – has maintained the consistent level of popularity enjoyed by the Queen. And on the occasions that the needle on the popularity gauge has flickered, it has not been because she has done something. It has been because she has *not* done something. Complacency, as she well knows, is the greatest threat. She has not earned the esteem and affection of her people by standing still. She has done it by changing almost everything while leaving one crucial element untouched: herself. As one of her closest confidants puts it: 'Everything's changed except the headscarf.'

Former Prime Minister, Tony Blair, believes that two factors have planted the monarchy where it is today. 'The first is the Queen's almost imperceptible modernisation of the institution in a way which has been very canny. Whilst yielding up very little of the monarchy's mystique, she has made it come to be seen as a much more grounded part of national life. The second thing is a maturing of public attitudes.' He believes that the former 'liberal elite' who felt that the monarchy had no place in a modern country now see it as an asset. 'People have looked at their political institutions and thought: "Well, we want to elect our government but if the choice is a president that doesn't have any of that mystique and those roots in our tradition and history, then, frankly, we'd prefer to stick with the monarchy."'

But people will only think that way as long as the monarchy continues with this 'imperceptible' change. Sometimes, it has been a case of adapting to events and playing catch-up with the wider world. Sometimes, there has been quiet but radical reform of the monarchy from within. Something else has happened during this reign, though. The monarchy has also undergone a deliberate rethink of what it is actually *for*.

Since the late nineteenth century, the standard handbook of constitutional monarchy has been the set of royal rights and obligations defined by the Victorian political thinker Walter Bagehot in his work *The English Constitution*. It was Bagehot who decreed that the Monarch must 'sign her own death-warrant if the two Houses unanimously send it up to her' and distilled the Sovereign's powers into 'three rights' – the right to be consulted, the right to encourage and the right to warn. This is the job specification which has been drummed into successive royal generations. The Queen herself grew up learning it from both her father and her tutor, Henry Marten.* But, in recent years, an additional aspect has quietly been added to the job description.

'During the nineties, we looked at everything,' says a former Private Secretary. 'We needed to find out where we should be going. We could always see great public affection in, say, Manchester, but we weren't connecting nationally. We had to ask: "What the hell are we supposed to be doing?"' The answer, in very simple terms, was articulated by another political thinker whose best known observations on the state of modern politics have been through the medium of television comedy. In his role as co-creator of *Yes, Minister* and *Yes, Prime Minister*, Sir Antony Jay has

* A senior master at Eton College, Marten regularly visited Windsor Castle during the Second World War to teach Princess Elizabeth about the constitutional duties that lay ahead. Despite his disconcerting habit of addressing a solitary Princess as 'Gentlemen', Sir Henry's lessons were much appreciated. In 1945, he was knighted by George VI in front of the entire school.

not merely entertained but has helped shape modern thinking on the dynamic between elected politicians and unelected servants of the state. Although best known as a comedy writer, he has written extensively on the science of business (his *Management and Machiavelli*, first published in 1967, remains on the syllabus at Harvard Business School). He is also the writer of two of the most important royal documentaries ever made. In 1969, he wrote the script for *Royal Family*, the first film in history to show the Windsors at home and in private. To many British and Commonwealth viewers, the sight of a Royal Family barbecue or the Queen buying an ice cream for Prince Edward remains as vivid in the mind as the other broadcasting sensation of that summer – the moon landings. It was Jay who also co-wrote the script for the 1992 film, *Elizabeth R*. Most viewers will remember the intimate footage of the Queen with her grandchildren at Balmoral, of Ronald Reagan hunting for decaffeinated coffee on the Royal Yacht and the full grandeur of the state visit by an emotional Lech Wałesa. Better still, some of the commentary was provided by the Queen herself.

Jay also wrote a book to go with *Elizabeth R*. By his own admission, most people were more interested in the photographs than the words. But the text had a profound impact at Buckingham Palace. One former Private Secretary describes it as 'the best monograph on the monarchy of our times'. In it, Jay breaks down the Queen's constitutional role into 'formal official functions' – signing legislation and so on – and a list of fourteen 'informal official services' from 'continuity' to 'focus of allegiance'. He also suggests ten principal qualities which the public have come to expect of the Monarch – including 'political impartiality' and 'attendance to duty'. He combines them all to define a new dual role for the modern Monarch. The Queen is head of state, of course, with all the rights and constraints of the sort ordained by Bagehot. But Jay also gives her a new title – head of the nation. It is an equally important role but one with a much more personal dimension. Unlike the head of state role, which is clearly defined and happens automatically – appointing prime ministers, receiving state visitors, etc. – the head of the nation duties are down to each individual monarch. 'They can be done well, or adequately, or badly, or not done at all,' writes Jay. 'They are the ones concerned with behaviour, values and standards; the ones which earn the respect, loyalty and pride of the people. If the Sovereign becomes just another occupant of a high office of state with no more relevance to people's daily lives and inner feelings than the Lord Chief Justice, then that crucial link between nation and state will be seriously weakened and will perhaps break.'

This new job description struck an instant chord at the Palace. 'It was the mid-nineties and we were constantly questioning ourselves about everything,' says a very senior official, now retired. 'This made sense. We had just never thought of the monarchy like that.' And so the Queen and her advisers quietly annexed this new 'head of the nation' title and added it to that of 'head of state'. As they sought to move the monarchy forwards from the unhappy rows about money and marriages which dominated the early nineties, here was a simple two-pronged answer to the question: what is the monarchy for? It was a definition which has since helped to shape the entire way the Palace goes about its business. It also chimed with the resurgence of what the historian Frank Prochaska has called the 'Welfare Monarchy' with the Royal Family at the forefront of the voluntary sector.

To this day it is the sentiments of Jay rather than Bagehot which open the Palace's official introduction to the 'Role of the Sovereign' on the Queen's website: 'The British Sovereign can be seen as having two roles: Head of State, and "Head of the Nation".' The latter is explained as follows: 'The Sovereign acts as a focus for national identity, unity and pride; gives a sense of stability and continuity; officially recognises success and excellence; and supports the ideal of voluntary service.' You won't find any of that in the Coronation Oath or the history books. But the Queen takes her 'Nation' role just as seriously as, say, her Coronation vow to 'preserve inviolable the settlement of the Church of England'.

It is the 'head of the nation' role which requires the hard work and delicate judgement. Jay believes that the Queen has been a natural from the start. 'Her success is rooted in face-to-face contact,' he says. 'It's all about looking people in the eye, hand to hand. It's a personal thing and she has been doing the legwork and laying foundation stones and planting trees and opening things and being seen like that for sixty years. And there is a ripple effect. Even if she only asks someone where they're from or what they do, that person tells a hundred people. I think this face-to-face work – not just relying on the electronic media – is somewhere close to the heart of this tribal loyalty. You need to be seen.' In 1964, a Harris poll revealed that 60 per cent of the population had actually seen a member of the Royal Family in the flesh. Cultural shifts, modern media, apathy and the impositions of modern security will have reduced that figure. But, after two decades of straw-polling by the author, it is still safe to say that it comfortably exceeds the number who have laid an eyeball on, say, their local MP.

Monarchy has always been a long game. As the Duke of York, British trade ambassador for a decade, points out, it could not be any other way.

'We are not interested in short-term issues. You can't do anything in the short term. It's all dependent on relationships. That's what the Queen's been doing for sixty years. The more you do it, the greater your experience, the greater the ability to lead, to change, to manage, to listen, to learn, and it's that ability to impart that knowledge and experience that, I think you'll find, every single member of the family is so grateful for.'

Sir Antony Jay certainly does not see himself as a latter-day Walter Bagehot (whom he admires greatly) but simply as a student of human nature. He believes that the emotional power of monarchy is as strong as ever and that anyone who thinks it's out of date in a twenty-first-century Britain is deluded. 'It is entirely irrational to ignore the irrational,' he says in the study of his pretty Somerset farmhouse. 'Almost everything about government is rational – paying tax, legislation and so on. But there is this irrational area – the Church, ceremony, pageantry. Ritual is hugely important. We are not just a ritualistic country but a ritualistic species.'

The former Cambridge scholar explains that he simply formed the idea of the Monarch's parallel state/nation roles after long conversations with successive private secretaries to the Queen. 'When we talk about a country we mean three things,' he says. 'There is the state – which is the overarching structure with a permanent identity. There is the government – which runs things, provides change, causes division and institutionalises conflict. Then there is the third element and it is the most neglected one – the nation. We all have social emotions. We need to feel part of something, we are tribal. I feel part of my school, of my university, of my regiment, even of the BBC – all things which involve shared experiences. People have died for that feeling, going over the top in the trenches because "you're with your mates". That is what being a nation is about. And that feeling of nationhood is harnessed to the state through the Royal Family.'

He points to the scenes of calm, unscripted unity following the death, in 2002, of Queen Elizabeth The Queen Mother as an example of that sense of nationhood. And he cites America's Watergate scandal and the 2009 saga of British MPs' expenses as good examples of the difference between a monarchy and a republic. In 2009, there was widespread fury when it was revealed how hundreds of MPs had been spending their allowances. Parliament's reputation sunk to a post-war nadir. This sort of episode, Jay suggests, causes deeper convulsions in a republic where the government and the state are seen as one and the same. Watergate remains a good example.* Because the President was the head of state, the whole

---

* President Richard Nixon resigned from office in August 1974. It emerged that he had attempted to block investigations into the burglary of his political opponents' offices in Washington's Watergate building.

scandal was far more traumatic for the country than if he had only been head of the government. So, by having a constitutional monarchy, says Jay, a country like Britain is better placed to digest a political crisis. 'We can have a terrible political scandal but not end up despising the state because it's the monarchy, not the government, which links nation and state,' he argues.

David Cameron certainly believes that Britain's abrasive political culture demands a substantial counterbalance. 'You have to have symbols of national unity that bring the country together, particularly if you have an aggressive confrontational political system,' says the Prime Minister. 'The fact that you have such a unifying figure for the nation makes it [the monarchy] immensely strong. Because this bit of the constitution is accepted and works, changes of government don't lead to constitutional crises or banking crises. We don't question our constitution every time something goes wrong.'

The Queen's success is not simply down to staying power and shoe leather. It also owes much to canny judgements at crucial moments. Despite the rosy glow which colours any cursory sweep of this reign, the Queen has not enjoyed one long, easy, golden era punctuated by a dark spell during the nineties. Her sixty years on the throne have consisted of three episodes of sustained success and two periods of recurring difficulty. Almost two-thirds of her reign could be classified as 'contented'. But more than a third – twenty-three years – could be described, to some extent, as 'troubled'.

As the news broke of the death of George VI on 6 February 1952, the world wished the new young Queen nothing but good luck. No change of monarch in recent history had been accompanied by such a combined sense of loss, goodwill and optimism. The reign of George V began with rumours of alcoholism and a criminal libel trial to quash charges of bigamy (a London-based French journalist, Edward Mylius, had accused the King of a secret marriage to an admiral's daughter in Malta; Mylius got twelve months). The accession of Edward VIII was mired in uncertainty and led, in short order, to the unhappy accession of George VI. But there were no outstanding issues, no whispered doubts about the accession of Elizabeth II. The fact was that post-war Britain, drab, battered and still on rations, badly needed a tonic and a fresh sense of direction. To see the throne pass from an avuncular symbol of dogged wartime resistance to a glamorous young mother married to a man of action was richly symbolic. Had George VI been succeeded by a son, would the mood have been as sentimental? Perhaps – but probably not.

Princess Margaret described the revivalist fervour of Coronation

Britain as a 'phoenix-time' for the nation. 'Everything was being raised from the ashes,' she told the royal biographer Ben Pimlott. 'There was this gorgeous-looking, lovely young lady, and nothing to stop anything getting better and better.' The new reign was off to a breathtaking start. 'The crowds were incredible,' Prince Philip said years later, reflecting on the reactions during that 1954 world tour. 'The adulation was extraordinary. You wouldn't believe it.' Perhaps it all started too well. The only way things could go from this euphoric peak was downhill.

The first 'golden period' of the reign could be said to have come to an end at the Glorious Goodwood race meeting of 1956 where the Queen was presented with a proclamation requiring her signature (she did not, as legend has it, sign the thing on the haunches of a racehorse). It was a document calling out the Army Reserve. Britain's disastrous intervention in the Suez Canal Zone had begun.* As the Suez crisis unfolded, Prince Philip embarked on a world tour in the Royal Yacht which attracted world attention for the wrong reasons after the wife of his equerry, Mike Parker, sought a divorce. Just a year earlier, Princess Margaret had abandoned plans to marry her late father's equerry, Group Captain Peter Townsend, because he was a divorced man. Now, the resurgence of the toxic D-word so close to the throne ignited rumours in the foreign press and even prompted the Palace to issue a statement denying any 'rift' in the royal marriage. By now, however, the monarchy had more serious rumblings to contend with. Following Anthony Eden's departure as Conservative Prime Minister at the start of 1957, it was left to the Queen to appoint a new one. These days, a ruling party would simply choose a new leader and the Queen would appoint that person as Prime Minister. Back then, she was expected to do the choosing, too. All sovereigns must stay above party politics. So, it was particularly disagreeable to be dragged into the internal politics of one particular party. Her solution was to ask an internal committee of Conservative grandees to sound out opinions in the party. The verdict was clear enough and the Queen duly summoned Harold Macmillan, an Old Etonian married to a Duke's daughter, ahead of R. A. 'Rab' Butler, seen by many as the more meritocratic choice. The conclusion drawn by a section of the press and public was that the Queen had been party to some cosy aristocratic stitch-up.

A few months later, the Coronation honeymoon was finally over. A small-circulation conservative magazine, the *National and English Review*, devoted a special issue to the future of the monarchy. This might have made little

* In 1956, after Egypt's Colonel Nasser had nationalised the Suez Canal, Britain and France reached a secret arrangement to support an Israeli attack on Egypt. A global backlash forced a hasty and humiliating withdrawal.

impact beyond its 4,500 regular readers but for an extraordinary critique of the Queen herself. The author was the magazine's editor, Lord Altrincham, a liberal-minded young Tory peer. He attacked the 'tweedy' courtiers around the Queen and made unfavourable comparisons between George V's 'classless stamp' on his reign and the Queen's 'debutante stamp' on her own.

What offended people across the social spectrum, however, was the sneering tone of his attack on the Queen herself – her voice, her way of speaking, her 'priggish' demeanour. Altrincham (who would later renounce his peerage to become plain John Grigg) was physically attacked in the street while some of his colleagues in the Lords advocated various medieval punishments. Yet his broader complaints about a detached and complacent Court struck a chord. Many years later he would even be congratulated in public by a former Private Secretary to the Queen for performing a useful service to the Crown. This was the era of Angry Young Men, the beginning of the 'end of deference'. The old Establishment was finding its ways and values were no longer swallowed whole by a pliant media. By the early sixties, the government was becoming mired in sex and spy scandals, notably the Profumo affair.*

The young guns of the new television age were now firing difficult questions at politicians instead of asking ministers if they had anything they 'might like to say to the nation'. The monarchy was not unscathed. The Royal Family was fair game for the edgy new genre of television satire. Sir Antony Jay, who joined the BBC in 1955 and went on to work with rising stars like David Frost, remembers the mood well. 'Just after Suez, there was the beginning of a whole new line of questioning. Suddenly, Eden was not a great figure. Suddenly there were crises. Our own feelings about things like Profumo were unmitigated glee. We were delighted to see the back of these useless, nineteenth-century-style aristocratic idiots. What we needed was the white heat of new technology and all that.'

The early sixties brought great happiness for the Queen and Prince Philip with the birth of Prince Andrew, in 1960, and Prince Edward, in 1964. But all the time there was the uncomfortable sense of old certainties being chipped away. In 1963, the Queen and her officials were genuinely shocked when she was booed at the theatre during the state visit of the King and Queen of Greece. The booing was aimed at the visitors, not the hostess, but such a scene would have been unthinkable ten years earlier. It was the Queen herself who was the target of jeering in Canada. As Britain edged closer to the future European Union at the expense

---

* In 1963, the War Minister, John Profumo, resigned from public life. He admitted lying to the Commons about his relationship with Christine Keeler, a model who had been sharing her affections with a Russian naval attaché.

of old Commonwealth allegiances, so royalist affection was dwindling overseas. The crowds on her 1963 tour of Australia were a fraction of the turnout in 1954.

Following Macmillan's resignation through ill health, there were fresh media accusations of royal intrigue when the Queen had to choose a new Conservative Prime Minister. Sir Alec Douglas-Home, a Scottish landowner and a friend of the Royal Family, was even grander and 'tweedier' than Macmillan. The process had been a shambles. Confined to a hospital bed, Macmillan had been advising the Queen on whom to choose as his successor even though he had already resigned and thus had no constitutional right to do so. But having been advised that Douglas-Home was the Conservative Party's considered choice, the Queen had no choice but to summon him. The media, now more combative than ever, went on the attack. 'You have to remember that we in our world were very anti-monarchy, anti-Establishment,' recalls Jay. 'We would do everything we could to be snide.'

The anti-Establishment movement did not have long to wait. After the 1964 general election, the Queen had her first Labour Prime Minister. Harold Wilson would prove both sympathetic and respectful but some of his ministers were almost contemptuous in their dealings with the Palace. Richard Crossman, as Lord President of the Council, made a point of arriving five minutes late for Privy Council meetings in order to keep the Queen waiting. And all the time, the monarchy – staid, dependable, old-fashioned – appeared to be at odds with the iconoclastic spirit of the sixties. The vast majority of people were not agitating or attending pop festivals but simply getting on with their jobs and their lives. Even so, the monarchy was seen as rather dull. And, short of a revolution, the greatest threat to the throne has always been indifference.

By the late sixties, more innovative voices began to prevail at the Palace. Instead of treating the media as an irritant, the Queen agreed to let the cameras in to produce two broadcasting landmarks – the first royal documentary, *Royal Family*, and the televised investiture of Prince Charles as Prince of Wales. These were turning points in so many ways.

The whole world seemed an increasingly dangerous and volatile place. Vietnam was on fire and the Cold War threatened cataclysmic horrors. At home, Northern Ireland had just imploded. The Royal Family not only seemed to offer reassurance and stability, they also seemed to have undergone a transformation. They were no longer aloof, 'tweedy' and out of touch. Suddenly they were human and dynamic. Dare one say it, in fact, they were what you might call modern.

The Queen had appointed a more professional, more adventurous team around her and it was working. The steady post-Suez decline had been halted. The 'contented' years were back. She would go on to enjoy a period of happy, uncomplicated romance with the public. There would be political rows over royal finances and the Commonwealth but they had little bearing on the mutual affection between the Monarch and the people. In 1973, the television cameras – and thus the public – were given pride of place at the wedding of Princess Anne, setting an entirely new tone for Royal Family events. The Silver Jubilee of 1977 restored the monarchy to a new high. The economy might have been on the brink of collapse but at least Britain had something to celebrate. For a whole new generation it was something of an awakening. 'I have a very strong memory of 1977,' says Prime Minister David Cameron, 'of a proper village party with trestle tables.'

When the Lord Mayor and the City of London held their jubilee feast for the Queen at the Guildhall it was a far cry from 1954. They limited themselves to the catering company's second-choice menu (salmon trout, beef and melon) at £13.50 a head.*

In his speech, the Lord Mayor of the day, Sir Robin Gillett Bt, took a rather gloomy view of the first twenty-five years of the reign. A former Royal Navy officer, he lamented that Britain had turned 'swords into ploughshares' and that, in the Commonwealth family of nations, it seemed as if 'all the children had grown up and sought, as children do, to spread their wings and leave the nest'. The Queen, however, had taken the throne in the opposite direction. Saluting the advent of the walkabout, he declared: 'To humanise the monarchy without detracting from its essential mystique and to bring it adapted but intact into this modern world requires exceptional talents with which Your Majesty has been amply endowed.'

Thus was the monarchy seen as both traditional and progressive in equal measure. The Coronation-style street parties which broke out all over Britain involved every generation and would be repeated in honour of the weddings of the Prince of Wales (1981) and Prince Andrew (1986). Soon, the Queen was being upstaged by grandchildren and glamorous daughters-in-law. She did not seem to mind one bit, although this did not go unnoticed by her officials. Another stunning royal documentary, *Elizabeth R*, was arranged to mark her fortieth anniversary on the throne, this time with a much greater focus on the Sovereign. What could possibly go wrong? And yet, within the space of nine months in 1992, it all went very wrong indeed. Marital breakdowns in tandem with renewed attacks on the royal finances would cause far greater damage than anything sustained between Suez and Woodstock. 'We were running out of respect

---

* Once again, more was spent on tobacco (£500) than on flowers (£430) or an orchestra (£195). And, once again, it was 'beer and sandwiches', at £1 a head, for the BBC.

and money,' admits one senior Royal Household adviser of the time. 'We were stuck in the mire.' And that was before a neglected builder's lamp ignited a wall covering. The fire which destroyed much of Windsor Castle at the end of 1992 lent an almost biblical sense of catharsis to the Queen's troubles. 'There is a certain symbolism in the fact that the Windsor fire should have been caused by a spotlight burning away a curtain,' reflects Sir Antony Jay. The Queen would call it her *annus horribilis*, yet the unhappiness would last much longer than a year.

As we shall see, though, it was a period which ushered in some of the greatest royal upheavals in a century. Some far-sighted reforms were already quietly under way. Others were pushed through in ways perhaps inconceivable in happier times. 'When the press started turning against the Palace over marriage, money and the castle,' recalls one former Private Secretary, 'that concentrated people's minds wonderfully.'

If monarchs are judged on their performance in adversity, this was when Queen Elizabeth II earned her laurels – far more so than in the early years when it required little more than a smile to bring any nation to a jubilant standstill. Here, to use Princess Margaret's phrase once again, was a genuine 'phoenix-time'. Out of the ashes of Windsor Castle there grew a renewed sense of royal vigour. For a monarch approaching her seventieth birthday it might have been tempting to retrench or even retire, as all her contemporaries had already done. Instead, she followed the pattern of the late sixties: stay calm, think again, listen to new ideas.

Buckingham Palace was opened to the public. Behind the scenes, the Royal Family started to discuss its own *raison d'être* at a gathering of family members and senior officials known as the Way Ahead Group. As in the late sixties, the profile of the executive cadre started to change once more. The Private Secretary's Office is the engine room of the monarchy. At any given time, there are three private secretaries – ranked in order of Private Secretary, Deputy Private Secretary and Assistant Private Secretary – one of whom is always in attendance. One day in 1996, a high-flying civil servant from Downing Street arrived to take the number three role. Mary Francis, a Cambridge historian and previously Private Secretary to John Major, became the first woman ever to reach the top tier at the Palace.

'I was told the Palace wanted someone with a background like mine,' she recalls. 'It was the first time they'd had a woman and the first time they'd had someone from a Treasury or Civil Service background as opposed to the Foreign Office or the Forces. They wanted someone to help think about change and future strategy.'

She found some of her new colleagues as unusual as they, no doubt, found her. 'I had never met a group of people for whom military background was far more important than anything to do with university,' she recalls. 'There was a recognition that they actually needed the injection of some rather different people.' But she also realised that she was working for a boss who was 'entirely pragmatic' about the challenges ahead.

Her colleague and Deputy Private Secretary Robin Janvrin was already driving what she calls 'the change agenda'. Among the new projects was the creation of a Co-Ordination and Research Unit – the CRU – to monitor the spread of royal activity and act as a royal think-tank. 'More and more people were being brought in with a more analytical approach,' Francis explains. 'We got a very talented diplomat from New Zealand and we used headhunters to hire in a few bright lads and lasses – the sort of people you might get to be special advisers – to work for him.' If they uncovered some awkward home truths, says Francis, then so be it. 'The research unit found some very interesting things. For example, the amount of time the Queen and the Duke of Edinburgh spent visiting private schools compared to state schools was disproportionate to the distribution of children in the country and, when they visited a private school, they were spending longer when they got there. It turned out that they were visiting the manufacturing sector far more often than the services sector – because it's easier to visit people making widgets whereas 80 per cent of the economy was actually in the services sector. It was a case of getting into these issues and writing it down in a wholly dispassionate way. That was the kind of thing that would then get discussed by the Royal Family at the Way Ahead Group.'

As a result, the Queen's 'head of the nation' role soon became more and more proactive. 'The change was gradual but it was quite considerable,' explains Francis. The Queen's diary was a case in point. 'When I arrived, the Queen's engagements were decided by looking through the invitations. By the time I left, it was a case of asking: what are the important things going on in the country that our Queen should recognise and how can we put together some visits that will do that?'

Charles Anson, the Queen's Press Secretary of the period, says that the reformers were pushing at an open door. 'We all agreed that we needed to get ahead of the media and not always be reacting,' he explains. 'There were lots of visits to hospitals and old people's homes, walkabouts and so on. But where were the issues of modern Britain and how was the monarchy signalling that it knew and cared about these? Then we asked the Lord-Lieutenants [the Queen's representatives in the counties] for ideas. Subsequently, we started drawing up a programme and finding the right people. It might not always be right for the Queen to do something completely new but could the Prince of Wales pick up some of these modern themes? And so it went on.'

Another senior Household official likens these years to the meltdown which hit the financial sector in 2008. 'You could say it was a case of managing change by disaster. Our attitude was almost: "We must use this crisis well." Both the Duke and the Queen could see that things couldn't remain the same. So when people suggested something like the CRU, they were right behind it. Sometimes, you get a moment where you can do things you couldn't otherwise do.'

As far as the media and much of the world was concerned, all this was of minor importance compared to the marriages of the Queen's elder sons, both of which came to an end in the Family Division of the High Court in 1996. The sudden death of Diana, Princess of Wales a year later would present the Royal Family with a personal tragedy and also the gravest crisis of the Queen's reign. 'That's when the stakes were highest,' says one former Private Secretary. 'I can't honestly say that I thought it was going to be the end of the monarchy but the serious republican element thought there was a chink in the armour and they were going for it.' Once again, as we shall see, the Queen's instinct, experience and a capacity for judicious change would prevail. So, too, would the reservoir of goodwill built up through nearly half a century of assiduous devotion to duty. A week after the Princess's death, a MORI poll showed that public attitudes towards the monarchy were just the same as they had been before and have continued to remain since (give or take a couple of percentage points): 18 per cent in favour of a republic, 73 per cent in favour of the monarchy and 9 per cent unsure.

It is a remarkably consistent figure, as any pollster will confirm. Indeed, it has barely changed since the giddy days of Coronation Britain when the Queen could do no wrong and yet 16 per cent of people still favoured a republic. Whatever changes people wanted to impose on the monarchy in that unhappy autumn of 1997 – and they were never short of suggestions – one thing was resoundingly clear. The vast majority did not want to see it disappear. The Princess's death was followed, within weeks, by the golden wedding anniversary of the Queen and Prince Philip. Addressing a lunch given by the Prime Minister, the Queen acknowledged that monarchs did not always find it easy to read the public mood, 'obscured as it can be by deference, rhetoric or the conflicting currents of public opinion. But read it we must.'

By now, the Queen, her family and her officials had a clear target at which to aim five years hence. As one ex-aide puts it: 'The Golden Jubilee was the culmination of several years of thinking: what would it take to close the door on the nineties?'

The Queen was almost endearingly keen on avoiding 'a fuss' over the fiftieth anniversary of her accession. A huge fuss, of course, was inevitable but her officials did not want an event which was in any way contrived. 'A lot of effort went in to making it look unplanned,' admits one. Any suggestion that the Palace was attempting to whip up synthetic support for a battered institution could have proved very damaging. In any case, royal officials were confident that the event would gather its own momentum. Some were privately relieved when the press started predicting a lukewarm public response. 'PALACE FEARS JUBILEE FLOP' said *The Times* in January 2002. With such low expectations, the jubilee could only go from strength to strength. It did so before the celebrations had even started, albeit in sorrowful circumstances.

On 9 February 2002, the Queen's sister, Princess Margaret, died at the age of seventy-one following several years of poor health and a series of strokes. Less then two months later, the Royal Family was in mourning again. The public response to the death of Queen Elizabeth The Queen Mother on 30 March 2002 took everyone – left, right, royalist, republican – by surprise. As she lay in state in the Palace of Westminster, police soon had to divert the queue to the west of Parliament, over the Thames and back down the other side. 'As soon as I saw the length of the queue to walk past Queen Elizabeth's coffin in 2002, it spelt to me that the troubles were now passed,' says a former Private Secretary. 'In fact, it dumbfounded me. I was one of the school who thought that she was a wonderful old lady but she was nearly 102. Even I did not expect queues as far as Blackfriars.' At one point, the line of mourners went even further, stretching from Westminster, across the Thames and eastwards towards the Tower of London. Informed that they faced a twenty-four-hour wait to file past the coffin, some simply shrugged and replied that they would wait.

The Golden Jubilee tour finally began in the Cornish rain on 1 May 2002. The crowds were modest at the opening fixture in Falmouth but the reason became clear a few hours later when the Queen entered Truro. It transpired that most of the county had descended on the cathedral city. From Northern Ireland to New Zealand, it was a similar story all year. 'The whole tone was looking forwards,' says one of the senior architects of the jubilee. 'It was about "her" thanking "us".' David Cameron, then the new Conservative MP for Witney, remembers the surge of affection. 'People were wondering: "Is it going to be a big event? Not sure." And suddenly there was this massive thrust and everyone got involved. In my constituency I went to several events and they were all brilliant and totally oversubscribed. Every village street party, every single barbecue suddenly had 25 per cent more people than they could cope with.' The Golden Jubilee concerts – one classical, one pop – in the grounds of

Buckingham Palace were screened around the world and drew more than a million people to central London to listen outside and watch the fireworks. Concorde flew down the Mall. 'God Save The Queen' rang out on Brian May's electric guitar from the Palace roof. Exactly ten years after the *annus horribilis*, the monarchy was back on track.

For all the occasional problems, the years since 2002 fall into the 'contented' category, culminating in the marriage of Prince William to Catherine Middleton before a global audience thought to rival – or exceed – an Olympiad. On a personal level, the Queen must have been equally thrilled to see the marriage of her eldest granddaughter, Zara Phillips, and the christening of her first great-grandchild, Savannah Phillips.

It has all served as a splendid prelude to an extraordinary celebration which has only happened once before – in 1897. It will be supervised by a passionately royalist Prime Minister who camped in the Mall to watch the 1981 Royal Wedding – 'I was in the best place, just where the Mall meets the statue outside Buckingham Palace' – and David Cameron has no doubts that the country will be doing much the same to mark the Queen's sixtieth anniversary on the throne: 'The Diamond Jubilee will be much bigger than anyone expects.'

This jubilee is an event which allows us to stand back and see the nineties in context rather than as the prism through which this reign has often been assessed. The jubilee helps us to reflect on the happiest and most miserable periods of the reign and to see that the euphoria of the mid-fifties was no more sustainable than the seemingly endless run of disasters a generation later. Instead, we can assess the success of this reign by the state of the institution sixty years on. If we take the Queen's full title – Her Majesty Elizabeth the Second, by the Grace of God, of the United Kingdom of Great Britain and Northern Ireland, and of Her other Realms and Territories, Queen, Head of the Commonwealth, Defender of the Faith – then there are unquestionably cracks and fissures in the institutions which she leads. The Church of England is divided over gay clergy, women bishops and overtures from the Vatican. The United Kingdom is less united than at any stage since Irish independence with four legislatures beavering away in London, Edinburgh, Cardiff and Belfast. Great Britain, the original 1707 Anglo-Scottish partnership, is less entwined than at any stage since the Act of Union. In the 2011 elections it was the separatist Scottish National Party which won an outright majority in the Scottish Parliament. In 2012, the party began planning for a referendum which could, in turn, lead to an independent Scotland. The Commonwealth is larger than ever yet increasingly flabby and inconsequential as it seeks a twenty-first-century role for itself. Of all the Queen's responsibilities, her 'other Realms and Territories' might have been the likeliest area for dissent. But, despite a handful of failed plebiscites, republicanism is an occasional issue in occasional areas – it surfaced suddenly in Jamaica in early 2012 –rather than a constant grievance. Few expect a country like Australia to retain the Crown in the long term. Yet, when offered an opportunity to replace the monarchy in 1999, the people voted to retain the Crown. Even among ardent republicans there is a strong personal affection for the Queen. And when much of Australia sat up into the night, gripped by the wedding of the Duke and Duchess of Cambridge in April 2011 – with that country's republican Prime Minister in the Westminster Abbey congregation – it was abundantly clear that the issue is, for now, a non-starter.

So, sixty years on, we find the constitutional garden in an untidy but not an unruly state. But there is an important point to be made here. There is virtually nothing that the Queen could have done to alter any of these situations. Indeed, all that can be stated with any degree of certainty is that things would be worse if it were not for her. That is certainly the objective view from overseas.

'The Commonwealth would certainly not exist in its present form without her,' says President Mohamed Nasheed of the Maldives (before being ousted in 2012). Born in 1967, this Liverpool University graduate became one of the world's youngest heads of state and the first elected leader of an Islamic archipelago republic which could disappear if sea temperatures rise by just a few degrees (he famously held the world's first sub-aqua Cabinet meeting in 2009 to highlight the problem). A one-time political prisoner who supplanted a dictatorship with a vigorous democracy, Nasheed is a canny, hard-headed politician. And he is not being sentimental when he says that his country, like many other former colonies and protectorates, can feel rather proprietorial about our Queen. 'She's our Queen as well, in a way. In our minds, she's not necessarily just English. She doesn't really have a nationality,' Nasheed explains. 'She is very different from British monarchs in the past because she's the first monarch to have engaged the world, not as an imperial ruler but someone who is out there to look after us in a sense.' He is equally enthusiastic about the Prince of Wales.

In Britain, it is certainly worthy of note that, even at its lowest ebb, the modern monarchy has not encountered anything resembling a coherent opposition. There has always been a republican lobby of some sort and it is possible – indeed, probable – that, given a personal choice, a majority of Labour MPs would prefer an elected head of state. In the fifties and sixties, republicans tended to rally around symbols – the Queen's head on stamps, Scotland's sacred Stone of Scone beneath the Coronation Chair and so on.

Today, they prefer to focus on cost and lifestyle. The most visible mani-festation of contemporary British republican thought is a pressure group called Republic which includes a small number of MPs, celebrities and public figures. A frequent complaint among its supporters is the absence of public debate on the issue but, in recent years, its public profile has risen considerably. Its efforts to present a constructive intellectual case for constitutional reform do not always chime with the class-war rhetoric of some of its supporters, but it offers some original perspectives. Contrary to the sour-grapes stance usually adopted by anti-monarchist groups at the first flutter of bunting, Republic's leader issued a statement welcoming Prince William's wedding on the grounds that it would kick-start fresh debate on the role of the Crown. On the wedding day itself, the organisa-tion even staged a rather forlorn 'Not The Royal Wedding' party in London's Red Lion Square. But it has its work cut out. The sense of national exhilaration as the new Duke and Duchess of Cambridge walked out into the world on that April morning was ample proof of that.

'People were worried about what was going to happen during those difficult times in the nineties,' says Sir John Major, Prime Minister for much of that period. 'But there's a difference between the often grudging reception which parts of the media and the republican fringe give the Royal Family and the deep, instinctive roots that you find when you go around the country. The monarchy has re-established itself in a quite astonishing way. Its value is incalculable. It gives us a unique identity. And that is maximised by the Queen because she has been there for so long. I find it impossible to contemplate a Britain without a monarchy. I simply cannot picture it.' He has noticed something else, too: 'It's regarded, these days, with much less awe and much more affection.'

His old foe and successor agrees. Indeed, Tony Blair believes support for the monarchy is arguably now stronger than ever: 'Whereas those who supported the monarchy in times gone past did so out of a very deferential respect for the institution, nowadays it's a far more rational, sustainable calculation that, all things considered, it's better for the country.' David Cameron puts it more starkly: 'There's no republican debate in this country.' Jack Straw, a former Labour Cabinet Minister and a critic of the monarchy in the early nineties, agrees.

Certainly, the old republican argument that monarchy, equality and progress are somehow incompatible is wearing thin. The 2011 United Nations Human Development Index assesses 170 countries according to fundamental living standards. Of the top ten, seven are constitutional monarchies and the Queen reigns over three of them – Australia (second), New Zealand (third) and Canada, (eighth). In top spot is the kingdom of Norway.

In Britain, a clear majority of people support the status quo. 'The polls are always about 80 per cent in favour of the monarchy to various degrees,' explains Sir Antony Jay. 'And you have to remember that the fervour of the 20 per cent who are anti-monarchy has nothing like the intensity of feeling which exists among the keenest members of the 80 per cent.' The Palace's own private polling, as ever, puts the figure at a steady 70 per cent in favour with 15–20 per cent against and the rest undecided. Regardless, it's a level of support beyond the dreams of politicians. As David Cameron puts it: 'We'd all love a bit of that!'

But the Queen, the Prince of Wales and their advisers are acutely aware that republicans don't usually produce republics. The greatest threat to the monarchy is itself. As the Duke of Edinburgh himself has sagely observed: 'Most of the monarchies in Europe were really destroyed by their greatest and most ardent supporters. It was the most reactionary people who tried to hold on to something without letting it develop and change.' The Queen is not immune to criticism from the most fervent royalists who, from time to time, believe that she is not acting in her own best interests – by failing to block some fresh transfer of powers to the European Union, perhaps, or acquiescing in the loss of the Crown or the 'royal' prefix from the letterhead of a public institution. She is certainly not oblivious to these concerns. If they are filling her post bag, no one will hide them from her.

But, standing back once more, it is her capacity to promote consensus which is a hallmark of her reign. 'She is a great non-executive,' says a very senior courtier. 'We find it in families with aunts and uncles and godparents. They are the non-execs who provide the support, wisdom and guidance on the sidelines while the parents fight it out in hand-to-hand conflict with the children. The Queen is playing that role at the heart of our constitution.'

As for the monarchy itself, it is now in robust health. We see an institution that is secure, solvent, confident and active. And she stands at the head of a Royal Household which is no longer dominated by a particular old school or regimental tie. Indeed, if there is one obvious 'old-boy network' at work inside the Palace today, it consists of alumni of the University of West London. Previously Thames Valley University (and West London Polytechnic before that), it now runs the Palace's very own Butler Diploma course and has educated far more members of staff than, say, Eton or Oxford. And they are not all boys either.

Presiding over all this is a sovereign whose level of experience has no equal among modern heads of state. In the mid-fifties, some talked excitedly of a 'New Elizabethan Age'. Amid the austerity and the bomb craters, it seemed naively optimistic. Perhaps, though, future generations, will talk of 'New Elizabethans'. Sir John Major certainly thinks so. 'The phrase trips happily off the tongue!' he argues. 'And we have seen nothing like it, except for Victoria. When historians look back in five hundred years, they won't find more than a handful of monarchs who will have served as long as our Queen.'

Yet the span of her reign is now so vast that those 'New Elizabethans' will actually straddle three centuries. The term may be too broad to serve as any sort of useful social or historic categorisation. As a little girl, Princess Elizabeth talked kings and queens with George V who had himself sat on the knee of Lord Palmerston. Today, the Queen has a British Prime Minister younger than any of her own children. During that 1954 tour of Australia, she attended reunions of Boer War veterans in every state. In Sydney, she even met Harold Wearne, ninety-one, who had fought in the Sudan War of 1885. Today she pins decorations on soldiers who were in primary school at the start of the twenty-first century.

As Prince William acknowledges, you have to be approaching seventy to be able to recall any other face on the banknotes and postage stamps. Sir John Major concurs: 'There are 6.8 billion people in the world, and over six billion of them have known nothing but the Queen as the British Monarch all their lives.'

It is precisely because of her long reign and the steady pace of her public duties that she is seen as someone whose world is shaped by tradition and convention. 'As soon as she gets a new diary, her Private Secretary can more or less fill half of it up straight away just like her Private Secretary would have done in 1952,' explains Ronald Allison, former Press Secretary to the Queen, pointing to the set-piece calendar of Easter Court at Windsor, Holyroodhouse every summer, the Cenotaph in November and so on. 'So, in one sense, nothing has changed. And yet, everything has changed.'

Certainly, when we see the famous East Front of Buckingham Palace or the Round Tower of Windsor Castle or a corgi or a sentry box or a Christmas broadcast, we sense continuity, permanence, dependability. That's the whole idea. What we don't see is an institution which has had to adapt just as much as the world beyond. It has managed to do so without us noticing – ever changing yet never changing. And that is all down to the shrewd leadership of an innately conservative woman who has also proved to be the very model of a modern monarch.

# 2

# *Herself*

*'You make it up a lot as you go along.'*

The water is splish-sploshing over the sides of the swimming pool. Built in the thirties, it was designed with relaxation in mind rather than earnest distance swimming by multiple bathers. There are no marked-out lanes. Unlike swankier, funkier corporate keep-fit clubs, there is no music system, no sauna. It's a bring-your-own-towel affair. The heavily tinted glass means that if you happened to walk past this corner of Buckingham Palace, you would not have a clue what lay within. But inside, privacy extends to little more than a couple of shower curtains.

But there will be no complaints from the users. Who cares if a few mod cons are missing? All are conscious that they are enjoying what is unquestionably one of the most exclusive perks in London.

For many years, this was royal-only territory. Diana, Princess of Wales, and Princess Margaret were keen users. The Duke of Edinburgh taught his children to swim in this pool. Today, the swimmers might be an entire cross section of Palace life – an equerry, a chauffeur, a secretary from 'up the road' at Clarence House or St James's Palace. Sometimes, they are joined by the most senior non-royal figure in these parts, the Lord Chamberlain.

It's the same story next door. The corridor may be painted in an institutional green but there can be few offices in central London with an en suite squash court. The Duke was playing on this very court as he waited for the birth of his eldest son (in the days when expectant fathers had to stay out of the way). These days, anyone can play. The reigning Palace squash king is the retired Royal Naval officer who runs the Princess Royal's office.

How times have changed. Not so long ago, any staff found exercising in here would have been fired, if not court-martialled. Edward VII sent a courtier away in disgrace for using a comb instead of a hairbrush. His son, George V, refused to allow jazz, cocktails and ladies with painted fingernails to intrude upon his Court. A horse belonging to George VI was not allowed to breed with another horse on the grounds that its owner was a bookmaker. And yet, today, cleaners and peers of the realm might be splashing side by side in the Queen's pool a few yards from where the Sovereign is discussing affairs of state with the Prime Minister. So how on earth was the Queen – and the Duke for that matter – persuaded to approve this below-stairs revolution? Very easily, it turns out.

'I went to see her and explained why it might be a good idea for staff welfare and she just said: "Yes, try it,"' says Air Vice-Marshal Sir David Walker, Master of the Household, and, as such, the man in charge of running all the royal residences. When a plan is well argued and well presented, the Queen's response can be very straightforward. The Earl of Airlie, the former Lord Chamberlain, recalls a similar reaction when he submitted his proposals for the most far-reaching restructuring of the Royal Household since the Victorian era. He discussed them at great length with the Queen, at the end of which a decision was needed. 'She just said: "Get on with it."' He finds that a slow response is a pretty reliable indicator that the Queen does not like an idea. 'If you write a paper, it will be back in short order. If she doesn't like what you've said, you might not get an answer so quickly,' he explains. 'But when you are talking to her about difficult subjects, somehow or other *she* makes *you* feel better when you leave the room.'

Ask anyone who knows and works with the Queen to describe her and they will begin by emphasising how different she is from her public persona. She is 'very funny', 'a great mimic', 'pin sharp', 'doesn't miss a thing', 'very feminine', 'better with men' . . . But the public persona – solemn, remote, inscrutable – is not so much a persona as a professional demeanour which has served her well. If she was known for her vivacity or exuberance, people would be disappointed and curious on the inevitable occasions when it was not there. Expect regal and you will always get regal. We know that there is a private Queen, just as there is an ordinary man beneath the bearskin and the red tunic. But if we think that this private Queen is simply a more relaxed, humorous, animal-loving, racing-mad country cousin to the public model, we are very much mistaken. As her prime ministers have learned, one should never make any assumptions.

'There is a quite mistaken view of the Queen that she is just a small-c conservative. And that's not true,' says Tony Blair. 'She's just very protective of the monarchy. What I found to be her most surprising attribute is how streetwise she is. Frequently, throughout my time as Prime Minister, I was always stunned by her total ability to pick up the public mood and define it in the conversations I had with her. She completely understood what was going on and had a very clear ability to analyse people and their strengths and weaknesses very quickly.'

Sir John Major was also struck by the Queen's quiet worldliness: 'There's very little she hasn't seen. In my own experience, there is almost nothing that ruffles her. She's a good student of human behaviour.'

Prince William, the Duke of Cambridge, believes that, for all the advisers dispensing wise counsel to the Queen throughout her life, much of her success has been down to following her own gut instincts. It is a strategy which she has passed on to the younger generation. 'It's very much the case that she won't necessarily force advice on you,' he says. 'She'll let you work it out for yourself. She's always there for a question or two; for whatever it is you might need. But, just as she probably had to do, she feels that you have to work it out for yourself, that there are no set rules. You have to make it work. You have to do what you think is right. And she's a prime example of that. She had to carve her own way and she's done it fantastically for sixty years.'

Prince Andrew, the Duke of York, learned the royal ropes the same way. 'You have to find your way, develop your interests. There is never any direction,' says the former Royal Navy Commander and former business ambassador. 'But you've then got to be given the guidance and help to be successful. She's always given hugely important consideration and advice. I don't think any of us would have done anything in isolation.' He also points out that the Queen treats her discussions with her children and grandchildren just like her audiences with her politicians. There will be no round-the-dinner-table discussion about what was discussed one-on-one during the afternoon. 'It's one of those odd things. It's exactly the same as the conversation the Monarch has with the Prime Minister. That is a conversation between the two of them and only the two of them. The same thing is true with the other members of the family. None of us actually discuss the conversations that each of us has had.'

In a society where the reality show and phone-in have made a virtue of being noisy and opinionated, the Queen is a rare advertisement for the power of silence. 'Where she's been brilliant is in her quietness,' observes Charles Anson, her former Press Secretary. 'In a very noisy world where people constantly want to express themselves or overreact, what the Queen has done has been the opposite. She is not a celebrity. She's not at all shouty. You get back, perhaps, to that part of the brain where a child wants reassurance from a mother or father. They might call their parents "old squares" but, deep down, they want the quiet reassurance from the parental figure.'

Propping it all up is a faith which dates from childhood but was substantially reinforced soon after her father's death. The Archbishop of Canterbury, Dr Rowan Williams, believes that one of his predecessors,

Geoffrey Fisher, played his part. 'Before the Coronation, Geoffrey Fisher prepared a little book of meditations and prayers for her to use daily,' says Dr Williams. 'I think she really treasured that. She showed it to me once at Windsor – it's in the library there. I just have a hunch that the period before the Coronation was very, very formative for her and for the way she's approached everything since. It was a time when serious-ness kept breaking in.'

But the Queen's staff also know that nothing helps a bold idea along like a spot of levity. She has a keen sense of the ridiculous. After meeting a Scottish ice-cream manufacturer in 2007, she was fascinated to hear that he had developed a robotic milking operation for his cows. The Queen asked the Keeper of the Privy Purse, Sir Alan Reid, to investigate. Might it be feasible to build an automated milking shed at Windsor? Keepers of the Privy Purse have had many strange duties to perform through the centuries but none has ever had to become an expert on remote-controlled manure sweepers and bovine waterbeds. The Queen was not only fascinated by it all but close to hysterics when Reid explained how the cows would congregate in a 'loafing area' prior to milking. 'The way it was described, it was as if the cow would sit and read a magazine or wander around chatting,' says one of those involved. 'She loved it.' The plans sailed through, the £900,000 milking shed is now up and running and anyone invited to stay at Windsor for the weekend will be given a very animated guided tour – from the proud owner.

After more than thirty years in the Royal Air Force, Air Vice-Marshal Sir David Walker understands chains of command better than most. He was previously in charge of 14,000 men and women as head of RAF training. Yet he regards the Queen as the best boss he has encountered. 'She is far more accessible than most senior officers I've worked for. She's got a good mind for detail and if you want to see her, you'll get to see her.' As the man in charge of all royal hospitality, he knows that the Queen wants to be consulted on all new ideas. 'She'd tell you if it was a stinker.' A state banquet might look like a time-honoured set piece but every aspect of it will be revisited every time. It's hard to rearrange the furniture much at a place like Windsor where the St George's Hall table is said to be the longest in Britain. But the Queen always likes to fine-tune the arrangements. A few years ago, she decided that state banquets were, simply, going on too long. She discussed it with the Master and a solution was found: lose the soup. 'It saves twenty minutes,' says Walker.

The Secretary of the Master's Department, Michael Jephson, is used to suggestions from the very top when he is compiling guest lists for a reception. Sometimes the Queen will ask him to invite an interesting person she has just heard on the radio. She has a similar eye for detail as an employer. 'She is very beady. She has an uncanny way of knowing exactly what is going on,' says the current Lord Chamberlain, Lord Peel. 'I wasn't prepared for the level of in-depth knowledge.' The loyalty of long-serving staff to the Monarch is reciprocated. 'She really does feel as if she is part of a team and sometimes it shows,' says a former senior official. In particular, she will not tolerate rudeness towards her own people.

Many of her staff – and those who come up *against* her staff – talk about her pragmatism. She can display what former Prime Minister Tony Blair has described as 'a certain hauteur' (it would be surprising if a monarch could not) but she is not stuffy.

Some have found that the best way of dealing with over-protective, second-guessing royal officials is to bypass them altogether and go straight to the top. It's a high-risk strategy but sometimes it's the only way, as the television producer Edward Mirzoeff discovered when he was filming the great 1992 royal documentary, *Elizabeth R*. The final scene was to be the Ghillies' Ball at Balmoral – the social highlight of the Queen's stay in the Highlands. It had been a fraught day. The ballroom was so gloomy that Mirzoeff had been forced to scrounge a vanload of lighting from his local ITV rivals in Aberdeen. He had even enlisted the van driver as a 'sparks' to light the room before the Royal Family arrived. Finally, after his crew had only been filming for a few minutes, Palace staff intervened. Mirzoeff was informed that his time was up. The cameras had intruded for quite long enough. Mirzoeff admits that he 'nearly lost it' with the courtiers: 'I thought: "This can't happen." So I dashed across the dance floor and went straight up to the Queen – and said: "Ma'am, we have to keep on filming."'

He remembers the 'Bateman looks'* as he committed the ultimate dance-floor faux pas. But it worked. 'I simply cannot tell you how marvellous she is in a situation like that,' says Mirzoeff. 'She said to me: "Fine, well just carry on." And we got our ending. In fact, I had problems with everybody at one time or another making that film – except her.'

As the royal biographer Kenneth Rose observes: 'One of the most pertinent mottos of the Household is "Better Not".' The same is not true of the boss. After more than thirty years of sponsoring one of Ascot's plum royal fixtures, the King George VI and Queen Elizabeth Stakes, the diamond giant De Beers decided to step down. Only one company

---

* The pre-war cartoonist H. M. Bateman, a royal favourite, specialised in scenes of excruciating social ineptitude.

was prepared to come forward with the requisite pot of money. And Betfair, an online betting company, was not what some of the Jockey Club grandees had in mind. But there was no objection when the suggestion was put to the overall boss of Ascot Racecourse. As one official explains: 'The Queen accepted the reality. If no one else is willing to sponsor something, then there is no choice.' What used to be called 'Diamond Day' became the 'Betfair Weekend'.

In any tricky situation, officialdom's immediate instinct is to follow precedent. The Queen, on the other hand, is more inclined to follow common sense. Sir John Major recalls a clash between the two mindsets in 1994, on the eve of the fiftieth anniversary of D-Day at Portsmouth Guildhall. 'The Queen had been placed next to two European royals, and President Clinton and President Mitterrand had been placed well below the salt at the other end of the table,' he remembers. Clearly, at an event marking the Allied liberation of France, it would look faintly ridiculous to have the two principal players at the wrong end of the table. But the protocol people were in no mood to budge. 'The fairly frosty response from an official was that elected presidents were lower in protocol than monarchs!' Major recalls. So his Private Secretary contacted the Queen's Private Secretary who consulted the Queen. 'The Queen's reply, broadly, was: "Of course, people will expect President Clinton and President Mitterrand to sit beside me and, in any event, I see my cousins all the time." So the two presidents did indeed end up flanking the Queen.'

The following year, she dispensed with protocol again when the leaders of the free world arrived in London to mark the fiftieth anniversary of VE Day. The capital was full enough already without dozens of extra motorcades. As a result, the crowned heads and presidents were herded on to a couple of hired passenger coaches. Some of the overseas protocol departments were appalled. But the world leaders didn't seem to mind. As King Hussein of Jordan was heard to remark: 'This is the first time I've ever been on a bus!'

The Queen presides over a total workforce of around 1,100 – ranging from farmhands to management consultants – putting the monarchy somewhere on a par with a small government department. It's an operation which has gone through precisely the same changes in employment and health and safety law as every other employer. These days no one there refers to 'the Court', except when referring either to the daily notice of royal activities called the Court Circular or the Diplomatic Corps. All diplomats are still formally accredited to the old royal address, the Court of St James's.

Internally, the royal domain is referred to as the Royal Household or simply as 'the Palace'. The 'tweedy courtiers' derided by Lord Altrincham in his audacious 1957 salvo against the *ancien régime* have been replaced by a younger, meritocratic and entirely professional executive team. Gone, too, are the old job descriptions like 'lady clerk'.

The Queen does not send or receive emails personally but she is well aware of Facebook, YouTube and Twitter, having insisted on full demonstrations before the Palace went live on all three. When she was invited to visit the British offices of Google in 2008, her hosts cheekily asked if they might use the royal effigy on the website's main page (the 'Google doodle' in e-speak). The Queen's head is one of the most closely guarded pieces of intellectual property in the world, restricted to stamps, currency and Seals of Office. Her Private Secretary put the idea to her. 'Why not?' came the reply. For one day only, the second 'g' in Google was replaced with the Sovereign's head.

Anyone who actually puts pen to paper and sends a letter can rest assured that, unless it is a busy period around a birthday or a major anniversary, their thoughts are likely to go all the way to the top. Bundles of ordinary letters are sent up every morning. They may be hostile, sympathetic, grateful or, simply, desperate. 'The Queen loves her mail and does not like to be shielded,' says senior correspondence officer Sonia Bonici as she prepares to send up the latest batch, some of which is not entirely complimentary about one member of the Royal Family. The Queen will see it all. As she said in 1992: 'It gives one an idea what is worrying people and what, actually, they feel that I could do to help. There are occasions when I *can* help. I can pass things on to the right authorities or I can even write to various organisations who will look into it. But I have always had this feeling that letters are written to *me*.'

The Royal Collection, which, for much of the reign, was run by just a handful of staff (including Soviet spy Anthony Blunt) is now the largest department of the Royal Household. Its 320 staff keep its one million works of art in perfect condition and circulating round the world's museums and galleries without a penny of subsidy. The Queen can't sell any of it; she holds the collection 'in trust for the nation'. Hence, it is she alone who approves the loan of every single object, be it an Old Master or a coal scuttle. The Queen is also the nominal boss of the Royal Collection's twelve gift shops in London, Windsor and Edinburgh, all of which generate vital income to maintain the collection. They sell everything from guardsman pyjamas for children to organic dog biscuits and royal postcards. The bestselling postcard used to be one of Diana, Princess of Wales. Today, it is the Queen herself. It's not the youthful film star

Queen of the mid-fifties, either. It's today's Queen, dressed in her full state finery on the day of the State Opening of Parliament. It's the image most people have – and like to have – of the Queen: constant, regal, benign, authoritative, feminine, true. It's an image which underlines the two most important by-products of constitutional monarchy: stability and continuity.

Yet it's also an image of a royal radical. It shows the Monarch who expelled the debutantes, invented the walkabout, opened up the Palace, tore up the rulebook on bowing or curtseying and hosted a pop concert at the age of seventy-six. This is the Monarch who has just opened a café in the Palace garden (albeit one where the cappuccinos come with a chocolate-powdered crown sprinkled on top). 'She is actually more open to new ideas now than ten, twenty or thirty years ago,' says one senior official. In 2010, the Keeper of the Privy Purse, Sir Alan Reid, received a request from Disney to take over the state apartments of Kensington Palace for the launch of the studio's seventh 'Princess' movie, *Rapunzel,* later retitled *Tangled.* Disney also wanted to stage a global celebration of all its princesses, going right back to Snow White. Where else but a real palace? Ten years ago, say staff, the response would have been a definite 'No' – if indeed the suggestion had ever been put to the Queen. On this occasion, after all the pros and cons had been laid out, the Queen was rather intrigued. 'Seems like a good idea,' she replied, giving Reid the nod. So how does she juggle these twin personas? How has a self-assured but intrinsically shy person who likes familiarity and routine – and is less confrontational than all her modern predecessors – also been the House of Windsor's very own royal revolutionary?

Princess Elizabeth Alexandra Mary of York was born on 21 April 1926, to be followed four years later by her sister, Margaret Rose. Her parents, the Duke and Duchess of York, had expected to lead a dutiful life on the periphery of the Royal Family and imagined that their daughters would do the same. Three events would change all that and shape the girl who would be Queen nearly twenty-six years later. The first was her father's sudden promotion from dutiful second son to King following the Abdication of 1936. The second was the Second World War, during which a little girl locked in a castle emerged into a beautiful young Princess at the wheel of an army truck. The third was the arrival of a dashing young Royal Navy officer with impeccable royal connections but no home. And having succeeded to the throne in 1952, the Queen has not merely moved it along with the times but has transformed it. The courtier who nodded off at the tail end of Victoria's reign and woke up in the early

1950s would have found few changes beyond some cars at the back of the Royal Mews and the advent of telephones. Had the same courtier nodded off and reawoken after a further half-century, he might have expired on discovering footmen in the Monarch's pool and secretaries borrowing the Royal Box at the Royal Albert Hall. On the other hand, he might be relieved to discover a monarch who had actually changed very little over the same period, her sense of duty and her love of horses, dogs and Prince Philip completely undimmed.

'The Queen realises that the world is changing, that the country is changing and that this must be reflected within the Household,' says a close colleague of many years' standing. 'But it needn't necessarily reflect her personal life. That's where she would dig her well-known heel in.'

Royal truths, taught on a grandmother's knee, certainly hold fast today. Queen Mary – along with George V – believed in settling upon a style and sticking with it. 'Queen Mary remained frozen into the fashions of 1913 and that's why she wore the toque and a stiff piece of buckram under the dress so that she could load herself with jewels,' says the historian Kenneth Rose. 'The King insisted on her having this rigid, old-fashioned appearance because he didn't like change.'

The Queen is similarly wedded to a certain style. Once teased by some fashion commentators for her floral patterns and sensible shoes, she is now held aloft as a fashion icon. 'She is, simply, one of the most elegant women in the world,' declared Miuccia Prada when the Queen's state visit to Italy in 2000 reached Milan. The sentiment was echoed by an entire room full of brand names including Missoni, Fendi, Ferré and Krizia ('The Queen is above fashion,' purred Mariuccia Krizia). Even the *Guardian* felt moved to salute the Queen on its front page the next day.

The Queen's own interest in fashion and jewellery, as in so much else, might be described as practical. All her shoes, for example, have a large square heel because she has discovered that it spreads the pressure more evenly than a point and thus makes standing up all day more tolerable. The royal designer, Hardy Amies, was always in awe of the Queen's ability to put on a tiara while walking downstairs. She has refreshingly uncomplicated views on clothes. According to Sarah Bradford, the Queen told a milliner: 'I can't wear beige because people won't know who I am.' A Private Secretary who misinformed her about a dress code with the result that she turned up in day clothes to find everyone else in 'full fig', was later admonished gently with the words: 'I think we were a little underdressed.'

However, the Queen is well aware that her choice of clothes can be critical to the success of an engagement. The green ensemble she wore for her arrival in Ireland in May 2011 set the tone for one of the most successful state visits of modern times in an instant. She had not reached the foot of the aeroplane steps before Irish commentators were joyously saluting her 'emerald' hat, coat and dress (the official Palace designation of 'jade' was largely ignored). The following night, her evening dress for the state banquet was decorated with 2,091 embroidered shamrocks and an Irish harp in Swarovski crystals. By the end of the tour, her dresser, Angela Kelly (herself of Irish descent), had become something of a national celebrity in her own right.

On any visit, she must dress up. It's not vanity on her part. It would simply offend her hosts if she did not. When the royal party got soaked at a military parade in Northern Ireland in 2010, there was no change of clothes available. As everyone thawed out indoors, the Queen declined a chair. 'I'll stand,' she said, explaining that by drying out on her feet her clothes would not be creased for the official lunch. A rare but historic wardrobe blunder took place just after the Coronation in 1953 when the Queen travelled to Scotland to be presented with the Honours of Scotland wearing an ordinary day dress. Many Scots took great umbrage. She might be Queen Elizabeth II of England but she was Queen Elizabeth I of Scotland. If she was to receive its sacred honours, then they believed that she should look the part and wear evening dress, if not Scottish Coronation robes.

The oversight was blamed on her Private Secretary, Sir Alan 'Tommy' Lascelles. Nearly fifty years later, as the Queen was preparing to open the newly created Scottish Parliament in 1999, she took no chances. For the first time, she had a woman as one of her private secretaries, Mary Francis, and the former senior Downing Street aide was pleasantly surprised to be involved.

'The Scots don't forget,' Mary Francis recalls. 'But there was no question of the Queen wearing Coronation clothes this time. So we commissioned a Scottish dress designer and, unprecedentedly I think, the Queen asked me to join her and her dresser when they had the discussion with the designer, which was very nice.'

The result was a three-part creation by Scotland's Sandra Murray featuring a dress of light green wool, a long-sleeved mauve coat of silk and wool and an Isle of Skye scarf. Not a word of Scottish displeasure was heard.

For years, the Queen's wardrobe was the fiefdom of the invincible Margaret 'Bobo' MacDonald, the former nursemaid who had been with her since she was a baby.* These days, the Queen seldom troubles the

---

* Known as 'the QE3' by the crew of the Royal Yacht, 'Bobo' was so close to her mistress that Palace newcomers would be warned: 'Don't upset Miss MacDonald or you'll ruin the Queen's day.'

big-name designers, preferring to leave her outfits to a small in-house team led by Angela Kelly. Diners at a certain Belgravia restaurant often do a double take when they spot the Queen with her wardrobe team enjoying a lively ladies' lunch in the corner. Kelly is one of a small inner sanctum of trusty intimates who loosely fall into three camps: staff (including the Windsor stud groom who looks after the Queen's personal horses and her pages), senior officials (including her Private Secretary) and ladies-in-waiting (two of whom have notched up a century's service between them). 'The Queen doesn't really have a "best friend", it's just not her,' says a trusted aide.

Another Queen Mary dictum is as true as ever: avoid over-familiarity. 'If the Queen ever feels affronted about something, she has the perfect answer,' explains Kenneth Rose. 'She just stares at the person with open eyes, absolutely no expression.' Even experienced staff occasionally find that they have transgressed the unmarked line through what might seem an innocuous remark. A former official recalls: 'Once, when everyone had just come back from their Christmas holidays, I said to the Queen: "Did you have a nice Christmas?" I got a very cold stare back. It was the kind of remark that you would make to anyone else but you were not encouraged to make to the Queen. Everybody had the same experience. You'd think: "Wow, we're getting on really well." And then she'd do something that just reminded you, that just pushed you back at a distance.'

It was not a mark of displeasure or rudeness. On another occasion, all was explained: 'The Queen told me that she was very influenced by Queen Mary who had given her tips about how you behave as a Queen. One of them was that you never allow yourself to get too close to your advisers. It was very clear in the Royal Family generally, but the Queen was very strong on this.'

To outsiders, it can seem a peculiar code of behaviour but the royal/courtier working dynamic is a unique one. 'You're not there to be their mate. You mustn't cross the line for very good reasons,' says Elizabeth Buchanan, Private Secretary to the Prince of Wales until 2008. 'When I got there, I was startled by how much you get to know about their life. People see things that are very intimate. A huge amount of trust is put upon your shoulders and it has to be respected. People might say to me: "How is Charles?" And I would think: "I don't know anyone called Charles." And I really would not think of him as "Charles". That's why titles are crucial. If you don't buy into that basic respect, then the whole thing's going to wind up very quickly. It's the same with ministers who want everyone to call them by their first name. It disrupts the relationship very quickly.'

No one, however grand, is immune from the royal 'stare'. Queen Mary – 'probably the last woman to believe in the Divine Right of Kings', says Kenneth Rose – once reduced Loelia, Duchess of Westminster, to jelly with a killer stare. The Duchess had kissed her hand and left lipstick on the royal glove. London's embassy circuit is still talking about the recent annual diplomatic reception at which one diplomat arrived late and missed his allotted place in the introduction line. Rather than miss out on his handshake and chat with the Queen, he pushed into the line further down. It was not a wise move. Not only was there no chat but he received 'the stare' and was promptly escorted away by officials.

A former Cabinet Minister, who periodically found himself on duty with several members of the Royal Family, admits that there was 'this invisible line between formality and informality' and not much guidance. 'Because we're in the modern world now, I find myself wondering: "Is this appropriate?" And I think, on balance, that it probably is; that if we choose to have a monarchy, it *is* different from other systems and they're never off duty. There isn't an entirely private life except within their own family.'

It's part of the royal paradox. We want our monarch to be just like us and yet we want her to be different. 'To be part of the nation and yet apart from the nation is always a difficult balance,' Sir John Major acknowledges. She may be the most famous woman on earth but those close to the Queen testify to a robust sense of position, though not of self-importance. And she has an implacable aversion to insincerity, however well intentioned. The Queen cannot abide pretence. A former Private Secretary recalls suggesting what might almost constitute a gag. 'I wanted a joke in this speech about *Private Eye* – it may have been using the phrase "Shome Mistake" – and she just said to me, very firmly: "It just isn't me to talk about *Private Eye*." All the private secretaries had the experience of recommending her to do various things when she was out and about and more than once she said: "I don't think that's quite right." It was a firm touch.'

One of those private secretaries was the late Lord Charteris who recalled drafting a speech for her which began: 'I am very glad to be back in Birmingham.' The Queen read it, picked up a pen and crossed out the word 'very'. It was not a slight to Birmingham. It was simply that – in her eyes – it smacked of insincerity.

'She's just not a consummate actress like her mother,' says a member of the inner sanctum. The late Queen Mother, it must be said, had no qualms about dispensing a little superfluous praise. When a storm forced an emergency landing in a godforsaken Canadian outpost called Cold

Lake in 1985, the locals were even more delighted when she declared: 'Ah, Cold Lake. I've always wanted to come here.'

It was Lord Charteris who remarked that the Queen 'combines her mother's charm with her father's shyness'. She has endured the public spotlight more than anyone else alive but has never enjoyed it greatly. 'You never feel that she courts popularity. Sometimes you rather wish that she did more,' says a former Private Secretary. 'But her judgement is impeccable. By not courting it, she is more popular than if she did court it. She's not an ambulance chaser.'

Prince William is emphatic on the subject. 'She cares not for celebrity, that's for sure,' he says firmly – and approvingly. 'That's not what monarchy's about. It's about setting examples. It's about doing one's duty as she would say. It's about using your position for the good. It's about serving the country and that really is the crux of it all.'

Once or twice, the Queen's reticence has not served her well. Ask senior Palace figures past and present to list the blunders of this reign and none will get beyond the fingers of one hand. But two examples usually recur: Aberfan (the Welsh village where 144 people, 116 of them children, died beneath a collapsing slagheap in 1966) and Lockerbie (crash site of the Pan Am Boeing 747, downed by a terrorist bomb in 1988). In both cases, the Queen was criticised for her slow response to the disaster. She did not visit Aberfan until six days after the tragedy and did not attend or send a member of her family to the Lockerbie memorial service in January 1989. In both cases, she would subsequently acknowledge to her advisers that she – rather than they – had got it wrong. Her critics at the time inferred a lack of compassion. In truth, say those who know her, it is down to a deep reluctance both to intrude upon private grief and also to show raw emotion in public. Those who accompanied the Queen to Aberfan – where she had tea with a family who had lost seven members – say that she was in tears. Few have seen her so distressed as when she visited Dunblane following the 1996 massacre of sixteen children and a teacher. 'It was almost unbearable,' says a member of her team that day. 'But you wouldn't catch her betraying that in public. It was done behind closed doors.' All those who have worked closely with the Queen point out that one of her greatest assets is what they call her 'negative judgement', her capacity to say 'No'. As Bagehot argued, sound constitutional monarchy is often about 'well-considered inaction'.

'She's as good at deciding what she doesn't want to do as saying what she does want to do,' explains Charles Anson. 'The Queen's got good instincts. She's open to new ideas if people make a convincing argument but she's not necessarily going to suggest it herself. That's natural – it's the nature of constitutional monarchy.' Nor does the Queen like arguments. Her preferred method of expressing disapproval of an idea is to ask a lot of questions about it. Another way of dispensing a gentle thumbs-down is to deploy a time-honoured phrase: 'Are you sure?'

'The Queen has the most incredible capacity to listen and to learn,' says the Duke of York. 'She is not above society. She's in it and reflects it. That comes through experience and I think we've all learned from her experience. All of us are in a long-term relationship with society and, as it were, the people.'

Few creatures of habit are more habitual than royalty. It's hardly surprising when your life is pre-ordained by the rituals of the national and religious calendars. Easter equals Royal Maundy. November equals Cenotaph. Christmas equals broadcast to the Commonwealth and so on. Royal memories can be elephantine. As William Shawcross has pointed out, the late Queen Mother retained a lifelong dislike for Dutch landscapes because they had lined the walls of the Palace air-raid shelter during the war. And having stayed at Chatsworth, the Duke of Devonshire's Derbyshire seat, at the height of the Abdication crisis, the unhappy associations meant that she never stayed there again during the remaining sixty-seven years of her life. But she was equally robust in her loyalties, be they to the Black Watch, the Eton College Beagles, the Sandringham Women's Institute or a teapot presented to her by a British Rail steward. It followed her on her travels for ever after.

The curious, often stifling pace of royal life means that the Queen craves those moments when she can 'blend in' and enjoy what other people might call 'normality'. As the Duke of York puts it: 'We're not that much different to anybody else. It's just a slightly different reality.' A favourite event is the Royal Windsor Horse Show, partly because it was where she competed in ordinary competitions as a little girl but also because it is somewhere she can wander around in a headscarf, being part of a crowd rather than its object.

On her return from the 2002 tour of Australia, the Queen thoroughly enjoyed an hour in the duty free section of Singapore Changi Airport while her plane refuelled. 'It was a secure area, no one was expecting her and she had a lovely time browsing at the Clarins counter while Prince Philip went off to look at gadgets,' says one of the royal party. 'Those sort of moments, that we take for granted, mean a lot to her.' It is why she remains so close to favourites like stud groom Terry Pendry and dresser Angela Kelly. 'They talk to her about day-to-day life in the real world,' says one member of staff.

Similarly, the Queen's loved ones find her endearingly envious of their own relative freedom to have conversations or express opinions which might be acceptable for a member of the Royal Family but not for the Sovereign. 'There are occasions when the Queen will say to you, "Oh you didn't do that, did you?"' laughs the Duke of York. 'And I know full well that it's a comment: "Oh, I wish I'd been able to do that."' Because it's removed the issue one step from the Monarch and allowed something to be said.'

Like anyone, the Queen has her likes and dislikes. Most are well known – horses: good; spicy food: bad, etc. She likes driving fast but hates seatbelts. She likes charismatic, confident men around her but prefers female staff to be more subtle and less demonstrative. As one former senior adviser puts it: 'She was born in the twenties and brought up to believe that men get on with things whereas women exercise power through quiet influence, not shaking their fists.'

When she has made up her mind about something, it does not easily unbend. The most obvious manifestation of that is the corgi. The current royal menagerie includes Labradors, retrievers, spaniels – not to mention cows, sheep, parakeets and a pigeon loft – but it is the corgi which has reigned supreme in the Monarch's affections since her father, then Duke of York, bought the first royal corgi, Dookie, from a local kennels in 1933.

The Queen continues to share her father's keen eye for decorations, an interest she has in common with most members of the Royal Family. As well as inheriting an extensive repertoire of honours, she has also created her own Royal Family Order. Outsiders may imagine that gongs are liberally sprinkled among relations and staff like confetti. As one courtier explained to royal biographer Gyles Brandreth: 'The Queen is the Fount of Honour so it is hardly surprising those closest to the fount get splashed.' But the details of who has (and has not) been awarded certain honours continue to fascinate royal Kremlinologists. Neither the Duchess of York nor Princess Michael of Kent, for example, has been offered the (women-only) Royal Family Order.

No courtier ever underestimates the importance of symbols. Senior officials still shudder as they recall the saga of the flagless Palace mast in the days before the funeral of Diana, Princess of Wales, in 1997. First a handful of mourners, then the papers, followed by the phone-ins, the politicians and finally the Queen's own senior advisers advocated a half-mast Union flag. But the Queen stood resolute in defence of symbolism. Only a Royal Standard should fly above the Palace, she decreed with mounting (and uncharacteristic) fury, and no death, including her own, should lower it. Mary Francis says that the flag saga was the only occasion she could recall of the Queen expressing real anger. Eventually, the Monarch was persuaded to amend tradition (today, the Union flag does indeed fly in the absence of the Standard) but not before a very senior adviser was heard to say: 'I have been scarred by the Queen.'

But if she is such an arch-traditionalist, how come so much has changed on her watch? One senior adviser puts it down to the Queen's ability to 'compartmentalise', to keep her head of state persona separate from her private life. 'If you propose a change or amendment and it is well argued, she would be gracious and sensible and say: "OK, yup, fine,"' he says. 'But "OK, yup, fine" doesn't necessarily mean "I agree."'

The opening of Buckingham Palace – originally to fund fire repairs at Windsor Castle and now to fund the Royal Collection – was a case in point. Sir Malcolm Ross, former Comptroller and architect of great state occasions for fifteen years, recalls that, ultimately, the decision to open up was a straightforward if momentous one. 'It was a necessity, not a choice. It was a very well-presented case and it was made clear to the Queen that it wouldn't affect her personally. Now she always enjoys looking round the Palace exhibition before it opens because they are always finding and displaying things even she has not seen. She likes meeting people who say: "It was lovely to see the Palace."'

Sandringham, in Norfolk, is a prime example of somewhere that doesn't change yet remains at the forefront of new ideas. The dining room may not have altered much since the late Queen Mother changed the colour scheme to light green in 1938. And the Royal Pigeon Loft continues to exist because George VI liked it and used to take Princess Elizabeth there as a little girl. But whereas he used to sell estate apples to Marks & Spencer in King's Lynn, the Queen takes great pride in her brand-new apple juice factory which distributes all over the country. She has even manned the bottling line herself.

The Queen believes in tradition, as long as it has a point. 'Protocol and ceremonial – and they're brothers-in-arms – must be relevant,' says Sir Malcolm Ross. 'You shoot yourself in both feet if you produce an event which is frankly nothing more than an historic re-enactment. It's got to be relevant.'

As old certainties and social norms recede, so the Queen is actually more open to suggestions than ever. Contrary to conventional wisdom, the older she gets, the *less* stuck in her ways she becomes. It is not necessarily what one expects of the longest living monarch in history. But, then, her age is often overlooked. That stock image of Queen Victoria is one of an elderly woman, forever in mourning clothes and a lugubrious state of retrospection. We have a stock image of the Queen, too. But while she has now outlived Victoria by several years, we still see her as active and engaged. It is an image that has barely changed in thirty years. Given that the Queen seems to carry on doing the same old things at the same pace all over the world year in year out, she seems to be at a perpetual stage of life; a lady of a certain age but not an *old* lady.

Jim Callaghan wisely observed that, for better or worse, each generation forms a composite view of the face on the coins: 'Every monarch makes his or her own niche in people's minds and hearts and this Queen has done that.'

We see a purposeful woman in a headscarf, perhaps with dogs or horses; we see a woman with a shy smile and a handbag walking down streets full of over-excited mothers and tongue-tied children; we see a proud woman dwarfed by extremely tall men in uniform and bearskins; we see a solemn woman in crown and robes processing through Parliament.

They are all images which betoken that dependability, loyalty, common sense, calmness. They might, with another person, suggest grandeur, coolness, detachment, elitism. And what is a monarchy if not grand, aloof and faintly untouchable? Yet those are not the impressions left on the vast majority of people when they see the Queen. Rather, they feel like the young academic who had just met the Queen during her tour of a science exhibition in 2010. 'I'd never given her much thought but it was a lovely opportunity to meet her,' he said afterwards. 'Then a few of us went for a drink and I realised I was shaking. My heart was pounding. And it dawned on me that I'd just done something extraordinary.' Despite being an extremely bright, articulate young man in the front line of medical scientific research, he could not recollect a word of what he had said during the encounter, nor could he offer any rational explanation for his state of benign shock. It was most unlike him, he said, but he was not bothered. Because he had just met the Queen.

Most organisations or businesses run by the same person for nearly sixty years become static, if not ossified. So why has this one been gathering momentum in the other direction ever since the Queen reached what most people would regard as retirement age? It's not only the result of what some call the 'Diana effect', although officials readily concede that one important legacy of the Princess was a greater informality and a recognition of the need for 'emotional change'. It's also down to a more general loosening of the royal collar.

'She doesn't want to do the same old thing any more,' says a former Private Secretary. 'She likes shorter greeting lines and fewer of them, more young people.'

She is smiling more these days, indulging her own interests a little more. If an awayday to the regions errs more towards horses and children than trade promotion, so be it. There is less of a beady eye on the clock – a far cry from the super-punctual Princess Elizabeth who took to prodding her mother's Achilles tendon with an umbrella during the 1947 South African tour to keep the royal show on schedule. 'She's quite often late for things now, not that anyone's complaining,' says one veteran royal correspondent. Of course they're not. Slowly, almost imperceptibly, the aura has changed. The Queen has now acquired the status of national treasure. There is nothing contrived about this metamorphosis whatsoever. It simply began in early 2002 following the death of Princess Margaret, followed swiftly by that of the Queen Mother.

'Finally,' says a family friend, 'she is seen as a grandmother.' Sir John Major echoes a popular Household view: 'At about the time the Queen Mother died, the Queen effectively became the "Mother of the Nation".' While the Queen Mother was alive, the Queen had been caught between the royal generations, the sensible, serious one trying to keep the younger members of the family under control while keeping a protective eye on the free-spirited mother. A delightful and good-natured sense of filial exasperation emerges from the latter stages of William Shawcross's official biography of the Queen Mother. When the Queen installed a stairlift to assist her mother with the steps at home, she received no thanks. Instead, the Queen Mother would make a point of travelling downstairs on the contraption and walking back up. Attempts to cajole her into a golf buggy for walkabouts only worked after someone had the bright idea of painting the thing in her racing colours. Nor was there any respite from her spending. A particularly eye-watering bill from a racing trainer arrived on the Monarch's desk with a little handwritten postscript: 'Oh dear'.

In the eyes of the public and the media, the Queen Mother was the living embodiment of the 'Blitz spirit' and she could do no wrong. Yet the same sentiments did not extend to the Queen. She was respected and admired almost universally, of course, but there was not that same sense of indulgence. The Monarch was not a twinkly-eyed old granny. She was a world leader.

In the last few years, though, there has been an unconscious reassessment. We don't necessarily think of the Queen as being very much older, just increasingly exceptional. 'She doesn't present herself as an old lady,' observes former Lord Chancellor Jack Straw. Now that the First World War generation has disappeared and the veterans of the Second World War dwindle to a noble handful, it becomes ever more extraordinary to think that the Monarch who sits and mulls over the state of the nation with David Cameron on Wednesday evenings used to do the same with Winston Churchill. When President Sarkozy of France and Britain's Gordon Brown neglected to invite the Queen to mark the sixty-fifth anniversary of the D-Day landings in Normandy, there was a public outcry. But it was not confined to Britain and it was not a row about 'snubs' or diplomatic niceties. It just seemed extraordinary to omit an invitation to the one surviving head of state who actually wore uniform during the Second World War.

The Queen's visit to Virginia in 2007 to mark the 400th anniversary of the English arriving in Jamestown generated true euphoria. To have a monarch was exciting, naturally. But that wasn't the point. The big deal was the fact that the Queen and Prince Philip had been guests of honour at the 350th.

Similarly, the packed United Nations Assembly which rose to its feet to salute the Queen in 2010 was not applauding her words. The main attraction was the fact that this particular speaker had already stood on the same stage to address the same organisation long before half of today's delegates were born. Her reign not only spans twelve British prime ministers but also twelve American presidents and six popes.

Just like her late mother before her, though, the Queen does not welcome attempts, however well meaning, to curtail her engagements.

So, does anyone ever try to say: 'Your Majesty, would it not be a good idea to take it easy?' 'We all do,' Prince William replies with a smile. 'We all try and sit down with her. My father and her children say it a lot to her. For the grandchildren, it's a bit difficult for us to say, "Take it easy" when she's so much older than us and has done so much more. We do hint at taking some things off her but she won't have anything of it!'

What about the word 'retirement'? 'I've never heard it,' says the Duke of York. 'It's not that it is "not open for discussion". It's just that it's not necessary. There's just a great deal of concern to make sure the Queen's programme is managed in a suitable fashion.'

Today, people are often surprised by their own emotional response to the mere sight of the Queen. A typical example occurred as she arrived at the 2010 Wimbledon Tennis Championships after an absence of thirty-three years. 'Oh God,' announced a woman in the crowd, astonished by her own vulnerability, 'I think I'm going to cry.'

'I always believed that, much as she would miss her mother, the Queen would actually find life in public easier,' says a former senior adviser. 'In the past, you had the throne being squeezed by the dazzling young generation and the dazzling old generation. Now, the Queen has inherited the mother-of-the-nation role and William is looking like a paragon while it is Prince Charles in the middle. It's a very tough role. And I think the Queen found it quite tough sometimes.

'Of course she misses her mother every day because they talked every day, they wrote letters to each other all the time. They were a tremendous double act but it wasn't a comfortable role for the Queen, always to be told how marvellous her mother was.'

He sums up the Queen's approach to the job today as follows: 'There's a serenity about her. But I think if you are of an age, you have a pretty old-fashioned faith, you do your best every day and say your prayers every night – well, if you're criticised for it, you're not going to get much better whatever you do. What's the point of worrying?' Ruminating on the way the Queen has reigned for more than half a century, Prince William believes that his grandmother has few grounds for regret. 'For her, it must be a relief to know that she has furrowed her own path and that she's done that successfully and that the decisions she's made have turned out to be correct. You make it up a lot as you go along. So to be proven right when it's your decision-making gives you a lot of confidence. You realise that the role you're doing – you're doing it well; that you're making a difference. That's what's key. It's about making a difference for the country.'

The Queen, on the other hand, sees nothing remotely remarkable in the way she approaches her role. Having spent some time accompanying her around Nigeria during a Commonwealth tour in 2003, Jack Straw, then Foreign Secretary, could not help reflecting that the Queen was only five years younger than his own mother. At the end of one day, he remarked: 'Ma'am, if I may say so, that was very professional.' 'Foreign Secretary,' the Queen replied, 'I should be, given how long I've been doing it.'

Recent years have been very good ones for the monarchy and the build-up to the Diamond Jubilee even more so. And herein, perhaps, lies the most important factor behind this new-found serenity. All bosses or commanders thrive when their organisations are successful. And the monarchy is not just back on track and prospering. It is breaking new ground.

Few members of the Queen's family or her staff had seen her as enthusiastic about a royal tour as she was in May 2011 during the first state visit ever made to the Republic of Ireland. This was a diplomatic watershed, a genuinely historic exercise in reconciliation and friendship which achieved more in four days than years of political horsetrading. No one else could have pulled it off. This was, arguably, the Queen's most important state visit since her tour of Russia in 1994 or the day that Britannia sailed in to newly democratic South Africa in 1995. Here was a stirring reminder of the healing power of monarchy. And the Queen was visibly thrilled. It was almost as if she was saying: '*This* is the point of me.' The fact that her hosts also included three famous racing studs on the royal schedule made it as near-perfect a state visit as one could contrive.

'She was so excited about it and really looking forward to it. It was quite sweet,' says Prince William proudly, pointing out that whereas he himself could 'nip in' to Ireland relatively easily, it had been off-limits to the Queen all her life. 'Normally, with a lot of tours, there's a certain amount of apprehension but also "I've done this before". But this was like a big door opening up to her that had been locked for so long. And now she has been able to see what's behind the door.'

But, he says, the Queen will have derived much greater satisfaction from the bilateral successes achieved during this visit than from satisfying any personal ambitions. There were certainly plenty of personal subtexts to this tour, not least the murder of Prince Philip's uncle, Lord Mountbatten, by the Irish Republican Army during a family holiday in County Sligo in 1979.* Yet neither the Queen nor Prince Philip made any direct reference to it. 'It's "personal" v "duty". There's a big differ-ence,' says Prince William. 'As far as she was concerned, in terms of the relationship between Britain and Ireland and the Troubles, it was time to move on from that. What's happened has happened and no one wants to cover it up. We must make sure all the right things are done and that the right people are said sorry to or vice versa. But it was not about her losing Lord Mounbatten when she was younger. It was about the bigger picture. And the bigger picture is close relations between the state of Ireland and the UK.'

The Prince's ready grasp of the diplomatic imperatives not only shows a wise head on young shoulders. It is another contributing factor to the Queen being, in the words of one bishop, 'the happiest I have ever seen her'. She can now look far into the future with confidence. She is supported by the most experienced Prince of Wales in history but can also take great pride in the calibre of the next royal generation down the line.

Only a matter of days before the Irish visit, Prince William and Catherine Middleton embarked on life together as the Duke and Duchess of Cambridge. Some of those at the wedding reception had never seen

---

* It was not just the death of Lord Mountbatten which appalled the Queen and the Royal Family. The bomb hidden inside his fishing boat also killed his fourteen-year-old grandson, Nicholas Knatchbull, his mother-in-law, Doreen, Lady Brabourne, and a fifteen-year-old local boy, Paul Maxwell. Nicholas's parents and twin brother, Tim, were so badly injured that they were unable to attend his funeral.

such an effervescent Sovereign. One describes her as 'positively playful'. 'She was, literally, skipping,' says another.

Six weeks before that wedding, Prince William travelled around the world at the invitation of the prime ministers of Australia and New Zealand. They wanted a senior royal representative to meet victims of a series of natural disasters. The five-day trip was arranged at short notice and the Prince was back on duty soon afterwards. 'I slept for quite a bit and then I went straight back in to work,' says the Anglesey-based RAF search and rescue pilot. 'Then she sent me the most wonderful letter saying "Congratulations" and "Well done, you did well down there" which meant a lot to me. It's funny but when you get a letter from her or a bit of praise, it goes a long, long way, more so than anyone else saying "Well done" to you. It's mainly because there's such gravitas behind those words.'

The regal aura can certainly humble the most distinguished visitors to the Palace. Cool-headed recipients of the most illustrious decorations can be a bag of nerves in the royal presence. But it is interesting to learn that the Queen commands the same reverence among her own heirs and successors. 'Even within the family [it happens],' admits Prince William. 'I say to people "she's my grandmother to me first and then she's the Queen." Words that come from her, I take very personally and I really appreciate.'

The future monarch certainly considers himself extremely lucky to have both his father and his grandmother to consult on the job that lies ahead. No trainee sovereign has ever had so much experience on which to draw. 'My relationship with my grandmother has gone from strength to strength,' he says. 'As a shy younger man it could be harder to talk about weighty matters. It was: "This is my grandmother who is the Queen and these are serious historical subjects." As I've got older, she's become an even more important part of my life so it's much easier. And obviously, with the wedding, she was a massive help.'

The Queen, he acknowledges, was a wonderful ally as the young couple started making wedding plans – only to discover that officials had been preparing lists without asking him. 'For instance, I came into the first meeting for the wedding, post-engagement. And I [was given] this official list of 777 names – dignitaries, governors, all sorts of people – and not one person I knew.' The Duke, Prince William, chuckles as he recalls his own sense of helplessness in the face of this earnest if well-meaning interference. 'They said: "These are the people we should invite." I looked at it in absolute horror and said: "I think we should start again."'

It was the Queen who came to his rescue: 'I rang her up the next day and said, "Do we need to be doing this?" And she said: "No. Start with your friends first and then go from there." And she told me to bin the list. She made the point that there are certain times when you have to strike the right balance. And it's advice like that which is really key when you know that she's seen and done it before.' The list was duly 'binned'. And a grateful Prince William absorbed another useful lesson in striking that delicate balance between 'personal' and 'duty'.

On other wedding matters, however, he rapidly learned that there was absolutely no room for manoeuvre. 'I wanted to decide what to wear for the wedding,' he recalls. As a commissioned officer in all three Services and a serving member of the Royal Air Force, the Prince certainly had a few choices. Except that he did not. 'I was given a categorical: "No, you'll wear this"!'

Having just appointed the Prince to the position of Colonel of the Irish Guards, his most senior military appointment – and one of *her* Guards regiments to boot – the Queen was quite clear that her grandson should be getting married in his Irish Guards uniform. 'So you don't always get what you want, put it that way,' he laughs. 'But I knew perfectly well that it was for the best. That "no" is a very good "no". So you just do as you're told!' Besides, as a serving officer in Her Majesty's Armed Forces, he could hardly disobey an order from the Commander-in-Chief.

The Prince admits that there are so many things that he would like to ask the Queen about. But he is both conscious of the demands on her time and the fact that she is a great believer in learning through experience. 'It goes back to trying to work it out for yourself,' he explains. 'I know that if I ask her questions, I'll be expecting one thing and something else will happen.' Does the Queen give him a long briefing before a big trip like his 2011 tour of Canada? 'I prefer to do a "post-debrief" than a "pre-debrief",' he replies. 'It's a bit easier and there are no hidden expectations.'

But he finds it comforting to know that there is such a repository of wisdom and experience to consult: 'There's no question you can ask and no point you can raise that she won't already know about – and have a better opinion. She's very up for that sort of thing. And for me, particularly, being the young bloke coming through, being able to talk to my grandmother and ask her questions and know that there's sound advice coming back is very reassuring.'

History has only yielded three octogenarian monarchs. By the age of eighty, neither George III nor Victoria played a particularly active role in the life of the nation. The Queen, on the other hand, has barely amended her schedule from that of twenty years ago. Students of the Court Circular might have spotted a gentle reduction in the number of afternoon engagements; slightly shorter state visits overseas; slightly more events at Windsor Castle (home); slightly fewer at Buckingham Palace (the office). But it's mere tinkering compared to Victoria's withdrawal from public life or George's decrepitude.

Officials do not talk of the Queen winding down or cutting back on her duties. They say that she is 'making better use of her time'. No wonder our stock image has not changed all these years. So what is the secret of her durability? The answer would seem to be a combination of health, faith and attitude – plus Prince Philip.

Lord Charteris, one of the most colourful royal private secretaries of the twentieth century, summed it up as follows: 'She sleeps well, she's got very good legs and she can stand for a long time. The Queen is as strong as a yak.' She certainly hates any suggestion of infirmity. Sailing round Scotland in the Royal Yacht in its final years, the Queen was infuriated to come down to breakfast and read newspaper rumours of a heart condition. She had been spotted attending a Harley Street clinic for a routine check-up and the press had jumped to conclusions. The next morning, *Britannia* was due to visit a lighthouse. A member of the entourage describes the scene: 'There are all these camera crews there, having read about the Queen's heart problem. We get to the lighthouse and the Queen, on her own initiative and without warning, goes whoosh – straight up to the top. When she gets to the top of the lighthouse, she waves down at the cameramen. End of story.'

Having enjoyed good health throughout her life, she is not always entirely sympathetic to those around her when they fail to keep up. The Queen was more bemused than concerned when Margaret Thatcher started feeling faint at the annual diplomatic reception: 'It was always intolerably hot at that diplomatic reception as there was no air. It had been a long day and Mrs Thatcher had to sit down,' remembers one of the royal party. 'The Queen went sailing by like *Britannia* and just said: "Oh, look, she's keeled over again."' As Sir William Heseltine, a former Private Secretary whose Palace career spanned almost thirty years, from the sixties to the nineties, puts it: 'The Queen has a great capacity for measuring herself.'

He recalls the final stages of the Queen's Silver Jubilee tour which concluded in Northern Ireland. The terrorist threat was at its highest level and there were serious misgivings at Cabinet level about this final exercise. After tens of thousands of miles and millions of people, the added tensions were taking their toll on the royal party. Sir Martin

Charteris (then not yet a peer) had already decided that this would be his final bow and that he would retire at the end of the Ulster tour.

'They were nervous days. Merlyn Rees [Home Secretary and former Northern Ireland Secretary] was a bag of nerves and trying to stop the Queen doing things; but she was determined to go round and meet everyone,' says Heseltine. 'The Queen said goodbye to Martin Charteris and he formally took his leave on the last day. I have a picture of Martin and me. We look at the last stages of exhaustion. But the Queen could have done a couple more days.'

The stress of royal duty is seldom discussed, not least because it invites the inevitable riposte from the commentariat: 'Stress? Those royals don't know the meaning of the word.' It is true that no plane or train is ever going to leave without them; job security is not an issue; they will never endure the scream-inducing frustrations of lost luggage, parking tickets and call centre idiocy. But royalty is a life, not a career. 'The Queen knows she doesn't have to go on the Underground or queue for a bus or deal with the other daily hazards of our lives,' says Ron Allison, former Press Secretary. 'And that is part of what makes her determined to do her duty as she sees it, to go to Belfast in the pouring rain.' And while politicians and celebrities by definition have an appetite for the spotlight, the same is not true of the Royal Family. George VI loathed public-speaking – as the 2011 Oscar-winning film, *The King's Speech* reminds us – and his successor is not much more enthusiastic. Yet speeches are expected and speeches must be delivered. If the Queen's engagements have become more adventurous over the years, the same could not be said for her speeches – usually safe and giving little of herself. This is in part down to the fact that she normally speaks 'on advice', her words crafted by ministers and civil servants as well as her own officials and herself. On occasion, they can combine to produce a great speech, such as her words of reconciliation during her state visit to Ireland.* Her message of condolence to the United States following the 9/11 atrocities contained a phrase so astute that it has now entered the language of bereavement: 'Grief is the price we pay for love.' Most of the time, though, she and her speech-writing team err firmly on the side of caution. 'The Queen is not keen on – and possibly not capable of – making off-the-cuff speeches,' says one

---

* Even Sinn Fein president Gerry Adams acknowledged the 'sincerity' of the Queen's Dublin speech in which she declared: 'To all those who have suffered as a consequence of our troubled past I extend my sincere thoughts and deep sympathy. With the benefit of historical hindsight we can all see things which we would wish had been done differently or not at all.' Her opening words – 'A Uachtaráin agus a chairde' (President and friends) – prompted the Irish President, Mary McAleese, to exclaim: 'Wow!'

former adviser. 'She thinks it's dangerous, which it obviously is. But particularly with an American audience, I find myself wishing she'd let go – which, of course, the Prince of Wales is very good at. Her instinct is to be very cautious.' And why not? For someone who has never had a politician's craving for the microphone, a lifetime of compulsory oratory must, at times, have seemed a formidable burden.

A rare example of serious regal fatigue came in the immediate aftermath of the investiture of Prince Charles as Prince of Wales in 1969. It had been a summer of relentless royal activity, including the screening of the most eye-popping royal documentary ever made, *Royal Family*. The Prince's investiture was the first made-for-television royal event, a pantomime of ancient druidry and medieval homage set on a sixties film stage with a chi-chi perspex canopy. But it was taking place against a backdrop of nascent Welsh separatist terrorism. The members of the Royal Family were doing their best to look on the bright side. As the Queen later told Noël Coward, she had been 'struggling not to giggle' because, at the dress rehearsal, the crown she had placed on the Prince's head was too big and 'extinguished him like a candle-snuffer'.

'There was a fairly tense atmosphere the night before with bombs going off as we were on the Royal Train,' recalls a former member of the Royal Household. At one point, a bomb hoax stopped the train altogether. As it chugged towards Caernarvon on the morning of the event, the onboard television was showing old footage of the investiture of the last Prince of Wales and the Queen Mother tried to lift the mood. 'Oh, you've missed it, darling,' she joked as the Prince appeared for breakfast. 'It's already happened.'

But there was no hiding the news of a bomb explosion thirty miles away (it had killed two men, believed to be its makers). Another blast could actually be heard by the royal party as a bomb went off in a Caernarvon goods yard and, come nightfall, a soldier would be killed in a car explosion. Added to the political and security tensions was the fact that this was all being watched around the world. It was arguably the biggest set-piece royal event since the Coronation but without the same all-embracing sense of goodwill.

Once it was over, the Prince of Wales began a tour of Wales but the Queen returned immediately to London. She then took to her bed for several days while the Palace issued a statement saying that Her Majesty had suddenly developed a 'feverish cold'. The royal physician, the late Sir Ronald Bodley-Scott, advised the cancellation of all engagements, including a trip to the tennis at Wimbledon where the Queen had been due to watch the ladies' final between Ann Jones and Billie-Jean King.

A senior Palace official now admits that it was not a cold at all. It was nervous exhaustion. It would be six days before the Queen was seen in public again. This turns out to have been a genuine and very rare case of royal stress.

If the Queen and her family are conscious of the danger lurking in every crowd, they do not show it. But it is hardly conducive to job satisfaction. 'Logic tells you to deal with assessed threats,' says a former member of the Royalty Protection team. 'But history tells you that the greatest threat is from fixated lunatics.'

Queen Victoria survived six assassination attempts. Her second son, Prince Alfred, Duke of Edinburgh, was shot and badly wounded during the first royal visit to Australia in 1868 and the future Edward VII escaped uninjured from shots fired by an anarchist in Brussels in 1899. In March 1974, Princess Anne escaped a kidnap attempt by an armed loner during which her protection officer was shot three times.* The Princess proved an imperturbable target. On being ordered out of her car by the kidnapper, she replied 'not bloody likely'. After reading a confidential report, Prime Minister Harold Wilson noted in the margin: 'A very good story. Pity the Palace can't let it come out.' Both the Queen and the Prince of Wales have been the targets of gun attacks – Her Majesty during the 1981 Birthday Parade and the Prince in a Sydney park in 1994. In both cases the bullets turned out to be blanks fired by disturbed youths, though no one knew that at the time. In 2010, the Rolls-Royce carrying the Prince of Wales and the Duchess of Cornwall to the Royal Variety Performance was attacked when it strayed into the path of a riot. The couple pressed on with the engagement. 'There's a first time for everything,' the Duchess remarked on arrival.

The risk is not just on the streets. In 1982, the Queen had the unimaginable shock of being woken by an intruder in her bedroom. A series of police blunders meant that she had to keep Michael Fagan, another mentally disturbed loner, talking for ten minutes until a chambermaid entered with the cry: 'Bloody hell, Ma'am. What's he doing in there?' 'I don't think the Queen ever got the credit for what she did then because it was almost too embarrassing to talk about it,' says Ron Allison. 'That, to me, is still the most extraordinary single event which has happened to the Queen.'

Her own mother endured the same horror – 'my heart stood still' – when a deranged deserter emerged from behind her curtains at Windsor Castle in the darkest days of the Second World War.

* Her bodyguard, Inspector Jim Beaton, was later awarded the George Cross, the highest decoration for bravery beyond the battlefield. Now retired, he remains in regular contact with the Royal Family and helps to run one of the most exclusive clubs in the world, the Victoria Cross and George Cross Association

A secretive team within Scotland Yard now maintains a 'Fixated Persons Index' but history would suggest that it can only be of so much use. And quite apart from all the oddballs and random thugs at large, there is the list of *known* threats, such as particular terrorist organisations. Police sources admit that, just months after the fire at Windsor Castle, there were credible intelligence reports of an IRA plan to attack Buckingham Palace using mortar bombs. The Queen was informed but refused to countenance a change of strategy, let alone a temporary move.

'The Americans or the Israelis have a completely different approach,' says a senior royal security source. 'They don't do risk. Their response is to put down a lot of heavy fire. But we try to manage out the risk. And, in any case, the Royal Family want invisible protection. It's partly because they are in what they call "the happiness business" and partly because they don't want people moaning about how many people they have around them.' In the late nineties, the Queen's Private Secretary, Robert Fellowes, actually appealed to chief constables to instruct their officers to be less heavy-handed when policing royal events.

It is another variation on the royal paradox. How dare they demand all this expensive protection? But we must protect them at all costs. It certainly earns them sympathy from any politicians who have been in a similar situation. 'I had protection for thirteen years,' says a former Labour Cabinet Minister. 'And while the police are great people, they're in your space – literally. My wife was praying for the time when it was all over. But it's a life sentence for the royals.'

The royal biographer Elizabeth Longford wrote that the Queen's life is 'rooted in physical and moral courage'. For royal sang-froid it is hard to match the Queen's remark when a concrete block was dropped on her car from a Belfast tower block in less peaceful times. Shrugging her shoulders, she observed: 'It's a strong car.'

Much of this robust stoicism is inherited, no doubt. And much of it must have its roots in a wartime childhood during which the family lived in constant fear of German assassination and kidnap plots. The wartime correspondence of Queen Elizabeth The Queen Mother, recently revealed in the Shawcross biography, shows a family as worried, fearful and uncertain as any other, except that they also had Winston Churchill dropping round to give them the full, bleak picture. The letters are endearingly honest, modest, sometimes funny – 'Tinkety Tonk, old fruit. Down with the Nazis!' – and often very moving. In a particularly touching one, as the doodlebugs start raining down on London in 1944, the Queen gives instructions to Princess Elizabeth on what to do in the event that she (her mother) is 'done in' – 'Keep your temper and your word . . .' Even in her darkest moments, though, the wartime Queen never contemplates retreating to safer territory. It is an example which has been faithfully followed by her daughter.

The Queen does not like confrontation, least of all with her prime ministers. But she is prepared to quarrel over issues which involve her own safety. So when the British Government urged her not to visit Canada in 1964 because of separatist unrest, she ignored the concerns and went. In 1979, her New Zealand Prime Minister, Robert Muldoon, urged her not to attend the Lusaka Commonwealth summit as the city had recently been bombed by Rhodesian planes. She ignored him, too. Most controversial was her proposed visit to Ghana in 1961. An outbreak of bombs and civil unrest during the days beforehand led to widespread concern in Britain. Many MPs and most of the media were demanding cancellation. The Prime Minister, Harold Macmillan, was half minded to call it off – Parliament was all for postponement – and later called it 'the most trying week of my life'. It came close to a constitutional crisis since the Monarch is supposed to follow the Prime Minister's advice but, in this instance, the Monarch was having none of it. The Queen was adamant. Reflecting on the episode afterwards, Macmillan wrote: 'If she were pressed too hard and if Government and people here are determined to restrict her activities, I think she might be tempted to throw in her hand . . . She loves her duty and means to be a Queen and not a puppet.' Aside from the fact that the Queen felt a certain obligation, having called off the visit two years earlier (not unreasonably, given that she was pregnant with Prince Andrew), she was also well aware of the geopolitical situation. Ghana, until recently a British colony, was being wooed by Khrushchev's Soviet Union. Macmillan and US President John F. Kennedy were determined that its prickly dictator, Kwame Nkrumah, should remain friendly to the West. So was the Queen. As she told Macmillan: 'How silly I should look if I was scared to visit Ghana and then Khrushchev went and had a good reception.'

In the event, the tour was a huge success. Macmillan picked up the telephone to President Kennedy and gleefully announced: 'I have risked my Queen. You must risk your money.' A month later, the US agreed to back the mighty Upper Volta dam scheme. The Soviet seduction of West Africa was off.

Whenever the prospect of saturation security raises itself, the Queen has been heard to reply: 'I have to be seen to be believed.' At a recent private lunch, her view was, as ever, rooted in practicality. 'I'm not afraid of being killed,' she said. 'I just don't want to be maimed.'

Looking through the Queen's life, the only things which seem to have unnerved her have been mechanical. She never liked Concorde much, using it just four times. And for many years she refused to travel by helicopter, not least because the former Captain of the Queen's Flight, Air Commodore John Blount, was killed in one in 1963. It was not until her Silver Jubilee year of 1977 that the Queen was finally persuaded to get into one and that was only to cross part of Northern Ireland following terrorist threats on the ground. Now that the only aircraft at the permanent disposal of the Royal Family is a rented Sikorsky helicopter, she uses it regularly. In any case, she is surrounded by chopper pilots. Prince Philip learned to fly a helicopter in 1956, Prince Andrew was a helicopter pilot with the Royal Navy and both Prince William and Prince Harry have followed suit – with the RAF and the British Army respectively. The Prince of Wales has even been involved in a helicopter emergency landing (although it managed to avoid the press). 'We were flying out of Exeter Airport at the end of an awayday,' recalls Elizabeth Buchanan. 'We said goodbye to the Lord-Lieutenant and we took off. I was pouring a glass of water and I noticed it was going sideways and then the pilot very calmly said that an engine had gone down and we would have to go back and make an emergency landing. I thought: "Well, maybe I'll get a footnote as someone who died in a royal crash." But the Prince's main concern was that he had people coming for dinner and he knew that he would be going home by road. He just said: "Oh hell, I wanted to go round the garden before dinner."'

At high points or low, the routine of royal life can sometimes be stifling, not that the Queen will complain. 'In more than twenty years of working for her, I've never heard her say, "That was the most boring day ever" or "Gosh, that Lord Mayor was a bore,"' says a former Private Secretary. 'If one was unwise enough to say, "It looked as if it was heavy going at lunch, Ma'am" or something like that, she would say: "Didn't you realise that chap's father was the son of my father's valet?" or something. She would have found out something that interested her. I don't think that I ever saw her go to sleep in the middle of an engagement. I think she's been recorded as having done it once.\* It is staggering if you think of it. I was caught sound asleep in the middle of a native dance in Canada, I remember. I'd gone the whole way. It's self-discipline if you want to sum it up.'

The Queen would be inhuman if she did not find that some of her encounters bordered on the narcoleptic. But, as Prince Philip has observed: 'The Queen has the quality of tolerance in abundance.' She

---

\* The Queen was seen to fall asleep very briefly at Düsseldorf's Heinrich-Heine University during the 2004 state visit to Germany. It happened during a lecture entitled: 'New insights into biology and medicine with the use of magnets'.

also has the ability to absorb the tiniest details from the most mundane situation. As Sir Malcolm Ross observes: 'It's one of the amazing skills she has. She'd come out of an investiture and say: "Did you see the man in the red socks?" And I'd think: "How did she see him?" She came out once and said to me: "Why was there an extra director of music in the gallery?" The man was hardly showing because he was sitting down. He was a new bandmaster and wanted to see the ropes. But she'd missed nothing despite having 120 people to concentrate on.'

The eye for detail keeps everyone on their toes. Ron Allison says that the Queen would sometimes help him do his own job. During one church service she spotted a rogue photographer creeping into a spot where he should not have been. With little more than a raised eyebrow and a slight jerk of the head, she caught Allison's eye and directed him to the miscreant.

Just as she will find something unusual in the most formulaic situations, so the Queen loves the unexpected. 'As a diplomat, you're always worrying that something will go wrong,' says Lord Hurd. 'But you don't realise that the Royal Family lead such curious lives that they're longing for something to go wrong. That's the late-night conversation: "Did you see that chap with his shirt undone? Did you see the man on the left fall over?" . . .'

But while the Queen enjoys the occasional unscripted glitch, she is also sensitive to the embarrassment of others. If someone makes an innocent mistake, however glaring, she would rather press on than dwell on it. There was an excruciating moment in May 2011 when President Barack Obama raised a toast to the Queen at the end of his state banquet speech but then carried on speaking. By now the orchestra of the Scots Guards had already started playing the National Anthem and it was too late for either of them to stop. When both had finished, the Queen simply turned to her guest and said: 'That was very kind.'

On arriving at an engagement in Lanarkshire, she noticed that her then Lord-Lieutenant, Lord Clydesmuir, was having considerable trouble extracting both himself and his sword from the official car to do the introductions. The Queen cut through this intractable ceremonial impasse by marching up to the greeting line, hand outstretched, with the words: 'My Lord-Lieutenant appears to be having difficulty in getting out of the car, so I'd better introduce myself. I'm the Queen.'

During their Downing Street years, John and Norma Major held a dinner to mark the eightieth birthday of Sir Edward Heath. 'The Queen came and Ted fell asleep between Norma and the Queen,' says Major fondly. 'I remember saying to Her Majesty: "Ted's fallen asleep." And she said: "I know, but don't worry. He'll wake up soon." And he did. And the Queen just merrily went on chatting to him.'

Throughout her reign, there have been complaints that the Queen does not smile enough. Lady Pamela Mountbatten, royal cousin and former Lady-in-Waiting, has pointed out that if the Queen smiled for all of the people all of the time, she would have developed a twitch by now.

Edward Mirzoeff, who spent most of 1991 filming her at close quarters, says that the Queen's mood – and her smile – depends on the feedback she is getting from those she meets. 'There were good days when she would get a good response and everything would flow,' he recalls. 'But there were days when people would be overcome by the moment and it would dry up. On a good day, she scintillates and she is aware of that – and she likes it when that gets captured on camera.'

'The Queen is absolutely exhilarating, you know,' says a regular royal guest. 'That po face hides an acute intelligence and sense of humour.'

There was nothing sycophantic about the laughter when she addressed the leaving party for her former Private Secretary Sir Robert (now Lord) Fellowes. 'Robert is the only one of my private secretaries I have held in my arms,' she declared (she knew him as a baby). The Queen loves dry asides, like the one from another Private Secretary, Sir William Heseltine. As she cleared up after lunch in a Balmoral log cabin, he prompted much royal mirth by remarking: 'Queen Elizabeth swept here . . .'

On occasions, her problem can be containing her mirth rather than exhibiting it. A visit to Trinity College, Oxford, earlier in the reign went magnificently askew when the Lord-Lieutenant, the Earl of Macclesfield, fainted during lunch, followed swiftly by his wife, who thought he had died. As Miles Jebb recounts in his history of the Lord-Lieutenants, a college servant tripped over in the confusion, dropping a tray of drinks. Summoning up Herculean reserves of composure at the end, the Queen remarked: 'We've had a wonderful lunch. Bodies all over the place!'

Sometimes, it's an innocent phrase which has the Monarch chuckling all the way home, such as the remark from a mayor of Dover as he was showing her some ancient regalia in a glass case. 'When do you wear it?' she asked. 'Only on special occasions,' he replied. Sir Malcolm Rifkind MP, the former Conservative Cabinet Minister, was accompanying the Queen to Stirling Castle during his days as Secretary of State for Scotland. 'There'd been this restoration work going on and she asked the foreman: "When will this all be complete?" Back came the reply: "It won't be in your time, Ma'am." She dined out on that!'

A piece of well-judged humour can go a long way. It is the

time-honoured duty of a senior government whip, always known as the Vice-Chamberlain of Her Majesty's Household, to write what is known as a 'message'. It's a daily account of the day's proceedings in the House of Commons written for an illustrious readership of one – the Sovereign. During John Major's Conservative administration in the mid-nineties, the task fell to Sydney Chapman, MP for Chipping Barnet.* As the Tory party's 'Back to Basics' morality crusade foundered on a succession of personal scandals, the MP found himself lost for appropriate words one day. 'It was a very quiet day in Parliament,' says Chapman. 'There were all these scandals going on so I composed this message, in the traditional third person way, saying that even Her Majesty's Vice-Chamberlain had dreamed that he himself was involved in a scandal and had been caught writing secret notes to a married lady of great importance living in a large house. I thought I might have overstepped the mark. But it obviously went down all right because I later got a very nice call from someone at the Palace saying: "Everyone here wishes they were Sydney Chapman right now."' It clearly didn't do him any harm. When he finally stepped down from the job, he had the unusual distinction of being offered an instant knighthood.

It is often said by – and of – those in authority that it is lonely at the top. There are times when the Queen prefers to seek the company of her dogs or horses. She will sometimes have pressing matters on her mind which she is constitutionally forbidden from sharing with those closest to her. But she enjoys taking a collegiate approach to the job. 'She reckons she is part of the team,' says a former Private Secretary. 'She's a marvellous colleague. I learned a hell of a lot from her about patience; about attention to detail without being too pernickety; take time to make up your mind – but when you do, don't be fickle and don't swing like a weathervane. And there's an unquestioning loyalty to the people who work for her. People underestimate how loyal she has to be sometimes to her own people.'

Perhaps it's a subliminal military thing. The Queen comes from a Forces family and has served in uniform herself. The Royal Household is the nearest thing she has to a regular command. And when her people are in action, she likes to be part of that team rather than an observer. The sense of team spirit is never more pronounced than on tour.

In the days when the Royal Yacht *Britannia* was afloat, there was sometimes the atmosphere of a works outing. Ron Allison recalls that

* The Vice-Chamberlain also serves as a hostage whenever the Queen opens Parliament. He or she must remain at Buckingham Palace until the Sovereign returns. As Sir Sydney Chapman admits: 'It's not much of a swap.'

everyone would have their own roles to play. Arriving on board *Britannia* could be alarming for a visiting guest. Allison and Air Commodore Archie Winskill, then Captain of the Queen's Flight, would be expected to generate a mood of informality. 'I wouldn't say we were Court jesters, but if the Queen was entertaining on the Yacht, we would break the ice a little bit. It was not anything ever approaching rudeness but we might pull each other's leg so the others present could realise it was OK to unwind.' And, at the end of a long day, the Queen liked to kick off her shoes and catch up on all the inside information from her fellow players in the royal production. 'She wanted to be part of it. She didn't miss a thing,' Allison recalls. 'Back on the Yacht, she might say: "I noticed you seem to be getting along very well with the local journalists here." I'd say: "Yes, Ma'am." She'd say: "And I saw you helping that very blonde lady working for the local press . . ."'

The Queen always has her Foreign Secretary or a senior Foreign Office minister in attendance on these trips. Lord Hurd, a veteran of many, says that he always enjoyed the royal post-mortem at the end of the day. As well as enjoying her commanding officer role on tour, the Queen will sometimes adopt a maternal role towards her troops. Lord Hurd was suffering from a particularly heavy cold during the 2004 state visit to Russia. 'The Queen sent me to bed,' he laughs. 'I was suffering and she said: "I think your place is in bed, Foreign Secretary." She prescribed the equivalent of Lemsip and I quickly recovered.'

This royal team spirit was never more necessary than during the most chaotic state visit of the reign. In 1980, the Queen's Mediterranean tour concluded with the first state visit to Morocco and the court of the autocratic and unpredictable King Hassan II. The true tale of what the media would call the 'Tour from Hell' has never been told before. But it is a useful illustration of all the various regal skills with which the Queen has reigned over the last sixty years.

Her trip to Morocco came as the last stop on a two-week tour of Italy and North Africa. The trip had already presented the Queen with some novel challenges, not least an interesting main course in Algeria. 'I saw the extraordinary sight of the Queen confronted with a roast lamb but no implements,' says Lord Hurd, the Foreign Office minister in attendance. 'It was very hot so she looked around for a spoon or a fork or a knife to attack it but there was no such thing. And then she got the idea she was supposed to claw at it with her hands and she did.'

Even this, however, was scant preparation for her next stop – Morocco. 'It was a unique state visit in that nothing that had previously been arranged actually took place as arranged,' says a Foreign Office official who was part of the tour. 'And if it did take place at the time that it was arranged, it took place in a different place, probably several hundred miles away.'

Having survived a number of assassination attempts, including a massacre at his own birthday party just nine years before, Hassan II was deliberately erratic in his movements. 'He was a catlike figure. You almost felt that he might pounce on you at any minute,' says one British diplomat. 'The only way you could approach him was through the Minister of the Court, a chap called Moulay Hafid who was really the Grand Vizier. He was a quite terrifying figure in a fez and dark glasses who would only speak to the Queen's Private Secretary, Philip Moore. He didn't bother with diplomats.'

Even the late Philip Moore, a former England rugby international, was powerless to keep control of the schedule from the moment the Queen arrived. Lunches were moved from one palace to another at a moment's notice. In one instance, an open-air affair, it hardly happened at all. The King disappeared to issue reprimands and orders to his chefs, leaving the Queen sitting in the sun for most of the afternoon until he reappeared, followed by some food, at around five o'clock.

At the King's state banquet, the Queen arrived in full regalia on time only to find the royal palace in question closed. It was left to the debonair Lord Rupert Nevill, Private Secretary to Prince Philip and a close family friend, to jolly along the British royal party for nearly an hour until the King arrived. As the King redefined the term 'lady-in-waiting', Lord Rupert managed to procure a dry martini and pass it through the window of the car to the Queen. She endured all these slights with cheerful equanimity. However, what she would not tolerate was the King mistreating her own staff. At one point, during another belated meal, the King turned to the Queen, pointed to Robert Fellowes, then her Assistant Private Secretary, and said: 'That's the person who's responsible for this terrible muddle.' It was at this point that the Queen delivered the immortal retort: 'I'll thank you not to speak about my staff like that.' As a British diplomat puts it: 'That was the end of the conversation.'

There was a further sovereign-to-sovereign bust-up later on the same day as the Queen was due to reciprocate the King's hospitality by taking him to see a British-funded Leonard Cheshire centre for the disabled. 'The King was also the Commander of the Faithful,' explains a member of the entourage. 'He thought that sort of thing was beneath his dignity. So he told the Queen that it was too late to go to the Leonard Cheshire home and he would take her back to her palace.' The Queen was having none of it. 'Well, you can stop the car in that case,' the Queen told him.

'And I'll go with my security people.' The convoy duly delivered the Queen to the charity.

There was nothing anti-British or anti-Queen in the King's behaviour. He was famously erratic with all his guests. Years later, Queen Sofia of Spain described her own visit to Morocco as 'a nightmare' and accused the King of lacing her food with lamb, despite knowing that she was a vegetarian. Queen Elizabeth II of the United Kingdom seems to have had a relatively easy ride. Certainly, some of the British entourage were almost starting to enjoy the surreal nature of the situation. Members of the British media were less amused. 'I've never been so b\*\*\*ered around,' the BBC's Keith Graves told the Queen's Press Secretary, Michael Shea. 'You think you've been b\*\*\*ered around?' came the reply. 'What about us?'

The comedy of manners reached its climax on the last night as the Queen prepared to host her farewell banquet for the King on board *Britannia*. 'The Minister of the Court turned up and said the King would be grateful if the banquet could be postponed for a few hours,' Lord Hurd says, still slightly incredulous at the thought. 'The real reason was that he was nipping about from one palace to the other for security reasons.' At this point, the Queen would have been within her rights to sail off there and then. Instead, she calmly explained that the event could not be postponed. 'She was not being bullied into changing the time of the banquet because all the guests had been asked for such and such a time,' says Lord Hurd. 'But then she said: "I will perfectly understand if His Majesty is late."'

The King was a mere fifty-four minutes late. But there was a further problem: gatecrashers. 'The King arrived with some princes, mainly cousins, who had not been invited. So we had to find a lot of extra knives and forks,' says Lord Hurd. According to another guest, the King arrived with iceboxes of food for himself, terrified that someone might try to poison him. He was also furious that the honorary British decorations granted to some of his family – and all agreed long in advance – did not include knighthoods.

The Queen, meanwhile, had grown quite fond of the old ogre. 'It was very revealing,' says one member of the Royal Household. 'She had brought some toys for the King's children. So she said to him: "Now, Hassan, have you given those toys to your children yet?" And he said: "No, I haven't had time." "Oh, Hassan!" she cried in despair. "You are hopeless!" And it was very touching. He took it on the chin from her!'

As Lord Hurd recalls, the King was actually afraid of the Queen. Hassan II might have been a terrifying autocrat to his people but even he could recognise a fellow sovereign who was not to be messed with. Over dinner, the King did his best to charm the Queen but remained angry with her officials over the missing knighthoods. 'He started hissing at me about how I had to arrange for the British ambassador to be sacked,' says Lord Hurd. 'The poor man was going to be knighted the following day on the deck. I was completely new. So I consulted Prince Philip who burst into laughter and said: "You do absolutely nothing and wait until tomorrow."'

Sure enough, the storm blew over. 'The next day, everything was smiles,' says Lord Hurd. 'We took our leave, and there were presents of carpets and so on.' Out on *Britannia*'s deck, the British ambassador, Simon Dawbarn, became Sir Simon – and went on to spend another two years in Morocco.

The Queen sent an immediate thank-you letter to King Hassan praising the 'extremely warm and generous hospitality' and adding: 'We have been especially touched by the way in which Your Majesty took such a personal interest in our programme.' It had been a textbook example of how not to organise a state visit and came very close to being a diplomatic disaster. At a time of renewed tensions in the Middle East, Britain certainly did not want a high-profile falling-out with one of the more pro-Western nations in the Arab world. But the visit was saved by the Queen herself. She had refused to lose her temper under extreme duress. Equally, she had refused to compromise on certain points of principle – defending her staff, supporting good causes, not letting people down. To this day, it remains a diplomatic masterclass. What's more, it provided the Royal Family with enough anecdotes and horror stories to last for years. It certainly wasn't dull. 'In a funny sort of way, it was good fun,' says one of the Queen's team. 'You know, I think she actually rather enjoyed it.'

# 3

## *Her Greatest Challenge*

*'We had to get sex and money off the agenda.'*

Prince William would probably prefer to be somewhere else. Not only has he had to put on a dark suit for one of the hottest afternoons of the year but England's footballers are involved in a crucial match. As President of the Football Association, the future Duke of Cambridge would rather like to be watching the game, if not in person then in front of the television. Instead, thirty-seven minutes into the match, it is time to abandon the radio commentary in the royal car and walk into the Royal Festival Hall to meet seven hundred of the cleverest people on earth. Ten Nobel Laureates and the inventor of the World Wide Web are among those waiting to see him. Even for a chap with three A levels and a 2:1 in geography, it's going to require extra reserves of small talk. There is no question of trotting out old faithfuls like 'And what do you do?' when the bearded gentleman in the moth-eaten jacket may turn out to be the pre-eminent world expert on DNA.

Fortunately for the Prince, he is not on his own. This is a family excursion. In fact, apart from his own wedding some months later and traditional state occasions like the Queen's Birthday Parade, few events will draw a bumper royal turnout to match this one. It's the 350th birthday party of the world-leading British institution, the Royal Society, an organisation so grand that it does not need to say what it is the Royal Society *of*. It is so exalted that this is not a party but a 'convocation'. The rarefied atmosphere is justified. It is a unique scientific institution. Founded by Charles II for 'improving natural knowledge', the society's members have included Isaac Newton and Charles Darwin and 74 of the current 1,400 members are Nobel prizewinners. For most of its 350 years, the Royal Society has enjoyed a close and fruitful relationship with the monarchy. Today its members will underline that bond by welcoming three generations of the Royal Family and admitting Prince William as a Royal Fellow. It will be a proud day, too, for the society's patron, the Queen.

The Prince looks relaxed for one who is about to address a full house at the Royal Festival Hall. 'I don't know why I'm here,' he tells the welcoming committee modestly. 'I'm left-handed as well so I could be the first person to smudge your 350th anniversary book.' It's a good ice-breaker. Everyone laughs. The Duke of Kent is already here. The Princess Royal dashes in at the last minute, breezily explaining that her train broke down at Swindon. Suddenly everyone stiffens. The Queen and Prince Philip have arrived. They are escorted by Lord Rees of Ludlow, Britain's most decorated scientist and the Master of Trinity College, Cambridge. Aside from his peerage and knighthood, Lord Rees has held the ancient position of Astronomer Royal for fifteen years and holds the Order of Merit, an honour limited to just twenty-four of the most distinguished intellects in the land. His college boasts the Prince of Wales and thirty-two Nobel prizewinners among its alumni. Today, which happens to be his sixty-eighth birthday, Lord Rees wears another hat – President of the Royal Society. Even he looks a little nervous.

First things first. The royal party and the society's council line up for a photograph. It is an extremely distinguished line-up. Of the 27 people in the picture, 26 have a title – ranging from Queen to professor. Even the odd one out, Mr Philip Ruffles, has the letters CBE FREng FRS RDI after his name. The organisers have commissioned a special fanfare for the entry of the Queen into the auditorium. A *Ben Hur*-style crash of trumpets brings the world of science to its feet and the royal party proceeds to the stage. It's a curious ambiance. Remote-controlled helium-filled penguins float around the auditorium. Laid out before the Queen is the mace, a gift from Charles II, and an inkstand, presented by George III. There is also a bell which was presented by the Queen herself on the society's 300th birthday. She and Prince Philip are the only people in the room today who were also present back then. The secretary recites the Fellowship citation for Prince William. He is to be recognised for his 'developing leadership role' and his 'ability to stimulate interest in science in young people'. The Prince dips a feather quill into his great-great-great-great-great-great grandfather's inkwell, signs the 350-year-old book without smudging his entry and moves to the lectern. 'My generation,' he declares, 'will have to engage with science more fully, perhaps, than any that has preceded it.' He also observes that both his father and grandfather had to wait until the age of twenty-nine to receive this accolade, adding: 'I am twenty-eight which just shows what a geography degree can do.'

The applause is generous, but not out of mere politeness. Today ensures a timely renewal of an ancient bond between the scientific world and the Crown. This is important because there is one very obvious absentee today. The Prince of Wales is also, as Prince William observed, a Royal

Fellow of the Royal Society. Officially, he is unable to watch his eldest son receive the initials 'FRS' because he is making a speech to the Consumer Goods Forum half a mile away. However, it is no secret that there has been a bit of a spat. The Prince and the Royal Society have very different positions on the subject of genetically modified foods. Prince Charles is firmly opposed; the society is cautiously supportive. That's why the scientists are so pleased to see the heir to the heir to the throne here today. Even if the society is out of royal favour during the next reign, it should be back in the loop during the one after that.

It is not the day for a scene, of course, although the point is made. In his wide-ranging speech of welcome to everyone, Lord Rees finds room to observe that 'we must confront' those who fear that genetic crops 'may run away too fast'. Much is unsaid today. The occasion is the nearest thing to a public celebration of another milestone. It is also the 350th birthday of the constitutional monarchy – 350 years since the Restoration summer when the Roundheads were kicked out and Charles II returned from exile to take the throne. By any standards, it's a big anniversary. But it has been almost entirely overlooked. Aside from a £5 collectors' coin from the Royal Mint, there is to be no official recognition of the birthday of the modern monarchy. The Queen's Diamond Jubilee is approaching and she doesn't want to overdo the royal anniversaries (this is a monarch who scrapped a set of stamps to mark her own seventieth birthday on the grounds that she didn't want 'a fuss'). Today's event will be the nearest this monarch gets to acknowledging the Restoration.

The scientists are delighted by all the royal attention. Royalty is sometimes dismissed as an irrational anachronism. But here are some of the most rational brains alive and they don't agree with that sentiment. 'I wouldn't call the royals irrational, except perhaps one who I won't mention,' says Lord Rees impishly afterwards. 'They are of great symbolic importance. The Duke of Edinburgh has been a very strong advocate of science. Prince William may not be a scientist but his interest in science makes his position here an important one – for him and us.' Science Minister David Willetts ponders the historic parallels. 'It's very interesting – this rational, open-minded organisation sharing a date with the Restoration of the monarchy,' he says. 'It just shows that the monarchy is not associated with obscurantism and darkness but openness and light.'

Prince William's football match has long since finished by the time he leaves. As he walks to his car, the President of the Football Association receives his first match report courtesy of a well-refreshed man in the crowd who has spent the afternoon in a pub and shouts a summary of events across the throng. The next day's papers are all dominated by football news. A few carry pictures of Prince William at the Royal Society although the words focus on the fact that he was not watching football. There will be few complaints at the Palace, though. This event neatly illustrates today's royal landscape: three generations in the age-old royal business of saluting excellence. It's dutiful, worthy, unshowy. And the absence of the Prince of Wales is not mentioned in any publication. A few years ago, there would have been sensational headlines about a 'snub' or a 'royal rift' above reports that the Prince was at odds with his family or the scientific establishment or the government or all three. These days, his views on GM crops are so well known that they are no longer news fodder. Similarly, no one would dispute his devotion as a father. His speech to the Consumer Goods Forum – on how the retail industry can help the environment – receives respectful notices in the retail media. But, crucially, his no-show is a non-story.

The last few years have been a happy period in the British royal narrative, with a spectacular wedding to mark the end of one chapter and the start of another. By continuing to do what she has always done without any obvious concession to age, the Queen is no longer merely respected but almost revered. Her children seem content in well-established public roles. Her first wave of grandchildren are all safely through the assault course of adolescence and getting on with life. Prince William is happily married and, along with Prince Harry, thriving in the Forces. Another newly-wed, Zara Phillips, has fought her way to the top of international equestrianism and was named BBC Sports Personality of the Year in 2006. 'The Queen's standing is extremely high and the Prince of Wales is happy,' says a retired senior aide. 'A few people sound off about some of his pronouncements but it doesn't shake the whole foundation. He's a stable figure who's been right on a lot of things. Now, the future is secure with William. He is a very traditional, conventional figure but he has got the Princess's touch with people. They think: "This guy is cool."'

There was, though, a decade of storms and turmoil before the current spell of sunny weather. Some of the trouble was foreseeable, some of it not. That the monarchy is where it is today is largely down to the way it faced up to the challenges of its darkest period since the Second World War – the nineties.

'This wasn't a place where they wanted much change,' says one of those who was in the thick of it during those years. 'The two issues which were besetting the monarchy and distracting attention from the good job the Queen was doing were, as ever, sex and money. We had to get sex and money off the agenda.'

As far as 'sex' goes, there was little the Queen and her advisers could do about her family's private lives. The failed marriages of her three elder children (the Prince of Wales and Princess Royal have since remarried) are well chronicled. Psychologists and agony aunts will be debating the royal component to these events for years to come but, ultimately, these were personal misfortunes.

The confluence of unhappiness which ran through 1992 – the separations, the scandals and the fire – may have led the Queen to describe it as an *annus horribilis* but much of it was beyond her control. She could, however, tackle the other crisis bedevilling the monarchy through the final years of the twentieth century – money. And she did. The result has been a restructuring of the royal finances on a scale not seen since George III. After sixty years on the throne, the Queen no longer depends on Parliament to provide public funds to keep the monarchy afloat. It is now supported by the property market.

The mid-eighties had appeared to herald a royal golden age. First, the Prince of Wales married Lady Diana Spencer in 1981. A kindergarten teacher thirteen years his junior, she was the shy, doe-eyed youngest daughter of the Queen's former equerry Earl Spencer. Pretty, scandal-free and naturally child-minded, the new Princess of Wales had grown up on the fringes of the royal world and knew the royal form. Equally, she could deploy an easy informality with total strangers. Prince William was born a year later and Prince Harry arrived in 1984. Prince William was old enough to be a pageboy in 1986 when Prince Andrew married Sarah Ferguson, a boisterous girl about town with a job in fine art publishing. On his wedding day, the Queen created her second son Duke of York. The new Duchess had also grown up on the royal periphery – her father, Major Ronald Ferguson, was polo manager to the Prince of Wales. Like Lady Diana, she had endured the misery of divorcing parents as a child. And, like Lady Diana, she was heralded by the press as a 'breath of fresh air' upon the royal scene.

Two daughters, Princess Beatrice and Princess Eugenie, were born in 1988 and 1990. That 'fresh air' blew fast and strong. To nods of media approval, the young royal couples had interests and friends far beyond the traditional royal territory of country sports and country houses. A new culture of glamorous fundraising was evolving on the back of Britain's economic revival. Charity was cool. And so was royalty. The Prince of Wales had already made a substantial impact on national life with his Prince's Trust, providing grants for the young and disadvantaged so that they could learn a skill or get a project off the ground. In 1986, ten years after the original, he founded the Prince's Youth Business Trust to lend start-up funding to young people who couldn't get a loan. Its success rate soon surpassed that of any High Street bank. Across the charity sector, traditional tombolas and tin-rattling were all very well but fundraisers discovered that there were richer sources to be mined. This was the age of the Sloane Ranger, the yuppy and the television 'personality'. And they came flocking when royalty was involved. A black-tie ball or a sponsored event with a royal endorsement – especially from 'Lady Di' or 'Fergie' – would reap huge dividends. The boundaries between royalty and celebrity soon became increasingly blurred. While the younger members of the Royal Family proved to be glamorous, happy and productive (in every sense), the nation was delighted to indulge them.

Fortunately for the monarchy, all this taffeta triumphalism coincided with the arrival of another newcomer on the royal scene. He was not a glamorous trendsetter. He would turn few heads outside royal circles and yet he would have a greater impact on the mechanics of the monarchy than almost anyone since Prince Albert.

When future historians compile their lists of eminent New Elizabethans, few will omit David George Coke Patrick Ogilvy, 13th Earl of Airlie. An exact contemporary of the Queen, Lord Airlie played with her as a child. It is even said that one of the Queen's first words was 'Airlie' – her name for Queen Mary's Lady-in-Waiting, Mabell, Countess of Airlie (the grandmother of the present Earl). Lord Airlie's father ran the Queen Mother's household for several years and his younger brother, Angus Ogilvy, married the Queen's cousin, Princess Alexandra. His wife, Ginny, has been a very popular Lady-in-Waiting to the Queen since 1973. Few Palace-watchers were very surprised, in 1984, when Lord Airlie was appointed Lord Chamberlain. It's a post often likened to that of royal non-executive chairman. The Private Secretary may be the all-important daily conduit between the Queen and her various governments around the world, but he still answers to the Lord Chamberlain. If there is a problem anywhere in the royal fold, it is the Lord Chamberlain's duty to know about it. It is also his duty to offer what the last incumbent, Lord Luce, called 'fearless advice' to everyone, including the Queen. If anyone could do that, it was David Airlie. 'I have known her all my life,' he acknowledges shyly. 'She knows me warts and all.'

Flawlessly connected and with a pair of Scottish castles, Lord Airlie might, on paper, resemble the 'tweedy courtier' of years gone by. But there was nothing sentimental about the Queen's choice of Lord Chamberlain. For twenty-three years he had been a dynamic figure in the City and commerce, spending the previous seven years as chairman of the investment house Schroders plc, before accepting the summons to the Palace. One of those pressing for Lord Airlie's appointment was William Heseltine, soon to be the Queen's Private Secretary. 'It was because I knew of his very successful career in business and banking that I thought he would make a very good non-executive chairman,' says Heseltine. Another member of the Royal Household still regards it as a watershed: 'David Airlie came along and saw everything. He was just the person because he was a real insider.'

Lord Airlie was not joining the Royal Household for a quiet life. 'I left Schroders on 30 November and came to Buckingham Palace on 1 December,' he recalls. 'Getting to know the set-up took a bit of time. It's quite a complicated organisation. I spent a lot of time listening because I began to form the view fairly early on that changes needed to be made.'

A tall, genial man, he combines a donnish eye for detail with an assured military bearing (a former Scots Guards officer, he later became Captain-General of the Queen's Body Guard for Scotland, the Royal Company of Archers). He rarely gives interviews. When he does, he speaks frankly. Having inspected every level of the Palace soon after his arrival, he had much to say. The Palace, he feared, was in danger of running out of money.

'The Royal Household were not adopting what might be called best practices. Civil List expenditure was outrunning revenue. It was quite alarming. Something had to be done and it couldn't wait. Those two factors led me to suggest to the Queen that we ought to do an internal review from top to bottom.'

The Civil List was the annual fund to cover the Monarch's duties as head of state. Most of it went on salaries and none of it went to the Queen herself. Nor did it include the Prince of Wales and his family who were funded by the Duchy of Cornwall, the ancient property portfolio which provides the heir to the throne with an independent income. What the new Lord Chamberlain had in mind was radical stuff, particularly so since, on the outside, the royal picture looked so rosy.

When Lord Airlie was appointed, the Prince and Princess of Wales were happily adjusting to life with two little boys while matrimony beckoned for the Duke of York. Today's Lord Chamberlain, Earl Peel, remains in awe of what happened next. 'Lord Airlie took it upon himself to call the heads of department together and read the riot act,' says Lord Peel. 'He said: "This is unacceptable. We're not working to properly controlled budgets. There is not the proper level of cooperation between departments and I wish to see change." And that didn't half rattle a few cages, I can tell you.'

If the courtiers of the day thought they could see off this boisterous new arrival, they were wrong. Nothing of any importance happens at the Palace without the Queen's say-so. Not only did she approve the plan but she decided to give Lord Airlie special authority to bring it about. For a monarch who had diligently sought to emulate her father and grandfather for more than thirty years, it must have been a painful moment. Some sovereigns cannot wait to stamp their own mark on the throne. Edward VIII was hiring, firing and redecorating within days. Not so the Queen. Sensitive to the memory of her father and to her mother's bracing views on all forms of change, she liked the status quo. But, on this occasion, wise monarch outweighed dutiful daughter. 'The Queen is obviously a natural conservative but she is very canny and she thought about it very carefully,' says a senior official of the era. 'When you're monarch, you live in an ivory tower. You're the boss. But if you're a decent, thoughtful monarch, you want to hear what other people say.' Future historians may look back on this as one of the most astute decisions of the reign. Lord Peel calls it a 'defining moment' in the one-thousand-year history of his job: 'David Airlie went to the Queen and he said: "Your Majesty, I really need your permission, in effect, to act in an executive capacity." And the Queen approved that. And so we saw the Lord Chamberlain really beginning to form policy within the Household in a way which had probably never happened before.'

The Palace of the mid-1980s was a computer-free zone and not exactly teeming with original thinkers. Indeed, some believe that the mindset had scarcely changed since the reign of Queen Victoria. 'Prince Albert was a great force for change,' says one who remembers the Royal Household of the 1980s, 'but after Prince Albert had gone, it went to sleep until David Airlie became Lord Chamberlain.'

A new arrival recalls it as follows: 'A nice Household in tweed jackets and grey flannel trousers enjoying delicious teas and nice, set programmes; drinking copiously; having a lovely time. What it needed was more professional people. It's always been in the nature of royal courts that you hang around, you backbite, you look for the next event in the social calendar, you shoot and you fish. But what was needed was people who *did* things. We're all like dogs. Some dogs are lapdogs and like sitting around. Some dogs like chasing rabbits and rats. We needed to recruit those that were good at chasing rabbits and rats and give them the money and the set-up to do it.'

Lord Airlie and some of the Queen's most senior officials had a plan. If the monarchy could become more efficient, the government would give it greater control over its own financial affairs. 'We wanted to become masters of our own destiny,' explains Lord Airlie. Sir William Heseltine says that relations with the government paymasters were becoming more and more strained. 'It was always going to be a running sore and none of us liked being run by the Treasury,' he remembers. 'More and more, the Treasury had become the masters and they were controlling everything from the stable boys' pensions to the salary of the Lord Chamberlain.'

Greater efficiency would also help counter the embarrassing annual headlines about royal 'pay rises' every time the Civil List was increased. Heseltine remembers his futile attempts to explain to the press that the Civil List was not 'pay' for the Queen: 'Even from the very beginning, with all that romance about the "New Elizabethan Age", there were always voices against the cost of monarchy and they were getting louder. Why did the Queen have to be "paid" so much? The press were always insisting that the Civil List was the Queen's pay. As Press Secretary, I tried for years to disabuse them of the idea but it was to no avail.'

The Civil List arrangement went back to 1760 and George III. He struck a deal whereby the government would fund the monarchy in exchange for all the profits from the Crown Estate. And back in 1984, Lord Airlie could see potential disaster. The Civil List was providing £5 million a year and it was not enough. Inflation was rampant, and if the monarchy did not get more money, it could become insolvent. But why should the government give more money to an Edwardian organisation which was still employing an army of footmen, handing out a 'soap allowance' and serving a sovereign routinely described as 'the richest woman in the world'?

'I didn't want to go to the Treasury for more money until we were a tight ship because who knows what they might have said?' says Lord Airlie. 'So that was the catalyst for bringing in Michael Peat.'

If Lord Airlie was the conductor, Michael Peat was the orchestra. Educated at Eton and Oxford, he came from chartered accounting aristocracy – a son of the eminently respectable firm of KPMG Peat Marwick, auditors to the Royal Household. He was no stranger to the quirks of the Palace. When Peat's father was called in to audit the royal accounts, officials would arrange for a tablecloth and silver to be laid out in the Privy Purse Office. In those days, it was not appropriate to ask an accountant to lunch in the Household dining room. A generation later, his son was consigning that way of thinking – and eating – to the royal dustbin. At the same time, he was producing ideas which would cause apoplexy all the way from the pantry to the ballroom.

Lord Airlie remembers the speed with which Michael Peat and his small team worked their way through the entire Royal Household – and the tension as they produced their recommendations. 'Michael did this, believe it or not, in six months and I worked very closely with him. We'd just done the same thing at Schroders and I was very conscious that it stirs the pot. Human beings just don't like change very much. It upsets people personally because they think they're being got at.'

Michael Peat duly presented a 1,383-page report containing 188 recommendations. 'Individually, they weren't very significant. Collectively, they were very important,' says Lord Airlie. Within the Royal Household, they were not merely viewed as important. Some caused uproar. Most proposals were hard to argue with – the introduction of combination boilers at Buckingham Palace or the use of hydroelectricity from the Thames at Windsor. The proverbial institutional joke 'How many people does it take to change a light bulb?' was no laughing matter. The Palace was spending £92,000 a year on changing light bulbs. In due course, the proposals would lead to one of the most important single innovations of the entire reign: the transformation of the Royal Collection from a dusty curatorship into a self-financing, world-class assembly of great treasures employing hundreds and viewed by millions. Some plans, however, caused tension, not least the idea of portion control – fixed helpings – in the five rigorously segregated staff dining rooms. Worse still was the suggestion that those five dining rooms should merge into one. As with any big change, it's the small details which cause the greatest pain. For many years, the Ascot Office, which had the less than onerous task of vetting those admitted to the Royal Enclosure during one week's racing each June, had been located at St James's Palace rather than Ascot Racecourse. Michael Peat's conclusion that the office should vacate St James's led to almost comic levels of resistance, much of it led by the Queen Mother.

'I remember thinking "What's all this fuss about the Ascot Office? Ascot is only one week once a year,"' recalls a member of the Household. 'Then I looked into it and it was a hornet's nest. I didn't want to go near it. These were just the sort of neuralgic issues which very traditional institutions can go nuts about. The Belgians have a saying: "Put a pebble in a man's shoe and he ceases to ask questions about the meaning of life." It was like that with the dining rooms and the Ascot Office. It could enter the bloodstream and no one could talk about anything else for days.'

Another source of institutional angst was a proposal to open up the use of the Royal Box at the Royal Albert Hall. On those nights when it had no royal occupant, the box could be used by senior members of staff. Michael Peat's recommendation that the privilege should extend to all ranks generated months of heat and fury.

'If you were a footman or a clerk, that was a big difference in perks,' says one of the modernisers. 'But it was an open sore for years.'

Whatever the Queen thought – and many imagine that she was entirely happy with the status quo – she could see the need for change. At the end of 1986, the Lord Chamberlain presented her with the Peat Report. 'The Queen saw it, gave it her approval and just said: "Get on with it,"' says Lord Airlie. 'She was hugely supportive and I should say that Prince Philip also played an important part. He came up with all sorts of ideas and you had quite a job arguing him out of it if you didn't think they were good ones. He challenges you!'

Lord Airlie was adamant that there should be no job cuts, merely natural wastage. Even so, parts of the institution were appalled that their routines might have to change for the first time since Queen Victoria. In the Royal Mews, they were still wearing Victorian state livery. In the kitchens, they were still cooking with Victoria's pans. Despite the opposition, Lord Airlie won the day. 'He was a spectacularly good commanding officer if I could put it like that,' says one senior official from those days. Lord Airlie admits that it was not easy. 'They were a great bunch of people,' he says. 'But, on the whole, they reacted uncomfortably. I had meetings and if you want to make a criticism of me, it is that I should have held even more.' He accepts that, even today, there are some who still resent the modernisation which he and Michael Peat brought about. 'The important thing,' he points out, 'is that it changed attitudes.' The report certainly changed one crucial attitude: that of the government.

As the costs started to come down, the Treasury was impressed. These courtiers, it seemed, weren't so bad at running their own finances after all. During the early seventies, things had got so bad that a House of Commons Select Committee had recommended the nationalisation of the Duchy of Lancaster and the Duchy of Cornwall (which, respectively, provide the private income of the Queen and the Prince of Wales) and putting the most senior members of the Royal Family on state salaries. The rest would be 'sacked'.

Nearly twenty years later, at the tail end of Margaret Thatcher's tenure as Prime Minister, the Royal Household had now shown that it could be trusted to take greater control of its own money. But the Palace was still dependent on an annual Civil List handout. 'It was pretty unsatisfactory,' says Lord Airlie. 'It was a period of high inflation and every year, when it was reviewed, it was "The Queen's getting another pay increase." We wanted to be in a position to manage the Household affairs on a much longer-term basis. You can't plan for one year. You want to plan for much longer.'

So he went to the Treasury with a plan: if the monarchy was given a ten-year deal then, for better or worse, it would get on with it.

It was a big risk. By 1989, the Monarchy's Civil List allowance had crept up to more than £6 million. In 1990, Lord Airlie wanted to fix a single figure for the next decade. If inflation surged, then that fixed sum might be hopelessly inadequate in a few years' time. If so, the Queen would have to go begging to the Treasury. The Palace's financial credibility would be shot to pieces and the monarchy really might end up with Whitehall civil servants running the Household.

Lord Airlie and his team were effectively gambling the financial future of the monarchy against the future rate of inflation. The sum agreed was £7.9 million, a figure based on average inflation over the previous ten years. It looked good, but Lord Airlie admits that these were nervous times.

Parliament would need to agree the new deal. And the Labour-led Opposition might have raised hell had Mrs Thatcher not discussed it with the Labour leader, Neil Kinnock, in advance. In a rare display of unity, Thatcher and Kinnock organised an old-fashioned stitch-up. On a July afternoon in 1990, the House of Commons was given a few hours' notice and just twenty minutes of parliamentary time to discuss the plans. Even so, there was no rejoicing in the Palace camp. 'I have to say that I was quite concerned we hadn't done a good enough bargain because inflation was going to go further,' says Lord Airlie. To his eternal satisfaction, he was wrong. 'What actually happened was inflation went down. We needed a bit of luck. It worked. It really did work!' It worked so well, in fact, that the monarchy would not need a rise for another twenty years.

Lord Airlie and his team had struck another deal at the same time. They were allowed to take over the maintenance of all the royal palaces. Up to this point, it had been the job of various government departments. But why should it be left to civil servants to fix a hole in the roof? Michael Peat, with his keen eye for institutional blubber, was soon trimming away. 'We think like the housewife. She knows how to run her house,' says Lord Airlie. 'We knew more about these palaces than they did.' Within six years, the success of the new property system would persuade the government to take the royal transport budget off the civil servants and give that to the Peat team, too.

As a result, the nineties would see the overall royal bill run completely counter to the rest of the state's expenditure. The whole royal show – including Civil List, maintenance and travel – cost £65.5 million in 1991-92. By 2000, that cost would be down to £38 million. Palace officials were wise enough not to expect any applause. They had pulled off a management triumph but the outside world was not paying any attention.

Those twin issues of 'sex and money' were now dragging the monarchy into new and more dangerous territory. In media terms, clever stewardship of the light bulb budget was irrelevant compared to increasingly lurid stories about the younger members of the Royal Family. These, in turn, had kick-started an entirely different debate: why was the Queen not paying income tax?

In every organisation people can usually look back to an incomprehensible event which makes everyone roll their eyes, shake their heads and go very red or very pale. All those record labels which turned down the Beatles must have had their painful post-mortems. Likewise the publishers which gave the thumbs-down to J. K. Rowling's Harry Potter. Most of the country, the Queen included, have asked similar questions about the brains in charge of the banking sector when the collapse of Lehman Brothers took the world to the brink in 2008. In the Royal Household, the Beatles–Potter–Lehman moment is still the day, in 1987, when Prince Edward put on Tudor fancy dress and cajoled certain members of his family to take part in a televised game show.

'Oh God!' winces a former Private Secretary, eyes closed, body stiffening, as if awaiting an unpleasant injection. 'An unmitigated disaster,' sighs another. Such is the reaction, even today, to the words *It's a Royal Knockout*.

It was an idea born of good intentions and a myopic understanding of public opinion. Having graduated from Cambridge, Prince Edward had joined the Royal Marines only to resign before completing the infamously unpleasant basic training. It had been a bold decision to choose arguably the toughest unit in the Forces and an equally bold step to walk away from a corps whose Captain-General was his own father. Few of those who set out to become a Royal Marine succeed, a fact largely overlooked by an unsympathetic press. Undaunted, the Prince was keen to make his mark elsewhere. He decided to recreate the once-popular show *It's a Knockout*, where rival teams in fancy dress have to compete in various custard-pie-style comedy capers. He would recruit his siblings as team leaders and sell the media rights to generate large sums for charity. In the process, it would show that the younger members of the Royal Family were unstuffy and happy to let their hair down in aid of good causes. Who could object?

The Prince and Princess of Wales smelled trouble straight away and declined. But the Princess Royal and the Duke and Duchess of York signed up. Whether they genuinely thought it was a good idea or whether they were simply being sympathetic to Prince Edward after his setback with the Forces is unclear. But with a healthy royal line-up secured, there were plenty of celebrities keen to join in, too – singer Tom Jones, footballer Gary Lineker, racing driver Nigel Mansell and many more.

In retrospect, it might seem extraordinary that neither the Queen nor her advisers found a way of quietly suffocating the project. 'I think like all parents, she finds it quite hard to say "no" to her own children,' says one senior official charitably. 'We all do.' Another says that the Prince had been 'very sneaky' in planning the event. 'We all tried to stop it,' he says, 'but it had been organised already without the knowledge of anybody in the Household. The only person who could have stopped it was the Queen and she wasn't prepared to do it. I bet she now wishes she had. It was a step down the slippery slope. It brought ridicule on the organisation.'

At one level it was a genuinely well-intentioned piece of prime-time fun with celebrities pelting and dunking other celebrities during a series of harmless faux-gladiatorial contests. However, a large section of the population found it condescending. The sight of members of the Royal Family in medieval costumes cheerleading all this buffoonery was not merely incongruous but somehow inappropriate, with echoes of a latter-day Petit Trianon.

The organisers had also made a fundamental error in their handling of the media. Exclusive rights to the action had been sold to one newspaper while the rest were left to watch it on television in an adjacent press tent. The journalists who had been barred from the big event were, therefore, somewhat underwhelmed before the thing had even started. When it was over, a weary but exhilarated Prince Edward arrived for a post-match press conference, expecting some amiable banter. He had put months of work and effort into what, after all, was a colossal exercise in charitable fundraising. Having described the occasion as 'one of the best fun afternoons that I have ever had', he asked the journalists if they had enjoyed themselves, too. A phalanx of stony faces stared back. 'Well thanks for sounding so bloody enthusiastic,' he snapped. 'Did you watch it? What did you think of it?' Before anyone could answer, he then stormed out. Any lingering sense of goodwill towards the project left with him.

From that point onwards, the behaviour of the younger royal generation was the subject of increasingly caustic media coverage. Anything which smacked of extravagance or questionable taste was highlighted. The Yorks' new home at Sunninghill Park was an early example. The absence of royal mourners at the memorial service for the Lockerbie bomb victims in 1989 was held up as evidence of royal disengagement from the rest of society.

Being a junior member of the Royal Family can be a thankless task. The trappings are there, of course, but you are destined for an ever-diminishing role as younger generations are born closer to the centre. But how wide is the orbit? At the Palace, the Green Book – the Royal Household directory – extends the Royal Family as far afield as Lady Saltoun, the widow of the Queen's distant cousin and late Highland neighbour, Captain Alexander Ramsay of Mar. The Court Circular, however, chronicles the official activities of just sixteen members of the Royal Family, the latest addition being a future Queen, the Duchess of Cambridge. They are each supported by an office and by the national network of Lord-Lieutenants. The rest do their own thing at their own expense. The dividing line can be confusing. Prince Edward, now Earl of Wessex and seventh in line to the throne, gave up his own television production company, embraced traditional royal duties and now, with his Countess, represents the Queen all over the world. Princesses Beatrice and Eugenie, fifth and sixth in line, are of a different generation and will lead private lives. Princess Alexandra, thirty-ninth in line and falling, performs around ninety engagements a year. Peter Phillips, eleventh in line, is a full-time marketing man and performs none.

The Queen has remained steadfastly loyal to the wider cousinhood, meeting many of their costs and including them in all the major royal events. She still invites them all on to the Palace balcony after her Birthday Parade. A plan to reduce the numbers there was drawn up by the Private Secretary's Office and discussed at one of the family's Way Ahead Group meetings in the mid-nineties. 'One of our joint recommendations was that when there were balcony appearances, there shouldn't be hordes and hordes of people standing there,' says one of those involved. 'But the Queen wasn't prepared to accept that. So it didn't happen.' Even officials at Westminster Abbey, the most loyal and royal church in the land, have suggested to the Palace that royal protocol verges on the excessive when nearly twenty people styled 'HRH' turn up and the clergy are expected to genuflect to all of them. The Queen, however, is not in the business of downgrading her relations. Nor does she encourage one-upmanship between them when it comes to official duties. Palace staff insist they keep no list of who does what, arguing that they want to avoid a 'league table' of royal activity in the papers. It's a charming pretence, of course. A few seconds on a Palace computer could produce the results.

George V was obsessive in keeping a table of all family activity and would read out the results each Christmas. These days, however, the task is left to Tim O'Donovan, a retired insurance broker from Datchet, Berkshire, who methodically goes through the Court Circular every day of the year, tots up all the results and publishes them in a letter to *The Times*. What everyone in the family acknowledges, however, is that, in

(*Previous page*) The State Opening of Parliament. The Queen has only missed it twice
(the first time, she was expecting Prince Andrew; the second, Prince Edward).

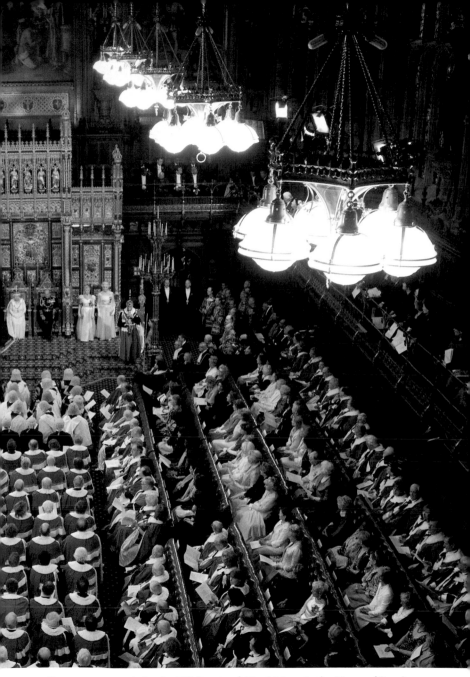

Everyone must wait for the MPs 'to attend Her Majesty in the House of Peers'.
The Pages of Honour and the Cap of Maintenance are to the Queen's right.
Her ladies-in-waiting, the Sword of State and her heralds are to her left.]

The Birthday Parade

(*Left*) The oldest Monarch
and the oldest Consort
in British history return
from Trooping the Colour.
Although the Queen was
85 in April, this is her
official birthday. The Duke
of Edinburgh was 90
the day before.

(*Right*) The customary
salute from the Red Arrows.

(*Below*) The extended
Royal Family – including
the latest recruit to
frontline royal duties.

Pope Benedict XVI begins his 2010 Papal visit to Britain with the official welcome at the Palace of Holyroodhouse. In 1961, the Queen made the first state visit to the Vatican.

UNITED KINGDOM HEADQUARTERS

(*Above*) The Head of the Armed Forces opens the new Joint Headquarters in Northwood.
(*Below*) Wearing a gold coat, shawl and hat made by her dresser, Angela Kelly,
the Queen tours Abu Dhabi's Sheikh Zayed mosque at the start of her 2010
state visit to the United Arab Emirates.

(*Above*) Welcome to Singapore (*Left*) As the Queen visits Ireland for the first time, the excitement is too much for one resident at the National Stud. (*Below*) The State Banquet for President Barack Obama at Buckingham Palace. The Queen's reign has already spanned twelve US presidencies.

future, the 'active' royal unit will be much smaller – the Monarch and the Consort plus children and spouses.

For now, though, the Queen is grateful for the work which her cousins do on her behalf. But her reign has seen a complete transformation of life on the royal fringe. The Gloucesters are a good example. Prince Henry, Duke of Gloucester, was the younger brother of Edward VIII and George VI. He was looking forward to a military career until the Abdication crisis of 1936 promoted him to third in line. Should anything have happened to George VI, the Duke would have been Regent to Princess Elizabeth until she came of age. Within a year, he had been withdrawn from his unit, accelerated from major to major general and was destined to spend the rest of his days unveiling plaques. His no-nonsense military small talk is still the stuff of Palace legend. Opening a flower show, he remarked: 'What a bloody big marrow. Glad I don't have to eat it.' And when a state visit involved an excursion to *Tosca* at the Royal Opera House, the Duke of Gloucester was heartily relieved as Maria Callas finally tumbled over the battlements. 'Well, if she really is dead,' he informed the occupants of the Royal Box, 'we can all go home.'

Although he remarked that his memoirs should be called 'Forty Years of Boredom', he never complained. His elder son, Prince William of Gloucester, sought to break the royal mould during the sixties and pursued a career in the City and then the Foreign Office. 'I am just a rather junior appendage to this extraordinary institution called the monarchy,' he once explained. But duty duly called for this eligible bachelor. Having returned home to help his elderly parents with the running of the family's Northamptonshire estate, he admitted: 'It looks as though I shall spend the rest of my life shooting small birds and sleeping with larger ones.' William's tragic early death in a plane crash in 1972 propelled his younger brother, Prince Richard, from life as a professional architect to that of a trainee 'royal'. Following his father's death in 1974, the new Duke of Gloucester took on most of his father's old patronages. But the nature of the job was changing. With the Duke of Edinburgh leading the charge, many members of the Royal Family were switching from a titular role to a semi-executive position in some of their organisations. Today, they still unveil plaques but they might also attend the board meetings. It's a change which has suited today's Eton and Cambridge-educated Duke of Gloucester well. In addition to some of the more traditional military and agricultural patronages, he is an active, hands-on supporter of organisations involved in architecture, disaster prevention, health and building technology. He also takes a mischievous pride in his patronage of the Richard III Society, a body dedicated to the rehabilitation of the most

notorious Duke of Gloucester in history. The latest model has flirted
with controversy himself, using his maiden speech in the House of Lords,
in 1984, to attack the tobacco industry and to argue that the government
should do more to tackle it. His Danish-born wife, meanwhile, is patron
of more than sixty organisations and a particularly active figure in the
field of musical education. None of their children, however, will lead a
'royal' life.

The Duke's heir, the Earl of Ulster, a soldier married to a doctor, has
no royal style, no royal home and will not take on royal duties when he
succeeds to the title. But for now, the present Duke, a grandfather and
proud bearer of a Senior Railcard, continues to maintain an active royal
schedule shaped not by tradition but largely by himself. He performs
around three hundred royal engagements around the world each year.
These events will never attract much interest from the national media
but they are much appreciated by the school children, diplomats, nurses,
veterans, scientists and whoever else happens to be on the receiving end
of royal and national recognition in the shape of the Duke. It is much
the same across the royal spectrum. The family call it 'supporting the
Queen'. It has long been the core business of royalty, accounting for
thousands of events involving hundreds of thousands of ordinary people
every year. But it counted for little as recession and post-Cold War
uncertainties hung over the start of the nineties.

In February 1991, as British forces prepared for war in the Gulf
following the Iraqi invasion of Kuwait, the *Sunday Times* devoted its
leader column to one of the most withering attacks on the Royal Family
for many years. The article contrasted two sides of British youth – those
in uniform going into battle versus fringe members of the House of
Windsor going on holiday. Beneath the headline 'Royal Family At War',
the column declared: 'It is the exploits and public demeanour of the
minor royals and nearly royals which causes most offence.' The examples
listed were flimsy. Evidence for the prosecution included some party
snaps of the Queen's nephew, Viscount Linley, and recent Parisian trysts
involving the Princess of Wales's brother, Viscount Althorp. Both were
private citizens and neither was any sort of burden on the state. The
impression created, however, was of a privileged, debauched elite being
propped up by the taxpayer.

There were heated scenes on phone-ins and chat-show sofas as royal
defenders voiced their support for the monarchy. The Palace press office
produced an extensive list of royal engagements involving troops in the
Gulf and their families. Even so, for a monarch so bound up with the
Armed Forces, this was wounding stuff. Complacency had set in after

the sunny years of weddings, babies and the Silver Jubilee. Suddenly, parts of the media had diagnosed a royal 'problem'. And it was all wrapped up with that even more damaging non sequitur: 'Why is the Queen exempt from tax?'

In broadsheets and tabloids alike, the tax issue quickly gathered momentum. The Queen's exemption was not some clever accounting wheeze. Nor was it an ancient privilege. It had only been established for half a century, having been agreed with her father by Prime Minister Neville Chamberlain in the wake of Edward VIII's abdication. George VI had incurred huge expenses paying off his brother but it was decided that a tax break was far tidier than agreeing a new Civil List arrangement. The Civil List option would have involved pushing the deal – very publicly and painfully – through Parliament. A tax deal, it was concluded, would produce the same result but could be done quietly. And, in due course, the Queen inherited the same system. Now, decades later, it had suddenly become a live issue after the details were revealed in a television documentary. Similarly, there was a new media vogue for 'rich lists' in which the Queen was routinely portrayed as the multi-billionaire owner of the Crown Jewels, Windsor Castle and the Royal Yacht. She could no more sell these than the Prime Minister could flog Big Ben but the impression had taken root. In the absence of any official figure for the Monarch's private wealth, the guesswork could be spectacular. Charles Anson, her Press Secretary at the time, remembers the mood only too well: 'Day after day, every other story would be followed up with "What's more, the Queen doesn't pay tax."'

What the media did not know was that the Queen had already been pondering the same issue herself. Behind the veneer of calm, the Palace was in turmoil. 'It was a difficult subject,' says Lord Airlie. 'There was media pressure. But on very important things like this, the Queen, rightly, doesn't wish to be rushed. I always say: if you're being pressed by the media, count to ten.' Lord Airlie and the Palace reformers were not only thinking about ways of paying tax but had a further plan: if the Queen took the rest of the Royal Family off the public balance sheet and paid for them herself, a lot of heat would go out of the arguments about 'minor royals'. The Queen had already been doing this for her cousins, the Kents and Gloucesters, for fifteen years. The cost for the rest of the Royal Family was running at £1.8 million. 'We were thinking the whole thing through very carefully,' says Lord Airlie. 'We had to make sure she could afford it.'

The Queen receives most of her Privy Purse (private) income from the annual surplus of the Duchy of Lancaster, an ancient estate covering

46,000 acres of countryside and a few urban sites including some prime
land around London's Savoy Hotel. In 1992, it was producing £3.6
million a year. The Queen would have no trouble paying tax on those
revenues, of course, but what if she was also supposed to pay for everyone
else out of the same pot? The whole point of the Privy Purse was to
give the monarchy some independence from government. How long
before the entire royal machine became entirely dependent on public
funds, a sort of pageantry sub-division of the Civil Service? These were
the sort of worst-case scenarios which had to be examined as Michael
Peat and his team did their sums. In the media, some royal supporters
offered the lame argument that the Queen, as the living embodiment of
the Crown, could no more tax herself than prosecute herself. But the
fact was that previous monarchs *had* been taxed. What's more, the Queen
was minded to go ahead. There was one stumbling block, though – the
Prime Minister. He was not convinced. 'The fact of the matter is we
would not have required the Queen to pay tax. I *did not* require the Queen
to pay tax,' says Sir John Major firmly. So here was a faintly hilarious
situation: a non-taxpayer trying to give money to the Inland Revenue
*against* the wishes of the government.

Charles Anson remembers the strange contrast between media heat
and Cabinet cool: 'John Major didn't want to do it. Even the Treasury
were reluctant. But the media, not just the tabloids, were absolutely on
a roll about tax.'

'I don't think any Prime Minister knows what it's like to be pushed
in that way,' says one of those involved. 'I mean, consistent tabloid pushing
at the monarchy's privileges was becoming pretty wearing. The Queen
was clever enough to see the advantages that if she did pay tax, a lot of
heat would go out of the financial pressure on her.'

John Major was not the only one advising caution. Queen Elizabeth
The Queen Mother was continuing her guerrilla war against the
modernisers from within her Clarence House redoubt. Her stern opposition to the creation of lady members of the Order of the Garter had
only just subsided following the installation of Lady Thatcher, a firm
favourite. Now she had caught wind of the tax discussions. Once again,
the Clarence House guns were primed. The Queen Mother was not
merely opposed to tax reforms for the sake of it, she was also fearful
that any change might reflect badly on her late husband who had secured
the original tax exemption from the government. The Queen dispatched
her Private Secretary, Sir Robert Fellowes, to outline the details to her
mother. 'When I finished,' he told William Shawcross, 'there was a long
pause and then she said, "I think we'll have a drink." In other words,

she thought it was completely wrong but she didn't want to hear about it.'

The Queen none the less followed her instincts. Her advisers had done their sums and had shown her that it was viable. In the end, Sir John Major came round to the idea, too. 'There were cases for her to do it,' he says. 'Those cases were advanced by the Palace. We discussed it. I agreed with it.' He would have loyally supported the status quo. But it was the Palace which was driving the changes. 'We worked hard on this,' Lord Airlie recalls, 'and, in February 1992, we entered into a discussion with the Inland Revenue.' There would need to be exhaustive and secretive investigations to establish what was taxable and what was not. But the process was under way. Nine months later, it would turn out to be a godsend.

It was exactly forty years earlier, in February 1952, that the Queen had acceded to the throne as she sat in a concealed treehouse, watching the wildlife stir beneath a Kenyan dawn. Now, in February 1992, she did not want any sort of Ruby Jubilee celebrations. She had even vetoed a fountain in her honour in Parliament Square. She had, however, agreed to another epic royal documentary, *Elizabeth R*. Unlike the ground-breaking 1969 film, *Royal Family*, this equally dazzling 107-minute film was more focused on the Queen herself. The portrait of a dutiful mother, grandmother and head of state proved to be an award-winning hit. But any hopes that it might calm the rattling of media pitchforks at the Palace gates were to be dashed within weeks. The year had started with awkward newspaper revelations of photographs confirming a friendship between the Duchess of York and a Texan businessman. Of greater concern was the rift between the Prince and Princess of Wales. It was becoming an open secret. During a tour of India the same month, the Princess's solo (and wistful) appearance at that peerless symbol of love, the Taj Mahal, had been calculated to send out a message to the world. She could not have been louder or clearer had she used a loud hailer.

The following month, Britain was embroiled in a particularly tight general election campaign. Having replaced Margaret Thatcher as Conservative leader less than two years earlier, John Major was seeking a mandate from the people. After thirteen years in opposition, Labour, under Neil Kinnock, was running him close. During any campaign the monarchy is expected to carry on quietly without upstaging the democratic process. Throughout this election, however, the royal story continued to take centre stage. The death of the Princess's father, the 8th Earl Spencer in March 1992, was followed by stories of further rows between the Prince and the grieving Princess. In the same month, it was announced that lawyers had drawn up separation plans for the Duke and Duchess of York. The decision was not entirely surprising given the recent reports about the Duchess's private life but the election was duly consigned to the inside pages again. The story continued to grow following official confirmation of the separation and an unimpeachable BBC report that 'the knives are out for Fergie'. The Queen, for whom all this must have been profoundly distressing anyway, felt honour-bound to apologise to the Prime Minister for all these distractions. 'I remember a call to Number Ten at the Queen's request being made very rapidly,' says one of those in the crossfire.

John Major won the election and politics duly returned to a more familiar, steady pace. Not so the monarchy. The procession of extra-ordinary royal revelations was merely gathering momentum. In April, it was announced that the Princess Royal had commenced divorce proceed-ings, the first of the Monarch's children to do so. In June, the remaining veneer surrounding the Waleses' marriage was eroded by the publication of *Diana: Her True Story*, Andrew Morton's account of the Princess's unhappiness. At first, the Princess assured Robert Fellowes – her own brother-in-law – that she had never spoken to Morton. When it transpired that she had communicated with him via an intermediary, Fellowes offered the Queen his resignation. It was refused.

The Highlands offered the Queen no respite during her annual spell at Balmoral. First, came the *Daily Mirror*'s publication of intimate photo-graphs of the Duchess of York and her financial adviser beside a French swimming pool. In the same month, the *Sun* reproduced transcripts of a three-year-old conversation between the Princess of Wales and her friend James Gilbey in which she spoke candidly about her unhappiness within the royal fold. Within five months, a similar conversation between the Prince of Wales and Camilla Parker Bowles, the future Duchess of Cornwall, would be laid bare in similar fashion. Come the autumn of 1992, an important tour of South Korea by the Prince and Princess would place the couple under the international spotlight. The visit proved to be a commercial and diplomatic success but a public relations nightmare. The media scrutinised every handshake and greeting line like marriage guidance counsellors.

Even when the couple were photographed looking solemn at a war cemetery, it was reported as another case of domestic unhappiness. 'It's a cemetery,' groaned one despairing press officer, attempting to put a wreath-laying in perspective. 'What did you expect? Cartwheels?' But there was no changing the narrative. And nor was it entirely wrong. This would be the last tour the Prince and Princess would undertake together. Soon after their return, the Queen was dealt another blow, one which would become emblematic of this abysmal run of events. On 20 November, a team of builders working on the north-east corner of Windsor Castle went for their mid-morning break, leaving a curtain draped over a scorchingly hot work lamp.

Within minutes, the greatest of all the royal residences was ablaze. The building work had at least emptied that particular part of the castle of both people and contents. But the blaze could not be contained. The only member of the Royal Family in residence, the Duke of York, helped coordinate a brisk and efficient evacuation of all the treasures in the path of the flames as they crept upwards and outwards through the 1,500-room castle. Priceless works were passed hand to hand down human chains to rest beneath open skies. Mercifully (for the works of art, at least), Windsor was spared a downpour that afternoon. Having rushed down from London, the Queen joined in herself. 'It was just awful for her,' says Lord Airlie. 'Awful, awful, awful. It was a dark, miserable drizzly November day and here was this fire roaring across this fantastic building.' He shivers at the recollection of the Queen watching the flames tear through her childhood home. 'Needless to say she was incredibly stoical about it all.' But what sort of impact would all this have on her? Her staff were worried. 'For a woman to lose her house, her nest, is very traumatic. A lot of her heart is at Windsor,' says Charles Anson. 'And the Duke of Edinburgh was on an official visit overseas when it happened. Obviously, the Queen had to come back to Buckingham Palace on the evening of the fire and about six of us went to her private entrance thinking: "Prince Philip isn't back yet and it will be quite a lonely thing for her coming back by herself on a day like this." And I remember feeling distinctly nervous about it, because what do you say? So, she came in and we all murmured: "We're so sorry, Ma'am." And she was brilliant. She looked very calm and said: "The maddening thing is I've lost my voice. I have a cold and the smoke has made it so much worse." We all said how sorry we were again and she said: "It was ghastly but we managed to save the pictures." This wasn't put on. She was just going to weather it.'

Her true thoughts will not be known until a future biographer is granted access to her papers in another reign. But we get a glimpse of the torment of those weeks from the words she wrote to the Queen Mother after spending the next few days with her at Royal Lodge: 'It made all the difference to my sanity after that terrible day.'

Those who thought the fire might mark some sort of closure to a sorry royal chapter were wide of the mark. 'That fire started other fires,' says Lord Airlie. With the remains of the great medieval chamber of St George's Hall still smouldering, the government set about reassuring the nation that all would be well. The National Heritage Secretary, Peter Brooke, inspected the Windsor damage and promised that all would be restored to its former glory by the state. But he had misjudged the mood of the nation. Such had been the corrosive effect of all the stories about marital strife and royal finances that a substantial part of the country did not share Brooke's avuncular spirit of generosity. 'I am not easily shocked,' says a former Private Secretary, 'but I was more shocked by the reaction to the Windsor fire than anything else. And I think most people who worked with me would have subscribed to that. Peter Brooke said exactly the right thing but was pilloried for it.'

A grudge was afoot and it had clearly spread beyond the traditional confines of left-wing orthodoxy. Much was made of the fact that Windsor was uninsured. The fact that its contents are priceless was irrelevant. Why, asked the commentators, should the rest of the country be expected to buy household insurance when the Queen evidently had not?

'Peter Brooke was a very nice man and I always felt very sorry for him,' says Lord Airlie. 'He made this speech to the effect of "Don't worry, Ma'am. We will put this right." And this lit another flame. The weekend was pretty miserable in the media.'

Papers which were traditionally supportive of the Queen now turned. The *Daily Mail* wrapped the fire, the tax issue and the catalogue of scandals into a national crisis beneath the headline: 'WHY THE QUEEN MUST LISTEN'. Condemning Brooke's announcement, the paper went on: 'The impression given is of an out-of-touch Government pandering to the wealthy insensitivity of an out-of-favour Royal Family.' Writing in *The Times*, Janet Daley summed up this new sentiment with a much-quoted sentence: 'While the castle stands, it is theirs, but when it burns down, it is ours.'

'I thought the media reaction to the Windsor fire was mean in the extreme, and I was quite shocked,' says Sir John Major. 'Windsor Castle is a national asset. To claim that it isn't seems to be mealy-mouthed in the extreme.'

The fact that the vast majority of Windsor Castle, the largest inhabited castle in the world, was not a royal residence was a fact which was deliberately overlooked. Around two hundred people – clergy, conservators, housekeepers, conference organisers, retired army officers and their families – live beneath its thirteen-acre roof in a close-knit community centred around the castle and its great chapel. The section of the castle destroyed by the fire was actually the collection of state and semi-state apartments which had been open to the public since the mid-nineteenth century. To this day, these rooms draw in up to a million tourists a year. None the less, minds were made up. Those spoiled royals had lost their luxury bolthole so they could damned well pay for the repairs themselves.

Four days later, at a City of London lunch to mark her fortieth year on the throne, and planned long before any of all this, the Queen made one of the most telling speeches of her reign. It is most widely remembered for her reference to an *annus horribilis*, her delivery all the more dramatic thanks to the state of her voice. Indeed, it nearly didn't happen. Laid low both by her cold and by smoke inhalation, the Queen had contemplated calling it off and told Sir Robert Fellowes: 'I can't make a speech today. I haven't got a voice. Prince Philip will have to do it.' Fellowes was clear that if anyone was going to deliver these words, they had to come from the Queen herself. A compromise was reached: she would deliver the speech before and not after the Guildhall luncheon (setting a precedent which is observed at lunches and banquets to this day, thus allowing the Queen to enjoy her food rather more). The most significant section of the speech was her acknowledgement that 'no institution . . . should expect to be free from the scrutiny of those who give it their loyalty and support, not to mention those who don't'. Its significance stunned the audience. 'I sat up pretty sharpish in my seat,' Lord Hurd recalls. 'It was portrayed as a cry for help,' says a former Private Secretary, 'but she was trying to say, "You're not just dealing with me and my family. You're dealing with an institution and you really are knocking it about a bit." I think she felt her children were getting a very hard time at the hands of the press and she would almost sooner it was all directed at her. She wanted a little bit of common sense and less hysteria.'

In the prevailing climate, there was no guarantee that anyone would listen. Back at the Palace, the Queen's advisers decided that it was time to pre-empt further attacks. The original plan had been to finalise all the new tax details with the Treasury and the Inland Revenue and announce the Queen's new financial arrangements the following March. 'The Revenue only had two or three people working on it in total confidence. And we were practically there,' says Lord Airlie. But over the weekend, between the fire and the *annus horribilis* speech, the decision was taken to get it all out in the open as quickly as possible. Some would later crow that the monarchy was caving in to the tabloids when, in fact, the decision to pay tax had been taken nearly a year before. But, in the circumstances, it seemed better to clear the decks.

'The timing couldn't have been worse because we hadn't tied up all the strings. We had to move very fast,' says Lord Airlie. 'The work had been done. It would have been nice to spend some time going through it quietly but the Queen had the *annus horribilis* speech the following day and a really terrible cold. So we had to take her through it very quickly. She was absolutely marvellous about it, she was very practical, she understood it. It was a very good example of how practical she can be.'

Just two days later, John Major stood before the Commons to announce that the Queen had voluntarily agreed to pay tax like anyone else. She would also reimburse the government for the Civil List costs of all the Royal Family except the 'old guard', the Duke of Edinburgh and the Queen Mother. It was a substantial reform announced in dramatic circumstances. In Parliament, there was cross-party agreement that the Queen had done the right thing.

Three months on, the details were announced in full, along with what would be one of the most important creations of this reign – the Royal Collection Trust. A registered charity, it was established to maintain and conserve this world-class assembly of paintings, sculpture, furniture, guns, clocks, jewels, porcelain, books, armour, Fabergé eggs and much, much more. Then, as now, it also had a mandate to 'enhance the public's appreciation and understanding' of the collection. There could no longer be any suggestion that any of it somehow 'belonged' to the Queen herself. It was now very clear that successive monarchs only owned it on behalf of the nation. John Major unveiled the plans to the Commons while Lord Airlie and Michael Peat took the unprecedented step of holding a press conference at St James's Palace.

There was a vast amount for the press to absorb, not least the shock of being invited into the Picture Gallery of St James's to hear the Lord Chamberlain give a frank assessment of the Queen's private wealth. The spirit of glasnost sweeping across Eastern Europe had arrived in the Mall. Dismissing wild media estimates of between £100 million and billions, Lord Airlie announced: 'Her Majesty has authorised me to say that even the lowest of these estimates is grossly overstated.' The sum, it emerged, was somewhere around £60 million.

The new arrangements were far from straightforward. The Queen was going to pay tax of her own volition but the law could not actually force her or her successors to do so. The most controversial issue was the fact that sovereign-to-sovereign transfers would be exempt from inheritance tax. This, the Prime Minister had stipulated, was to ensure 'a degree of financial independence from the government of the day'. There were practical reasons. Monarchs cannot make conventional inheritance plans, they can't retire and they can't hand over the business or the family home to their successor at an appropriate point. What's more, assets like Sandringham and Balmoral are both official and private residences. In the Commons, Major warned that they might fall victim to 'salami slicing' without the exemption. The Labour leader, John Smith, was not entirely convinced by the exemption but the plans were generally accepted amid some lively tumbril talk from the left.

The press response was, predictably, mixed. In most cases, there was a sense that a line had been drawn under the mayhem of recent years. The *Sunday Times*, cheerleader for reform, sensed history in the making. 'Never, since the English civil war,' it declared, 'has there been such a determined royal campaign to woo public opinion.' If that was a little over the top, so, too, was the *Mirror*'s vindictive personal attack centred on the inheritance tax issue. 'HM THE TAX DODGER' ran the headline. 'The Queen is set to become Britain's biggest tax "dodger" – paying as little as £2 million on her vast fortune,' wrote the paper's political editor, Alastair Campbell. Within five years, he would be turning up for meetings at the Palace, reincarnated as the Prime Minister's Press Secretary. On this occasion, he managed to reduce some of its residents to tears. Even after the hammering of the preceding year, members of the Royal Family and their staff were shocked to see the Queen depicted as Fagin on the front of a national paper. Finally, at the end of April 1993, Lord Airlie had one further innovation to announce. For the next five years, Buckingham Palace would open to the public during the summer to finance the rebuilding of Windsor. The taxpayer would not be footing the bill. As the editorial column of *The Times* concluded the following day: 'The opening of Buckingham Palace is an imaginative step in the renovation of the House of Windsor.'

In these uncertain and ill-tempered days, it was too soon to realise the extent of what had been achieved. Through a sustained series of reforms which, at times, must have grated with her innately conservative nature, the Queen had none the less persisted with the most fundamental financial overhaul of the monarchy in two centuries. It had taken nine years to move from the framework of an Edwardian house party to an organisation ready for the twenty-first century. And it would take at least another ten years for a new culture of professionalism to bed in. But money was now off the mainstream agenda. Sex, on the other hand, was not.

Within days of the inferno at Windsor, the Queen's *annus horribilis* speech and the announcement about tax, the Prime Minister had another bombshell to deliver to the Commons. While it was greeted with studied solemnity in Parliament, it was to become an enduring topic of conversation at the saloon bar, the watercooler and the playground gates for the rest of the millennium. 'It is announced from Buckingham Palace that, with regret, the Prince and Princess of Wales have decided to separate,' John Major said. 'Their Royal Highnesses have no plans to divorce and their constitutional positions are unaffected. This decision has been reached amicably, and they will both continue to participate fully in the upbringing of their children.' To this day, the former Prime Minister refuses to elaborate beyond his original statement. 'These things were not in my memoirs. They will not be in the papers I leave when I die. I'm not talking about them now. I won't talk about them in the future.'

The following weekend, there was actually some cause for celebration as the Princess Royal remarried in an almost obsessively low-key ceremony at Crathie Church, near Balmoral. Her new husband was the Royal Navy officer and former equerry Commander Timothy Laurence. Even the harshest royal critics were unable to find fault with the most inexpensive royal wedding in history. Instead of opening up Balmoral Castle for a proper wedding party, the bride and groom held a two-hour reception of soup and sandwiches in a castle function room and enjoyed a thirty-six-hour honeymoon in an estate lodge before returning to work. The contrast with the 'fairy-tale' wedding spectaculars of the seventies and eighties could scarcely have been more pronounced.

Just as the public had devoured every detail of the Prince Charles and Lady Diana romance, so they would be treated to every sorry step in its demise. The so-called 'War of the Waleses' would be the dominant royal theme throughout the nineties. Real history was also taking place in these years. The Queen was leading historic missions to countries which, in many cases, had never seen a British sovereign before. Only the Pope had managed to draw greater crowds to central Warsaw than those which came out for the Queen in 1996. Despite kinship with the tsars, no British monarch had ever set foot in Red Square until the Queen arrived one grey autumn day in 1994 (sadly, it was empty, nervous Russian security chiefs having evicted the public). In the same year, as democracy took root in post-Soviet Estonia, the new Estonian coalition government included a royalist party. Its leader believed that the best guarantee for the country's long-term democratic freedoms was a constitutional monarchy. A letter was dispatched to Buckingham Palace asking if Prince Edward – still single and establishing a role for himself – might consider becoming King of Estonia (in much the same way that Prince Philip's Danish grandfather had been invited to become King of Greece). The Queen and her youngest son were both touched by the offer; here was a pleasant morale-booster, a reminder that some parts of the world regarded the monarchy as more than just a glamorous soap opera. But the offer was politely declined.

No one can recall a happier start to a state visit than the moment the Queen stepped off the Royal Yacht on to a Cape Town quayside to be greeted by Nelson Mandela on a March morning in 1995. And one of the first acts of Nelson Mandela's presidency had been to return South Africa to the Commonwealth. It would prove an enduring friendship. The fiftieth anniversaries of D-Day, VE Day and VJ Day were powerful and evocative moments when the Queen and her family were the perfect focal point for a complex range of national and international emotions. 'We are just war relics,' the Queen Mother joked to the Queen after their VE Day anniversary appearance, along with Princess Margaret, on the Palace balcony. As Churchill might have said: some war, some relics. These were huge occasions involving millions of people all over the country. Whatever the private domestic problems of the House of Windsor, it was still a phenomenal force for national unity.

But always in the background – and very often in the foreground – there were the tensions between the Prince and the Princess of Wales. Equally sensitive was the relationship between the Princess and the institution from which she was obviously detached and yet to which she was also inextricably attached through her sons. 'The Princess was a political hot potato and several papers were championing her,' says a former senior official. 'The Queen needed to be careful, constitutionally, because there was a lot of support for this hot potato.'

Added to that were the tensions between the Queen's staff at Buckingham Palace and the Prince of Wales's officials who had set up a fiercely independent operation at St James's Palace. The Prince's new team were determined to rebrand their man their way and resented what they regarded as old-school interference from 'over the road' at the Queen's office. As the Prince's environmental messages became more forceful, his mother's advisers became more uneasy. Says one: 'We got a lot of: "If the Prince wants to talk about the environment he will do so and he'll clear it with the Department of the Environment. So get off our backs. We're grown-ups. We can deal with the government." It was that sort of tone.'

It did not take much to resurrect the chilling spectre of the *annus horribilis*. 'You might have wonderful D-Day or VE Day anniversaries but then along came *Panorama* in 1995,' says Charles Anson. 'Suddenly we were right back in there and it raised all those worries again. It took a long time to get rid of that sense of neurosis, a sense that round every corner there's a problem.' The Princess of Wales's interview for BBC1's

*Panorama* in November 1995 was a turning point for the Monarch. Its genesis, the Princess would claim, was an interview granted by the Prince of Wales the year before. In 1994, the Prince had allowed broadcaster Jonathan Dimbleby to produce a film and a book about his life. Both provided a colourful and compelling account of the unique nature of the Prince's job. Neither viewer nor reader could be left in any doubt about the depth of his feeling for the people who would, one day, be his subjects, nor for the broad range of causes he had chosen to champion. The entire multimedia exercise was overshadowed, though, by a few seconds in nearly two hours of candid and engaging close-quarters filming. The Prince's admission that he had remained faithful to the Princess until his marriage had 'irretrievably broken down' would be the enduring memory in the public consciousness. Some of his advisers had believed that the admission would help to 'clear the air' after years of speculation about his relationship with Camilla Parker Bowles. Instead, it merely moved the speculation to a new, more frantic level, begging the fundamental question: what next? The Queen and the Duke of Edinburgh were dismayed, not just because of the Prince's candour on screen. More wounding was the accompanying book which gave the impression that the Prince had endured an unhappy childhood. As the book was serialised in the *Sunday Times* over several weeks, the drip-feed of revelations managed to eclipse everything else the monarchy was attempting to do at the same time, including that long-awaited historic state visit to Russia. At Windsor Castle, the sense of frustration boiled over in public. 'I've never discussed private matters and I don't think the Queen has either. Very few members of the family have,' the Duke of Edinburgh said crisply on the eve of the royal departure for Moscow. The Queen Mother harboured similar reservations. As she would tell Sir Eric Anderson (former Provost of Eton and royal confidant) years later: 'It's always a mistake to talk about your marriage.'

The most damaging result of the Dimbleby book/film, however, was that it invited some sort of response from the Princess's side. Here was her *casus belli*. A year later, amid great secrecy, she prepared her riposte courtesy of the BBC and its *Panorama* programme. This was not to be a profile of her life and work. Whereas the Prince had been very careful to avoid any criticism of his wife in his programme, the Princess's interview was an extended dissection of her marriage in front of a global television audience. Worse still, she cast doubts on the Prince's prospects as King. It was time for the Queen to act. Up to this point, the Queen and Prince Philip had gone out of their way to be conciliatory to their daughter-in-law. Now, though, the Sovereign could not stand by. Not only did she write to the Prince and Princess urging them to seek a divorce but the Palace released a statement to say that she had done so. That way, there would be no funny business by the spin doctors for both parties who had been busy of late. The Queen wanted her position to be absolutely clear. Shortly afterwards, the lawyers went to work and, on 15 July 1996, their divorce was stamped in the High Court, just three months after the Duke and Duchess of York had gone through the same process.

Despite the outward impression of business as usual, the Queen was well aware that the monarchy could not possibly stand still if it was to regain its place in the nation's affections. However much she disliked change for change's sake, she was mindful of a popular and oft-quoted Palace mantra, lifted from Giuseppe di Lampedusa's 1958 novel, *The Leopard*: 'If things are going to stay the same, then things are going to have to change.' After all, a radical Labour government was on the horizon. The creation of the Way Ahead Group, the committee of the senior members of the Royal Family and their officials, was part of this process. Post-*Panorama*, the committee began addressing the most fundamental issues. Nothing was off-limits. A few weeks after the Waleses' divorce, it convened at Balmoral to discuss issues such as male primo-geniture and Catholic succession to the throne. These were matters for governments, not monarchs, to decide but the Queen and her advisers wanted to have clear, considered positions on the matters should they arise instead of being forced into knee-jerk responses by events. Staff in the Private Secretary's Office were charged with examining every aspect of the monarchy's work. 'In a sense, it was an exciting time,' a member of the team recalls. 'It took the 1990s for us to ask ourselves: are we doing the right things?' It also helped to maintain a sense of perspective. Charles Anson describes the mood: 'Mary Francis [the new arrival who would rise to the position of Deputy Private Secretary] had recently been in a very senior position in the Private Office at Number Ten. She would come to the morning meeting in the Palace and ask: "Why do we spend every morning talking about Fergie?" I thought: "My God, I've got sucked into this as well." It was a wake-up call. We should have been talking about what the monarchy should be doing, not how the Duchess or Diana would be hijacking the media.'

The Queen was adamant that there should be no sense of competition with the Princess. Even so, it was sometimes hard to avoid the impres-sion that the Princess was in competition with the monarchy. In the autumn of 1996, the Queen was due to pay a state visit to Thailand to mark the Golden Jubilee of King Bhumibol. Upon her return, the Prince of Wales was to make important inaugural royal visits to previously

uncharted royal territory across Central Asia. But after the Foreign Office
and the Palace had fixed the final plans, the Princess announced that she
would attend a charity ball and lunch in Sydney slap bang in the middle of
it all. Most of the media opted to go with her. The more conservative
elements within the Palace and Parliament became increasingly alarmed
as the Princess turned her attention to landmines. At the start of 1997,
she was branded a 'loose cannon' by a junior defence minister after calling
for a world ban on the weapons – and was promptly applauded by the
Opposition. Her stance was very popular but, given a clear party political
divide on the issue, it was an inappropriate intervention from a member
of the Royal Family. Except she was no longer a member of the Royal
Family and, following her divorce, was no longer styled 'Her Royal
Highness'. So what exactly was she? What sort of role should be expected
of the non-royal mother of the future Sovereign? And what were the
appropriate limits to her new non-royal status?

      She never had the chance to find an answer. In the early hours of 31
August 1997, she died alongside Dodi Fayed and the French chauffeur
who had been driving them through Paris. The following seven days
would test the monarchy to the same extent as the whole of 1992. The
events of that week – the human tragedy, the hysteria directed against
an absentee monarch, the tensions upon the Queen's return and the
resounding finale – have been the subject of extensive court hearings,
books, documentaries and even an Oscar-winning film. What has not
been heard before is the story of those who were actually on the inside.
For more than ten years they have kept their counsel. Even now they
remain modest, although they are quietly proud of what was achieved.
'I was worried. I was worried,' says Lord Airlie, who, as Lord Chamberlain,
was responsible for pulling the entire funeral operation together. 'It was
a very uncomfortable time. The Windsor fire was more difficult because
it went on burning in so many different areas whereas, sadly, the funeral
arrangements just had to be done. To be quite honest, we hadn't got time
to think of anything else. We just got on and did it.'

      The Palace had several carefully prepared blueprints for every sort of
royal funeral. Every six months there had been internal rehearsals and
military-style exercises for precisely this sort of eventuality. Cut the Royal
Household and it would bleed khaki. Except that, once again, the Princess
defied all known categories.

      'We didn't use any files,' says Lord Airlie. 'We didn't look at them. I
said, "No." We started again.'

      The man with the blank sheet of paper was Lieutenant Colonel
Malcolm Ross, late of the Scots Guards. His official title was Comptroller,

Lord Chamberlain's Office. In practice, he was the man in charge of all royal ceremonial and pageantry.

'The Princess was thirty-six years old, no longer a member of the Royal Family but never off the radar,' says Ross. 'And because of her immense popularity, we all underestimated everything. The first day was spent getting the Prince of Wales out to Paris and getting the Princess's body back. And we were in completely uncharted waters because there are certain legal requirements and we had never brought a dead member of the Royal Family back to this country.'

Having repatriated the Princess in royal style, the funeral preparations could begin in earnest. 'We sat in Buckingham Palace until two in the morning,' says Ross. 'I went home to St James's Palace and there were a thousand or so people kneeling around the Queen Victoria Memorial with candles and it was the most moving thing I've ever seen in my life. It was an incredible atmosphere – calm and serene. That was before the media got it. Then, of course, the fury started.'

Pent-up public emotion needed a target and an outlet. To begin with, it was directed at the paparazzi who had been pursuing the Princess's car through Paris. But then it started to be directed at the Royal Family and the Queen herself. The Royal Family were collectively criticised for the fact that Prince William and Prince Harry had been taken to church the morning after their mother's death, for the fact that the Princess was not mentioned during the service, for the queues to sign books of condolence at St James's Palace and for the absence of a flag at half-mast above Buckingham Palace. There were explanations. The boys had wanted to go to church. The Church of Scotland service was a matter for the minister. As Tony Blair observes in his memoirs, *A Journey*, the Queen was doing what she felt was right: 'I knew the Queen would have felt that duty demanded that the normal routine was followed. There would have been no Alastairs [as in Alastair Campbell, the Prime Minister's Press Secretary] in the entourage suggesting that possibly mentioning the tragedy might be sensible. The Queen is a genuine not an artifical person . . . there is no artifice in how she approaches things.'

The omission of Diana's name from the service still baffles many. But those who know the Queen would have been equally surprised had a Church of Scotland minister been instructed, at her bidding, to insert specific prayers into his service. As he explained later, he had not mentioned the Princess by name out of concern for her sons. 'My thinking,' the Rev Robert Sloan told reporters, 'was that the children had been wakened just a few hours before and told of their mother's death.' More than a decade after the Princess's death, the minutiae of that week continue to polarise opinion.

The books of condolence, meanwhile, were an untested innovation; the more that people became aware of their existence, the greater the numbers wanting to sign one. As for the Palace flagpole, it could only fly the Royal Standard – and never at half-mast for anyone, the Queen included. These might have seemed minor points from the detached perspective of Balmoral but they rapidly took on totemic importance for the increasingly emotional crowds in London. Just as the issues of fire damage, tax and marital discord had been conflated into a single crisis in 1992, so these perceived slights took on far deeper significance now: here, said the critics, was proof that those 'remote royals' just didn't care. The problem was compounded by a new phenomenon. The Palace had not been the focal point of twenty-four-hour rolling television news before. Without regular helpings of fresh material to digest, the media beast would continue to regurgitate old information. There was no shortage of people in Kensington Gardens and the Mall to offer opinions. And the more angry they became about a missing flag, the more it occurred to other people that, come to think of it, they, too, were cross about the flag. None of this was lost on those inside the Palace. A senior member of the Metropolitan Police team on duty that week sums up the mood: 'In the Mall, I saw a Jesus with a crucifix on his back meet a bloke carrying a flagpole with a flag at half-mast on his back. They greeted each other like old friends and it didn't even look unusual. That was the atmosphere we were dealing with.' One old member of the Household believes that if the Queen had been at Windsor rather than in the Highlands it would have been a different story. 'You can feel as if you're in another world at Balmoral,' he says. 'And she was.'

Inside the Palace that initial sense of shock on day one was soon replaced by a steely unanimity of purpose. 'It was an occasion when people pulled together like you could never imagine,' Sir Malcolm Ross remembers. 'We had daily conferences with the Archbishop or his representatives, the Dean of Westminster, the Commissioner of Metropolitan Police, the Head of the Army and so on. Lord Airlie chaired it and was going round the table saying, "Can you do that by lunchtime today?" "Yes," said the Commissioner. "Yes," said the Archbishop. "Yes." "Yes." "Yes."' Nor was the Royal Family as detached from it all as the critics suggested. The members of the funeral committee gathered in a Buckingham Palace drawing room each morning and were regularly joined by Prince Philip on a conference telephone. As one of those present recalls: 'Prince Philip was being a typically crisp and efficient chairman from Balmoral and saying: "Hang on, why not do this, or do that?"'

The new Prime Minister himself was earning plaudits – even from old foes like the *Daily Telegraph* – for protecting the monarchy. Some had winced at Tony Blair's demotic language in lamenting 'the People's Princess' hours after her death but his stature continued to rise as he defended the Royal Family from the brickbats. It needed it. Tabloid headline writers and the left-wing broadsheet commentariat had found rare common cause. The Royal Family, they declared in increasingly shrill tones, simply did not understand modern Britain. Proclaiming the dawn of an 'emotional revolution', an editorial in the *Independent* even suggested the following: 'What would really do the monarchy good, and show that they had grasped the lesson of Diana's popularity, would be for the Queen and the Prince of Wales to break down, cry and hug one another on the steps of the Abbey this Saturday.' In retrospect, it seems hilarious. At the time, less so.

Despite his mantra of 'New Britain', Tony Blair realised that his primary duty was to protect 'Old Britain', as the monarchy was being portrayed by much of the media. At the height of the flag hysteria, he urged people to show sympathy for the Royal Family and to understand that the Windsors were 'trying to cope in a tremendously difficult situation'. As he writes in his memoirs: 'I really felt for the Queen.' He describes how he worked closely with the Prince of Wales to persuade the Queen that she had to come to London, to be seen and to address the nation. Contrary to the way in which these events would be depicted in the film *The Queen*, the Prince of Wales played a key role in helping the monarchy turn the corner. 'I respected her [the Queen] and was a little in awe of her,' writes Blair. 'But as a new Prime Minister, I didn't know her or how she would take the very direct advice that I now felt I had to give her. So I went to Charles.' The Prince was in full agreement with the Prime Minister and, up at Balmoral, the Queen duly concurred. It would change the national mood completely. Looking back on it all now, Blair says that the Queen 'rightly' viewed some of the public and media hysteria as 'irrational'. At the same time, she came to a pragmatic view about it. 'She completely got the fact that it had to be met, at least a little part of the way,' says Blair. 'And once she did, she did that very, very adroitly.'

At the same time, though, Blair's emissary to the Palace planning meetings was getting a mixed reception. Just five years earlier, Alastair Campbell's 'HM THE TAX DODGER' story in the *Mirror* had left some of the Royal Household in tears. Now he was back in the role of helper – or, as his own diaries suggest, as saviour. In his view, the Palace was hopelessly out of date and out of its depth. As one of those who attended the daily meetings recalls: 'It was the big Alastair Campbell takeover: "We'll take it over. She was the People's Princess" and all that.' The Downing Street team were advocating a 'People's Funeral' with the public marching behind the coffin. Campbell refers to it as his 'Pied Piper' idea. The police and the Royal Household were less enthusiastic. 'There would have been a major disaster if we'd followed Campbell's idea to have a "People's Funeral". His ideas were insane,' says one of the Metropolitan Police planners. 'The first was to have the cortege with all the people following behind. One of the officers in charge said to him, "How many people do you want to kill?" All the people would have got to Parliament Square but you can't turn a huge crowd like that. They would have ended up spilling down on to the Underground.' The other Downing Street suggestion was for the coffin to be carried around Trafalgar Square. The police took an equally dim view of the likely crowd surge within the square. According to Palace and police sources, Number Ten then took a back seat and left the pageantry experts to put together this historic medley of ancient and modern.

Not so, according to Campbell's memoirs. He acknowledges that his 'Pied Piper' plan was vetoed by the police but says that the Royal Family and its staff needed his 'constant assurance that they were keeping in step'. He also quotes their repeated gratitude for all his insights. The monarchy certainly was (and still is) grateful for Downing Street's support during one of the worst weeks of modern times. But, at times, Campbell seems to misinterpret genuine expressions of warm appreciation – which the Palace does very well – as signs of inadequacy.

If he was unaware of the tensions he was creating, others remember things differently. 'He was ejected,' says one of the Palace planning team. 'Robert Fellowes handled it beautifully and I think he took Alastair Campbell outside and effectively removed it from his grasp.' It must have been handled very well as each side would forever after speak warmly of the other and there are no lingering resentments. In his memoirs, Blair describes Fellowes as 'a thoroughly sensible man', adding: 'I don't know what he really thought of Diana – I think he saw both sides to her, loved the side he loved and shrugged at the other – but he was a professional and as you sometimes find with well-bred upper-class types, a lot more shrewd and savvy than he let on.' Fellowes, in turn, would invite Campbell to the Buckingham Palace leaving party which the Queen gave him on his retirement.

While 'Pied Piper' ideas were being quietly smothered, there were more practical decisions to be taken. The Princess's coffin, it was agreed, would be carried on a gun carriage, despite the military / royal overtones. 'I wanted people to be able to see the coffin,' says Sir Malcolm Ross. 'If we were going to have this mass of people in London, a hearse and a low vehicle with glass between the public and the coffin was not the spectacle we were trying to achieve.' Ever since the horses bolted at the funeral of Queen Victoria, coffins on gun carriages have traditionally been pulled by humans from the Royal Navy. Ross, however, decided to give the horses the chance to redeem themselves after nearly a century and called in the King's Troop, Royal Horse Artillery. 'You can whistle up the King's Troop in ten minutes but you try and get two hundred sailors. Not a chance.'

The smallest details could require mini-summits. The authorities at Westminster Abbey were happy to have Sir Elton John singing his lament for the Princess and yet they had reservations about the inclusion of Verdi's Requiem on the grounds that it was a secular piece of music (the Abbey relented). 'I had Plácido Domingo on the line from San Francisco asking if he could take part,' says Ross. 'I said: "So sorry, the job's gone."'

By now, the two main concerns for the organisers were the reaction to the Queen's impending return to the capital and the size of the crowds at the funeral. The Palace team had come up with three suggestions which, according to police sources, avoided a serious crowd control issue or even loss of life. The first had been the extension of the funeral route by starting from Kensington Palace, the Princess's old home, rather than St James's Palace. The second was the erection of giant television screens in London parks to ease congestion around Westminster Abbey. The third was the decision to publicise a processional route for the hearse all the way through London and up to the Princess's ancestral home at Althorp, Northamptonshire.

All eyes were now on the Queen's arrival from Balmoral to meet the crowds and address the nation. Much of the midweek anger had vanished as quickly as it had appeared following the sudden – and astonishingly composed – appearance of Prince William and Prince Harry with their father amid the mourners and flowers outside Kensington Palace. Newly released details of the funeral arrangements also gave the rolling news channels plenty to chew on.

Even so, some of the most experienced members of the Royal Household still look back on that moment as the most pivotal of the Queen's entire reign. As one retired aide puts it: 'The stakes were at their highest when the Queen made that broadcast after she came down from Balmoral. She did it live which was a crucial decision by her. It was a high-risk thing but she did it brilliantly. Then she made another very important decision. It was her initiative – what she wanted to do and felt she should do. And that was to walk outside the Palace and bow to the coffin as it went past. A very big moment, that, actually.'

Any lingering doubts about the core strength of the monarchy were dispelled as much of the world watched the Queen deliver her tribute to her late ex-daughter-in-law. 'What I say to you now as your Queen and as a grandmother, I say from my heart,' she said (the 'as a grandmother' phrase was a genuine Alastair Campbell contribution). The following day, as she led her family out of the Palace gates to lower their heads as the coffin passed by, few could doubt the significance or sincerity of the gesture. The Sovereign, who traditionally bows to no one, had not merely shown leadership and humility. She had also displayed genuine majesty.

'The important thing is that at the end of the day on that Saturday, it went all right,' says Lord Airlie. Drawing on a metaphor from his days in the City, he adds: 'You may well find in years ahead, that that crisis, that awful situation, was the very nadir of our stock market. Look back and it's probably true. But the monarchy has come through.'

Two years later, the Royal Family assembled for another royal wedding. The marriage of Prince Edward to public relations executive Sophie Rhys-Jones did not bring the capital to a euphoric weekday standstill but took place on a Saturday afternoon in the family church, St George's Chapel, Windsor. There was none of the bunting and street-party mayhem which accompanied the weddings of the Prince's brothers back in the eighties. This was not supposed to be another 'fairy-tale wedding'. The world could watch and yet it was not expected to get involved. Even so, Windsor Castle, now restored to greater grandeur than before, rose to the occasion beautifully. The two main television networks cleared their schedules to pack it all in and stations around the world carried the event live. The choice of Windsor made it emphatically a family affair, not a state occasion. The scale matched the mood perfectly. Similar thoughts led the Prince of Wales and Camilla Parker Bowles to choose St George's Chapel for the blessing of their wedding in 2005. The whole occasion was marked by sensitivity, given the divorces on both sides, the Prince's future position as Supreme Governor of the Church of England and the death of Diana. There were problems with the location of the civil marriage ceremony* and even the date. Come the day, though, there was a carnival atmosphere around Windsor. Here was a stylish and inescapably modern occasion in an impeccably ancient setting with a buzz and

* Plans for a civil ceremony in the castle had to be shelved when it transpired that the castle would need to obtain a wedding licence and, subsequently, make itself available for general wedding hire. The event took place in the Town Hall, minus the Queen. Her absence denoted her disapproval of the arrangements, not of the marriage. She attended the service of blessing in St George's Chapel, hosted the reception and made an affectionate speech with a racing theme. It was the day of the Grand National.

a warmth epitomised by the obvious happiness of Prince William and Prince Harry. A line had been drawn. The world wished the Prince of Wales and the new Duchess of Cornwall well. It was time to move on.

For the Queen herself, the Golden Jubilee of 2002, with its sad start and its stupendous crowds, surpassed all expectations. As she was cheered through the packed streets of Windsor three years later on her eightieth birthday, the Queen's position as the new Mother of the Nation was beyond doubt.

Henceforth, the Royal Family would be looking forwards. True, the Duchess of York would continue to cause the occasional bout of royal apoplexy, most notably when caught trying to sell royal access to an undercover reporter. There are some who believe that she should now relinquish her title, not least because it was the Queen Mother's during the Queen's formative years. But the general feeling is that the harm she inflicts is on herself – and that it might even fulfil a necessary role. Sir Antony Jay, observer of royal fortunes across four decades, shares a favourite theory of the late Lord Charteris – the importance of royal lightning conductors. 'Every royal family needs a wicked fairy, someone to pick on,' he points out. 'It's a displacement activity. It was Princess Margaret then Princess Anne then Princess Michael of Kent. The press tried it on with Prince Harry and nightclubs for a bit but it didn't work. Now it's Prince Andrew. You always need someone to be picked on.'

But as well as wicked fairies, every royal family needs a few happy endings, too. The sense of euphoria which accompanied the wedding of Prince William to Catherine Middleton in April 2011 surprised even the most optimistic royalists. Following the announcement of the couple's engagement the previous November, there was a palpable sense of restraint, of not wanting to tempt fate, among the press and the British public alike. A recurring media theme was that the people had been hoodwinked by a fairy-tale wedding thirty years earlier and they did not want to be duped again. The rest of the world, however, took a less cautious view. Here was a great new chapter in the one-thousand-year story of the world's most famous family. Why not just enjoy every moment?

Come the day, a 10,000-strong media contingent from all over the world watched a million people in central London enjoy a day of uncomplicated exuberance. Across Britain, all that doubt and caution simply evaporated. People suddenly found themselves much more excited than they had expected to be. The sight of Prince William and Prince Harry travelling to the Abbey together evoked powerful memories of the two boys making that heartbreaking walk behind their mother's coffin in 1997.

Here they both were fourteen years on – two dashing young blades waving and smiling at near-hysterical crowds in their immaculate army uniforms; a credit to Diana, to the monarchy and the country.*

Catherine Middleton's radiant happiness on the arm of her father, Michael – a man displaying his own Olympian powers of composure – struck an instant chord with the public. Some commentators had previously tried to project the union as a clash of class and culture, the girl from the happy, entrepreneurial Home Counties family being tossed into an unbending, snobbish world obsessed with pedigree. All of a sudden, those Jane Austen conspiracy theories simply collapsed. Everything about the occasion bespoke a genuine, solid love match, an impression reinforced by the armies of lip-readers employed by Fleet Street to translate every inaudible aside. 'I am so proud you're my wife,' the new Duke of Cambridge whispered as he helped the new Duchess into the State Landau outside the Abbey. Since boyhood, Prince William has carried a colossal – at times overwhelming – burden of expectation. That burden, at least, could now be shared.

And despite the inevitable comparisons with the wedding of Prince Charles and Lady Diana Spencer thirty years earlier, the backdrop was reminiscent of a different event. The 1981 royal wedding took place in an era of cloudless skies. During the build-up to this wedding, though, there had been a miasma of negativity. There were grumbles about the expense of it all (even though the cost to the public purse amounted to 0.2 per cent of the bill for the 2012 London Olympics). There were complaints from the modish left that another burst of Charles-and-Di-style razzmatazz was projecting an outdated image of Britain. Just days before the wedding, the Deputy Prime Minister, Nick Clegg, announced that he was planning to end male primogeniture in the Royal Family and allow the eldest child to succeed to the throne, female or male. It's a recurring cross-party idea and became the subject of a more serious commonwealth discussion later in the year. On this occasion, it merely succeeded in kick-starting a debate about the entire monarchy on the eve of a wedding.

There were rows about the guest list too, notably the absence of invitations to the two former Labour prime ministers Tony Blair and Gordon Brown. The omission carried uncomfortable, subliminal political messages – even if none was intended. To many, it smacked of a snub. The problem was that the two surviving Conservative ex-premiers, Lady Thatcher and Sir John Major, had been included. The Clarence House team charged

---

* While Prince William was dressed as Colonel of the Irish Guards, Prince Harry wore the Household Cavalry uniform of a Captain in the Blues and Royal.

with drawing up the guest list had decided to include all members of the Order of the Garter, on the grounds that Prince William was a Knight of the Garter himself. Lady Thatcher and Sir John were members of the Order. Blair and Brown were not. This was no 'snub'. It was just an oversight – 'a cock-up', as a senior Buckingham Palace aide acknowledged. Blair had met Prince William many times and had gone out of his way to defend the monarchy at its lowest ebb. Brown had not only been scrupulous in his dealings with the Palace but, as Chancellor, had chaired the committee which created a permanent public memorial to Diana, Princess of Wales. With the monarchy, perceptions of neutrality are as vital as the exercise of neutrality. If the guest list could include every Lord-Lieutenant and the footballer David Beckham, it could surely have included two former prime ministers. But the overarching concern was one of tone. The marriage was taking place against a backdrop of economic hardship and substantial cuts in public spending. The situation was certainly not as bleak as the conditions of post-war austerity which prevailed in 1947 when Princess Elizabeth married Prince Philip. But now, as then, it was vital for the monarchy to strike a happy balance between spectacular pageantry and common sense.

And yet, all these worries simply melted away by mid-morning on 29 April 2011. The moment the bride arrived at the altar in her masterpiece of lace and ivory satin by Sarah Burton at Alexander McQueen the occasion was already a monumental triumph. It had the bonus of making Britain feel a great deal better about itself at a time of economic malaise. And in that regard, the closest comparison was not the ballyhoo of the royal weddings of the eighties. This one, rather, echoed that unexpected revivalist hit of the previous decade – the Silver Jubilee of 1977.

Overall, inter-generational royal relations have seldom been better. Once at loggerheads, the Prince of Wales's staff and the Queen's officials now liaise, dine and even work out together on a daily basis. Michael Peat, the architect of all those royal reforms on behalf of the Queen, was knighted and went on to become the Prince's Private Secretary, a move which helped to harmonise the two operations. In 2011, after more than twenty years of royal service, he finally announced that he would return to the private sector, to be replaced by William Nye, a senior civil servant. The Prince has rearranged his household at Clarence House to replicate the structure of Buckingham Palace, complete with a Master of the Household. But the Queen is well aware of the need for each generation to exercise a sensible independence from the one in front.

So while Prince William and Prince Harry had previously depended on their father's staff at Clarence House, they have now set up their own office next door in a corner of St James's Palace. The Queen also pays for Prince William to have his own independent constitutional adviser in the form of Sir David Manning, former British ambassador to Washington.

Long before their wedding, the Prince and his bride-to-be had been renting a farmhouse together in Anglesey following his posting there with the RAF. As man and wife, however, they also needed a new London base. The new Duke and Duchess of Cambridge could hardly be expected to share the Clarence House bachelor flat with Prince Harry.* A modest apartment in the private wing of Kensington Palace – where the Duke spent much of his childhood – was allocated to them.

However, there was no question of Prince Harry moving out of the shared office. The two Princes remain extremely close and several guests at the evening party after the wedding were reduced to tears during Prince Harry's irreverent but poignant tribute to the big brother who had helped him through the turmoil of their mother's death. Today, the Duke, the Duchess and the younger Prince plus nine office staff all work out of a small terraced house which had previously been earmarked as accommodation for the Lord Chamberlain. Guests are greeted by a bust of the Queen and a portrait of Edward VII next to a very ordinary kitchen where the royal residents and the staff share a coffee machine, a kettle and a table covered in newspapers. Brynnie, a friendly working cocker spaniel belonging to senior aide Helen Asprey, is part of the furniture.

The single stairwell (there are no backstairs for staff) is dominated by a Franz Winterhalter portrait of Queen Victoria and lined with smaller military prints and a view of Windsor from Eton. It is smart but not grand. There is an easy informality and a bustling sense of purpose as young assistants trot between floors bearing correspondence or dress samples. If the Duke of Cambridge is between official engagements, visitors are as likely to bump into him wearing chinos, open-neck shirt and tank top as to find him in a suit.

Space is tight, though. This may be the headquarters of the most famous young couple on earth but they don't just share the same first-floor study with each other. They share it with Prince Harry, too. And because there is only room for two desks, the trio are reduced to what, in modern officespeak, is known as 'hot-desking'. 'It's not a problem as they're hardly ever all there at the same time,' explains a member of staff. While the Private Secretary works in the room next door, the other

* Fraternal living arrangements were fairly relaxed. It was reported that the brothers had resorted to marking their initials on the soles of their shoes. Otherwise, one might walk off in the other's footwear.

officials and assistants occupy the floor above. Here, the atmosphere is even more informal, the walls lined not with works from the Royal Collection but delightful sketches of the Princes as very young children. It's a small, close-knit operation without the trappings of larger royal households – equerries, ladies-in-waiting, orderlies and so on. And at this stage in his life, that is precisely how the next monarch but one likes to keep it.

With the domestic situation happy and settled, it is money which has crept back up the agenda again. Today, it is a matter for Sir Alan Reid, Keeper of the Privy Purse since the Golden Jubilee. An international management consultant from the same KPMG stable as Sir Michael Peat, Reid has quietly introduced an entirely new financial structure for the monarchy. In 2010, exactly 250 years after the creation of the Civil List – an anniversary studiously ignored by everyone at the Palace – the old system was torn up. The ten-year Civil List deal had come to an end and Reid and the Coalition Government both agreed it was time for a simpler plan. Instead of receiving a fixed head of state allowance from the state plus complicated grants for maintenance and travel, the monarchy would receive one lump sum every year – a percentage of the Crown Estate's annual profits. Announcing the plans in June 2011, the Chancellor, George Osborne, said that the initial share would be 15 per cent – to meet a projected royal bill of £35 million. But the figure, he added, could be adjusted up or down. What's more, it would have a new name. The term 'Civil List' would be consigned to the history books. The new deal would be called the Sovereign Grant.

Once upon a time, the Sovereign had taken the entire Crown Estate pot. In 1760, George III swapped it all for the Civil List. Now, 250 years later, the monarchy would live on a slice of that original pie. It seemed like a good deal all round. The Royal Household had finally achieved Lord Airlie's dream of being 'masters of their own destiny'. Parliament would have scrutiny of the whole royal budget via the National Audit Office. But, looking to the future, there are risks, too. The Crown Estate is a dynamic property developer in a tough market. Any unpopular decisions – and it has made many – may now rebound directly on the Queen. What's more, the new deal was announced in the teeth of a dire economic crisis. And, unlike most of the public sector, the monarchy had already spent the previous twenty years cutting costs. Thus, there was less flab to lose. Yet Reid has already identified new cuts, not least by securing a place on the Royal Visits Advisory Committee. Previously, royal visits were decided by the Foreign Office and the royal visitor, while the bill was then sent to the Treasury for payment. Now that the cost must, instead, come out of the monarchy's central budget, Reid will in future be in a position to clip royal wings. It is unlikely that a state visit will ever be called off because of the transport costs. But if the choice is between sending a junior member of the family to the Pacific or hiring a new footman, it may help to focus the mind.

Lord Airlie is the first to admit that he and Michael Peat have not made things easy for their successors by stripping out so much of the fat during the nineties. 'I don't think we're that popular,' he jokes. Subsequent arrivals have observed that one side effect of the reforms was a surfeit of risk-averse, box-ticking accountants. 'It was a classic pendulum thing,' explains a member of today's Royal Household. 'There was no financial control in the 1980s and then way too much by the time of the Golden Jubilee in 2002. There were just far too many accountants reconciling their numbers with other accountants.' Another official recalls the way that, over time, the level of financial control was becoming counterproductive. 'If you had a good idea, you were told "no" straight away and then you had to fight to say why it was a good idea.' The risk-averse culture had got to the point that Palace staff could not even send or receive emails for fear of hackers. One of Reid's first moves on taking over the Palace's financial operations in 2002 was to slash the number of fellow accountants and install new computers.

The scale of the great Airlie/Peat reforms is not forgotten, however. 'What Lord Airlie did was brave, it showed great foresight and it was not an easy task,' says today's Lord Chamberlain, Lord Peel. 'I know the difficulties he faced and the opposition he encountered but he changed the face of the Household and since then it has evolved at a pretty rapid rate.'

The Duke of York is under no illusions that this rapid rate of reform is set to continue. 'This organisation went through a restructuring under Lord Airlie and I suspect there are going to be huge changes in the way things are done for the Sovereign Grant,' he says. 'The whole thing is going to have to change and it's a question of how that's done. There won't be a compromise solution. There will be a solution that best meets the needs of the time.'

None the less, in her Diamond Jubilee year, the Queen can look back on a minor royal economic miracle. When she came to the throne in 1952, her income from the Civil List was £475,000 – equivalent to 60 per cent of the Crown Estate's profits – not to mention all the other allowances. The entire Royal Family was funded by the state and the Queen paid no tax. Today, the monarchy costs not 60 per cent but 15 per cent of the Crown Estate's profits. Aside from the Queen and Prince

Philip, none of the Royal Family receives an annuity from the state. And the Monarch is taxed. The Civil List, that central royal budget, has now been replaced. But for twenty years – from 1990 to 2010 – it never had an increase. In other words, the monarchy was the only arm of the state to exist on the same budget for two decades (by way of comparison, an MP's salary tripled during the same period). 'Business would think we were mad!' jokes the Duke of York. In the year of a £9.4 billion Olympiad, the Royal Household's budget for the entire Diamond Jubilee is £1 million – less than a thirtieth of the cost of a single, temporary Olympic basketball arena.

To the monarchy's critics, it will always be a 'luxury we cannot afford'. Since a presidency would presumably involve a national election (going rate: £80 million) this is a moot point. But the Royal Household is certainly in a stronger position to defend itself after the reforms of the last twenty-five years. If the Airlie/Peat revolution had not started when it did, who knows what further damage might have been done when those explosive issues of sex and money finally detonated at the start of the Nineties? 'It had to be done,' says Lord Airlie. 'And what would one say if it hadn't been done?' He would, doubtless, accept that the ultimate credit for the overhaul of Her Majesty's Household rests with Her Majesty – since she appointed him and gave him special powers in the first place. The Duke of York certainly thinks so. 'That comes from leadership from the top,' he says. 'Whether or not there were people in the institution who would have had that sort of bravery, I am not sure.'

There must have been times when the Queen wondered whether she was doing the right thing. With hindsight, she must have wished she had done some of them faster. There is no doubt that the monarchy had grown complacent through the eighties. The shadow of the nineties should hang near enough to ensure that the same mistake is not made again for a while. But the new Sovereign Grant is the culmination of one of the greatest royal upheavals since George III was on the throne – back in the days when there was still a monarchy over the Channel in France. As he gets up to leave, the most influential courtier of modern times allows himself a shy smile. 'It's all right now, you know,' says Lord Airlie proudly. 'It's all right.'

# 4

## Her People

*'The word "corporate" is a word the Queen does not like.'*

There is no fanfare. Instead, there is Ray Wheaton. One of Buckingham Palace's senior liveried staff, quick-witted Wheaton is the Page of the Chambers, a one-man reconnaissance patrol who moves through the Palace ahead of the Queen, checking with a beady eye that everything is as she expects to find it. As his face pokes round the huge mirrored door to the White Drawing Room, the assembled staff and guests stop talking, clear their throats and stiffen. Moments later, the Queen comes through the door looking purposeful and then her face lights up as soon as she is introduced to the first of her three hundred guests. Two hours later, she will have met every single one.

It's party time at the Palace. Tonight's guests include charity workers, financiers, a millionaire astronaut, doctors, nurses, a wine grower, a pop star – all of them with one thing in common: South Africa. A week from now, the Palace will be putting on a dazzling show of old-world pomp and modern hospitality to welcome the new President of the Republic of South Africa, Jacob Zuma.

The relationship between Britain and South Africa is a close and vital one. The British Government wants to underline this with a full state visit for Mr Zuma, just a year into his presidency. It is the British Government which decides who receives an invitation for a state visit – there are two each year – but the Queen will be the host. She must ensure that all visitors are treated exactly the same. Even so, she will have a particularly soft spot for this event. South Africa was the first foreign country she ever visited. She had never ventured beyond the Isle of Wight until, in 1947, she accompanied her father, mother and sister on a great post-war tour to what was then still part of the British Empire. It was in Cape Town, on her twenty-first birthday, that she pledged her life to the imperial family of nations in a broadcast which is said to have reduced Winston Churchill to tears when he heard it on the radio back in London. Douglas Hurd was with her as Foreign Secretary when she returned to Cape Town for the first time nearly fifty years later. 'That speech weighed on the Queen's mind,' he says. 'She was very conscious of it.' Today, South Africa is a key member of her beloved Commonwealth. There will be no shortage of talking points with Mr Zuma.

For the first fifty years of this reign, state visits were set in aspic. But now, at an age when most people would probably feel that they have got their entertaining down to a fine art, the Queen has decided to shake things up a bit. She believes that these visits could benefit from some extra razzmatazz in advance. So she has started holding warm-up parties. Not only does it get everyone more excited about the visit but it also gives her some extra insights into the nation she is about to honour. And tonight's reception offers plenty of those. The Queen is introduced to a little group which includes singer Annie Lennox, Labour politician Lord Mandelson and Mark Shuttleworth, the first 'African astronaut' (a software tycoon, he explains that his only qualification for space travel was that he 'bought a ticket off the Russians'). Talk turns to Nelson Mandela. The Queen remarks that the father of modern South Africa is still as bright as a button in his nineties although she's a little worried about his knees. All agree. Afterwards, Lennox admits that she herself is a little star-struck, an unusual situation for a pop star. Despite playing at the Golden Jubilee pop concert in the Palace gardens in 2002, this is her first meeting with the Monarch. 'She's beautiful, radiant. A very gentle person,' says Lennox, who greeted the Queen with a huge smile and a textbook curtsey. 'I thought she'd be a bit intimidating but she is very personable with a big twinkle in her eye.' Recalling her days as an anti-apartheid protestor, the scale of the journey suddenly sinks in: 'Here we are with the Queen celebrating the new South Africa. I'm rather emotional.'

London was the hub of the anti-apartheid movement in the days of white-only rule. A lot of old hands from the African National Congress are here tonight. 'I can't believe I was just talking to the Queen. Brilliant!' says Nduna Biyase, chair of the London branch of the ANC. He is not the only one enjoying the sense of the surreal. South African international footballer Quinton Fortune (formerly of Manchester United, now of Doncaster Rovers) thought it was a joke when his invitation arrived. The thirty-two-year-old midfielder was equally astonished when his manager gave him the night off to go to the Palace even though it would mean missing an important match (the boss must be furious with himself; at this precise moment, Rovers are losing at home to Leicester City). Fortune says that no one is more excited than his mother, sitting at home in South Africa and demanding a full report (she's not talking about the match). 'My mum can't believe it. South Africa is mini-England.' He is not the only footballer here. Gary Mabbutt, former Spurs and England defender, has long been an ambassador for the Prince's Trust and helped South Africa with its bid for the 2010 World Cup. 'Just look at this,' he marvels, surveying the room. 'Look at the job the Queen does. It's the same with Prince Charles. He does an amazing amount but the media never portray that side. It's always so negative.'

That's certainly a subject on which the two heads of state may have something to say. Mr Zuma's hectic private life has been dominating press coverage of the visit, with the press wondering which of his three current wives will join him on the trip. Tonight, one of his daughters by an earlier marriage is here. Nkosazana Zuma, twenty-eight, is a student of International Studies and Diplomacy at the University of London. When the Duke of Edinburgh learns that she is studying diplomacy, he promptly steers her towards the Foreign Secretary, joking: 'You can learn something from him.' She has been perfecting a curtsey in recent days, much to the amusement of her student friends, but fears that tonight's attempt was not a success. 'I think I got my curtsey wrong but the Queen didn't seem fazed at all. Someone told me that the staff are more uptight about protocol than the Queen.'

The staff are certainly out in force tonight. The more junior liveried staff are handing round the champagne and Sandringham apple juice. Two dozen of the most senior members of the Household – a cross section of ladies-in-waiting, private secretaries and equerries from the offices of almost every member of the Royal Family – are mingling with the guests in the Picture Gallery. They wear discreet blue name badges and scatter themselves among the guests, many of whom have arrived not knowing anyone. All the staff have had thorough briefings from the Master of the Household and his team. No guests are to be left awkwardly studying the paintings with no one to talk to. The party is buzzing, the bonhomie infectious. There has already been a reception line at the start so that everyone has been introduced to the Queen and Prince Philip. Ice broken (up to a point), the royal couple can now move around the room, their staff introducing them to random clusters of guests. And no one is more than a few feet from a Windsor because the Queen has brought along reinforcements. Tonight's royal turnout also includes the Duke and Duchess of Gloucester, the Duke of Kent and Prince and Princess Michael of Kent. It is quite a production, but nothing compared to the state welcome which is just a week away. President Zuma is well used to grand ceremonies and motorcades overseas. But his daughter Nkosazana has no doubt that this one will be in a different league. 'We have so many ties with Britain and it's a big deal for South Africa to be recognised by the Queen. And not everyone gets to ride in a carriage!'

Everyone at the Palace, from the Sovereign down, knows the importance of keeping it a 'big deal'. The Royal Household is about to go into overdrive, just as it will soon afterwards when President Barack Obama of the United States comes to stay. Short of a Coronation, nothing beats a state visit when it comes to glimpsing the full extent of the royal machine.

'It's a team effort and if we don't have that team effort, it doesn't work,' says Lord Peel. His job has been likened to that of the non-executive chairman of the Royal Household.* These days, every position at the Palace has a formal job specification, even the medieval post of Lord Chamberlain which comes with a 'wand' of office and a ceremonial key attached to the waist (no one knows what it unlocks). The Lord Chamberlain has many responsibilities: he has to 'ensure strategic direction to the Household . . . to ensure the Household runs smoothly as one integrated entity'; he is 'responsible to the Queen for ensuring that clear strategic direction is given to the Household' and he must also see to it 'that people of appropriate calibre and experience fill the senior posts'. He must 'support close co-ordination' between the Queen and the Prince of Wales and help to 'create a pleasant but professional atmosphere'. The job specification also notes that the successful candidate should be in his or her late fifties or sixties, retire by seventy and devote half a working week to the task in return for £82,000 a year. The ideal Lord Chamberlain should have 'a wise and balanced approach', 'experience of acting as a chairman', 'prestigious standing in the wider community' and 'some understanding of the public sector'. He should, ultimately, 'be reconciler, healer and facilitator'.

A tall, jovial Yorkshire landowner and direct descendant of Sir Robert Peel, the Tory Prime Minister and founder of the police, Lord Peel came highly recommended by the Prince of Wales. Prior to this position, he spent twelve years performing a similar role for the Prince at the Duchy of Cornwall (a position with the even more exotic title of Lord Warden of the Stannaries). A Lord Chamberlain needs a considerable degree of both tact and nerve. As in any family business, it is not always easy for an outsider to spell out home truths to family members who know the place a great deal better than he does.

'Whenever I go round any of the royal palaces I always have to have a lot of oil with me,' he jokes. 'You never know what's going to happen so I just spread it into the joints.'

He chairs a monthly gathering of all the heads of department – 'like a board meeting' – plus a weekly update every Tuesday morning. Having

---

* The Lord Chamberlain is not to be confused with the Lord Great Chamberlain, an entirely ceremonial and hereditary post which involves escorting the Queen at the State Opening of Parliament. The present Lord Great Chamberlain is the Marquess of Cholmondeley.

worked for the Prince of Wales for many years, he is very keen on making the Clarence House staff feel part of the wider royal team and regularly organises joint meetings and lunches for the Prince's officials and their opposite numbers. Football-minded courtiers have a phrase for this new pan-royal *esprit de corps*: 'Mon United'.

'They know each other, of course they do, but there is no substitute for actually looking across at somebody and having a proper conversation,' says Lord Peel. 'And I think we rely on computers too much these days. The human touch is sometimes lost.'

The Royal Household remains a sometimes confusing blend of old world and new, an early pioneer of alternative energy but also a place where, even in the twenty-first century, female office workers were quietly advised that trousers were 'inappropriate' office wear (the rules have now changed).

The contrast certainly made an impression on Lord Peel when he arrived in 2007. 'What surprised me most was the fact that underneath this formal façade was a highly effective, highly efficient modern system of work. It's a mixture – longstanding employees who bring a band of security to the system at the same time as young people coming forward with ideas and challenging the old systems. People are proud of working here and they like to show it off.'

Today's Royal Household is another world from the Court of, say, George I, whose retinue included a Polish dwarf and a feral child found in the woods near Hanover. The modern management culture actually compares favourably with the more forward-thinking ends of both public and private sectors. But it can still be a bewildering network of quirks and hierarchies. A team of forty-three still wear 'the livery' – red and black tailcoats for front of house, black or dark blue for the more senior attendants within. There may be a Yeoman of the Cellars and Britain's last fendersmiths. And yet, the more demeaning job titles – lady clerks etc. – have now gone. While there's a lot of talk about 'service', there are no 'servants'. It's 'staff'. And all of them, from Lord Peel to a trainee footman, have access to a twenty-four-hour helpline, a book club, self-improvement courses, one of Britain's most picturesque golf courses and the cheapest cappuccinos in London SW1, not to mention that Palace pool. Bottom-up communication is encouraged. On this wet spring morning, Lord Peel is in the process of following up an email suggestion from a junior member of staff who has a bright idea for new solar panels (the Sandringham Estate installed some of the first ever seen in Britain).

Once this was a place run by gentlemen amateurs. Today, it is proud to talk of 'professionalism' and 'excellence'. But there is one word which is not encouraged. 'The word "corporate",' says Lord Peel, 'is a word the Queen does not like. When we get on to the subject of the Household, she always says: "I understand the need for effectiveness, efficiency and so on but we mustn't be too *corporate*." Getting that balance is quite difficult really. I do agree with her. We don't want to be overtly corporate. It would destroy the very essence of what we're all about.' As Air Vice-Marshal Sir David Walker puts it: 'The Royal Household is not a business but we operate in a businesslike way.' Walker is one of the Royal Household's five heads of department. As Master of the Household, his is one of the two largest, covering everything which makes the royal residences tick – from maintenance to footmen to the kitchens. It is his department which is responsible for all forms of hospitality. The Queen may be the longest living monarch in British history but the monarchy is actually doing more entertaining now – in terms of receptions, theme days, special garden parties and charity events involving other members of the family – than when she was half her age. Hence the 50 per cent rise in hospitality in five years. Walker's workforce, however, has remained exactly the same, at 240. 'It's just a case of greater efficiency,' he says, explaining one bright idea which has helped his staff cope with the surge in activity. He simply trained the cleaning staff to assist the footmen on big occasions (the Queen has even approved two special liveries for the cleaners – a blue one for official events and a scarlet one for state occasions). At the same time, the footmen have been trained to do various cleaning tasks.

'It doesn't matter if you're commanding a hundred thousand people or a hundred,' he says. 'The same principles come to bear. The number of people you actually deal with is much the same. You deal with people through people.' Historically, the Master has always been a senior officer from the Services but Walker – the first from the RAF – was no stranger to the Palace when he arrived in 2005. Nearly twenty years earlier, he spent three years here as equerry to the Queen, a post which rotates between the three Services, each of which will send a rising star to spend three years acting as the Queen's diary manager, gift carrier and meeter and greeter. When Walker was doing that job, Michael Peat and his team of consultants were only just beginning their exhaustive overhaul of the Household and its ancient work practices. Many of today's jobs – like Palace maintenance – were done by civil servants, not royal staff. It was a quieter place. 'The world was different,' says Walker. 'The people were less diverse. It was a much smaller organisation. The Household has expanded hugely since those times. We were living in a much less litigious environment. It's more efficient now and doubtless some would say a few babies have been tossed out with the bath water. But I recognise it as a much better place.'

He remembers the rigid hierarchies of the five different dining rooms – the Household dining room (for 'members' of the Royal Household as the most senior staff are known), the officials' dining room, the junior officials' dining room, the stewards' dining room and the staff dining room – plus an in-house pub. It took more than a decade to change all that, with the strongest resistance coming from the junior end of the spectrum ('the office workers didn't want to eat with the cleaners', as one veteran of that exercise puts it). These days, all that is left is the Household dining room and the staff restaurant. Everyone, from top to bottom, eats in the staff restaurant, although the Household dining room is still used for meetings and the occasional guest lunch.

Walker is well aware that all this reform works both ways. Any changes, however small, in a traditional place like the Palace need to be handled carefully. 'People tell you they're agents for change. But it's one thing inflicting it on people and it's quite another thing being on the receiving end. In my experience, change, in general, is badly managed. Good change requires a lot of thinking.'

He points to the staff restaurant as an example. 'Wash your mouth out,' he jokes when a colleague refers to it as the 'canteen'. It is actually several first-floor rooms with the ambiance of a comfortable and slightly eccentric boutique hotel. There are eighteenth-century portraits, an exhibition of royal gifts – model ships, a silver tray presented by the Mayor of Kandy, a bronze of the Queen's beloved mare Burmese – and a selection from Prince Philip's cartoon collection. A large self-service area fills the space previously occupied by the Palace pub. A mural shows a blow-up of the menu card from the wedding breakfast for the Queen's parents: 'Consommé à la Windsor, Suprèmes de Saumon Reine Mary, Côtelettes d'Agneau Prince Albert, Chapons à la Strathmore, Jambon et Langue à l'Aspic, Aspèrges Sauce Crème Mouseuse, Fraises Duchesse Elizabeth, Panier de Friandises [sweets], Dessert [fruit], Cheese.'

Today's staff menu – slightly healthier and in English – is no shorter. However, staff are not expected to eat the whole lot: 'Lentil soup (suitable for vegans), chicken chasseur, veal and bacon pie, polenta with chilli and vegetables, baked potato, cold meats, apple crumble with cream, banana mousse, fresh fruit, yoghurt or cheese.' There are warnings about dairy, gluten and nuts but no prices. Lunch is included in the job package and is consumed in a large, open-plan dining room. It's all creams, beiges and soft carpet with free-for-all seating. Next door, beyond a Giles cartoon from the *Daily Express* of 1954, is an all-day café selling snacks and coffee beneath Coronation prints and a plasma screen showing Sky News. At 75p for a cappuccino, it's certainly mindful of the Queen's edict not to be too 'corporate'. Any profit – and there can't be much at that price – goes into the staff welfare fund.

Next door to this is the Breakfast Room which, in addition to a large portrait of Louis, duc de Bourgogne, has computer monitors for those – footmen, cleaners and so on – whose jobs do not come with a desk and a screen. With no Palace wifi on security grounds, online opportunities can be limited. This is where out-of-hours meals are served to the dwindling band of single staff who live inside the Palace in single-room, barrack-style accommodation on the upper floor (tonight, their dinner menu is 'chorizo chicken' and 'cassis delice'). The Master of the Household and his team are determined to get the live-in numbers down to a bare minimum. A block of offices above the Royal Mews has been converted into modern three-bedroom flats with shared kitchens and living areas. It's been a cultural rather than an economic decision. 'We've spent a lot of money so that staff don't live in this building. The majority go "home",' he says. 'They leave here, they go out of the door, they walk down the street and they re-enter their home. And that is very helpful from a psychological perspective. They're not so institutionalised.'

Perhaps the grandest part of the staff wing is the Jubilee Room, a large, airy corner room full of sofas, armchairs and a large leather footstool in the shape of a corgi. It feels like the library of a St James's gentleman's club. People are reading or sipping contemplative coffees. The Buckingham Palace book club meets in here. In the corridor outside, a book exchange is piled high with old paperbacks while the walls are lined not with Old Masters but with entries to the Royal Household art competition.

Not so long ago, the smell of smoke and beer would have hung heavy in this part of the Palace at certain times of the day. Now, as in every workplace in Britain, smoking is consigned to a yard at the back. And the bar is no more. The only alcohol served in the staff restaurant is a glass of wine to mark the birthdays of the Queen (at least she has two of them) and of Prince Philip. 'The culture of the organisation is completely different now,' says Mike Taylor, Assistant to the Master. 'Today, people are interested in the gym or in the pool or the squash court or the tennis court. They're not necessarily interested in going to the bar. They finish work and they go home and drink there if they want.' In 2003, after an undercover tabloid reporter had spent two months working at the Palace as a footman, he was forced to return various items which he had removed. While the management was furious at the deceit, there was, none the less, quiet satisfaction that one of the pilfered items had been the list of daily lunchtime drinks orders for senior members of the Household. Not one of them had requested alcohol. It's not all alcohol-free territory, however. There are staff bars at both Sandringham and Balmoral because of the distance to the wider world. Sandringham has never been booze-friendly. None of the estate villages has a pub and drinking is confined to social clubs. At Balmoral, though, there have been occasional problems with drinking among the staff who are brought from London to look after the Royal Family and its guests. The Highlands have never been as popular with the staff as with the Windsors. Some employees are unashamedly urban creatures who cannot see the appeal of a mountain hike in driving rain. It is by far the most remote billet on the royal rota. As a result, some preferred to spend their off-duty moments in the bar rather than enjoying the scenery.

A few years ago, the Master and his team decided more variety was called for. So, staff are now offered mountain bikes and kayaks. The Queen also lets them ride the estate ponies, the first time some employees have ever sat in a saddle. And for those who still cannot see the appeal of the Highlands, every staff bedroom has now been equipped with its own television using the proceeds from the Palace café. The Metropolitan Police have also noticed problems when recruiting volunteers for Balmoral shifts. 'You need to find city-dwelling policemen who are not scared of being out at night with the wind whistling in total blackness,' says a former officer from the royal beat. 'You'd be surprised how many don't like it.'

It's hard to dispel public perceptions of a *Downton Abbey/Upstairs, Downstairs* forelock-tugging culture in a place where frock coats are still part of the uniform and there is an entire department devoted to horse-drawn carriages. Sir David Walker is a stout defender of tradition and of terminology against those who think the Palace should do away with some of its ancient rituals. 'The Yeoman of the Glass and China Pantry still looks after the glass and china. We could, I suppose, rename him the Glass and China Manager but I don't think he'd be that pleased. Perhaps we'd be losing a little bit of where we've come from. Do we need a Master of the Household for that matter? What would they call me instead? General Manager, Administration and Catering?'

But, behind the scenes, the culture has been transformed. Walker is proud that his department recently became the first to be accredited to the government-endorsed Investors in People scheme. All the other Palace departments have since followed suit. Walker is also wary of complacency.

'You can't sit here and think you're absolutely excellent. There was a sort of feeling, perhaps, that we were terrifically good. But you can always do better. You've got to be constantly critical.'

To that end he decided his senior staff should visit a group of his old colleagues for whom complacency usually means death – the Red Arrows. The parallels between the RAF's formation flying team and, say, dishing out the canapés at Windsor is not immediately obvious. But Walker says it made a big impact on his team. 'The thing that impressed them most was the systematic approach the Reds have put in place to doing the same thing over and over again. During the season, they will do, say, a hundred displays. They treat each one as if it had never happened before and then they debrief themselves mercilessly. Everybody wants to identify where they have not done as well as they should have done. Now that's the culture we try to put in place here. We're not into self-flagellation but we're saying: "OK, we've done this event over and over again but we'll sit down and identify where it could have gone better." I tell you, every time, we find things we can improve on.'

The Master's own background is in aerial warfare. He makes no pretence to be an expert in cooking or napkin-folding. He splits his domain between two deputies. One, Lieutenant-Colonel Charles Richards, arranges the Queen's private and family entertaining, as well as all her appearances at the big annual events like Royal Ascot. The other is Edward Griffiths, a former senior executive with the Roux brothers' catering empire. He likens his job to running the 'hotel service' side of the Palace, although he is the first to make it very clear: 'We are a private house rather than a hotel.' It's a team of 135, split between F branch (food), G branch (general – footmen and so on) and H branch (housekeeping). And, until recently, they were virtually autonomous units. Jobs were for life. Promotion was a matter of waiting for someone older to retire or die. And no one ventured into someone else's territory. Having come from the outside world, Edward Griffiths was surprised. 'If you worked as a waiter in a hotel and walked past something on the floor and didn't pick it up because "it's not my job", then you wouldn't last very long as a waiter,' he explains. 'One thing I would say in defence of the old regime is that they always did their best to deliver. But there were all these people with these titles all doing things which were very closely linked. An underbutler would work in the pantry, cleaning china and glasses and laying tables but he wasn't involved in service. The attitude was "This is my job and you can't do that."'

All that has changed. Words like 'cross-training' and 'multi-tasking' have entered the Palace vocabulary. People like Lindsay Steele are now rising up through the ranks. She is one of the first female footmen, an entirely alien concept back in the days of 'lady clerks' and 'chambermaids'. No one has suggested tinkering with the title of 'footman', however. 'When people ask why not "footwoman" or "footperson", I say footman is part of history and to change that now would be to lose that,' argues Steele who was twenty-five and on front-of-house duty at a Michelin-starred restaurant when she spotted an ad for a footman in the *Caterer* magazine. A country girl from Cheshire, she says a love of history drew her to the idea of royal service. Three years in, she says the thing which has surprised her most is the variety of the job – from spit-polishing shoes, to making a 5 a.m. breakfast for a visiting finance minister to serving on the Royal Train. Her favourite off-duty moments have included pony-trekking and bingo at Balmoral (several staff cite the weekly bingo sessions as the best bit of their stint on Deeside). The highlight of her career, says Steele, was receiving a lesson from the Queen herself in how to revive the embers of a dying fire.

When friends ask her what a footman does, she has a ready answer: 'I start by saying it's similar to being a butler and if they don't know what that means I mention *Jeeves and Wooster*.' But what sets Steele apart from the footmen of yesteryear is not just the fact that she is a woman. It is that she is a holder of Britain's first university-endorsed Butler Diploma. What's more, she's now training to teach it.

The Royal Household has teamed up with the University of West London and the hospitality industry to produce a national qualification covering everything required of the modern Jeeves, from valeting to shooting lunches to cigar storage. Much of the syllabus was written by the Palace Steward (the most senior liveried figure in the Royal Household). Once, a boy would join the Household from school and work through to old age before reaching this position. The current Palace Steward is Nigel McEvoy, who joined as a trainee footman at nineteen when he realised he was never going to be a chef. He reached the top slot while still in his thirties and is just as much of a perfectionist as his predecessors. But that hasn't stopped him from embracing new ideas like radio earpieces at big events. His team may be wearing Georgian tailcoats but if the Lord Chief Justice is still waiting for his gravy while the Foreign Secretary's wife has already finished her *longe de venaison de Balmoral*, then someone needs to know pronto.

Edward Griffiths acknowledges that the more his staff are trained, the greater the chance that someone will poach them. 'I don't think it's a bad thing to have turnover. Fresh blood is vital,' he says. Some move on to big hotels or become butlers in private homes. 'It's important to understand that young people have a very different outlook from baby boomers like me who are writing the job adverts,' says Griffiths. 'They are far more interested in work/life balance than two generations ago. People are not coming to stay for ever. If they get a job here, it's very portable. Just saying that they have had three years work in the Royal Household – a lot of employers will look at that.'

Through internet recruitment, the Royal Household is increasingly seen as a mainstream employer rather than a throwback. Pay grades are now set in the mid-range of hospitality industry salaries. The Palace has an established work experience programme for hospitality students from four British universities plus one in Switzerland. One bright spark from Bournemouth University did his work experience here, graduated with a BA in hospitality, came back and, within a few years, has now risen to one of the most senior liveried positions.

Many – indeed most – arrive with other qualifications. The chances are that the cleaner dusting that bust of Prince Albert or the footman opening the car door will actually have a degree – in anything from history to psychology. No fewer than 70 per cent of housekeeping assistants are now graduates. The figure for footmen is only marginally lower at 60 per cent. Yet, considering that annual staff turnover in the Master's department is 5.5 per cent – in an industry where 50 per cent is not unusual – job satisfaction does not appear to be a problem. It is also accepted that staff can supplement their income doing out-of-hours freelance work for catering firms who need slick reinforcements with a safe CV. It is not unusual for a member of the Royal Household to turn up at a smart London house for dinner and find a colleague serving the drinks. Everyone knows, though, that there will be trouble the moment it detracts from the day job. If anyone needs to be reminded where their loyalties lie, says Griffiths, then their days are numbered.

Sir David Walker and Edward Griffiths are very keen on benchmarking – comparing this place with similar organisations. It's not easy to benchmark a fendersmith when you've got the only ones in the land but Griffiths explains that it's simply a question of comparing like with like. He uses embassies, hotels and large institutions to evaluate his own team. And there is always some sort of exchange programme going on. For example, a group of footmen have just been sent to study meet-and-greet techniques and 'guest history systems' at the Ritz. They will write a report on their return. It turns out that there is more of a science to this than might be imagined.

'If you study where people go when they go to a restaurant,' says Griffiths, 'most go back to a place where they're recognised, where the *maître d'hotel* says, "Hello, so good to see you again." These hotels have observed for a long period of time that a reception desk is a barrier. So the answer is not to wait for your customer to come in and then ask their name but to find out what time they are arriving.'

The Ritz spirit works in reverse. Staff from some of the big hotels will be invited to spend a few days watching a state banquet being pieced together. Seven years ago, the Palace joined a secretive club which wields huge clout in the food world and which recently elected Griffiths as its chairman. Nothing could be less calculated to attract interest than a body calling itself the Food Service Management Group. However, its members include the Houses of Parliament, banks, department stores, public institutions – anywhere serving food, in fact, apart from hotels and restaurants. All their deliberations are entirely confidential, but by pooling information, they can ensure that they are getting the best value from suppliers and staff alike. It sounds like catering's answer to a papal conclave. Perish the supplier who crosses this lot.

The Palace is an organisation which takes its food extremely seriously. The most popular page on the entire royal intranet system is the daily menu for the Palace restaurant. Everything from the soup of the day to the Queen's cottage pie will be prepared in the same kitchens under the auspices of the Royal Chef, Mark Flanagan. He had a tough act to follow when he arrived in 2002. His predecessor, Lionel Mann, was a much-loved Palace fixture who had spent forty-two years cooking for the Queen. In the old days, Flanagan would have joined straight from school and worked his way up from peeling potatoes. These days, the Queen recruits like any other mainstream business in the services sector. After many years with household names like Raymond Blanc and the Roux brothers, Flanagan was running the Wentworth Executive Club when he was invited to submit his CV to the Royal Household. He is now in charge of a kitchen team of 53, cooking up to 1,000 meals a day for the entire staff as well as for the Queen and her family. It is an operation that, on any given day, will involve preparing meals in up to four of the five royal residences (Buckingham Palace, Windsor Castle, Holyroodhouse, Sandringham or Balmoral). Along with the job comes automatic membership of a club straight out of P. G. Wodehouse. The Chefs des Chefs is restricted exclusively to the personal chefs of the world's heads of state. It is an assembly of some of the world's greatest cooks and yet does not contain a single celebrity chef. Nor does it include, say, the head chef from Number Ten Downing Street or the US Senate. You can only join if you cook for your head of state.

The club meets once a year – the latest gathering was in China – to swap ideas and promote members' national cuisines. It is particularly useful, in the run-up to a state visit, to have a hotline to the person who knows how the visitor likes his eggs. It's all very well asking the embassy but diplomats are usually too preoccupied to talk to the person at the stove. The forthcoming South African state visit will not present Mark Flanagan with any surprises. 'I know the chap who looks after President Zuma's residence very well,' explains Flanagan. 'I can contact him directly and say, "Is there anything you really need me to get hold of?" Sometimes people can be very guarded whereas I can get to the right people. They know what I need to know and when I need to know it.' Discretion, needless to say, is the club's primary rule. Flanagan is often asked what sort of food the Queen likes best. He won't say. Aside from adhering to a strict code of confidence, he points out that if everyone knew the Queen's 'favourite' dish, she would never be served anything else.

Flanagan epitomises the new Palace ethos in terms of people management. He is a member of the *Académie Culinaire*, a network of chefs who provide apprenticeships for newcomers. He always has two raw recruits in training at the Palace and, by the end of their three-year apprenticeship, they should be good enough to run a royal houseparty on their own. When the heat is on for a big event like a state visit, he will also offer 'chance of a lifetime' work experience to star pupils from selected catering colleges. Like Griffiths, he is glad that the Palace has moved on from the old 'job for life' culture. 'We actively encourage our young guys to go back out into industry rather than plot a more laid-back path here. It's a meritocracy here. We want to know what you can bring to the organisation.' But he is also adamant that all his staff absorb the old Palace traditions. This may be something as minor as cucumber sandwiches (not only are the crusts removed but they must be cut into squares, not fingers). It also extends to history lessons. 'There've been some fantastic chefs here. Carême – he was a legend. That's something I keep reminding the young ones. They say to me: "Who is this bloke?" And I give them a book and say: "Have a read of this." He's not like our celebrity chefs. He is still very much revered.'*

The kitchen staff are surrounded by history, particularly when working in the soaring medieval kitchens at Windsor. Royal cooking is another

---

* Marie-Antoine (Antonin) Carême, founder of *haute cuisine* and Royal Chef in the early nineteenth century, once produced a banquet of 909 different dishes. He invented George IV's favourite dish, Potage de Tortue à l'*Anglaise* (turtle soup), eighty tureens of which were served at his Coronation in 1821. Another formidable Frenchman was Réne Roussin, chef to George VI. Even a dish as elementary as kippers would have to be sieved, spread on toast and served on a folded napkin.

example of ancient and modern. The average Palace meal will probably have involved at least one antique saucepan plus the latest gadget from Japan. In the Georgian cooking halls beneath Buckingham Palace, one side of the main kitchen still has the original roasting spit and a huge wood-burner called Queen Mary's Oven, neither of which sees much action these days. But there is also a knee-high hotplate from the same period which is still in regular use because its low height allows two cooks to heave cauldrons of soup and stock pots on and off easily. Shelf after shelf is piled high with polished copper pans engraved with the cyphers of different monarchs. Many are from the reign of Queen Victoria; some go back to George IV. There is an enormous Edwardian trough specially designed for cooking turbot. Next door, in the 'Copper Store', is a pan the size of a baby's bath. Flanagan explains that he has invested in a lot of new stainless steel equipment but none of it can do the really big tasks and nothing beats copper for an even spread of heat.

An adjacent storeroom could be a cookery museum, full of magnificent old ice-cream *bombes*, tiny savarin moulds for finger-sized rum babas, jelly moulds for preparing the sort of blancmange mountains only seen in period dramas. It's all still in use. And alongside these gems is the most up-to-date catering machinery in the business. Flanagan's latest acquisition is a new *sous vide* water bath which gently melts the meat for his casseroles. Other innovations include the camera and the computer. Astonishingly, until recently no one bothered to write down recipes from particular banquets. In many cases, the only recipes consisted of a few notes and what was stored in the head of Flanagan's long-serving deputy and head chef, Mark Fromont. 'In the past, we would just rely on Mark's memory which is phenomenal. But now, we take a photograph of every-thing and do a standard operational manual which helps with training and consistency. In the past, you never took a photograph and if you didn't have handwritten notes, then it didn't happen.'

The kitchen structure is not unlike that of a large restaurant. Below the Royal Chef – who does more managing than cooking – is the head chef, the sous chefs (in charge of sections), the chefs de parties (who focus on specific areas – the sauce, perhaps, or the canapés), then demi-chefs de parties (juniors) and, finally, the apprentices. And there are no separate sections for royal food and staff food. On an ordinary day, the Duke of Edinburgh and the porter might end up with the same gravy on their roast chicken. 'We find it works much better if we engage every-body and there's no division between preparing staff meals and royal meals,' Flanagan explains. Of course, members of the Royal Family will order their own dishes. The kitchens are one part of the Palace where there is an 'open line' with the 'principals'. There is no need for a Private Secretary to get between the Queen and her boiled egg. If she has a special request, she may call down herself. But royal food is a tiny part of the operation. The chefs are much more likely to be doing lasagne for two hundred staff than cooking a salmon fresh from the Dee for the Princess Royal. 'At least 75 per cent of our role is about looking after the staff,' says Flanagan.

Monarchs have had chefs since time immemorial, but no monarch ever had something called a Head of Personnel until the Queen began the great shake-up of the Royal Household in the nineties. Before then, the task of running the staff had been left to a gentleman called the Establishment Officer, assisted by a couple of lady clerks and a few filing cabinets. These days, it is a twenty-five-strong operation run by Elizabeth Hunka, who arrived in 1999 after a career at the top of the commercial sector. She certainly does not feel as if she is helping an ancient organisation keep up with the rest of the world. She believes that the Royal Household is one of the most progressive workplaces of its size.

'To be a talented organisation you've got to pull in people from all quarters,' she says. 'We've widened it out now.' She lists some of the changes, not least the fact that 80 per cent of the five thousand job applications in the previous year came via the internet. For some people, she says, applying online is much less daunting than writing to the Palace. She is pleased but not satisfied with her diversity figures – 50/50 male/ female across the Household and 30 per cent female in the most senior positions ('broadly equivalent to Whitehall'). The Palace is 'in the fore- front' of equal pay scales between men and women. The overall number of staff from ethnic minorities is just under 6 per cent overall but nearly 11 per cent in financial areas. There are no corresponding figures for gay or lesbian staff – 'we don't ask' – but the Palace has never been seen as under-represented in that regard.

Union numbers have remained steady since unions were recognised in the seventies with a fifth of the staff split between three trade unions (Unite, Prospect and PCS). It's a particularly sociable workforce, too. The £5 per year Royal Household Football, Sports and Social Club incorporates staff from all the residences. Besides organising keenly fought sporting encounters with other institutions (the Corporation of London, perhaps, or the Bank of England), it arranges quiz nights and barbecues. It recently took over the entire upper tier of Tower Bridge for a staff ball. For employees who routinely run garden parties for eight thousand, such events are not unduly challenging. The cricket pitch and golf course

at Windsor Castle, plus the football pitch at Kensington Palace, are open
to all. As well as the twenty-four-hour independent counselling service,
there is the 'Well Being' service which sorts out maternity, paternity and
adoption leave and allows staff to 'buy' extra holiday. There are free
lunchtime and after-hours courses in 'customer care', 'finance for non-
financial managers' and even 'taming your grammar gremlins'. The
more dedicated can study for a Chartered Management Institute
qualification.

It has all been approved by the Queen, along with all the reforms to
the pension scheme and perks like a loan scheme for buying bicycles. 'I
think we do change rather well and that's led by the Queen,' says Hunka.
'I never get the sense she says no to something progressive. She's practical. I remember the first staff survey in 1999, which was a bit of an
unknown, and the Queen and the Duke were very keen to read the report.'

Hunka's boss is Sir Alan Reid, the man with the Palace purse strings,
hence that ancient title, Keeper of the Privy Purse. 'We are seriously into
training now and we get a huge amount of return for investing in people,'
he says firmly. 'But we needed to empower a lot of people and it's taken
years.' He was astonished to arrive in 2002 and find no external computer
links. 'It took three days to communicate with the outside world,' he
recalls. 'You'd get a letter in, you sent one back and everything was
happening unbelievably slowly. That was based totally on risk aversion.
That's why the risk-averse culture is so daft. The Queen is not remotely
risk averse.' The filmmaker Edward Mirzoeff would agree. Even more
frustrating than his evening at the Ghillies' Ball at Balmoral was his
attempt to film a 1991 Privy Council meeting for the same documentary,
*Elizabeth R*. The restrictions, he says, were almost comic. 'It should have
been very straightforward but the staff suddenly said: "You can cover
the first item of business but not the second or third so you'll have to
leave the room and come back for the fourth." This was crazy as the whole
thing only lasted a few minutes and would have been over by the time
we came back in with all our kit. We couldn't do it. I saw the Queen
talking to Robert Fellowes at the end of a corridor and I screeched up
to her and said, "Excuse me, Ma'am, but I've got a huge problem. We
can't go in and come out again." The Queen looked faintly puzzled and
said to Robert: "I can't see that there would be a problem." And so
Robert said: "No, I think that should be fine."'

The historian Kenneth Rose has studied royal risk aversion through
the ages and has a favourite story about two courtiers at Windsor looking
out of the window during the reign of George V. One says to the other:
'Don't quote me, but there's a blackbird on the lawn.' The Household

mindset has progressed somewhat since then. Reid says that he is all in favour of constructive innovations from today's younger staff, admitting that fresh ideas were less welcome in the not too distant past when retired generals ran most things round here. 'Someone in their second career is not the best pilot for change,' says Reid. 'They've done the dramatic stuff. They want to run a safe ship. And they're not getting the best out of junior staff. People used to think: "Everything is done superbly. Why put it at risk by letting footmen come up with ideas?"' By computerising every section of the Palace, he says, there has been a major shift in staff relations. 'A lot of people don't understand how technology breaks down management structures,' he explains. 'It's very easy for someone to send an email to the Private Secretary. He may not want to receive it necessarily but it's a lot easier than getting a fifteen-minute appointment with him.'

The Palace intranet site is open to all 1,100 employees. Relaunched in 2010, it is very much an organ of the staff rather than the bosses. More than forty different departments nominate 'editors' and, while it has yet to embrace blogging, it is never short of suggestions and is about to launch eBay-style royal classified ads. It is run by computer scientist Nicola Shanks who used to run websites for children's television characters like Bob the Builder and Angelina Ballerina. Now she is in genuine fairy-tale territory. Having moved from a tieless, jeans-and-T-shirt industry to the Palace, she has been surprised by the fact that the supposedly stuffy royal world seems to have more fun. 'I was struck by the sense of community – all the clubs and things that go on. Even compared to the media industry, it's very sociable.'

A random glance at the intranet pages shows a lot of charity and social events, including a fun run in sumo costumes and a sponsored golf marathon at Windsor. The Royal Household Book Club is turning its attentions to *The Hare With Amber Eyes* by Edmund de Waal and *Any Human Heart* by William Boyd. The Royal Household Film Club is about to show *The Adjustment Bureau* and *The Social Network* in the former cinema (it's been renamed the South Drawing Room but the old projector still works).

All this change has not always been easy. Privately, some lament the passing of particular perks or quirks. Few doubt that the Queen must have had misgivings herself. As the recurring refrain goes: 'The Queen does not like change.' Yet she is also well aware of when sentimentality must yield to necessity.

Throughout the Royal Household, no department was more resistant to the changes of the eighties and nineties than the Royal Mews. This is a part of the Palace which did not employ women until 2004. With its seventy stalls and an indoor riding school dating from 1766, it is a very grand but busy working equestrian centre and car depot in the very heart of London. It is also a major tourist attraction. The job of the Mews is to transport the Queen and her family by road. For 99 per cent of the time, this is done by a team of seven chauffeurs using a fleet of eight official limousines and several less conspicuous cars, all of which are based in a gloomy garage and workshop at the back of the Mews. On a handful of occasions each year, they travel by horse-drawn transport. This is done by around thirty horses which also enjoy larger, grander accommodation than anyone in the entire Palace.

Britain likes to pride itself on doing pageantry better than anyone else, and at the heart of any great state spectacle, you will usually find horses and carriages. The wedding of the Duke and Duchess of Cambridge was a superb example.

The Royal Mews has nothing to do with the Household Cavalry which comprises front-line army troops performing ceremonial duties between deployments. During most state visits – or royal weddings – it's the Household Cavalry which provides the gleaming, clattering, swaggering Sovereign's Escort which rides fore and aft of the royal carriage procession. The Royal Mews is the civilian operation which moves the Monarch and her family. But it is always run along military lines by an ex-army officer called the Crown Equerry. And given the Queen's love of horses and the Duke of Edinburgh's knowledge of competitive carriage driving (he wrote the modern rulebook), the Royal Mews always attracts keen royal interest. It was also a semi-autonomous province when Michael Peat and his consultants looked through the gates in the late eighties. The Crown Equerry of the day was Sir John Miller, a distinguished former Welsh Guards officer who was awarded the MC and the DSO within a month of each other for bravery in 1944. He could be similarly robust towards anyone interfering with the Royal Mews, which he ran for twenty-six years. As his *Daily Telegraph* obituary concluded in 2006: 'Miller was effortlessly polite and wholly devoted to his Sovereign – though he was rather less genial to those whose social position was unclear to him.' Fellow Welsh Guards officer Kenneth Rose has fond memories of talking to Miller shortly before a dinner at Windsor Castle. The Queen had planned a treat for her guests in the form of an after-dinner recital by Mstislav Rostropovich, then arguably the greatest living cellist. Miller was less than thrilled. 'I've had a very difficult day,' he informed Rose. Gesturing towards Rostropovich, he went on: 'See that fellow talking to the Queen? He's been playing his damned fiddle outside my office all day.' Miller was close to all the Royal Family, having introduced Prince Philip to carriage driving, the Prince of Wales to hunting and the Princess Royal to eventing.*

Such was the sort of opposition confronting the Palace reformers in the late eighties. Peat's accountants arrived to find incomprehensible accounting systems and baffling numbers of horses. 'Miller slammed the gates in Michael Peat's face,' recalls a former Private Secretary who witnessed the power struggle. 'And, dare one say it, he enjoyed the support of the Queen so it wasn't easy.' The issue was partially resolved when Miller retired in 1987, after more than quarter of a century at the Royal Mews, with the GCVO for his troubles.† Thereafter, the Royal Mews went into decline over several years. 'It was an awful shambles,' says one of those involved. 'Morale was appalling, standards were down. It was like a really bad military unit and the chauffeurs were very much the second-class citizens. Cars are much more use than the horses but they are not as sexy.' Finally, the discontent got so bad that the Queen had to act herself. In 1999, she decided that the Royal Mews really could not carry on being a royal department in its own right. Instead, it was placed in the care of the Lord Chamberlain's Office, the Palace's ceremonial wing. Today, the men-only tradition is over. Female grooms – 'liveried helpers' as they are known – make up more than a quarter of the staff and that figure is rising. Some female recruits have fitted in extremely well, quite literally. Many of the uniforms for the big occasions – known as 'state liveries' – are 150 years old and can cost thousands of pounds to replace. Designed for the frame of a nineteenth-century groom, many are too small for a well-built twenty-first-century male but often suit a female outrider very well.

The Mews is thriving, as busy as it has been at any stage during the reign. One of its regular duties is to ferry new ambassadors and their senior staff to and from the Palace to present their credentials to the Queen. Some might argue that it's a pantomime ritual in the age of modern diplomacy but it's greatly appreciated by foreign envoys, even if they do have to dress up in evening dress at eleven in the morning. And they are more numerous than ever. In 1939, there were just two dozen

---

* Miller, who had a superstitious streak, would never sleep the night before a state occasion. He was particularly worried ahead of the Queen's Birthday Parade in 1981 – scheduled for 13 June. He would feel vindicated. Not only did a man fire (blank) shots at the Queen in the Mall but the Queen Mother fell and damaged her leg after the parade, the Duke of Edinburgh's horse went lame and his groom was injured in an accident.

† The GCVO, Knight Grand Cross of the Royal Victorian Order, is the highest rank within the order, a decoration bestowed only on members of the Royal Family and a handful of the most senior and trusted officials.

embassies in London. Today, after the fragmentation of the old world order, there are now 157 (plus several embassy-sharing ambassadors from smaller countries). Every single ambassador will get the full Royal Mews treatment on arrival in London whether they have an embassy or not. 'The challenge is putting horses to a carriage built two hundred years ago and putting them out on the streets of London,' says Major Simon Robinson, Crown Equerry until 2011. He arrived via the King's Troop Royal Horse Artillery and the occasional stint as an amateur jockey for the late Queen Mother. 'People do what they're told but horses have a habit of letting you down if you don't train them properly.'

The Crown Equerry is in charge of the most spectacular aspect of every state visit – the carriage procession for the Queen and her guests. Just one or two badly behaved horses could scupper years of finely tuned diplomatic planning. And the Queen – who will have approved every detail of the procession in advance right down to which horses pull which carriage – spots absolutely everything. In 2007, there was a nasty moment as the Queen welcomed President Kufour of Ghana to Britain. Several thousand Ghanaians had lined the Mall with drums, trumpets and bright flags and launched into a riot of noise and dancing as the Queen's carriage approached. A few of the younger horses on duty were spooked. 'The crowd just went potty and there were horses rearing, leather twanging and bits of broken harness,' recalls Robinson. At one point, he had to ride alongside the Queen's carriage, grab the bit in the mouth of the lead horse and literally pull the animal past the crowds. Back at the Palace – 'I was in a muck sweat when we got down there' – he discussed what had happened with the Queen. 'She knew exactly what was going on,' he says.

Most of the time, of course, the Royal Family moves around by car. Four-wheeled operations fall to the Transport Manager, former policeman Alex Garty. The horse/car relationship is entirely amicable these days, although the chauffeurs are fond of reminding the coachmen that they drive the Queen 365 days a year rather than six. The horsey element like to point out, in turn, that they do all their own repairs and maintenance (the Royal Mews carriage restorers are among the finest in the world) whereas the chauffeurs are dependent on the AA or the RAC if they have a breakdown. The Royal Mews employs no car mechanics.

The two flagships of the car fleet are the State Bentleys, made for the 2002 Golden Jubilee using the pooled wisdom of the Association of British Car Manufacturers. Each weighs four tons, has no number plate (no need), no tax disc (no need) and no rear-view mirror (for privacy). Nor does it have leather seating throughout. Instead, it is designed like a stagecoach – leather seating for the driver (who would have been open to the elements) but cloth-covered seating for the passengers within. There is no satellite navigation system on display. The chauffeur will have learned the route already. But there will be an Ordnance Survey map of the relevant area which is always provided for the Duke of Edinburgh. The lack of gadgets was at the Queen's request. The makers offered her every conceivable sort of luxury accessory but all she asked for was a radio and a CD player.

The State Bentley can accommodate passengers of every dimension. Sadly, the same does not go for the driver. The designers built the front end of the car around the Queen's head chauffeur, Joe Last, including the bulkhead which divides the front and rear of the car. It means that the driver's seat cannot slide back any further. Last will retire after the Diamond Jubilee to spend more time with his Ford Focus. But his successor will need to be the same size. 'We'll be looking for a five-foot-eight replacement,' jokes Alex Garty. Most of the seven chauffeurs are ex-Forces, like Last, or ex-police, like Garty, and they are a loyal bunch. 'I've been here three years and we've never had a staff move,' says Garty. Sometimes, his team will find themselves in the back (the Princess Royal, for example, often likes to drive herself). They also test drive potential additions to the royal fleet. Every car manufacturer craves a royal endorsement. The criteria, though, can be unpredictable. A vehicle may have great acceleration, for example, but what's the hat room like in the back? All chauffeurs have been through regular anti-terrorist courses with both the Metropolitan Police and Devon and Cornwall Police who run white-knuckle high-speed evasion courses over Dartmoor. When a London mob attacked the Rolls-Royce Phantom VI carrying the Prince of Wales and the Duchess of Cornwall in 2010, no amount of driving skill could make up for the fact that the car was blocked in by protestors. Much loved by the late Queen Mother, it is not nearly as robust as the State Bentley and sustained a broken window. Since that evening, the use of the older vehicles in the Mews has been under review.

In addition to the two State Bentleys, the Queen keeps three other official 'state cars' in the main garage at Buckingham Palace – a trio of Rolls-Royces from 1988, 1977 and 1949 (the last, a Phantom IV, is known as the 'Old Beast'). All are in the claret state livery with the Queen's arms painted on the side. Next door, in a side garage, are three twenty-year-old Daimler limousines, often used for larger royal motorcades. They are also used for what are known as 'Red Crown Jobs'. When the Queen sends a representative somewhere on her behalf, the car carries a red crown instead of a royal standard. In among these eight official cars is what happens to be the Sovereign's own choice of unofficial vehicle – an entirely anonymous green Daimler Sovereign. Nearly seventy years after learning to drive at the wheel of an army truck, the former ATS mechanic still likes to drive herself. She is no slowcoach either.

Wherever she goes, however, the Queen will be followed by bodyguards. Indeed, there can be few heads of state who have accumulated quite so many different bodyguards over the centuries. Compared to, say, the Pope, who survives with the Swiss Guard to defend him, the Queen is positively overrun with loyal defenders. Quite apart from the Foot Guards and the Household Cavalry, the Queen is protected by the Honourable Corps of Gentlemen at Arms. All retired officers, they are a Henry VIII creation who turn up at state occasions in red coats and white-feathered helmets to guard the Queen with battle axes. They have a friendly rivalry with the Yeomen of the Guard who like to point out that they are the oldest of the lot, having been formed by Henry VII. All retired NCOs and warrant officers, the Yeomen wear scarlet doublets and each protects the Queen with a seven-foot halberd known as a 'partisan'. North of the border, she is guarded by the Queen's Body Guard for Scotland, the Royal Company of Archers, well-connected gentlemen of a certain age (in a green uniform) who protect her with bow and arrows, and also by the High Constables of Holyroodhouse (who wear a blue uniform and carry truncheons). While their loyalty is unsurpassable, their security value is less certain. Hence, there is a further strand of protection.

The real bodyguards are the men and women of the Metropolitan Police's Royalty Protection team, or SO14 as it is known (each Special Operations unit has its own 'SO' designation). With a staff of around five hundred, Royalty Protection is divided between static protection (guarding buildings) and personal protection officers (what most people would think of as bodyguards). These days, SO14 forms part of a structure called Protection Command along with SO1 (Specialist Protection) which protects politicians and VIPs and also SO6 (Diplomatic Protection).

In the late nineties, there was talk of streamlining the operation and merging the royal and political protection officers into a single unit. The idea was quietly squashed after senior Downing Street figures decided that they would rather retain their own police elite, thanks very much. It would certainly have been deeply unpopular in the ranks. Healthy rivalries exist between SO14 and SO1 over everything from exams and overtime to haircuts (which tend to be more extreme in Specialist Protection than Royalty Protection). But both pride themselves on doing the job without the combative, self-conscious machismo of some of their overseas colleagues. When it comes to genuine bodyguards, the less conspicuous the better.

It is the Master of the Household's Department and the Royal Mews which are the most visible aspects of the modern Court. They provide spectacle, pageantry and service. But a state visit would be pointless without a context. Every part of the Royal Household will be involved when a head of state like President Zuma comes to stay. The Queen's Private Secretary, Sir Christopher Geidt, will have sat on the Foreign Office Committee which agreed to issue the invitation in the first place. The Queen is always consulted on whom she has to stay even though, ultimately, it is not her choice. And she has had to put up with some pretty objectionable guests over the years. She was clearly uncomfortable with the government's decision to invite the Romanian dictator Nicolae Ceauşescu for a full state visit in 1978, so much so that she took drastic steps to avoid meeting him any more than necessary. While out walking her dogs in the Palace gardens, she spotted Ceauşescu and his wife, Elena, heading down a path in her direction. As the Queen told a lunch guest some years later, she decided that the best course of action was to hide behind a bush rather than conduct polite conversation. No guests have annoyed her more than the famously corrupt and unhinged President Mobutu of Zaire and his wife – the aptly named Marie-Antoinette – who paid a state visit in 1973. Mobutu's penchant for barmy titles and executing his opponents in front of large crowds must have made the small talk challenging. But what made the Queen angrier than some had ever seen her was learning that Mrs Mobutu had smuggled a small dog through customs. Worse still, the President's wife was ordering it steak from the Palace kitchens. 'The Queen was very, very angry,' says Ron Allison, the Queen's former Press Secretary. The trusted Deputy Master of the Household, Lord Plunket, was summoned by an incandescent Sovereign and told: 'Get that dog out of my house!' 'I don't know how he did it,' says Allison, 'but it was taken off to the kennels at Heathrow.' The late Martin Charteris, Private Secretary to the Queen at the time, recalled: 'She really was shaking with anger.'

However horrible the government's friends, it is the Queen's duty to be nice to them. As Sir Malcolm Rifkind explains: 'She is a servant of the state, as we all are, and she has no illusions to the contrary.'

At any given time, there is always a queue of world leaders wanting to meet the longest serving head of state in the Western world. 'Quite often, you get a message from a British ambassador that some head of government would like to visit the UK and expects to see the Queen,' says Rifkind. 'There is a recognised procedure for explaining, politely, that it is not possible at this moment in time.'

The Private Secretary will be the conduit for all these delicate decisions. He will also help draft the Queen's speech at the state banquet and, on overseas tours, be in attendance at all times. But the royal department which plans every minute of the itinerary and pulls the whole visit together is the Lord Chamberlain's Office. Despite its name, it is not actually run by the Lord Chamberlain but by a man called the Comptroller. Whether it's royal weddings and funerals, medieval ceremonies, arcane titles, ancient uniforms, fiddly protocol or the use of the Queen's cypher on a commemorative mug, then it all goes through the surprisingly young and pragmatic team that runs the LCO. As well as the Royal Mews, it oversees investitures, the Yeomen of the Guard, all the Queen's doctors, all the Queen's clergy and the annual River Thames ritual of Swan Upping. The department handles the two hundred or so honorary royal office holders – from chaplains to homeopathic pharmacists – who appear on the Palace horizon from time to time. If anyone needs an answer to some imponderable issue of etiquette – how should one wear the regalia of the CMG with a dinner jacket? – then someone in the Comptroller's domain will know.

Until a change in the law in 1968, it was also the Comptroller's job to license all plays and theatres on behalf of the Lord Chamberlain, laying down specific rules on nudity, swearing and the depiction of royalty (God was not allowed on stage until 1966 and nudes had to be motionless, expressionless and 'dimly lit'). In the febrile atmosphere of the late sixties, it appeared increasingly absurd that censorship of the West End stage should be left to a retired army officer at the Palace. The Comptroller of the day, Sir Johnnie Johnston MC, was of much the same opinion himself and there was widespread relief across the Household when the government was finally persuaded to abolish this royal role. Two decades later, during his shake up of the old Palace order, the Lord Chamberlain of the day, Lord Airlie, sought further change. He thought it would simplify things if the Lord Chamberlain's Office had a different name since it had very little to do with the Lord Chamberlain himself. His idea was to rename it the 'Ceremonial Department' for the sake of clarity and common sense. The LCO was having none of it. It gives some indication of the independence and clout of the Lord Chamberlain's Office that it can rebuff the Lord Chamberlain. 'The title of "Comptroller" is a complete misnomer,' says Sir Malcolm Ross, who had the title for fifteen years. 'I think the last person who actually understood it was Queen Victoria. But it is so ingrained at the Palace that it would have caused even more confusion to change it.'

Like everything else at the Palace, the pattern of the state visit has changed a great deal in the last few years. World leaders are busier these days so their visits are shorter. They want to cram in as much as possible. President Zuma is not only a dawn riser but wants to hold a business summit in the Palace Bow Room over breakfast. His wish is the LCO's command. 'We've got a concentrated bunch of big hitters,' says Jonathan Spencer of the LCO, 'and they'd much rather do it at the start of the day. Forget lunch.'

Unusual requests must be accommodated without so much as a raised eyebrow. Visiting US presidents now require a sound-proof communications hub so a blast-proof glass box is duly erected in the Regency Room whenever the Americans come to stay. When President Obama arrived in May 2011, the traditional state welcome had to be completely rewritten. His security advisers would not permit the usual greeting on Horse Guards Parade. Nor did they want their man travelling down the Mall in a horse-drawn coach with the Queen. Instead, he was driven into the Palace in his rocket-proof eight-ton presidential limousine and the welcome ceremony was staged on the Palace lawn.

The Obamas, like every state visitor, stayed in the Belgian Suite, Buckingham Palace's grandest. It also happens to be where Prince William and his bride spent their wedding night. The suite – it's actually a substantial two-bedroom, two-bathroom, two-stateroom garden apartment with a direct door to the Palace pool – was built to Edwardian standards. It has colossal baths and a splendid mahogany thunderbox adjacent to the main bedroom. But for one recent state visitor, however, it was inadequate. This particular head of state regarded baths as unclean and his substantial stature demanded rather more space than that afforded by the Belgian Suite's shower cubicle. A spacious but temporary power shower room was installed (at the visitor's expense).

Some of the most complicated issues are to do with protocol. Much as its critics portray the Palace as a minefield of superfluous rules and social booby traps, the monarchy is positively laid back compared to most heads of state. 'That's one of the great misconceptions. We have no rulebook, just guidance. We're less protocol-orientated here than a lot of people,' says Jonathan Spencer, pointing out that he has never come across any head of state who does not employ a 'head of protocol' whereas no such position exists in the Royal Household. 'If you want to see serious protocol, unbelievable minutiae, you need to look elsewhere.' He is too diplomatic to name names but old Foreign Office hands speak fondly of the Chinese, the Japanese and the French as Olympic-class protocol sticklers.

There are two remaining departments of the Royal Household which also play their own parts in every state occasion. The Privy Purse Office manages the cost of every event, even working out which meals should be charged to the Foreign Office's budget and which to the Civil List.

For every state visit, the Royal Collection will be involved, too. Its staff will put together an exhibition of art, letters, gifts and photographs – much of it from the Royal Library – illustrating the links between Britain and the visiting nation.*

Works of art from across the collection must be rounded up for the state banquet. They include vast candelabra, plates of silver gilt (silver covered in gold) and magnificent china such as the eighteenth-century Tournai service which will be used on this occasion. This is still a 'working' collection. These are not just museum pieces. Occasionally, they have to sing for their supper.

As the great day dawns, these treasures are stacked in boxes around the Palace Ballroom. Laying the table for a state banquet is one of the wonders of the hospitality world. And it takes days. Before a single one of the 1,026 Stourbridge glasses (each engraved with 'EIIR') or a single fork can be laid, the Yeoman of the Glass and China Pantry, Steve Marshall, must measure out all 171 settings with a ruler. It's a U-shaped table and the Queen and her ten guests along the base of the U will each have twenty-two inches of space but those seated down the sides will have five inches less. Everyone will have six perfectly spaced glasses (champagne for the toast, white wine, red wine, water, champagne for pudding and port) and napkins folded to one of the Royal Household's repertoire of designs. For tonight, a Dutch bonnet fold has been chosen.

Around the edges of the Ballroom, a formation of uniformed house-keeping assistants move backwards with light vacuum cleaners attached to their waists (reversing leaves no marks). The Palace Steward, Nigel McEvoy, is checking the service stations around the room. There will be nineteen of them, each with a team of four staff looking after nine people. Staff will carry hot plates with napkins rather than gloves, to avoid thumb marks. Everyone will be watching the discreet 'traffic light' system which McEvoy operates from tiny lights above the royal dais. The blue light means 'action stations' and the green light means 'get serving'.

The guests will receive 'butler service' rather than 'silver service'. This means the footman will offer them a large dish from which they may help themselves (with silver service, the server just gives you a pre-determined portion). 'It's just the way the Queen prefers it,' explains

---

* For the state visit of President Barack Obama, the display included some of Queen Victoria's diary entries deploring the slave trade ('To what can human nature descend . . .'), George III's handwritten lament that 'America is lost!' and a delightful letter from Queen Elizabeth to Princess Elizabeth describing a picnic lunch with the Roosevelts in 1939: 'HOT DOGS too!'

McEvoy. 'If they just want half, they can have half. They needn't say, "I'll have one of that and two of that" and they can still engage in their conversation while they're helping themselves.'

In addition to a full turnout of forty footmen, his serving staff will also include a dozen housekeeping assistants who will put away their vacuum cleaners and put on their new state livery for the night. Several former staff will come out of retirement for the evening to serve the wine, a duty which also involves serving the sauce. Everyone knows that the banquet will take an hour and fifteen minutes and the old hands know that the slowest eaters will be those at the far end where it is harder to observe the brisk pace favoured by the Queen. For that reason, the Master of the Household and the Comptroller are always seated down there at the two ends of the U-shaped table.

McEvoy will use his senior footmen to chivvy, very gently, any guests who are 'coffee-housing', Palace slang for talking too much. Tonight's 171 guests will include several members of the Royal Household. If any of them slow things down, they will be treated less kindly. A new Palace executive, attending his first state banquet, was mortified when a footman whispered in his ear: 'Her Majesty has noticed you're the last to eat.' He later discovered it was a joke but, by then, he had lost his appetite completely.

A glorious scent is emanating from the Ballroom Annexe where the Queen's florist, Sharon Gaddes, and her team are almost invisible behind twenty-five huge dustbins full of flowers. These are gradually becoming a hundred separate flower arrangements. There will be twenty-one of them – including more than a thousand roses – on the table alone. Gaddes has gone for a peach/red/gold theme to suit the rich decor of the Ballroom and has been here since the previous weekend sorting out deliveries of freesias, orchids (from Singapore), euphorbias, carnations ('you've got to have carnations'), lisianthus . . . It is March but all the foliage for the arrangements has come from Windsor Great Park, including forsythia, which is just in bloom. Even here, things have changed in recent years. Photographs of earlier state banquets show much smaller table arrangements embellished with the occasional palm tree. Today, the emphasis is on colour and impact. Gaddes likes to make a statement. When asked to produce a set of flower arrangements for a reception in honour of Arsenal Football Club, everyone assumed she would replicate the club's red and white colours. As a devoted fan of (blue and white) rivals Chelsea, she did nothing of the sort and decked out the state apartments in shades of blue. Today, she concedes that she may have gone too far with two riotously effusive floral fountains streaming down from giant urns behind the Queen's chair. If she doesn't trim them back a bit, the television cameras won't actually be able to see the Queen and her guests coming in to dinner.

A forty-one-gun salute in Green Park signals the moment when President Zuma finally arrives to meet the Queen and Prince Philip on Horse Guards. She introduces him to the Prime Minister, the Foreign Secretary, the Chiefs of the Services and half a dozen hats and chains before anthems and the inspection of the Guard of Honour. It's the Grenadier Guards today. Their Colonel, Prince Philip, escorts the President down the ranks.

Time for carriages and the Queen, dressed in a violet coat, and her guest, wearing sunglasses and thick gloves, step into the two-ton Australian State Coach, the only one in the fleet with an on-board generator to provide central heating and electric windows. It's the colder, older Scottish State Coach for the Duke and Thobeka Madiba-Zuma. The most recent of the three current Mrs Zumas (the President has married five times), she has only been a First Lady for three months. The Royal Mews team are in their state liveries with wigs tucked beneath their hats. It is already apparent that the South African suite (as a delegation is called) have a livery of their own. They are all wearing scarves in their national colours to celebrate their country's staging of football's World Cup. Given the Arctic temperature, it's a wise move. This is one of the largest suites in years – a seven-coach affair (most visits have five). The sixth carriage, a semi-state landau, includes Mr Ohm Collins Chabane whose title dwarfs anything the Royal Household can muster: Minister of Performance, Monitoring and Evaluation and Administration of the Presidency.

As they are all cheered down the Mall at jogging speed, the non-mounted staff speed ahead in cars to receive them at the other end – among them, in smart scarlet overcoats, the chockmen with blocks for the wheels and dustpans for horse exhaust. The carriages sweep across the Palace forecourt, through the arch and into the Quadrangle where the Band of the Welsh Guards strikes up with 'Nkosi Sikelel iAfrika', the South African national anthem. The Household Cavalry troopers guarding the Grand Entrance instantly and noisily clatter to attention, causing some of the assembled media to jump out of their skins. Dust billows above the rich, timeless sounds of hoof and wheel on gravel and cobble. Before the carriages have even drawn to a halt, the travelling footmen and outriders have gracefully hopped off their perches to hold horses and open doors.

Top hat in hand, the Duke assists Mrs Zuma out of their carriage. This is not an ideal moment for high heels. The rest of the entourage must wait in the cold while the Queen, the Duke and the Zumas pose for the official photograph on the steps. In the Grand Hall, the heads of all the Royal Household departments are lined up to greet the visitors. After all this Field of Cloth of Gold treatment comes a light lunch in the Bow Room. There are no speeches, no toasts and everyone sits at round tables of ten. It invariably works as an ice-breaker and everyone is far more relaxed by the time they emerge to swap gifts and look around the Palace. The Queen presents Mr Zuma with a mounted bronze stag and a book about deer stalking as well as the regalia of a GCB, Knight Grand Cross of the Order of the Bath. In return, Mr Zuma gives the Queen the modern South African equivalent – the Order of the Companions of Oliver Tambo Gold Class – and a chess set featuring Zulu and Xhosa warriors. Up in the Picture Gallery, the media have assembled to watch the host and her guest inspect the Royal Collection's exhibition of Anglo-South African memorabilia. The exhibits have been chosen carefully. This is not the occasion to bring out souvenirs of the Zulu or Boer Wars. Instead, the emphasis is on royal visits of modern times, including the Queen's great South African tour with her parents in 1947. On one table sits the artificial flower she took from her twenty-first-birthday cake in Cape Town and kept as a present for 'Darling Grannie'. There is a letter from Princess Elizabeth to Queen Mary, too: 'Darling Grannie, when I caught my first glimpse of Table Mountain I could hardly believe that anything could be so beautiful . . .' Fast-forward half a century and there is some fascinating correspondence between the Queen and Nelson Mandela, starting with his letter inviting her to pay her first state visit in 1995. He addresses her as 'Madam' and concludes: 'You will be most welcome. NR Mandela.' Her handwritten thank-you letter after that trip begins 'Dear Mr President' but finishes 'Your sincere friend, Elizabeth R'. This is certainly warmer than her usual sign-off to other Commonwealth heads of state – 'Your good friend, Elizabeth R'. By 1999, Mandela is actually starting his letters 'Dear Elizabeth' and signing them, 'Please accept, Your Majesty, the assurances of our highest esteem, Nelson'. No other president has called the Queen plain 'Elizabeth' for a very long time. Even if the visit of President Zuma is a soaraway diplomatic triumph, it is highly unlikely that he will be on first-name terms by the end.

Despite the presence of the press and her guests, the Queen is still captivated by all this evocative memorabilia of 1947, one of the most important years in her life: her first trip abroad, her twenty-first birthday, her engagement and her wedding. 'It's quite intriguing,' she says, studying a photograph of the White Train, the famous express which was supposed to speed the Royal Family across South Africa but had to stop in every town so that the King and Queen could be greeted by the waiting crowds.

'That was the fastest transport,' murmurs Mr Zuma. 'It wasn't as far as we were concerned,' the Queen recalls with a smile.

They stop to look at the original text of her famous twenty-first-birthday radio broadcast to the Empire. 'That's the speech I made,' says the Queen. 'I did it outdoors. You can't nowadays because there are too many aeroplanes.'

Mr Zuma looks on politely. That was the South Africa of another age, a tour during which the (white) South African government of the day prevented George VI from pinning medals on black servicemen. The visitors are much more interested as the exhibition progresses to the recent past. They look at souvenirs from the presidential inauguration of Nelson Mandela and the silk scarf which Mandela gave the Queen. The rest of the South African suite have now made their way into the exhibition, too. Many are still wearing their own World Cup scarves, having kept them on throughout lunch – a case of national pride rather than necessity as the Palace is perfectly warm. The Household team are not remotely bothered. If guests want to wear football scarves, so be it. Every delegation has its eccentricities. During the last Chinese state visit, one guest had to be asked, very politely, not to take his laptop into the state banquet. When the President of Mexico visited in 2009, some members of the Royal Household had to spend much of the evening guiding Mexican guests to and from the Palace smoking area.

Suddenly, there is an awkward moment. The exhibition includes the gift which Mr Mandela gave Prince Philip during his 1996 state visit to London. It's a chess set of African warriors. And Mr Zuma has just given the Queen . . . a chess set of African warriors. The President looks faintly embarrassed, as if to say: 'Why didn't anyone tell me that Mandela gave them a chess set?' The Queen deftly smoothes over any discomfort as she turns to Prince Philip and says clearly, 'That's yours,' thus making it quite clear that she is delighted to have one of her own.

Mr Zuma has an afternoon of homage ahead. He must pay his respects to the Tomb of the Unknown Warrior in Westminster Abbey and to the memory of ANC hero Oliver Tambo whose house and memorial in north London are now shrines for modern South Africans. The Queen, mean-while, has a banquet to give. No living head of state can have hosted more banquets but she always likes to check the arrangements every time. The staff know that it will be a very thorough inspection. Everything is ready, right down to the pineapples decorating the table, each of which opens up to reveal perfectly sliced rings within. All the grapes have been pre-cut into clusters of four. The Queen has noticed a problem as soon as she walks in with the Master and his deputies. There is a draught blowing at ankle level through the entrance to the Ballroom. 'I hope we can sort that out,' she tells Air Vice-Marshal David Walker. 'Our guests are coming from summer.' Standing at one end of the table, she casts a keen eye down the line of table settings. One of them seems very slightly off centre. 'I think the dressing is wrong. Down there . . .' The Master of the Household walks down the table as the Queen guides him along. 'No . . . not that one . . . no . . . there!' The Master stops and looks closely at the setting. It is fractionally out because it is on a join in the table. 'I could move all the others,' he says mischievously. 'No, don't do that!' the Queen laughs.

She checks her own place. President Zuma will sit on her right. Both will be making speeches and their microphones have been disguised in the foliage of the flower arrangement in front. 'Can you hear these?' she asks the sound man. He can. The Queen's attention is caught by Sharon Gaddes's towering vases (she could hardly miss them). 'Who did these?' she asks, clearly impressed. Gaddes steps forward and bobs. 'Where did you find all these roses?'

Gaddes explains that it's a mix of flowers from as far afield as Ecuador, Israel and Windsor. The absence of African exotica meets with the Queen's approval: 'There's no point showing them their own flowers.'

She notices that some of the candles are not vertical. 'They look skew-whiff. Will someone put them up straight?' The Yeoman of the Silver Pantry assures her that they have yet to be put in properly. 'I'm just worried about them falling out,' she remarks. 'Where was it they fell out?' Edward Griffiths reminds her that it was during a banquet given by President Ciampi of Italy and they reminisce fondly about the evening when loose candles set fire to the flower arrangements. As the Queen heads for the door, she feels that breeze by her ankles again. 'Who's in charge of the draught?' The Master has got the message.

Down in the kitchens, Mark Flanagan's team are already preparing the *Pavé de Saumon Glamis*, *Noisettes d'Agneau Narbonnaise* and *Sablé aux Pommes de* Sandringham. He must also prepare a vegetarian banquet for those with special requirements – and the surprisingly large number of guests who always 'remember' that they are vegetarian on the night. Tonight's alternative menu is Tomato Tart Tatin, Pan-Fried Polenta with Ratatouille and Lentil Salsa and Sandringham Apple Shortbread (unlike the main menu, the vegetarian menu remains in English). Upstairs, on the balcony, the chairs are laid out for one of the most extraordinary – though invisible – rituals of a Palace banquet. In a tradition harking back to the medieval custom of royal meals as public entertainment, two dozen people will have tickets to sit behind the

Band of the Grenadier Guards and simply watch the banquet. In the days of Charles II, the public would watch the Monarch and his guests wade through 145 dishes. Tonight's banquet involves just three – plus 'dessert', as fruit is known around here (coffee and petits fours will be served back in the drawing rooms). The 'audience' will be made up of members of staff, each of whom can bring a guest, and it's always extremely popular as the 'audience' have dinner thrown in. However, once seated no one is allowed to budge for the best part of two hours.

There will also be a separate phantom state banquet going on tonight, involving a dozen senior officials – usually a physician or two, a Private Secretary to a junior member of the Royal Family and a few diplomats. They will follow the same dress code, mingle with everyone else for drinks and eat exactly the same food. But they will eat it in the Royal Household Dining Room – the substitutes' bench for the banquet. That way, if any of the 171 guests on the seating plan are delayed, taken ill or suddenly called away, a replacement guest can simply be slotted in without any awkward gaps at the table.

Nearly half of tonight's guest list will be regulars – Cabinet Ministers and the senior diplomatic crowd in addition to members of the Royal Family and their most senior officials. The other half will be President Zuma's suite plus eminent people with strong South African links – the novelist Gillian Slovo, the chairman of Barclays plc and so on. While the President will be on the Queen's right, with the Duchess of Cornwall on his other side, Mrs Zuma will be on the Duke's left, with the Prince of Wales on her other side. The President's daughter Nkosazana has also had another invitation back to the Palace. The University of London diplomacy student will be near the top end of the table between Air Chief Marshal Sir Jock Stirrup and Lord McNally, the Liberal Democrat peer. There will be an even spread of royalty from end to end so that no one feels they are 'below the salt'. For centuries, the Royal Family would be seated in order of precedence at the top end. But the Queen changed all that in 2000 when the Queen of Denmark came to stay. She scattered members of her family to outlying sections of the table so that everyone was within hailing distance of an HRH. It's now standard practice. Tonight, the Duke of Kent, for example, will be far down one leg of the table, seated between the multi-tasking Mr Ohm Collins Chabane and the Archbishop of Canterbury's wife. The Duchess of Gloucester will be well down the other side, with Mr Nathi Mthethwa on her right and the Marquess of Cholmondeley on her left.

Nigel McEvoy's team have been handed detailed printed instructions. At the top table, the Queen will be served first, President Zuma second and Prince Philip third. There are plenty of special dietary requests at all nineteen service stations. A senior financial figure should not be served red peppers and his wife is allergic to salmon. One politician is 'no meat, no wheat' while another is 'no pork or melon'. The wine waiters are laying out a selection of non-alcoholic drinks – Diet Cokes, Malvern Water and Sandringham apple juice.

The international media arrive before any of the guests and are shepherded through to the South Drawing Room. Tonight, once again, it reverts to its original role as the old Palace cinema. A large television monitor will relay proceedings back to the press.

Every guest is introduced to the Queen, the Duke and the Zumas before making their way through to dinner in little groups. They all know where they are sitting because they are handed a little booklet with a list of all the guests and a seating plan. Even so, it can be a little unnerving being one of the first guests into a huge Ballroom so the band strikes up a series of jaunty numbers, starting with 'Out Of The Blue' – otherwise known as the theme tune to the BBC's *Sports Report*. The Palace staff know that they can always rely on the Archbishop of Canterbury to lead the way like a good shepherd. There is an air of informality. The South African delegation are not wearing their football scarves tonight but cheerfully strike up conversation with footmen and butlers who are waiting to push in ladies' chairs and start serving. Samantha Cameron walks through talking to one of the Queen's ladies-in-waiting, Mary Morrison. David Cameron chats to Paddy Harverson, the Prince of Wales's Press Secretary.

Once all the non-royal guests are in, the Royal Procession forms up in the Music Room for the principal guests to come into dinner, men on the right, women on the left, with the Queen and President Zuma in front. Leading the way is the Lord Chamberlain, Lord Peel, alongside the Lord Steward, the Earl of Dalhousie, an entirely honorary figure who only appears at state occasions.

Until a few years ago, it was traditional for these two most senior courtiers to walk backwards into banquets. The practice was always a source of much mirth in the media and, to general relief, the Queen eventually took the view that her people could walk forwards. But reversing officials had their uses because it meant that they could keep an eye on the Queen and her guests and keep the procession moving at the correct pace for everyone. And since that is still useful, someone still has to walk backwards. It's another job for Ray Wheaton, Page of the Chambers. 'If we're going too fast for the Queen and the visiting head of state, then Ray will put his hands out and say, "OK, just slow down a bit,"' says Lord Peel. 'It's very funny but it's done for a very good reason.'

Tonight, Ray Wheaton steers the royal convoy into dinner right on time. The Queen is wearing a Stewart Parvin white satin dress and this, of all nights, is an occasion for what the Queen calls her 'best diamonds'. These are the twenty-one diamonds arranged into a necklace and bracelet and presented to Princess Elizabeth on her twenty-first birthday by the people of South Africa. She is also wearing Queen Alexandra's Russian Fringe Tiara and her new chain of the Order of the Companions of Oliver Tambo. The President is in white tie and the red sash of the Order of the Bath. However cold he was feeling earlier, he is now a little on the hot side. As he takes his seat next to the Queen, he repeatedly and nervously mops his brow. At least, he is spared the old routine for state banquets – speeches at the end of dinner.

The Queen has no need of her gavel. A short drum roll brings silence to the Ballroom. She touches briefly on her 1947 tour but focuses on the present and the future. Her speech has been written by the Foreign Office, hence a workmanlike text full of clunking phrases like 'a strong commitment to tackling together the global challenges of poverty, development and climate change'. But she concludes with an old African proverb: 'If you want to walk fast, walk alone. If you want to walk far, walk together.' She toasts her guests and the people of South Africa but the canny guests know not to drink their champagne just yet. The lengthy, two-part South African national anthem must be played first and then glasses are raised. The Queen and President Zuma both choose to sip glasses of water rather than Pol Roger champagne. The President then speaks, paying tribute to Britain's place at the 'forefront of a global movement for a free South Africa' in the days of the anti-apartheid movement. He points out that Britain is the largest investor in his country but this is a relationship built 'on the rock of human solidarity'. He toasts the Queen and the Duke and, this time, everyone knows that they have to wait until 'God Save The Queen' has finished. Finally, the banquet begins. Mark Flanagan's salmon is served by Nigel McEvoy's men and women. Air Vice-Marshal Sir David Walker keeps a careful eye from the far end of the table as all the senior members of the Royal Household turn to their guests, Prince Philip turns to Mrs Zuma and the Queen asks Mr Zuma how he is enjoying what will probably be one of the most memorable days of his life. And up in the dimly lit recesses of the balcony, two dozen onlookers sit and watch the new model twenty-first-century Court effortlessly deliver a thoroughly modern royal production which would have made the Georgians feel at home.

# 5

## Her Politicians

*'It's what she's* for.'

It is alternating between drizzle and a late spring sunset as a handful of selected television crews excitedly uncoil electric leads and set up their equipment in the Buckingham Palace Quadrangle. Plugs are passed through open windows to connect to ancient sockets within. The Palace wiring hasn't changed since George VI was on the throne but there's enough juice to fire up a few television lights and monitors. Normally, news crews are obliged to report from outside the Palace walls. But this is very different. After four days of post-election horsetrading, Prime Minister Gordon Brown has realised that he is not going to be able to form a government and has finally decided to resign. But he has to get a move on if he is going to do it tonight, because he has to resign to the Queen and she has a dinner engagement.

Tonight is a dinner in honour of the Queen's Gentlemen Ushers at the Turf Club and it has been in the book for a very long time. The Gentlemen Ushers are among the most loyal honorary members of the Royal Household, retired officers from all three Services who help orchestrate big royal events in return for little more than the train fare. The Queen is not going to let them down. It has been business as usual at the Palace all day. Earlier, the Queen had invited the 1st Battalion, Grenadier Guards, fresh back from Afghanistan, to parade on her lawn where she presented them with a new colour. While she prepares to head out for dinner, a steady flow of smart cars is coming the other way beneath the archway and crunching to a halt in the Quadrangle. The Princess Royal is hosting a dinner for supporters of one of her leading charities, Save the Children. Her guests at the Palace tonight will be received through the Grand Entrance, just like state visitors. If any politicians do decide to turn up, they will be steered to a side entrance called the King's Door. That's just the way it is. It may be the most important political moment of the twenty-first century so far but that is no reason to tear up longstanding engagements. If Brown does not want to prolong his own agony for another night and end up looking like a lonely loser clinging on to power, he needs to get himself down to the Palace – fast.

All of a sudden, people around the country are realising that the monarchy is not the rubber-stamping irrelevance its critics would have us believe. True, the Queen hardly has to make a decision. Once Brown has resigned, there will only be one candidate for whom she can send – the Conservatives' David Cameron. He may not be ready since he is still negotiating with the Liberal Democrats. But the Queen does not want the country left without a government all night.

The monarchy has already played an important role in this process. It has helped to fill the political vacuum of recent days simply by being there, waiting in the wings. The markets have remained stable. The public sector has got on with its job. Nothing has happened and, in these circum-stances, nothing is preferable to something. 'We have a system where a change of government – or a lack of one – doesn't lead to a constitutional crisis because the monarchy plays its part,' explains Cameron.

Although we will not even see the Queen during the climax of this saga, the fact that the central players have to enter and exit the highest office in the land via her gates underlines the entire point of the monarchy. As one former Private Secretary puts it, this is 'the grit in the constitutional oyster'. There is real drama as the news choppers hover in the middle distance. The fourteen media representatives in the Palace Quadrangle crouch over portable monitors on the gravel, waiting for indications of what will happen next. Producers frantically call up colleagues standing outside Downing Street asking for estimates – or even guesstimates – of what will happen and when. There is more rumour than fact stalking these precincts. Suddenly, on crackly screens, Brown emerges from Number Ten Downing Street and announces that he is off to tender his resignation. His wife, Sarah, appears and the couple walk a short way down the street, hand in hand with their two young sons who are making the first public appearance of their lives. It's a highly charged, emotional moment for the Downing Street staff. But it's the cue for action at the Palace. The reporters leap into position in front of their cameras, commentating on what happens next and the progress of the Brown motorcade through the rush-hour traffic, its path cleared by police outriders. He is still Prime Minister – for the next few minutes. He still gets the full treatment.

At 7.27, the Queen's Private Secretary, Christopher Geidt, her equerry, Wing Commander Andrew Calame, and tonight's Lady-in-Waiting, Lady Susan Hussey, appear from the King's Door to welcome Mr Brown and his wife out of their blue Jaguar Sovereign. Lady Susan is a picture of sympathy. She almost looks sadder than the soon-to-be-ex-Prime Minister. These are human moments, devoid of politics (Lady Susan appeared equally downcast when John Major departed). Mr Brown is escorted upstairs and straight in to see the Queen while Mrs Brown waits in an ante-room. She will be presented at the end. Word comes down that the children, sitting patiently in a blacked-out Ford Galaxy, have been invited in, too. There is an outbreak of melodramatics. A police driver moves the Galaxy right up to the King's Door as if depositing a master criminal at the Old Bailey. One of the Queen's pages comes marching across the gravel towards the cameras flapping his arms at the television crews in a way that clearly states: 'Thou shalt not film.' Two little boys who, moments earlier, were being paraded in front of the world's cameras in Downing Street, are now smuggled inside the Palace like a pair of secret agents. No one films them.

At 7.43, the now ex-Prime Minister walks out trying to smile. It is self-evidently a wrench. In the process of holding his head up high, he forgets himself, gets in the car first and leaves Mrs Brown to walk round and get in on the other side herself. As the Browns leave in their two-car motorcade, Mr Brown probably doesn't notice a parting gesture from the royal side. The Queen's equerry, standing on the gravel, performs a valedictory bow (even though there is nothing in the equerry training manual about bowing to ex-prime ministers).

Moments later, the Queen's (then) Press Secretary, Samantha Cohen, hands round notices on thick cream paper embossed with the Crown. They declare: 'The Right Honourable Gordon Brown had an audience of the Queen this evening and tendered his resignation as Prime Minister and First Lord of the Treasury, which Her Majesty accepted.' For the next half an hour, Britain has no Prime Minister at all. Should a meteorrite land or enemies invade, it's down to the Queen to take the initiative. David Cameron receives the call from the Queen's Private Secretary and begins the journey from the House of Commons to the Palace with his wife, Samantha. Reflecting on it all a year later in his Downing Street study, Cameron thinks that Brown rather rushed things. 'My view is it would have been easier if he'd spent the night here and had gone the next morning. But I think he felt "I don't want to stay here any longer than I should" and everyone at the Palace was very accommodating. From my point of view, it felt as if it was all happening in a tearing rush when it didn't need to.'

There is a sudden change of mood in the Quadrangle, bolstered by the weather. The drizzle subsides, the evening sun peers out and bathes the inside face of the East Front in a honeyed glow. But David Cameron is not yet Prime Minister. He does not yet enjoy the trappings of office. For the moment, there is no police motorcade for him. And so, while Britain and the Queen sit in limbo, the news choppers hover overhead transmitting pictures of the future Prime Minister sitting at traffic lights in Trafalgar Square. On he travels, stuck behind a commuter on a Vespa and a chap having a lesson in a BSM car. 'It was wonderful,' Cameron recalls. 'It was just terribly British. There's no other country in the world which has this sort of changeover. In America, they have this grand occasion weeks later. But we have a vaguely farcical moment where you're stuck in the Mall with people taking pictures, traffic blocking the car and I'm desperately wondering what I am going to say on the steps of Downing Street.'

As the traffic stops and starts, the reporters in the Palace Quadrangle are earning their keep, filling in time with every bit of trivia they can muster. The BBC Radio Five Live reporter tells her listeners that Cameron will be the first Prime Minister who is younger than all the Queen's children. BBC Television's royal correspondent, Nicholas Witchell, informs viewers that Mr Cameron will become the youngest Prime Minister since Lord Liverpool in 1812.

Cameron's silver Jaguar sweeps in at 8.10, followed by a couple of plain-clothes policemen in a BMW. 'As the car turns into Buckingham Palace, it's totally surreal. You can't believe it's happening,' Cameron recalls. 'You've seen this on the television so many times and you can't believe you're actually doing it.' The equerry and the page greet Mr and Mrs Cameron and usher them inside. He is taken up to the Private Audience Room where, officially, he 'kisses hands'. Except that he does not. 'It's a myth,' says Cameron. That will all happen the next day in a formal ceremony when everyone has a little more time and is a little less stressed. The Queen asks Cameron if he can form a government. Yet he has no overall majority and is still in discussions with the third-place Liberal Democrats. She has asked an interesting question. Looking back, Cameron jokes that it was not a straightforward answer. 'I like to think I was one of the first prime ministers in a long time who, when asked to form a government, instead of saying, "Yes, Your Majesty," said: "Well, I'll do my best. I'll get back to you!"'

It's not a long audience. As Tony Blair recalls in his own memoirs, new prime ministers tend to be tired and preoccupied and, in his own case, 'looking a trifle manic'. Before Cameron leaves, the Queen invites his wife, Samantha, to come in for a brief but friendly chat (Tony Blair recalls the Queen 'clucking sympathetically' with Mrs Blair about the sudden upheavals for the family). At the same time, the Queen's page comes out into the Quadrangle to alert Cameron's driver and policemen, who are chatting on the gravel, to snap into action. They're rapidly discovering a different pace of life already. The Queen's Private Secretary, Christopher Geidt (he has yet to become Sir Christopher), knows that the new Prime Minister must now face the world and offers him a short breathing space. As Cameron recalls: 'He kindly said: "If you want to use my office, there's time to collect your thoughts before the next step." So I popped into his office and thought a bit more about what I was going to say.'

At 8.35, the Camerons emerge from the King's Door. The Queen's tally of British prime ministers has now reached a dozen. The next tenant of Number Ten Downing Street escorts his pregnant wife to the right-hand door of the car and shuts it before walking round to the other side. He waves at the broadcasters on the way out. Within minutes, they are handed another piece of paper announcing: 'The Queen received the Right Honourable David Cameron this evening and requested him to form a new administration. The Right Honourable David Cameron accepted Her Majesty's offer and kissed hands upon his appointment as Prime Minister and First Lord of the Treasury.'

It's not exactly a surprise but it ends the uncertainties of previous days. As the reporters broadcast these words to the nation, they don't see another car quietly pulling away from the Palace's Garden Door. The Queen has kept the Gentlemen Ushers waiting quite long enough at the Turf Club. It's time for dinner.

The Queen's actual discussions with her prime ministers have remained locked in the vaults of their collective memories to an astonishing degree. But we have had many indications of the tone and atmosphere. The late Lord (James) Callaghan summed it up neatly when he said: 'What one gets is friendliness but not friendship. She's very interested in the political side – who's going up and who's going down. But not so passionate about the MLR|minimum lending rate|.'

Like most prime ministers before him, David Cameron genuinely looks forward to his Wednesday trips to the Palace: 'The audiences are very friendly, enjoyable occasions because it's just the two of you so you can say what you like and she can ask what she likes. As well as talking through what the government's up to, there is quite a lot of businesslike stuff – my travel, her travel, state visits and so on.'

Both the Prime Minister and the Queen like to roam well beyond affairs of state. When Cherie Blair was pregnant with Leo, one of the first people whom Tony Blair informed was the Queen.

Sir John Major found the Palace far more comfortable on the inside than it is perceived to be from the outside. 'What seemed remote from afar became warm and very human at close quarters,' he says. And he never felt any need to tiptoe round any subjects. 'Nobody else is present, except the occasional corgi. That trust is absolute. I never held back on anything I wished to say to the Queen and I believe that the reverse is equally true.' The audience, he believes, is a vital element of sound government. 'The Queen sees state papers but she doesn't know what is not yet committed to paper. She doesn't know what is in the mind of the Prime Minister. Without the weekly audience, that crucial line of communication would be broken.'

Those working close to the Queen all testify that she genuinely enjoys the daily business of politics. As one puts it: 'It's what she's *for*.' She is genuinely interested in the human dynamics of it all. It was the personal dimension, as much as the political, which intrigued her about the formation of her first Coalition Government. 'She asked a lot about it,' says David Cameron. 'She asked how we were all getting on.'

Prince William, who has already met many of the Queen's various prime ministers around the world, has no doubt that these audiences are appreciated equally by both parties. 'If you think how many meetings she's had with different prime ministers at different times it's incredible,' he says. 'Some of them must wish she would turn round and tell them what to do! But she always speaks very highly of having these meetings.'

During the British parliamentary year, the audiences are weekly (officially, the Prime Minister has 'an audience of the Queen', not the other way round). And every summer, the Prime Minister is invited to stay at Balmoral, attend the Braemar Highland Games (optional) and enjoy a Royal Family barbecue cooked by Prince Philip (not optional). It can be a strange experience. Tony Blair has written that his first Balmoral weekend was 'a vivid combination of the intriguing, the surreal and the utterly freaky' fortified by 'rocket fuel' cocktails and a breakfast, lunch and dinner 'out of Trollope or Walter Scott'. No wonder, he observed, the Royal Family eat sparingly.*

Blair's first visit was, understandably fraught, given the recent death of Diana, Princess of Wales.

Sir John Major has fond memories of walks down to the Balmoral cricket ground and of trips to tea at Birkhall. 'The Queen usually drove me there and we would have tea and cakes with the Queen Mother and I would admire her collection of Spy cartoons and look with awe at the

---

* Some have accused Blair of breaking the code of secrecy surrounding the meetings of monarch and Prime Minister by describing them in his memoirs. But there are no complaints from the Palace. While he may have indulged in some mildly indiscreet – and highly readable – scene-setting, he has been scrupulous in observing constitutional proprieties. We are still no closer to knowing what the Queen actually *thinks*.

stack of *Dad's Army* videos.' Later on, there might be a black-tie dinner or, more often than not, that barbecue cooked by Prince Philip and another member of the Royal Family. 'At the end of those very informal – and hugely enjoyable – evenings, the Queen and other members of the family would wash up and any guests who offered to do so would be politely repulsed,' says Major. But, in among all the pleasantries, there would also be a lengthy one-on-one audience, too. 'Nobody's around in August, so there's always a lot to catch up on in September.'

The Queen's political antennae extend far beyond her audiences and what she gleans from the media (newspapers and radio in the morning, television news at night). Every morning at eleven o'clock, she telephones her senior Private Secretary and asks an entirely redundant question: 'Are you free to come upstairs?' No Private Secretary in history, as far as anyone knows, has replied: 'Sorry, but I'm a bit tied up.' They will run through any events touching on the monarchy – casualties in Afghanistan, a Cabinet reshuffle in New Zealand, thoughts for the Christmas broadcast – and the Queen's diary. After half an hour, she will call down to ask her Deputy or Assistant Private Secretary if they might be 'free' and one of them will bring up the paperwork, including documents for signature. There are usually around a dozen and, depending on the document, she will write either 'Approved ER' or 'Elizabeth R' (the royal signature is known as the Sign Manual). It might be army regulations, royal warrants, Letters of Credence for ambassadors or a parliamentary Bill. It's more than a regal production line. The Queen will not read every clause but she will know exactly what she is signing. When this sort of stuff is coming across your desk day after day, you have a feel for the pace and nature of what is happening across your kingdom.

Every few weeks, she receives her Vice-Chamberlain, the government whip who is the House of Commons go-between with the Palace. He or she will turn up carrying the wand of office, a black staff which unscrews in the middle, and then relay various messages between MPs and the Monarch. These might involve the Queen's Speech or a House of Commons resolution to wish her a happy birthday. The Vice-Chamberlain must also write that daily 'message', the personal summary of what is happening in Parliament.

As we have learned, these may sometimes be light-hearted but they are also a reflection of genuine backbench feeling. The Queen doesn't want a constant diet of glowing reports about government triumphs. The message may be a closely typed side of A4 paper but it will be read and digested, along with a selection of state papers and anything else she finds in her Red Box. Every night at seven o'clock one of these battered briefcases – leather on the outside, metal within – will be sent from the Private Secretary's Office.

By eight the following morning, it will have been returned, with anything which has caught the Queen's eye underlined in red pencil. Inside is material for signature, material she is obliged to see (not least the top copy of the latest Cabinet minutes) and material she will be interested to see (a sheaf of Foreign Office telegrams, perhaps). On weekday evenings, the box is a smaller model known as a 'Reader'. It can be piled high, unless there is an evening engagement or a state banquet in prospect, in which case the contents may be reduced. But private secretaries are told that the Queen prefers to be given a little too much than run the risk of overlooking something important. At weekends, it's a larger model called a 'Standard'. Inside will be a broader selection of reading material plus weekly summaries from the Queen's fifteen other realms around the world. Some of the Canadian briefings will be in French (no translation is required; the Queen is fluent in French). But it will all have been processed and returned by Monday morning. Even when the Queen would rather not read something, she gets on with it regardless. 'A lot of material goes into her boxes, huge amounts of stuff about appointments that have to be in her name,' says former Deputy Private Secretary Mary Francis. 'It all goes in but not an awful lot comes back to you. She reads the Foreign Office telegrams and puts a tick on them, she reads the Cabinet minutes and puts a tick on them. You don't very often get a question or a comment. But you know it's all sinking in and almost certainly some of it gets played back when she meets the Prime Minister at her weekly meeting or has her audiences with new ambassadors.'

The Queen does not cut corners. If it's in her Red Box, it's there for a reason. 'She is very assiduous and careful about reading things and when you discussed things with her, she had read them very carefully,' says Francis. 'And she was on top of them – not in an academic, intellectual way but she had certainly understood them and spotted the main messages and the main issues.'

But why on earth is she expected to do all this? No one doubts the Queen's devotion to duty, so she will read whatever she is given. But is it really necessary for her to wade through the minutiae of appointments or legislation that she cannot amend? Why must she read obscure diplomatic dispatches or be presented with technical issues which are gibberish to all bar experts in the field? Some have suggested that she sometimes uses the Red Boxes as a diversionary tactic, an excuse to lock herself away. Mary Francis thinks it goes to the heart of what constitutional monarchy is all about. 'I often wondered what the point was, to be perfectly frank. But she is a constitutional monarch and there are points at which she has to engage – whether it's meeting the Prime Minister or other Ministers or making appointments. And it would be strange if the person who was doing those things was being kept ignorant of the workings of government and what was happening generally.' In other words, it might be a document of stultifying inanity or head-throbbing complexity. But if it passed through the political system without passing beneath the gaze of the Monarch, then she would quite simply feel that she had failed in her duty.

Besides going through new legislation – and turning it into law with a stroke of a pen – there is another political duty at the dustier end of the regal spectrum which the Queen is said to enjoy greatly. The Privy Council is the oldest legislative assembly in Britain and once served as the Monarch's Cabinet. Today, its work is no longer secret and it remains a means of pushing through a lot of low-level government business without involving Parliament. It can be both a wonderful and tedious hotch-potch of stuff – authorising new laws in the Channel Islands or issuing coins. It involves proclaiming Bank Holidays. Tens of millions of diaries cannot be printed until these are sorted out. The Queen must also approve the marriages of all direct descendants of George II under the terms of the Royal Marriages Act. Many of them will be leading ordinary lives and will never even have met the Queen. Some may not even be aware of the rule. Yet if they do not go through the Queen and the Privy Council, then, according to the law, their marriage is invalid and their children are, technically, illegitimate. Most couples with a royal ancestor are, of course, thrilled to get their union personally blessed by the Monarch but the Privy Council Office is aware of some exceptions. They need not fear a knock on the door from the wedding police, however. 'We don't go looking for them,' says one of the team. 'We take a pragmatic view. It's a case of don't ask, don't tell.'

A lot of Privy Council business involves amending the statutes of universities or anything with a royal charter (including the BBC). It also has a judicial wing which acts as the court of appeal for Commonwealth countries which have yet to construct one of their own. On rare occasions, one of these sober little gatherings in the 1844 Room of Buckingham Palace can, effectively, send a man to his death. Some countries which retain the Privy Council also retain the death penalty. The Council doesn't carry out sentencing, it merely judges appeals. But if it rejects the appeal of a murderer on death row in the Caribbean, then a condemned man is on his way to the gallows once the Queen has uttered a single word: 'Approved.' And it is her constitutional duty to do so.

There is no debate at these meetings. All the business has been prepared in advance and is usually over in five minutes. But it's by no means formulaic ritual. The Clerk of the Council always prepares a short explanation of every item of business for the Queen in advance. It might be a couple of sentences explaining the reasons for, say, amending the Charter of the University of Keele or freezing the assets of a terrorist suspect. There might be dozens of items but the Queen reads the lot. It's just like her Red Boxes. It's often dense, turgid stuff. But that's not the point. She believes that she would be falling down on the job if she did not know what it was she was actually approving at these meetings.

The Lord President of the Council – a senior Cabinet Minister who usually has a more onerous day job like Deputy Prime Minister – turns up with a trio of Government Ministers. The minimum required for any meeting is three Privy Counsellors.* They line up outside the 1844 Room and the Lord President goes in first for a few words with the Queen. When she is ready, she presses her buzzer and the rest of them file in, along with the Clerk, and they shake her hand.

The emphasis is on brisk efficiency, hence the fact that meetings are conducted standing up, a time-saving mechanism famously introduced by Queen Victoria. The politicians stand on one side of the Queen with their backs to the window while the Clerk stands on the other. The Lord President reads out all the orders on each page of what is called the List of Business whereupon the Queen replies 'approved' and everyone can turn the page.† When it's all done, the President will say: 'That, Your Majesty, concludes the business of today's Council.' The Queen might comment on one of the more interesting orders and then she rings her buzzer, the doors open and the ministers walk out. Because they are all Privy Counsellors, they are not expected to turn round on their way out and bow again like ordinary mortals. These people – with 'Right Honourable' before their name and 'PC' after it – are, historically, the Sovereign's trustiest advisers. They just leave.

'I always had the sense that the Queen really enjoys every aspect of it,' says former Clerk of the Privy Council, Alexander Galloway. He admits that the details of some rituals are so complicated that they can

* A member is called a 'Counsellor' rather than the more conventional 'Councillor'. Senior members of the Royal Family are appointed as Counsellors of State, two of whom must be designated to stand in for the Monarch whenever she goes abroad. The Queen was appointed one herself on turning eighteen. It was a sobering experience for a Princess who had led a relatively sheltered life. She was said to be particularly shocked by the details of a murder case.
† The Queen also has a set of Privy Council implements laid out before her, including sealing wax and a candle to melt it. It's a nice touch but a historic one. The reality is that all sealing is now done elsewhere with longer-lasting plastic.

fox the most experienced people in the room, namely the Queen and the Clerk. 'The great thing about being Clerk of the Privy Council is that if anyone asks you a question, it's almost certain that no one knows the answer,' he points out.

On half a dozen occasions during her reign, though, the usual calm of the Privy Council meeting turns into a cross between a circus and a medieval homage. It happens when a ruling party falls and a new government comes to power with a lot of first-time ministers. Not only must the Queen swear in a lot of new Secretaries of State but there are a lot of new Privy Counsellors to be created, too. 'It was like a baptism by hosepipe,' says David Cameron with a smile, recalling the day when he took his new Coalition to be sworn in. 'There was this wonderful scene – a lot of people getting into the Privy Council and then a lot of people kissing hands and accepting the seals of office too. So you had someone like the Lord Chancellor, Ken Clarke, who's had the seals of almost every office [Kenneth Clarke held no fewer than five different Cabinet positions during the Thatcher/Major years] and you had Liberal Democrats like Danny Alexander who never thought they'd ever get the seals of any office! Here was this giant queue of oath-takers. They go down on one kneeler, kiss hands and affirm the oath of the Privy Council and then get on another kneeler to become Cabinet Ministers and do the kissing and swearing again.' Just to add to the confusion, the Deputy Prime Minister, Nick Clegg, had to be sworn in ahead of the Prime Minister since he was also the new Lord President of the Privy Council. And without a Lord President no one else could be sworn in. Cameron goes on: 'My abiding memories of the day are of Nick Clegg going first and all the Lib Dems thinking: "Good God: we're running the whole country!" and of everyone getting seals of office except me. They come in these huge leather boxes with a key. And everyone gets one except the Prime Minister who just kisses hands. But it was all beautifully arranged, with a rehearsal and coffee and a very nice room at Buckingham Palace followed by a chat afterwards. Like all these things, the Palace do it very well and make everyone feel very special.' It is always a frantic few days after a change of government. Not only must the Palace round up the victors for swearing in but the Queen will also summon the losers for a formal farewell. By tradition, every departing Cabinet Minister is granted an audience when a government falls. 'It was a perfectly pleasant ten-minute conversation about the way things were going and then you got the smile and the handshake and that was it,' says one former Cabinet Minister. 'But it helps. It produces finality. It's a very nice recognition and you feel a little bit warmer that you've seen the Sovereign, even if she's only saying: "Thank you very much. Don't call me. I'll call you.'"

This complex collection of constitutional duties, conventions, obligations, quirks, anomalies and fathomless rituals is not laid down in black and white, of course. Walter Bagehot might have distilled some of the essentials of constitutional monarchy in his great work, *The English Constitution*, but he never said anything about Red Boxes or the Commonwealth or detachable wands or kissing hands. Yet this entire, often baffling interplay between the Sovereign and the political class is neatly encapsulated in one of the most colourful and spectacular days in the royal calendar.

The Buckingham Palace Billiard Room is packed. Accountants, secretaries, cleaners and several peers of the realm are gathered beneath the naval portraits and the china displays. They are all staring, spellbound, at the table – but no one is playing billiards. Laid out before them is a very handsome cross section of the Crown Jewels.

It is now a ritual before every State Opening of Parliament that Palace staff are allowed a glimpse of the royal regalia which will be used. Some of the old-timers are as captivated as a tourist entering the Tower of London's Jewel House for the first time to see the Crown Jewels. The Jewel House has a few gaps today. All the items now sitting here at the Palace have been replaced by signs saying 'In Use'. It may be disappointing for today's tourists at the Tower but it is a reminder that these treasures are not museum pieces. They are central fixtures in the great constitutional/theatrical production that is about to unfold.

'You're looking at over three thousand natural gems – diamonds, sapphires emeralds and historically some of the biggest in the world,' says the Crown Jeweller, Harry Collins, opening up a deceptively dull box to reveal the Imperial State Crown. In an hour or so, it will be on the Queen's head in the Palace of Westminster.

The post of Crown Jeweller – the highest accolade in the trade – is a part-time one and comes with a modest 'E II R' tie pin plus custody of some of the greatest treasures in the world. Collins was an interesting choice when he was appointed in 2007. He was not running a grand boutique in London's Bond Street but the family jewellery shop in Royal Tunbridge Wells. His passion for these pieces comes through loud and clear. 'The sapphire at the top has a lovely story,' he tells his hushed audience, pointing to the top of the crown. 'Edward the Confessor wore that sapphire in a ring all his life and he wanted to be buried with it. His wish was granted in 1066, so that stone was buried for a hundred years. It sends a shiver up my spine every time I think of it. And then a hundred years later, when they were moving his body, they exhumed him and it was decided to make his sapphire a Crown Jewel.'

Collins has similar stories about all the main jewels in this particular crown – the Black Prince's Ruby, Elizabeth I's pearls, the 317-carat Cullinan II diamond (itself cut from the largest diamond ever known).

There are so many people in so many different costumes that the Billiard Room could be the backstage area of an opera house or a film set. Two of the longest serving members of staff – chief clerk Paul Almond and stud groom Brian Stanley – will be Serjeants at Arms for the day. Dressed in the Victorian uniform of the Lord Chamberlain's Office, they will carry the two maces, symbols of royal authority, in the Royal Procession.

Several footmen have come out of retirement for the day to serve as State Porters. Dressed in thick scarlet overcoats, they will act as door-keepers during all the comings and goings.

Four nervous-looking schoolboys are wearing knee-length scarlet coats, white breeches and white stockings. They are the Pages of Honour who will carry the Queen's velvet robe, eighteen feet long and trimmed with ermine. They are usually the children of royal friends or officials but today's quartet includes a member of the Royal Family. Eleven-year-old Arthur Chatto is the younger son of Princess Margaret's daughter, Lady Sarah Chatto. The Queen is his great-aunt and, for now, he is eighteenth in the line of succession.

Conservative MP Mark Francois, the current occupant of the office of Vice-Chamberlain, is here in a morning coat with his black wand of office. He will spend the morning here as the Queen's hostage until she has safely returned from Parliament. It will be a pleasant captivity. Refreshments and a television have been laid on in the Regency Room. 'We don't do manacles any more,' explains a Palace official.

Suddenly, the atmosphere suddenly switches from coffee-morning banter to action stations. The Sovereign is on her way down from her apartments. No one in history has performed this ritual more often than the Queen. She has only missed it twice (through pregnancy), an attendance record to shame Queen Victoria who managed just seven State Openings in the last forty years of her life. Many of the Palace participants are veterans of this event. Even so, no one is blasé about the constitutional significance of the day and no one wants to make a mistake on live television, least of all the Monarch herself. Dressed in a Stewart Parvin state dress of apricot duchess satin embroidered with Paris beads and gold thread, her solemnity is infectious.

There are two carriage processions, the first one for the crown and the second for the Monarch. Royal Mews staff have been busy all morning hosing down the gravel to minimise the dust cloud from the two hundred horses passing through the Palace Quadrangle this morning (they include First Love, a spirited ex-racehorse of the late Queen Mother which gave her the last win of her life and which is carrying the Crown Equerry today).

All eyes are on the Monarch as she departs in the Irish State Coach with the George IV diadem twinkling on her head. It is a super-tiara, a substantial piece in its own right, though little more than a hairband in comparison with the Imperial State Crown which has gone on ahead.

All the Royal Mews staff are in their state liveries, of course. Coaching Instructor, John Nelson, in wig and tricorn hat, steers the Irish State Coach up the Mall, past Horse Guards and up to the Sovereign's Entrance at the House of Lords where the Royal Standard is hoisted (or, in royal parlance, 'broken') on high.

The Queen disappears into the Robing Room to put on her robe and the crown. A fanfare heralds her reappearance in the Royal Procession – which is missing one notable figure. For the first time since 1620, the Lord President of the Privy Council will not be taking part. The new incumbent, the Liberal Democrat leader Nick Clegg, is also the new Deputy Prime Minister and wants to be seen at the head of the brand-new coalition, not processing self-consciously behind fifteen heralds and pursuivants dressed as playing cards, as well as someone holding the Cap of Maintenance on a stick.

Inside the House of Lords, the peers chat quietly in their scarlet robes as they wait for the Monarch to take her seat on the throne. The MPs are in boisterous form next door in the House of Commons as they wait to be summoned through to the Lords for the Queen's Speech. They affect a noisy nonchalance in their lounge suits and day dresses, cheering loudly as the door is slammed in the face of Black Rod, the Queen's messenger from the Lords. It is all part of the ritual. The MPs always like to make it clear who is boss round here.

Having finally opened the door to Black Rod, they listen to his royal summons and stroll with little urgency through to the Lords. There's limited space at the back of the Chamber where it's standing room only, even for the Prime Minister. If this was a theatre, this would be the cheapest part of the house (in fact, under modern safety regulations, the MPs might even be thrown out for blocking the exits). Yet it is these latecomers in the ordinary workaday clothes, crammed in at the back with no seats and a lousy view, who have written every word of the script presented to the Sovereign with the three thousand jewels on her head. And for all its infernal complexities – there is still no definitive explanation, say, for the Cap of Maintenance after a thousand years of monarchy – this is an occasion with a very simple, fundamental message. And if it is unclear whether the Queen enjoys it very much, there is not an atom of doubt that she regards it as sacrosanct.

It goes without saying that the Queen is above politics. That's the whole point of the monarchy. But she is also human. She must have opinions and a set of values by which to judge issues, just like anyone else. So what are they? Politicians and political commentators sometimes presume to suggest what the Queen's private views might be on a particular issue, usually by second-guessing the opinion of a wealthy, small-c conservative member of the wartime generation with a deep affinity for the countryside. So, for those who live and breathe politics, it can be quite a surprise when they do encounter authentic, deep-rooted neutrality. Much as it may offend some politicians, it would seem that the Queen really does regard them as a single breed. Sir Godfrey Agnew, the revered Clerk of the Privy Council for more than twenty years, summed it up: 'The Queen doesn't make fine distinctions between politicians of different parties. They all roughly belong to the same social category in her view.' Sir Malcolm Rifkind – whose three Cabinet positions all involved working with the monarchy at close quarters – was struck by a remark the Queen made during one conversation at Holyroodhouse: 'The Queen said to me: "The Shah of Iran asked me if I had more years with Labour or Conservative prime ministers. And I said to him that I hadn't the faintest idea because I'd never thought about it." And I don't suppose she does. Because the party is the least important consideration. In all the times I was with the Queen as Scottish Secretary, Defence Secretary and Foreign Secretary, she never expressed a controversial political view of any sort whatsoever.'

The Queen's sixty years on the throne break down into 34 Conservative, 24 Labour and, latterly, a spell of Conservative/Liberal Democrat coalition. And if there are any observations to be drawn about her political outlook, then it seems fair to say that she enjoys the occasional outbreak of consensus. 'I think this Coalition is going to be rather good for the country,' she told a guest seated next to her at a lunch just weeks after the 2010 election. 'Since we live in a time of unprecedented change, let's try to make the most of it.' After more than half a century of pendulum politics between the two major parties, it was hardly surprising that the Queen should enjoy the novelty value of her first British coalition (with sixteen governments around the world, she's had one or two elsewhere). What's more, the uncertainty surrounding the 2010 general election served to remind the public about the monarchy's role as the guarantor of stability and fair play.

'The Royal Family absolutely love things that are different,' says Mary Francis. 'They love it when a chair falls over or the curtain doesn't open. It's a talking point. In the same way, a coalition is different – and it has quite clearly involved the Queen. It's put a lot of focus on the importance or potential importance of her role and what she might have to do. And that's quite reassuring.'

In the end, the Queen was not forced to decide between two rivals in the 2010 election. With neither the Conservatives nor Labour enjoying an outright majority, a stalemate might ultimately have required a particularly unwelcome decision by the Sovereign – another election. But the politicians sorted it out themselves. Once the Liberal Democrats were clearly going to share power with the Tories, then the Monarch was off the hook. But it could have been a difficult constitutional position if, after Brown's resignation, talks between the Tories and the Liberal Democrats then collapsed.

Before the election, senior civil servants and constitutional experts had started drafting a Cabinet Office manual. It would set out, in purely factual terms, the laws and conventions governing the relationships between Parliament, the government, the monarchy and so on. Surprisingly, perhaps, no such document existed before. With an election looming, the experts' priority was to prepare a draft chapter offering guidelines in the event of a hung Parliament. They looked at the situation in other Westminster-style parliaments, notably in New Zealand where a manual had evolved over the previous twenty years.

The new manual had no legal standing then and has none today either. It was not a rulebook but a guidebook (and a draft one at that). But it addressed the role of the Queen in a general election. It emphasised very clearly that it was down to the politicians to find a solution and that everything should be done to spare the Queen from picking a premier. 'The manual makes it clear that the Queen does not become a kingmaker,' explained one of its authors, Professor Vernon Bogdanor of Oxford University. 'It is not for her to bring the parties together, but, rather, to accept the outcome of negotiations.'

Today's party leaders are barely old enough to remember the desperate haggling after the general election of February 1974 (which resulted in a hung Parliament and the removal of Conservative Prime Minister Edward Heath), but the Queen remembers it only too well. And the last thing she wanted, in the event of a hung Parliament, was a frenzied media demanding some sort of magic solution from her. A dry but authoritative manual would be just the thing to calm everyone down and ensure sensible analysis of the situation. The Queen clearly approved of the document.

She made that clear a few weeks after the election when it was suddenly announced – with almost no notice – that she would be visiting the Cabinet Office in person, at her own request, for the first time. As constitutional referees, sovereigns are used to dealing with electoral winners and losers. They don't usually come to pay tribute to the ground staff.

The Whitehall civil servants are buzzing as the Queen is shown around the administrative nerve centre of the nation. 'I don't think people realise how exciting it is until it happens,' says Sinead Keller, twenty-nine. She works as a press officer in the Honours Secretariat, the bit of the Cabinet Office which handles the thousands of MBEs, OBEs and knighthoods dished out each year. She has been to investitures and has seen the impact that royal recognition has on other people. Today, though, she herself receives a handshake from the Queen. She is surprised by her own reaction. 'When the moment comes, it really does hit home. I'm not a great flag-waver but it's easy to underestimate how much affection there is for the Queen.'

There is also another subtext to today's visit by the Monarch. In recent days, the new government has been issuing stark warnings about the need for Civil Service cuts. Here is a gesture of royal solidarity with those who, like her, are constitutionally obliged to remain neutral.

Sir Gus O'Donnell, the Cabinet Secretary, has ensured a complete cross section of staff for the Queen. Lil Kibblewhite on the reception desk has been here twenty-two years and has a daughter and granddaughter working in the same building. 'I only got told this morning that I was going to meet her,' she says, clearly thrilled. Personal assistant Regina Adu heard a whisper yesterday and spent last night practising her curtsey.

Having introduced the Queen to some of the 'Transition team' behind his constitutional manual, O'Donnell takes her upstairs to sit in on his weekly meeting with the thirty-two permanent secretaries from across all the government departments. Today's agenda includes electoral reform and the imminent visit of the Pope. The meeting takes place in a dreary glass-fronted room with no view and decorated with a few prints from a staff photography competition. It may lack the grandeur of the Cabinet Room in Downing Street, yet these people are the most powerful mandarins in the land, supervising millions of civil servants. Some would say that these are the people who really run the country. And they are rather pleased by this sudden pat on the back from on high. At the end, O'Donnell takes the Queen down to the atrium and makes a short speech congratulating staff on the way they have 'responded to the challenges of transition' – but also paying tribute to the Queen's staff. As Whitehall officials cram every landing and peer down from the balconies and gantries, O'Donnell also has one more bit of good news. In this climate, he is in no position to proclaim a day's holiday or even a round of drinks, but he announces that the Queen has agreed to let him stage this year's Civil Service Awards – the public sector Oscars – at Buckingham Palace. She receives a rousing send-off. It's been a long few weeks for everyone.

Since Britain has no written constitution, some MPs have described this manual as the nearest we have to the real thing. It has affirmed the principle that, in the event of a hung Parliament, the existing government should cling on in a caretaker role until a new government can be formed and that everything should be done to spare the Monarch from having to choose it herself. Have we witnessed another subtle but significant shift in the balance of authority? Has the Queen quietly presided over a transfer of power at her own expense? David Cameron thinks not and believes that we should not get carried away. 'Gus O'Donnell and the civil servants have got very excited by the idea of a hung Parliament. They love it. And they're now trying to codify it by writing down what they think ought to have happened.'

Cameron believes that it is one of the great strengths of Britain's unwritten constitution that it can adapt to the unexpected, as it did when Gordon Brown resigned as Prime Minister while the other parties had still not decided whether they could work together. 'The British constitution, with its incredible flexibility and dignity, managed to morph around the problem. There might have been a major debate in other countries but we went ahead without anyone making a fuss.' The reason there was no fuss? There was an honest broker waiting at the Palace.

None the less, the position has changed during the Queen's reign. When she took the throne, she was *expected* to choose her prime ministers, however disagreeable the task. Now, the situation is different. Not only is she *not* expected to choose her prime ministers but it seems that she should only do so as a very last resort. She seems happy with the situation. David Cameron acknowledges that her role as 'kingmaker' has changed since the days when she had to choose Harold Macmillan and Sir Alec Douglas-Home as Conservative prime ministers but he sees that as part of a gradual historical process. 'Her role has been diluted because the Conservative Party now has a way of electing its own leader. If you take a three-hundred-year view, then those sort of powers have become more and more constrained. And that's even more the case now.'

The rest of us regard this sort of regal inertia as normal because it accords with our view of a non-interfering monarchy. But here is another hallmark of this reign. We think that the Queen does not interfere because monarchs are not supposed to interfere. In fact, previous monarchs were quite happy to quarrel with the government of the day and there are signs that a future one might, too. In taking a rigorously non-confrontational stance, the Queen is not the rule. She is the exception.

Edward VII complained to Downing Street when Sir Henry Campbell-Bannerman talked about 'the will of the people' on the grounds that his words had a 'republican' flavour. George V saw communist plots everywhere and would pick fights with his governments over the tiniest details, even reprimanding the Chancellor of the Exchequer, Lord Birkenhead, for wearing a soft hat. George VI was more than happy to voice his criticisms of the Welfare State in front of its creators.

The Queen, by contrast, has been served by a dozen British prime ministers – and more than 150 across all her realms. Yet it is hard to point to a single episode of disagreement on a point of policy. And she certainly hasn't criticised her politicians' fashion sense either, even when one of her prime ministers raised a brazen two fingers to the royal dress code. In 2002, the then New Zealand premier Helen Clark turned up for a state banquet in a trouser suit. The Queen, dressed in ball gown and tiara, merely stared and said nothing.

Her discussions with all her prime ministers, of course, are confidential. But there have been enough nudges, winks and third-hand accounts of these encounters to suggest that any serious dispute would have surfaced. We have no inkling of the Queen's thoughts on two of the issues which have polarised the nation more than most during her reign – the Suez crisis of 1956 and the invasion of Iraq in 2003. That is as it should be. But if we look at a comparable national fault line during the previous reign, such as Neville Chamberlain's policy of appeasement towards Nazi Germany, there was no doubt where royal sympathies lay. Chamberlain's appearance on the Buckingham Palace balcony with the King and Queen made sure of that. So when and how has the Queen expressed *any* enthusiasm or hostility towards a government policy? It has often been suggested that she came to blows with Margaret Thatcher during the eighties, following the Prime Minister's combative positions towards the miners' strike and the Commonwealth. As we shall see, however, even this never came close to the dispute it was said to be at the time. In which case, has she been a soft touch? Hardly. She has just done things differently.

The Queen has certainly been happy to raise objections over matters directly affecting herself. Her decisions to tour Ghana in 1961, Canada in 1964 and Zambia in 1979, in defiance of ministerial concerns about her safety, are cases in point. And when Tony Blair's government proposed abolishing one of the most ancient posts in the land – the Lord Chancellor – ministers were left in no doubt about the Palace's opposition to the idea. The Lord Chancellor was promptly reprieved. But on broader matters, an argument is not her style. Because of the confidentiality between monarch and Prime Minister, there may have been a foot-stomping, plate-throwing row with a premier which will only come to light many years hence. Then again, perhaps not. But the Queen certainly has her distinctive way of expressing disapproval or cajoling politicians into thinking again. It's simple. She just keeps asking for more information. When a Dean of St Paul's Cathedral once asked her what she could do if a Prime Minister made an appointment she didn't like, she replied: 'Nothing constitutionally – but I can always say that I should like more information.' It is a more gentle, some might say feminine, approach. And it has served her well.

A classic illustration is her subtle intervention involving a controversial housing dispute in 2010. The Crown Estate was planning to sell 1,230 homes across London to a private company. The sale would raise £250 million to improve its commercial property portfolio in central London but it was enormously unpopular with the residents who, not unnaturally, feared soaring rents and evictions in the hands of a private developer. Local MPs and councillors from all parties were highly critical of the plan. Sally Bercow, the wife of the Speaker of the House of Commons, wrote an article in the *Guardian* 'imploring' the Queen to stop it. In fact, the Queen had been inundated with letters from residents asking her to do just that. The Queen could not – any more than she could sell the Crown Jewels. While the Crown Estate belongs to her in name, its master is the Treasury, its profits are the Treasury's and for her to start dictating its business strategy would be to risk a constitutional row. But it now turns out that she certainly did not sit idly by. Instead, she asked the Keeper of the Privy Purse, Sir Alan Reid, to contact the Crown Estate and ask its commissioners why they were selling all those homes at that precise moment and what they were planning to do with the money. The Crown Estate replied that it planned to reinvest the money in Regent Street, claiming that it was an ideal time. The Queen was unimpressed. She replied that it could hardly be the ideal time to sell the homes of 1,230 families in the middle of a recession. All summer she deployed the same tactic she had described to that Dean of St Paul's: if in doubt, keep on asking more questions. We do not know the precise flow of corre-spondence thereafter. We do not know the internal discussions at the

Crown Estate. But we do know this: in October 2010, a new deal was suddenly struck whereby the houses were not sold to a private developer for £250 million. Instead, they were sold for £150 million to the Peabody Trust, a well-respected housing association. The controversy melted away. The residents got on with their lives. The chairman of the Crown Estate issued a statement saying: 'Everyone who cares about the future of affordable housing in the capital should warmly welcome this news.' And the politicians patted themselves on the back. No one thought to ask what the Queen had to say on the matter. Why should they? She could not possibly get involved in anything political. Could she?

So what does the Queen think of her prime ministers? We are unlikely to discover her views on her politicians until that future biographer is granted access to her diaries many years from now. Jim Callaghan made another telling observation, however: 'Each [Prime Minister] thinks he is treated in a much more friendly way than the one before, though I am sure that's not true. The Queen is more even-handed.'

Clearly, the Queen will always have a special regard for Sir Winston Churchill. How could she not? He was her first Prime Minister and an immense figure in her family's life. As the Queen Mother wrote to the Queen in 1954: 'What a privilege to have lived in his day – a truly great man.' At his state funeral in 1965, the Queen set the usual rules of precedence aside so that the Churchill family arrived after and left before the Monarch – a small gesture but one of immense significance at such a carefully choreographed event.

As for her other prime ministers, it is hard to venture beyond Sir Godfrey Agnew's assertion that, in the Queen's eyes, they are all much the same. Some clearly sensed that they enjoyed a special rapport with the Monarch. Harold Macmillan was fond of recounting his arrival at Sandringham after a frantic royal Christmas in 1959 and bumping into the old Duke of Gloucester. As Macmillan liked to remember it, the Duke exclaimed: 'Thank Heavens you've come, Prime Minister. The Queen's in a terrible state. There's a fellow called Jones in the billiard room who wants to marry her sister and Prince Philip's in the library wanting to change the family name to Mountbatten.'*

Another Prime Minister who liked to think he enjoyed a particular connection with the Queen was Harold Wilson, her first Labour Prime Minister and a man who went out of his way to protect the royal finances

---

* Princess Margaret duly married Antony Armstrong-Jones (later created the Earl of Snowdon) in May 1960 and the Royal Family's surname (though not that of the dynasty) was changed to Mountbatten-Windsor in the same year.

from would-be reformers. In fairness, Wilson had good reason to perceive that he had a 'special' bond, and not just because he increased the Civil List by almost half in 1975. 'Harold Wilson certainly felt he was rather a favourite,' recalls former Private Secretary Sir William Heseltine. 'Martin Charteris [Private Secretary from 1972 to 1977] once told him that the Queen called him "Harold" and called Harold Macmillan "Uncle Harold". I think he rather enjoyed the idea of being "Harold".' It was Wilson who shielded the monarchy from the left of his own party whenever there was a move to shrivel the finances or take the Queen's head off the stamps. And even at the very end of his prime ministerial career, he managed to do his monarch a favour. He had made the decision privately to resign from the job in 1975. But he sat on the announcement until March 1976, choosing the very same week that Princess Margaret was due to announce her separation from Lord Snowdon. As Prime Minister, he would surely have been consulted on the unhappy decision. The Princess was about to become the first senior member of the Royal Family to divorce since Henry VIII. Yet Wilson's news would certainly serve to deflect much of the media attention away from the Royal Family. 'We had a plan to announce it on the Friday when the Princess's children would be home from school,' recalls the Press Secretary of the day, Ron Allison. 'Then, on the Tuesday of that week, Wilson came in to tell the Queen that he was going to resign later that year.' Did he deliberately do the monarchy a favour? 'Maybe,' says Allison. 'Joe Haines [Wilson's Press Secretary] didn't miss many tricks.'

No one has ever spoken of a 'special' rapport between the Queen and Edward Heath, the Conservative Prime Minister from 1970 to 1974. She granted him exactly the same courtesy and respect as all the others, of course. Outside politics, however, the bachelor MP's only interests were music and sailing, neither of which were high on the Queen's list of small talk. Politically, he favoured new European alliances over old Commonwealth allegiances, which can hardly have pleased the Head of the Commonwealth. He also gave her a piece of advice which she followed – and forever regretted. In the run-up to the 1971 Commonwealth get-together in Singapore, deep divisions had opened up on the issue of South Africa. Heath felt that a bad-tempered summit was no place for the Monarch who might become dragged into an awkward row. 'He [Heath] just thought that this was going to be a very difficult, unpleasant meeting and that it would be better if she stayed away,' says Sir William Heseltine. 'But I know she always regretted it and steadfastly refused to contemplate the possibility of being absent from any later ones.' Once again, one wonders what the Queen's father or son would have done in the same situation.

She would have had a plausible constitutional case to ignore Heath. It is accepted that, at a CHOGM, she answers to none of her sixteen prime ministers but to the Secretary-General of the Commonwealth. In the event, she did as she was told.

Heath clearly believed that he was an open book to his monarch and, by his own standards of brisk inscrutability, he probably was. 'I believed in telling the Queen everything,' he said some time later. 'There was always an agenda drawn up in agreement with the Private Secretary. She had it on a card on the table beside her to make sure that the items were covered but I believed in telling her a good deal else of what was going on.' It doesn't sound like much fun for either party. 'I don't think he enjoyed his audiences at all,' says Ron Allison. 'I don't think he was wise enough to get full benefit from them. There was no small talk apparently. He was a very strange man.' Allison had been a BBC reporter immediately before moving to the Palace and had interviewed the Tory leader a few days before the 1970 election. He had found him in his London flat, alone and conducting a record player. Another former courtier, talking to Ben Pimlott, recalled: 'Ted was tricky. She was never comfortable with him.'

The relationship which has captivated most historians is that between the Queen and Margaret Thatcher, her first woman Prime Minister. It appears to have been one of strong mutual respect on both sides, despite sensational reports that the Queen was dismayed by Mrs Thatcher's position on certain issues. The Queen might have had private doubts about some of Mrs Thatcher's policies just as some of the new Tory free marketers might well have found some of the Palace old guard intolerably plodding and patrician. But senior ex-officials on both sides remain adamant that neither side would have dreamed of briefing against the other. 'I always felt that those stories were exaggerated. The Queen was always rather fascinated by the achievement of Mrs Thatcher in making such an impact upon the world,' says Charles Anson, who also worked for Mrs Thatcher at Number Ten in the early eighties. 'The Queen might be amused or startled by something Mrs Thatcher said but it wouldn't alter her judgement that she was a fantastic force to be reckoned with. And, constitutionally, the Queen just would not make snap judgements about her Prime Minister.' Similarly, Mrs Thatcher was appalled at any suggestions that she had upset the Queen. Not only would her curtsey border on the gymnastic but, to avoid keeping the Queen waiting, Mrs Thatcher would insist on arriving early for her weekly audiences.

If there was any sense of one side leaning on the other, it now turns out that it was the Queen who was actively exerting the pressure on the

Prime Minister. Sir William Heseltine recalls the 1979 Commonwealth summit where the future of the war-torn colony of Rhodesia – soon to become Zimbabwe – was on the table. Lord Carrington, then Foreign Secretary, had devised a plan to persuade the conference that solving the Rhodesia problem should be a matter for Britain and not the Commonwealth. But, first, he needed to persuade Mrs Thatcher to agree to his strategy. 'The Queen helped the Foreign Secretary bring Mrs Thatcher to accept the plan,' Heseltine recalls. 'The Queen was also very successful in smoothing the feathers of the African leaders who were upset by some of Mrs Thatcher's attitudes.'*

And there was no concealing the Queen's anger when President Reagan ordered American forces to invade the independent Caribbean island of Grenada in 1983 without anyone bothering to inform its head of state – the Queen. The Palace vented its fury on Number Ten but Mrs Thatcher's friendship with President Reagan counted for little. Grenada was no longer a British colony but an independent nation. Charles Anson, then a diplomat at the British Embassy in Washington, remembers it well. 'The Americans were not consulting us much in the final stages of the invasion. It all happened very quickly. You even had the Russian navy in the Mediterranean being scrambled because they heard America was attacking "Granada".'

A year or so later, Anson was back in America as the Queen's Press Secretary when there was a very different conversation with Mrs Thatcher.

'Looking at it from the other end, I was with the Queen in Kentucky at the time of the Brighton bombing.† In those early hours, it wasn't clear if the Prime Minister had been injured. And when it was clear she was OK, I remember the Queen being very concerned whether she should immediately go back to Britain.' Mrs Thatcher was having none of it when the two women spoke by telephone soon afterwards. It is said that her first words to the Monarch were: 'Are you having a wonderful time?'

Lord Hurd, a Government Minister through both the Thatcher and Major years, travelled all over the world with both the Queen and Mrs Thatcher. He never detected the slightest animosity on either side, although he says that the Queen was occasionally 'amused' by Mrs Thatcher's unyielding stance on a particular point. During the Thatcher years, the Queen allegedly said of her Prime Minister, in fond mock

---

* Lord Carrington's strategy worked and, following talks at London's Lancaster House, a ceasefire and independence followed. Zimbabwe's subsequent decline into a kleptocratic dictatorship is another story.
† In 1984, an IRA bomb exploded in the Prime Minister's hotel at the Conservative Party conference in Brighton and killed five people.

despair: 'Mrs Thatcher never listens to a *word* I say.' Mrs Thatcher, in return, found some of the royal ways equally baffling, not least the Queen's habit of washing up after Balmoral barbecues with her own bare hands. After one trip to the Highlands, she sent the Monarch a pair of washing-up gloves.

The Queen's dealings with her subsequent prime ministers – all men – appear to have been more straightforward. 'I found the audiences much more comfortable than I imagined,' says Sir John Major. 'The meetings always had a touch of formality, but it becomes a very easy relationship. And, inevitably, the more one exchanges confidences, the more comfortable it becomes. I don't want to give you the impression it's in any sense over-familiar. The Monarch is the Monarch and prime ministers are there as their public duty. But audiences were conducted very informally. They became a very relaxed series of exchanges.'

It was Major who had to help the monarchy through some of the darkest moments of the nineties. He had his own problems, too, not least the economic crisis of 1992. 'I was at Balmoral in the days leading up to Black Wednesday and other economies were in terrible trouble, too,' he remembers. 'I was talking to a European prime minister and it was a rather difficult conversation because there was a piper walking up and down on the lawn outside playing the bagpipes. And the prime minister kept saying "What's that noise? What *is* that noise?"'

As far as Major is concerned, though, some of the happiest moments of his Downing Street years were spent with the Queen, not least the fiftieth anniversary of D-Day on the Normandy beaches. 'When the Queen took the salute at Arromanches, officials tried to put a limit on the number of old soldiers who could be there and they failed absolutely. They were there in their thousands and thousands, all these elderly men who'd been in the war, lucky enough to survive it, proud of what they'd achieved. So long was the march past that we were terribly worried we would be beaten by the tide, but the Queen remained until every last soldier had passed. It was one of the most moving sights I have ever seen in my life. It was just magical. I've never forgotten it.'

The Queen's relationship with Tony Blair is perhaps the one which people feel they know best. That is because it was the subject of the film *The Queen*. The Palace will not confirm whether the Queen has even watched it. Tony Blair insists that he has not, although he fears that some people have taken it all a little too literally: 'Particularly in America, I'm constantly getting people saying to me "I did like you in that movie."'

Of all the Queen's British prime ministers, Blair has also been the most frank in describing the nature (though not the contents) of his meetings with the Monarch in his book *A Journey*. Recalling his first audience following the Princess's funeral, he writes: 'I talked perhaps less sensitively than I should have about the need to learn lessons. I worried afterwards she would think I was lecturing her or being presumptuous and at points during the conversation she assumed a certain hauteur; but in the end she herself said lessons must be learned and I could see her own wisdom at work, reflecting, considering and adjusting.'

The Blair years were undoubtedly challenging ones for the monarchy as the New Labour project took root after eighteen years of Conservative administration. The party's manifesto included some of the most dramatic constitutional reforms since the suffragettes, not least the removal of the hereditary peers from the House of Lords. Blair had made a specific point of including a line in his party's 1997 election manifesto: 'We have no plans to replace the monarchy.' The very fact that the point was made did not go unnoticed inside the Palace. So what was he thinking? 'We had no plans to change it so it didn't occupy a lot of our time,' says Blair, sitting in the offices of his new Tony Blair Faith Foundation in central London. But, looking back, he admits he can see why there might have been worries. 'We were doing a lot of changes. And because we were changing the House of Lords – getting rid of the hereditary peers – there was a worry among some that I was just a cleverer revolutionary. But, actually, I wasn't!' He also believes that part of the royal anxiety was simply down to lack of familiarity. Blair had got to know the Prince of Wales and his team during his time as Leader of the Opposition but the Queen's office at Buckingham Palace was another matter: 'I was a lot closer to Prince Charles than I was to any of the other royals at that time.'

Blair had never voiced any criticisms of the monarchy himself, although some of his Cabinet colleagues and backbenchers certainly had. In some cases, this had involved a spot of youthful rebellion – like the republican cross-Channel awayday to Boulogne to 'avoid' the 1981 Royal Wedding. Among those on board were future Labour luminaries Harriet Harman and Lord Mandelson. Senior figures like Jack Straw had also advocated urgent modernisation of the monarchy from the comfort of the Opposition benches. Once in office, though, they all rather appreciated their trips to the Palace. As Home Secretary, Jack Straw would even appear in morning dress for the swearing-in of bishops ('if there's a dress code,' he explains, 'you should follow it').

For many others on the Labour benches, though, removing a hereditary head of state was a logical aspiration following the removal of the heredi- tary element in the Lords. Palace wariness was heightened by the fact that the Royal Family had been dragged into the election firing line by a tiny issue which, none the less, was a headline-grabber on the campaign trail: the future of the Royal Yacht *Britannia*. The Conservatives had pledged to build a new one. Labour was opposed. Douglas Hurd goes as far as describing the entire saga as the greatest mistake of the Tory government in which he served.

In 1994, John Major's Conservative government announced that it would decommission the forty-one-year-old Yacht when she reached her next major overhaul. Ministers announced that they would retain an open mind on the merits of a replacement but there were few signs of enthusiasm. Given recent controversies over royal finances and domestic troubles, the Queen and the Royal Family remained silent on the matter.

The Yacht issue was definitely one for the government, whatever the family's own private thoughts. Sir John Major remains resolute on this matter: 'During the early nineties, the monarchy went through a very difficult time. Ask yourself this question: in the midst of the recession, with the British people facing economic hardship, how popular would it have been to announce a £50 million spend on a new yacht for the personal use of the Royal Family? How would that have been portrayed by the media? I had not forgotten the storm two years earlier when I announced the rebuilding of Windsor Castle.' He also argues that *Britannia* had been designed for a long-gone era of ocean-going royal tours. Air travel, he says, had rendered her semi-redundant.

There were sound reasons for building a new ship, however. When plans for *Britannia* were first announced in 1951, she was to be designed with a twin role in mind – royal residence and wartime hospital ship. The latter was never a serious option. Without a helipad, *Britannia* could never be a proper hospital ship and her royal status would always make her a target, however prominently a red cross was painted on the sides. Later on, however, she developed a serious peacetime role as a trade promotion platform. On any tour, she would spend more time on commercial than royal duties for the simple reason that it worked. No royal passengers were necessary. If a British trade delegation invited a bunch of Wall Street titans to a business breakfast in a New York conference room, then attendance would be sparse. Who wanted yet another hotel buffet? If the same guests were invited to the same meal in the dining room of the Royal Yacht, then a full turnout could be expected. Similarly, if a British ambassador in the Gulf invited his most senior contacts for a drink aboard the Yacht – and, crucially, included spouses on the invitations – then he was suddenly the most popular diplomat in town.

In 1993, British businesses based in India were informed that *Britannia* would be stopping in Bombay. Any companies with contracts ready for signature were welcome to invite their Indian opposite numbers to attend a signing ceremony on board – and in the Queen's own drawing room to boot. There were no members of the Royal Family within a thousand miles, yet the royal setting was enough. Deals which had been languishing for years suddenly enjoyed a new lease of life. Protracted haggling over the small print miraculously gave way to constructive dialogue. Minor legal squabbles were suddenly resolved. 'The Yacht thrashed about in the Bay of Bombay,' Lord Hurd recalls, 'and millionaires trooped aboard and signed up.' By the end, contracts worth £1.1 billion were signed. 'I went to a similar event with the Prince of Wales in Kuwait to educate the Kuwaitis about privatisation,' Lord Hurd continues. 'They all came on board, had a good luncheon and billed and cooed. It was a very, very valuable appendage.' On one trip, Rear-Admiral Sir Robert Woodard, *Britannia*'s captain, found himself receiving a bearhug from a West Midlands industrialist who had just sold a £1.5 million sausage machine on the back of a *Britannia* reception in the Caribbean.

Such occasions were a powerful antidote to the routine criticisms of the Yacht's £11 million annual running costs.

Sir John Major says that he explored all the commercial arguments. 'All kinds of different options were discussed and examined,' he says. 'As a trade vessel, the Royal Yacht still had quite a cachet. But when you examined it more closely, a good enough case couldn't be made. Would I, personally, have wished to retain her? Of course I would. But one has to be pragmatic about such things and I don't think such a decision would have been very helpful to the monarchy at that particular time. If it had been economically practical to keep her, without the risk of heaping more grief on the Royal Family, we would certainly have wished to do so.'

But the primary purpose of having a Royal Yacht was not an economic one. Nor was it that tired old catch-all excuse of 'security', although *Britannia* was undoubtedly a secure place to berth a monarch abroad. The main arguments for maintaining the Royal Yacht were political and emotional ones. Many people believed that Britain, as a maritime island nation, should have a national flagship, especially one that was recognised around the world. '*Britannia* was brilliant at projecting influence rather than power,' says one of our most senior ex-ambassadors. 'And we are in the influence game.'

Lord Hurd describes his ocean-going tours with the Queen and Prince Philip as the 'most pleasant' moments of his entire career as Foreign Secretary. 'With the Queen on board, it underlined the fact the monarchy was different and not like the Prime Minister,' he says. 'I travelled a lot with Margaret Thatcher and John Major and you were in hotels but it wasn't the same. There was a magic about *Britannia* which had nothing to do with magnificence because she wasn't a magnificent ship. She was a homely ship in the proper sense – and extremely effective – because the Queen was at home.'

Britannia had her enemies, though. Some MPs – mostly Labour but with some Conservatives among them – regarded her as an expensive, embarrassing anachronism. The Chancellor of the Exchequer Norman Lamont could find the £60 million needed for a replacement easily enough but he did not want the special pleading from every other arm of government if he produced it. His Treasury officials, never the most romantic breed, certainly disliked having this anomaly on their books. Within the Ministry of Defence there were top brass from all the Services who resented the special status of the Royal Yacht Service – a one-ship fleet. With much weightier matters on his mind, John Major pushed the whole issue to one side until the 1997 general election was imminent. With less than four months to go, the Defence Secretary, Michael Portillo, suddenly produced a new policy and got it past a weary Cabinet on the cusp of defeat: if re-elected, the Tories would build a new Royal Yacht. But Portillo omitted to follow one important convention regarding royal issues. He did not clear the plan with the Labour Opposition. As a result, Labour campaigners had every right to attack it. And they did. A much-loved royal institution was now a hot political issue. Day after day on the election trail, old-style Labour politicians like John Prescott made a virtue of scrapping what was presented as a millionaire's toy. The fact that *Britannia* had originally been commissioned by a Labour Prime Minister, Clement Attlee, was never mentioned.

As the Duke of Edinburgh observed to Gyles Brandreth some years later: 'Attlee did it properly. He got the Opposition on board.' The Duke was less impressed by the Tory tactics in 1997: 'Major was blocked by Lamont and didn't get the Opposition on board. And then Portillo got involved and made a complete bollocks of it. Absolutely idiotic.'

Lord Hurd accepts some responsibility himself. 'I blame myself somewhat because as Foreign Secretary I ought to have made sure that the Opposition – Blair and Robin Cook and so on – had some experience of *Britannia* and knew what it was about. But they didn't. They weren't asked to things on board. And that was a mistake because they threw away a huge asset for the country as a whole. They didn't have that experience of what the ship could do and why she was unique in the world.'

His contrition is well founded. It now turns out that it might all have been very different after Labour won its landslide victory in May 1997. 'I'll tell you this,' says Tony Blair, lowering his voice, 'I didn't want to get rid of it [*Britannia*]. After we'd agreed to get rid of it, I actually went on it and I remember, as I stepped on, thinking: "That was such a mistake to have done that." And I think it was Prince Charles who was showing me around and I could see him thinking: "Thank you for that."' With a new government buzzing with pent-up reformist energy, Blair did not have the time for this sort of eccentric distraction. Besides, Gordon Brown's Treasury advisers were desperate to kill off the Yacht once and for all. 'I don't put this on Gordon Brown,' he says, 'but the Treasury were saying: "This is just ridiculous" and so forth.' Tellingly, he adds that the Queen never raised the issue with him. Not once.

Politics aside, Prince Philip remains adamant that the Yacht did not need replacing. 'She ought to have had her steam turbines taken out and diesel engines put in,' he told an ITV documentary to mark his ninetieth birthday. 'She was as sound as a bell and she could have gone on for another fifty years.' As it turned out, she lasted just seven months into the new administration.

*Britannia* enjoyed one last world tour to provide Britain and the Prince of Wales with a dignified platform from which to hand Hong Kong back to China. Following her return, the Royal Family gathered in Portsmouth in December 1997 for a decommissioning ceremony. The Queen was not the only one seen to shed tears that day. This was not just a royal mode of transport. It was a home, full of memories of royal childhoods and family memorabilia – Prince Philip's collection of driftwood and all sorts of unusual trinkets and gifts which had no obvious place at Buckingham Palace or Windsor or anywhere else. It was in *Britannia* that the Queen kept a much-loved copper coffee table given to her in Zambia and an original set of G Plan furniture. The ambiance was that of a small country house – lots of understated style and plenty of character. Naval engineers had even designed the royal observation decks so that gusts of wind were vented downwards. That way, there could be no Marilyn Monroe moments with the royal skirts.

Finally, in April 1998, it was announced that *Britannia* would be towed to Scotland to spend the rest of her days as a tourist attraction in the port of Leith. She remains there to this day in the care of a charitable trust.

Perhaps *Britannia*'s innate problem was that she did her best work overseas, beyond the gaze of the taxpayers who paid for her. To this day, the rest of the world remains utterly baffled that the Queen has lost her maritime residence. 'I would like the British government to give her back her ship,' says President Nasheed of the Maldives. 'It's madness to take it away.' He even suggests, only half jokingly, a Commonwealth solution: 'I think we should all chip in!' In Britain, however, *Britannia* was associated with royal holidays – Cowes Week, the Queen's annual Scottish cruise and the occasional royal honeymoon. Perhaps it was a mistake to call her 'The Royal Yacht' in the first place. To many people the word 'yacht' has too many connotations of leisure and pleasure, of gin palaces, gold taps and Mediterranean fleshpots.

Perhaps it was all down to timing. *Britannia* needed either refurbishment or replacement at the very moment that royal fortunes were at a post-war low. Had anyone suggested getting rid of her a few years later, it might not have happened. 'I think if it had happened five years into my time,' Blair admits, 'I would have just said: "No."' In any case, *Britannia* was seen as a symbol of 'Old' Britain. Fresh symbols were required for a new era and a new century.

Two years later, on the last night of 1999, Blair welcomed the Queen to the opening of a bold new statement about 'New' Britain, its values and its place in the world. The Millennium Dome had cost twelve times more than a new Royal Yacht. It lasted a year before the shutters came down and the tumbleweed came rolling through. Years later, it would reopen as a successful concert venue. But it has never sold a single sausage machine.

The early years of the Blair government were some of the most tumultuous of the Queen's reign. Four months in, the new Prime Minister found himself helping the Royal Family through the febrile days which followed the death of Diana, Princess of Wales. As one member of the New Labour administration recalls: 'They'd come a little closer than they really felt comfortable with in having a major crisis. Ultimately, the people would have come back to them but it was a little shocking to them.

'New Labour had not had any reason to demonstrate closeness to the monarchy,' says Mary Francis. 'But this was the moment at which Tony Blair realised he had got to support the monarchy and see it through because it wasn't in anyone's interests to have the whole thing collapsing around his ears.'

A month later, the Queen's state visit to India turned into an embarrassing catalogue of diplomatic slights following injudicious remarks by her new Foreign Secretary, Robin Cook. Accompanying the Queen in Pakistan the previous week, Cook had let slip that he favoured an international solution to the disputed Indian territory of Kashmir. Pakistan was thrilled. India, which wants no such thing, was furious.

As a result, the Queen arrived in New Delhi to be greeted by gratuitous abuse in the Indian media. On the eve of her arrival, the Indian Prime Minister described her as the leader of a 'third-rate nation'. The Band of the Royal Marines, in town to accompany the tour, was suddenly disinvited from a reception for the Queen. The diplomatic atmosphere was disastrous from the off. As the British press laid the blame squarely with Cook, he took the extraordinary step of asking the Queen's Private Secretary, Sir Robert Fellowes, to issue a statement saying that the Queen was 'entirely satisfied with the advice from the Foreign Secretary'.

Since the Queen acts on the advice of her ministers, Fellowes had no choice. As, Kenneth Rose has pointed out, however, this set a dangerous precedent. If the Monarch could be made to speak up for a minister, what was she to say when she was no longer 'entirely satisfied' with him?

Just five months later, there was another cavalier approach to the old constitutional customs. The government decided to endorse a backbench campaign to introduce sex equality to the line of royal succession (Coalition Deputy Prime Minister Nick Clegg would attempt something similar thirteen years later, just before the wedding of the Duke and Duchess of Cambridge). The centuries-old rule that royal brothers should automatically jump ahead of royal sisters seemed about to be overturned following the introduction of a Private Members' Bill in the House of Lords by Lord Archer of Weston-Super-Mare (otherwise known as novelist Jeffrey Archer). The Home Office minister, Lord Williams of Mostyn, told Parliament that the Queen had been consulted and had 'no objection'. Cue uproar on the Conservative benches. The bible of parliamentary procedure, Erskine May, makes it very clear that the Monarch's view shall never be known let alone used to influence any debate. If we know what she thinks about one Bill, so the argument goes, then we might want to know her views on another. A select committee was duly convened to investigate whether a constitutional abuse had occurred. Lord Williams was absolved of wrongdoing on this occasion, but the government accepted that his words should not be taken as a precedent (in other words: 'This won't happen again.'). The Succession To The Crown Bill died a quiet death soon afterwards.

None of this could be described as throne-rocking stuff, but it showed a different mindset at work in government. The monarchy could not expect the old conventions and routines to carry on unchallenged. Sir Malcolm Ross, architect of major royal events for nearly twenty years, clearly remembers the change of mood at one of the first state occasions of the New Labour era. As usual, the Honourable Corps of Gentlemen at Arms, the Monarch's 'closest' bodyguard, were on parade – retired gents in plumed helmets and nineteenth-century uniforms. But the effect was lost on the new Foreign Secretary. As Ross recalls, with some amusement: 'Robin Cook was attending and the bodyguard marched on. Suddenly, the cry came from this very loud voice: "Who are these *extraordinary* old men?"'

(*Previous page, above and left*) Garter Day at Windsor Castle – a celebration of the oldest order of chivalry in Britain. Lunch is always followed by a procession of all the knights and a service at St George's Chapel. It was the Queen's father, George VI, who revived much of this medieval pageantry.

(*Facing page*) The most spectacular approach to Windsor Castle is from the Long Walk, to the south, as President Nicolas Sarkozy of France is discovering.

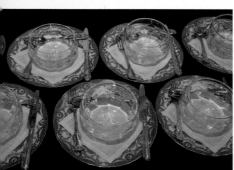

(*Above*) Toasting the President of Mexico; (*left*) finger bowls and Queen Victoria's Minton dessert service awaiting the fruit course; (*below*) words of welcome for the Sarkozys at St George's Hall, Windsor. The table is the longest in Britain.

A souvenir from staff at Aldgate Tube station during a tour of the City of London.

En route to a Palace investiture. The Queen is accompanied by her Lord Chamberlain, Earl Peel.

Familiar faces at the opening of the Falkland Islands Memorial Chapel at Pangbourne.

A Palace reception during the 2009 G20 Summit in London.

Formal and informal
moments for the G20
leaders and their host,
Prime Minister
Gordon Brown.

May 2010. Mr Brown's
successor, David
Cameron, becomes the
Queen's 12th British
Prime Minister. Across
her realms, there have
been more than 150.

(*Above*) The Royal Family's Highland retreat, Balmoral.

(*Below*) End of an era. The Royal Yacht (1953-97), enters Hong Kong harbour ahead of the colony's return to China. It was Britannia's last voyage.

Culture clashes were to be expected. What really concerned the Queen's senior advisers was Labour's programme of constitutional reforms, particularly the creation of a new Scottish Parliament and the proposals to remove the hereditary peers from the House of Lords. It was not the proposals themselves which were the issue. These were all well-debated policies which had been in the election manifesto of an all-conquering political party. The big question for the Queen's officials was how best to keep the monarchy entirely detached from these issues. The obvious hurdle was reform of the Lords. 'I have no idea what the Queen's personal views were about it,' says Mary Francis. 'But the Palace was sufficiently savvy to see that this was going to happen. The vital thing was to make it clear that having a monarchy doesn't rest on having a hereditary aristocracy. We had to de-link the hereditary principle in the Lords from the hereditary principle in the monarchy.' Their task was not helped by royalist commentators in the conservative press insisting that abolishing Earls and Dukes in the Lords was a threat to the monarchy itself.

Were Mary Francis and her colleagues grateful for all this loyal support from papers like the *Daily Telegraph*? 'No,' she says with a laugh. 'We did not want to be defended like that. The view was that a constitutional monarchy works without those bells and whistles and the vital thing was to make sure no one thought anything else.'

Tony Blair had the same concerns. 'There were some people who said: "If you start tampering with the hereditary principles here, it's only a short step,"' he recalls. 'Whereas my view was that it's not a short step. It's a completely different issue.' But he took care to make his views clear to the Queen. 'I used to have this conversation with her. My point was that I'm a classic representative of the modern view: I can't honestly justify my laws being made by people on the basis of [birth]. I can't do it. And, besides, it gives the Conservatives a perpetual majority in one of the Houses of Parliament. On the other hand, the monarchy is a completely different thing.'

The joint Palace/government strategy of 'de-linking' the monarchy from the 'toffs' actually worked rather well and the expulsion of the hereditary half of the Lords was achieved with no collateral damage to the monarchy.* What the Queen really thought, we do not know. Several senior ex-courtiers actually believe that the demise of the hereditaries

---

* The Lords has not lost all its hereditary peers – yet. In a last-minute deal to avoid parliamentary guerrilla warfare, the government agreed to let ninety-two stay on pending further reforms. There has also been a stay of execution for the Queen's two hereditary officials in the Lords, the Earl Marshal (a post held by successive Dukes of Norfolk) and the Lord Great Chamberlain (the Marquess of Cholmondeley). Both roles are ceremonial and neither man plays any part in politics.

from Parliament has been a great boon for the monarchy. Heredity is no longer an open political sore.

For Mary Francis and her colleagues, though, there was another equally precarious debate to avoid. Blair and his ministers were planning to create a new parliament for Scotland and an assembly for Wales. Whatever the end results, the Queen's primary concern was to keep the monarchy out of any rows about national identity. 'People spent a lot of time asking: how does it affect the Queen and her overall role in the country? I wouldn't say they were worried but they certainly wanted to make sure they got it right,' Francis recalls. As the Palace representative on the government working groups for all of this, Francis remained assiduously neutral. 'There was no inclination to challenge any of it,' she says.

While there was plenty of heated public debate over symbols and ceremonial for the new legislature. Who would be in the procession? Would that famous Scottish nationalist Sean Connery be turning up? Yet a thumping great piece of constitutional reform passed by with little public comment. The Queen was, in effect, to be demoted. She might have the constitutional right to hire and fire prime ministers of the United Kingdom but the new First Minister of Scotland would simply be handed to her on a plate by the Presiding Officer (or Speaker) of the Scottish Parliament.

Tony Blair will not go into detail but is clear that he had 'a lot of discussions' not only with the Queen but with her Private Secretary and the Prince of Wales. While the Palace was not challenging the government, this still had to be a consultative process. 'They weren't saying, "We don't agree with you." They were simply reflecting on it. I found that not only proper but also very helpful,' says Blair. 'There was a concern, which I shared, that devolution was one step on the path to independence. For the Queen, it wouldn't be great to be the Queen presiding over the break-up of the United Kingdom. So, I would explain my thinking on this which was that unless you offered this halfway house within the United Kingdom, you really would at some point find a full-blown march to independence. As it turned out, it never really happened and actually I think the financial crisis has probably removed any serious possibility. But I said to people throughout that this is a perfectly legitimate worry.' That worry would certainly become more legitimate, shortly after this discussion, when the Scottish National Party secured an overall majority in the 2011 elections to the Scottish Parliament. The Queen was reported to have sought a special briefing from Prime Minister David Cameron on the subject. Whether an independent Scotland retained the monarchy or not, any unravelling of the United Kingdom would be a seismic constitutional challenge for the Monarch.

Given the party's mandate at the polls, some of Labour's new young bloods felt that it was time to question and, possibly, do away with what they saw as outdated flummery. And the sentiment was not confined to the political elite. Within the Civil Service, there were plenty of radical young bucks who felt that a rare opportunity had come to shake out a lot of dusty tradition. So, when the parliamentary and royal authorities set about planning the State Opening of Parliament after Labour's repeat success in the 2001 election, some of those involved suggested a new form of ceremony. 'Why can't she come in a car?' asked one. Another wondered why the Queen had to deliver the Queen's Speech from her throne in the unelected House of Lords. Could she not address both Houses of Parliament in Westminster Great Hall? Tony Blair is adamant that these suggestions were not coming from his advisers, despite their zeal for modernising so many other facets of national life. 'The irony is it wasn't us. It wasn't the Alastair Campbells of this world at all. They couldn't give two hoots about it. There were people in the Civil Service who were desperate. They suddenly thought: "We've got a Labour government. For God's sake, if you're not prepared to take on all this flummery of the monarchy . . ." My attitude to it, despite what the press kept writing, was absolutely clear. The Queen's Speech is a great event. Why do you want her to turn up on a tandem? It's ridiculous. She's there in the carriage and it gets filmed around the world!' Blair says that he repeatedly had to ward off the meddlers: 'It would usually be some younger guy in the Civil Service talking about this and I would say: "No. I've got more important things to worry about and, in any case, I like it."'

He admits, though, that his own officials went too far in politicising the text of the Queen's Speech, putting incongruous technocratic jargon in the mouth of a monarch well into her seventies: 'The poor Queen was reading out New Labour twaddle. I said: "I've had enough of that. I'm not having that again." It was so embarrassing listening to that "New Labour, New Britain" stuff.'

Even so, the modernising mood rattled some of the Queen's representatives. The Duke of Norfolk, hereditary Earl Marshal and the organiser of state occasions at Westminster, authorised various tweaks to the running order and a minor reduction in the length of the royal procession. Suddenly there was no longer room for a few ancient fixtures like Silver Stick-in-Waiting (a senior officer in the Household Cavalry).

Overall, though, the dynamic between the monarchy and the government during the New Labour years can be seen as cordial and correct with the occasional stumbling block rather than a prolonged period of tension. In that regard, it was no different from the relationship between the Palace and the previous radical reforming administration – that of Mrs Thatcher. And it was by no means all one-way traffic. On one summer's evening in 2003, Tony Blair unveiled a Cabinet reshuffle which left politicians on all sides of both Houses of Parliament open-mouthed. He announced a shake-up of the entire judicial establishment, including the abolition of the post of Lord Chancellor, the head of the legal system. The Lord Chancellor was certainly a very powerful figure. Since he ran the judges, acted as the Speaker of the House of Lords and sat in the Cabinet, he had a foot in three camps – the judicial, the legislative and the executive arms of the state. It was a system which had worked pretty well since the Norman Conquest but New Labour's modernising tendency wanted to tidy it up.

By now, however, the Queen's officials were feeling more assertive. It was six years since the death of Diana, Princess of Wales, and royal confidence had been boosted by the Golden Jubilee of 2002. This was an occasion when the Palace felt entitled to square up to the government. After all, the Queen was entirely within her rights. Quite apart from running the entire judiciary, the Lord Chancellor is one of the five people entitled to decide if a monarch is sane enough to reign or if a regency is required. The Queen meets him (it's never been a her) in many different capacities and he is expected to look the part, too. On just his second day in office as Lord Chancellor, Jack Straw was astonished to receive a visit from the royal robe makers, Ede & Ravenscroft, who wanted to measure him for his Court dress and shoes. He was even more astonished when they suddenly produced a half-finished outfit. 'They had already been on to my tailor to get my measurements!' he says. Crucially, on top of everything else, the Lord Chancellor also holds one of the most colourful titles in the land. He automatically becomes the Keeper of the Royal Conscience. As one of the Queen's advisers puts it: 'The government were going to abolish the Queen's "Conscience". It was a jaw-dropper. No one had consulted her. I just don't think anyone had thought it through.'

Once, the Keeper of the Royal Conscience took on the King's responsibility for 'infants, idiots and lunatics . . . and all charitable uses in the kingdom'. Today, the job involves delicate issues with clergy. In retrospect, it was an extraordinary decision not to consult the Queen – one of her constitutional rights, after all – about the abolition of an ancient office with deep-rooted royal connections. We have yet to learn the precise chain of correspondence and events, but Palace sources are clear that the Queen put her foot down. Six years later, the departing Lord Chancellor of the day, Lord Irvine, gave some indication of what happened in a statement to a House of Lords Select Committee: 'I asked him [Tony Blair] how a decision of this magnitude could be made without prior consultation with me, the judiciary . . . and the Palace. The Prime Minister appeared mystified and said that these changes always had to be carried into effect in a way that precluded such discussion because of the risk of leaks.' Tony Blair remembers it slightly differently. 'Maybe there was more blowback than I realised. Maybe there was that concern,' he says. 'But my point was very very simple. I just kept saying this to everyone. The fact is the Lord Chancellor is also running a department of 10,000 people. I needed him in the department.' In the end, royal concerns prevailed. The shake-up of the judiciary went ahead but the Lord Chancellor was spared the chop. The Queen managed to keep the man who keeps her conscience.

In 2007, Tony Blair relinquished power to his next-door neighbour at Number Eleven. In years gone by, the arrival of Gordon Brown at Number Ten might have presaged some challenging dialogue between Downing Street and the Palace. On paper, Brown was easily the most left-wing Prime Minister of the Queen's reign. His political heroes included Oliver Cromwell and James Maxton, the anti–Establishment cheerleader of 'Red Clydeside' during the inter-war years (Brown wrote his biography). Brown had always made clear his distaste for formal state occasions, avoiding, whenever possible, white-tie state banquets and any setting which might oblige him to wear a kilt. When attendance was unavoidable, he would arrive in a lounge suit, regardless of the dress code. Yet, once in power, his relations with the Palace were very easy. There was still the odd gesture which smacked of gratuitous modernisation and rattled some of those at the Palace, not least the decision to drop the Royal Arms as the symbol of Britain's new Supreme Court. It opened in 2009 with a newly commissioned floral logo instead. By now, though, New Labour had largely sated its appetite for constitutional reform and Brown had a more pressing issue on his mind for most of his time in office – global economic turmoil. As Prime Minister, he dutifully turned out for all the appropriate events and was happy to wear full evening dress for the Queen (although he still managed to dodge the kilt). He had, in fact, forged an unlikely alliance with the Duke of Edinburgh as a young man. In 1972, the students of Edinburgh University elected Brown as their Rector (the chairman of the university court of management). Traditionally, this was a largely honorary post for a celebrity or eminent Scot. Brown was not only the first student to be elected to the post but also the youngest Rector in history. Senior staff were dismayed. Not so the Chancellor of Edinburgh

University, the Duke of Edinburgh. 'Of course, none of the academics or professional people who sat on the court wanted me to chair the university governing body,' Brown recalled in 2008. 'The one person who gave me enormous encouragement and support and recognised that the students wanted to have someone there to represent their interests was the Duke of Edinburgh himself.'

Brown had also got to know the Queen during his decade as Chancellor of the Exchequer and had come to appreciate his occasional audiences at the Palace. No Prime Minister has had the word 'dour' applied to him more often, yet Brown found plenty of levity in his chats with the Monarch. During his days as Chancellor, he remarked: 'One of the things people don't realise is she's got a tremendous sense of humour – something that people who don't know the Queen should appreciate. She'll be talking about things that make both her and me laugh. And her questions are designed to get the best out of you.'

However, there was one issue about which the Queen was, apparently, too diplomatic to ask questions: those Civil List arrangements which were due to end in the summer of 2010. As with *Britannia*, it was too close to home. And Brown was in no hurry to provide any answers. But the bald truth was that if nothing happened soon, the monarchy would run out of money. The Palace accountants and Treasury officials had been in constructive talks for months about the idea of financing the entire institution using a percentage of Crown Estate profits. But, whatever the solution, it would have to be approved by Parliament in what would, inevitably, be a heated political and media debate. In the end, Brown decided that it could wait until after the 2010 election and shelved all discussion of the subject. As things turned out, it would become a decision for someone else.

David Cameron, the Queen's twelfth Prime Minister, is the first to be related to her, albeit at a considerable distance. As the great-great-great-great-great-grandson of William IV via an extra-marital affair, he is the Queen's fifth cousin twice removed, a fact he was not actually aware of until he became Conservative leader and the genealogists promptly went digging deep into the heraldic mines. He saw her now and then in his youth, not as a very distant relative but as a prep school contemporary of Prince Edward. The Queen might have thought she had said farewell to her last Old Etonian Prime Minister nearly half a century earlier when Sir Alec Douglas-Home was defeated in 1964. Like every new arrival, though, Cameron was impressed by her intuition and her grasp of events, from the global to the parochial. 'She's always in touch, extremely sharp,' he says. 'She's always seen the latest ambassador who's just arrived or one of ours who's just left.'

However perplexing any political dilemma may seem to him, he is mindful of the wealth of experience sitting in the chair opposite him. 'In the great scheme of things, you are conscious that you are her twelfth Prime Minister,' he admits.

Within weeks of Cameron's appointment, Brown's unfinished business with the royal finances came to the surface. The ten-year deadline on the Civil List was due to expire just weeks after the election. Cameron and his Chancellor, George Osborne, were in no mood to duck the issue. They liked the plan to use a share of Crown Estate profits but were also about to announce the greatest public sector cuts in a generation. So they decided to maintain the existing Civil List funding arrangements until after the Diamond Jubilee while details of the new Sovereign Grant were thrashed out. Cameron regards it as an important long-term decision for the monarchy. 'There's a real opportunity to have a proper reform,' he says. It will always remain a sensitive political issue. Royal finances, however they are structured, are destined to be one of life's guaranteed headline-grabbers.

However, with a big royal wedding followed by a jubilee falling into his lap in his first couple of years in charge, Cameron's early royal encounters have been much happier than those of John Major and Tony Blair. His Coalition partner, Liberal Democrat leader Nick Clegg, made a brief foray into royal territory with his call for the laws of succession to be amended, just like Lord Williams of Mostyn thirteen years before. Clegg's argument for a Swedish-style system whereby the eldest child of the Sovereign succeeds to the throne, regardless of gender, attracted widespread support as it always does in any opinion poll. The monarchy has thrived under its queens – notably Victoria and both Elizabeths – and male primogeniture has few defenders. But any change to the rules of succession would not only involve the assent of every parliament in all sixteen of the Queen's realms; it would also open up a separate debate about the Act of Settlement, the legislation which excludes Roman Catholics or anyone married to a Roman Catholic from the line of succession. While it is blatantly discriminatory and offensive to some Catholics, it is also bound up with several other laws fundamental to Britain's constitutional settlement, including the very Acts of Union on which the United Kingdom is founded. To unravel one Act could expose all the others to adjustments by politicians less well disposed to the institution of monarchy. Successive Prime Ministers would dodge the issue until 2011 when David Cameron held a meeting with his counterparts from all the Queen's realms and agreed to take the first steps towards constitutional reform.

\* \* \*

In all her dealings with all her prime ministers, the Queen has been advised by the most important figure in the Royal Household, her Private Secretary. He may be outranked by the Lord Chamberlain. He may not enjoy the intimacy of a Lady-in-Waiting. But his office is the Monarch's link with the outside world. He is the gatekeeper, the filter, the timekeeper, the lookout and the first port of call for any advice. He must be both proactive and reactive. Far better to pre-empt a crisis than be landed with one. And he must think globally. He is the Private Secretary to the Queen of sixteen countries. If the Prime Minister of Belize or Australia needs an urgent chat with the head of state, then it all goes through the Private Secretary. Hence, he is actually one of three people at any given time – the Private Secretary, the Deputy Private Secretary and the Assistant Private Secretary. Whoever is in attendance at the time will be referred to as *the* Private Secretary. Royal titles were never designed to be straightforward. So he has sometimes been she, although no woman has ever held the top position in the Private Secretary's Office. 'The essence of the Private Secretary's task,' writes Professor Vernon Bogdanor, 'is to ensure that the machinery of constitutional monarchy works effectively.' David Cameron (who was taught by Bogdanor at Oxford) explains that his Permanent Secretary will have a chat with the Queen's Private Secretary before the Prime Minister's weekly audience. 'They put together an agenda and say, "You ought to cover these things" and that's what the Queen always has on a piece of paper next to her. But we'll stray into other stuff as well,' says Cameron. 'Then I tend to go and talk to her Private Secretary afterwards and we have a glass of wine in his office. If there are things we've agreed, I give him a good read-out.'

Not all prime ministers have taken such a collegiate view. Jim Callaghan was one of the most scrupulous observers of the code of confidentiality. When he emerged from his first audience to find the Queen's wily old Private Secretary Martin Charteris offering a whisky and a chat, he declined both on the grounds that he didn't drink and couldn't possibly discuss the meeting with anyone, not even the Queen's own Private Secretary.

Tony Blair, however, was always grateful for this sagacious go-between. 'One of the great advantages of the system is that before you go and see the Queen, or occasionally afterwards, you will sit with the Private Secretary for half an hour,' he recalls. 'It was Robin Janvrin for most of my time and he was very, very good with me and I got to know him quite well. The great advantage was that the private secretaries would sensitise you, they would say things maybe the Queen wouldn't quite want to say in that way. So I remember having discussions with Robin about the Lord Chancellor position where I was explaining it and I think he basically understood it. That allowed him to go back into his world and say: "Look, there is a reason for this . . ."'

As the political historian Professor Harold Laski once explained, the Private Secretary 'must know all . . . must be ready to advise upon all. Receiving a thousand secrets, he must discriminate between what may emerge and what shall remain obscure.' It is the Private Secretary who must deflect any blows aimed at the Sovereign, if necessary by absorbing them himself. If an engagement goes wrong or someone feels that their worthy cause has been neglected by the Royal Family, the Private Secretary will take the hit. After the Queen omitted an important reference to the Holocaust from her 1996 speech to the Polish parliament, her Private Secretary, Sir Robert Fellowes, threw his hands up when confronted by a baffled press corps. 'Blame me,' he declared. 'Just say it was all my fault.' (The computer printer had contained the wrong sort of paper, the key paragraph had fallen off the page and no one had spotted it.)

Another important defensive task for the Private Secretary is to protect the Monarch from those close to her. Mary Francis can think of a few examples: 'There were always people around who would make the Private Secretary's Office quite cross, trying to get to the Queen to bend her ear about something and probably not understanding that there was very little she could do about it.' The popular stereotype of the Private Secretary is of an over-cautious, over-protective, rather stuffy minder, forever second-guessing the whims of the Monarch. Such a candidate would not last very long. Charm, intuition, humour and an open mind are crucial. A little eccentricity is not unknown. A man like Sir Frederick Ponsonby, Assistant Private Secretary during three reigns and George V's Treasurer, might have refused to speak to anyone with shiny buttons or suede shoes, but he also turned his hand to writing film scripts and hatched a madcap scheme to recover King John's treasure from the Wash. Several of the Queen's crop of private secretaries (eight so far) have possessed hidden talents – for painting, sculpting and dry stone walling among others. As Kenneth Rose has pointed out, the art of a good courtier is to be alert to the very major and very minor issue at the same time. Thus, on the eve of the Battle of Passchendaele in 1917, George V's Assistant Private Secretary, Sir Clive Wigram, found himself resolving the pressing issue of whether lady munitions workers should shake the Queen's hand during a factory visit. Sir Arthur Bigge, later Lord Stamfordham, was one of the greatest royal advisers of modern times. While he could be the most ferocious nit-picker, he also supervised the transformation of the Saxe-Coburg-Gothas into the House of Windsor. 'He taught me how to be a King,' said George V.

Sir Michael Adeane, the Queen's longest serving Private Secretary, summed up the twin imperatives of the job: 'It is no use thinking you are a mandarin. You are also a nanny. One moment you may be writing to the Prime Minister. The next, you are carrying a small boy's mac.' The Queen inherited her first Private Secretary, Sir Alan ('Tommy') Lascelles, from her father. Outwardly brisk and fearless (he had won the Military Cross), he was also a fiercely intelligent man. His hatred of self-importance extended to denying a peerage for himself. 'He was a terrifying man if you met him in a corridor,' recalls a junior member of staff from that era. 'That glare – and those beetling eyebrows. I think he was the scariest of the lot.' Lascelles was also determined to obstruct any attempts by the Duke of Edinburgh to encroach on his patch. While this spurred the Duke on to create his own dynamic role in public life, it would also leave him with a long-standing wariness of the Private Secretary's Office.

Lascelles departed soon after the Coronation, to be replaced by his deputy, Sir Michael Adeane – himself a grandson of Lord Stamfordham. If there was a degree of nepotism at work, it was no substitute for ability. Other Royal Household positions – the Master of the Horse, for example – might depend on connections. The Private Secretary, though, had to earn his keep. Adeane had a first-class History degree from Cambridge and (for all their 'tweediness') had assembled an equally cerebral team around him. Outwardly, Adeane appeared a model of courtierly under-statement. On being accosted by Prince Philip's biographer Basil Boothroyd one morning, he listened politely for a minute or two, before saying: 'I do hope you'll forgive me but I've just heard that my house is on fire. I wouldn't mind but as it's a part of St James's Palace . . .' He was a nimble political tactician, assisting the monarchy through some delicate territory, not least the choice of two prime ministers in the days when the Queen was expected to select them. He also defended the monarchy from what, at the time, represented the gravest threat since the Abdication. The 1971 House of Commons Select Committee on the royal finances was the one which argued that the Queen should become a salaried public official, that the Queen Mother should be pegged to a Prime Minister's pension and that the Duchy of Cornwall should be nationalised. Following Adeane's interventions, the monarchy emerged with none of the above and a doubling of the Civil List.

His nineteen-year tenure would come back to haunt his successors some years later when one of the great Palace scandals of the reign came to light. In 1979, the Prime Minister, Margaret Thatcher, informed the Commons that the former Surveyor of the Queen's Pictures, Sir Anthony

Blunt, had been a Russian spy. Adeane, it transpired, was informed of Blunt's treachery in 1964 and had brokered a deal with the Home Secretary. If Blunt divulged his spy contacts to the intelligence services, he would be allowed to stay in post until retirement and the government would be spared another spy scandal. It seems inconceivable that the Queen was unaware of the arrangement In the finest traditions of the office, it was the Private Secretary's Office which took the criticism.

Next came Sir Martin (later Lord) Charteris, a brilliant, innovative and impish figure who was happy to admit that he had been rather in love with the Queen from the moment he met her in 1950. A prolific snuff-taker, he would have to be brushed down by a footman several times a day, particularly ahead of his daily meeting with the Queen. But behind the eccentric veneer lay an arch-moderniser. On his watch, television was embraced as a tool and was no longer regarded as a hazard. The monarchy was seen as less aloof, more accessible. 'Conscious decisions were taken that things needed to change,' recalls Ron Allison, the Queen's Press Secretary at the time. 'Key to this, and never to be underestimated, was Martin Charteris, the wisest man I ever met.' Charteris's finest hour was the Silver Jubilee of 1977. His successor, Sir Philip (later Lord) Moore, was a more reserved figure but one of life's all-rounders – shot down during the war, he was an Oxford exhibitioner, England rugby international and high-flying diplomat before joining the Royal Household. He was also the last Private Secretary of the wartime generation. He died in 2009, moments after sitting bolt upright in bed and declaring: 'Come on, Moore, pull yourself together.' Old-school to the last.

What might be called the new generation of private secretaries started with Sir William 'Bill' Heseltine, a rising star in the Australian Civil Service who served as Press Secretary before joining the Private Secretary's Office. He was closely involved in the appointment of Lord Airlie, the Lord Chamberlain who would usher in the most radical internal reforms for a century. He had to keep the Palace in step with Downing Street during the Thatcher years but was equally solicitous of the Opposition. One of Mrs Thatcher's last acts as Prime Minister was to reach that Civil List deal which would endure for the next twenty years. But, as the *Britannia* saga would prove years later, big-ticket royal items must have cross-party support. And the Labour Party was enjoying something of a revival under Neil Kinnock. 'I did something fairly novel,' says Heseltine, now retired and living in Western Australia. 'I'd only met Kinnock at a few functions. And when he became Leader of the Opposition, I said: "Would you like to come and have dinner with me one night?" And he said: "Can I bring Glenys?" I said: "Of course." And we had a rather jolly little dinner at home – just his wife and myself and my wife – and we established a workable relationship.' That relationship certainly helped when the time came for Heseltine and Lord Airlie to visit Kinnock to explain the Civil List proposals. 'He was very good about it, too,' says Heseltine. 'He asked one or two pertinent questions, because, like Harold [Wilson], he had his discontented people on the left who would make a bit of a fuss about it. But he was very supportive.'

Heseltine departed just before the calamitous downturn in royal fortunes which would become known as the *annus horribilis*. That would turn into what one of today's senior courtiers describes as a *decadus horribilis*. As the Queen led the monarchy through what were undoubtedly the worst years of her reign, her chief adviser was Sir Robert Fellowes. An unflappable optimist, his default mode was cheerful pragmatism. He had also known the Queen since childhood, having grown up at Sandringham where his father ran the estate. All of this would prove indispensable during the crises which started with the derailing of the Duchess of York in 1992 and reached a nadir with the death of Diana, Princess of Wales five years later. As a cousin of the former and brother-in-law of the latter, Fellowes was often in a difficult position but, equally, he was well placed to offer frank advice all round. This might often be garnished with a sporting metaphor. 'We were on the seventeenth green,' he would remark when anyone suggested that the Queen had been forced in to paying tax. Having seen the institution through the worst of the storms, he was succeeded by his deputy, Sir Robin Janvrin. A former Royal Navy officer and diplomat, he had already been introducing a new, more professional approach in the wake of the Airlie reforms. More women rose to senior executive positions across the Royal Household. Senior professionals were seconded from industry and Whitehall. As the death of the Queen Mother and the Golden Jubilee drew a clear line under the recent past, royal confidence returned. As one official puts it: 'Up until then, it felt like a reign of two halves – Act One: good, Act Two: bad. Then, suddenly, we were into Act Three.'

Act Three has now outlasted the dismal years. A brilliant royal wedding has served as a prelude to an historic milestone seen just once in history, more than a century back. As the Diamond Jubilee raises the Queen even higher in the pantheon of great monarchs, her senior staff have gladly receded into virtual obscurity. Today's Private Secretary, Sir Christopher Geidt, is very happy to be the most low-profile incumbent of the reign, seldom photographed, never quoted. A former diplomat and Balkans expert, he has quietly finessed a tri-generational approach to the business of monarchy while altering the Queen's own schedule to one more suited to the oldest monarch in history. It has been done so imperceptibly that her workload actually *rose* during 2010 – 444 engagements, 69 more than the year before.

'It's not about cutting back. It's about managing her time more effect-ively,' explains an official. 'So, yes, she needs to meet the new ambassador for Belarus. But how long does she really need one-on-one with him?' The Duke of York suggests that it could also be a case of curtailing some of the travelling: 'There's no getting around the fact that she's got to go to the CHOGM [the Commonwealth Heads of Government Meeting]. You can get her there in comfort but the issue is the time zone.' Sitting in his airy Buckingham Palace office overlooking the Mall, the breeze flapping the net curtains over the open window and wafting in the sound of a brass band, the Duke adds that more and more future engagements are likely to be scheduled for home: 'I think you'll probably find that there is more going on here because it's easier for the Queen to do it here than having to travel miles and miles all over the world. It's a sensible way of doing it.' Just as the soup course has been quietly excised from the modern state banquet to shave twenty minutes off the evening, so every moment of the royal day is being constantly audited for savings. Under Geidt, the Palace has a created a new research unit, called the Secretariat, which is routinely charged with exploring new ways of doing the same old thing. Yet nothing has changed at all in terms of the most important constitutional duty of every monarch – her discussions with her Prime Minister. The Queen began her reign advising, warning and consulting a Prime Minister who received his army commission from Queen Victoria. Today, she deals with a man who was two years below her youngest son at prep school.

# 6

## Her Image

*'One doesn't want to look like everybody else.'*

It was perhaps the most extraordinary piece of royal film ever shot – a genuine, gale-force royal domestic right in front of the camera. The Queen was not merely cross. She was losing it, hurling shoes and threats and sporting equipment and venting the sort of regal fury that, in another age, would have cost someone their head. The object of all this fury was the Duke of Edinburgh who, in the circumstances, made the sensible but uncharacteristic decision to run away. Little wonder this jaw-dropping scene has never seen the light of day. More surprising, perhaps, is the fact that, to this day, few people even know about this bizarre royal bust-up. For that, the Queen can thank both an obliging Australian camera crew and one of the most gloriously curmudgeonly characters to serve in the Royal Household in her entire sixty-year reign. But Commander Richard Colville DSC, Press Secretary to both George VI and the Queen, certainly earned his keep that day on 6 March 1954. By then, the Queen was halfway through her eight-week tour of Australia. That, in turn, was just part of a six-month post-Coronation round-the-world voyage, the greatest royal tour in modern history. But, inevitably, on a journey of this scale, there were tensions along the way and they surfaced as the young royal couple enjoyed a weekend's break from the introduction lines and the near-hysterical crowds which had characterised the tour.

They had come to stay on the shores of the O'Shannassy Reservoir in Victoria where the Metropolitan Board of Works had placed an executive chalet at their disposal. The lake had been freshly stocked with fish. The authorities had shipped in extra supplies of koala bears in case the resident population should prove reclusive. The Queen and Prince Philip had just two engagements over the weekend – a trip to church and a brief session with a camera crew which was in the course of filming Australia's first full-length colour feature film, *The Queen in Australia* (it would play to packed cinemas for months after her departure). On this particular Sunday afternoon, the Queen was due to be filmed looking at some kangaroos and as many koalas as could be found. Senior cameraman

Loch Townsend had already arrived with his deputy, Frank Bagnall, and a sound recordist. They were starting to look at their watches. The afternoon light was fading. 'Christ, when are they bloody well coming?' muttered Townsend, at which point the door of the chalet flew open. Bagnall followed his professional instincts and turned on his camera. But what happened next was not in the script. Out dashed Prince Philip, with a pair of tennis shoes and a tennis racquet flying after him. Next came the Queen herself, shouting at the Prince to stop running and ordering him back. And still the camera kept on turning. Eventually, as Townsend later recalled, the Queen 'dragged' her husband back into the chalet and the door was slammed.

If the camera crew were wondering what to do next, they did not have long to wait. Angrier than a wounded buffalo, Commander Colville suddenly charged into view. Here was a man who thought it such a grave affront to royal privacy to film the Queen being driven through the gates of Balmoral that he had banned the BBC from doing so. On this occasion, he was Vesuvius in human form. Loch Townsend was a brave filmmaker who had been in action with his camera during the Second World War, but he was not about to enter mortal combat with the man British journalists knew as 'The Abominable "No" Man' – or, simply, 'Sunshine'. Townsend, by his own admission, surrendered on the spot: 'I said: "Calm down." I went up to Frank and I started unscrewing the back magazine and he said: "What are you doing?" I said: "Exposing the film, Frank. You may have finished using your balls but I've still got work for mine." I'll never forget saying that. And anyway, I unscrewed it. There was about three hundred feet of film . . . and I said: "Commander, I have a present for you. You might like to give it to Her Majesty."' Colville disappeared with the film and, soon afterwards, a member of staff emerged with beer and sandwiches for the crew. It was not long before the Queen reappeared herself, calm, serene – and very grateful. 'I said who I was and introduced Don and Frank,' Townsend recalled. 'And she said: "Oh thank you very much. I'm sorry for that little interlude but, as you know, it happens in every marriage. Now, what would you like me to do?"'

Townsend is no longer alive. He described this episode in detail to a resourceful historian writing a doctoral thesis called *The Glittering Thread* for Sydney's University of Technology in 1996. Though never published, it remains an extraordinary record of the mayhem of the 1954 tour. Its author, Dr Jane Connors, who went on to become a senior executive in Australian national radio, interviewed Townsend twice about his experience. We shall never know the real background to the row, but what comes through loud and clear is the dynamic between the monarchy and the media at the start of the reign. This was a tour during which a government delegation arrived at the Australian *Daily Mirror* demanding the surrender of a photograph of the Duke of Edinburgh with a drink in his hand. Yet within ten years, the Queen would be lampooned on British national television; within fifteen, she would have allowed cameras to film a family barbecue. Forty years after Loch Townsend was surrendering his film on pain of arrest, the heir to the throne would be screened around the world discussing the breakdown of his marriage. A year later, Diana, Princess of Wales, would be doing the same. By 2010, the Queen would be admitting television cameras to film *Masterchef* in the Palace kitchens and *Time Team* in the Palace gardens while the engagement of her eldest granddaughter would command the following headline in the *Yorkshire Post*: 'QUEEN'S GRANDDAUGHTER TO WED EX-FISH AND CHIP FRYER FROM OTLEY'.

For all her instinctive conservatism, this sovereign has steered the monarchy through more transition than any in modern times. And nowhere has that change been more dramatic or more painful than in the monarchy's dealings with the press. At the start of the reign, the media was an occupational hazard which had to be endured, much like rain at Royal Ascot. At the dawn of the Diamond Jubilee, it is regarded as a necessary tool for the business of reigning. On the basis of 'if you can't beat 'em, join 'em', the monarchy now produces online films about itself.

The Queen and her family certainly do not read all the media, nor do they watch it all, believe it all or believe that others believe it all. However, it is hard to dispute the theory propounded by Sir Antony Jay, architect of the modern royal job description, and Sir Bernard Ingham, former Press Secretary to Margaret Thatcher, who have both likened the modern media to an impressionist painting. If you study it up close, it is unreal and distorted. If you stand back and absorb it as a whole, it offers a vivid representation of reality. A senior member of the Household offers a good example. The Crown Estate recently bought a commercial estate in Slough, including a fast-food restaurant. The following day, a national newspaper carried an image of the Queen wearing an imaginary McDonald's hat and flipping burgers. Nonsense, of course. But not *utter* nonsense . . .

Today, very little happens at Buckingham Palace without the close involvement of the Press Office. It's a small operation given the amount of coverage generated by the head of state of sixteen countries and her family. The Queen employs ten people to handle media arrangements for herself and the wider Royal Family – a similar operation to, say, the press office for the Rural Payments Agency. Another nine people work at

Clarence House and St James's Palace dealing with the Prince of Wales, the Duchess of Cornwall, the Duke and Duchess of Cambridge and Prince Harry. The entire operation is the same size as that of the press office for the Big Lottery Fund – or roughly half that of the Health and Safety Executive. Mostly in their thirties, the royal team include a former zoologist, a former spokesman for Manchester United, an ex-journalist or two and former press officers from the public and private sectors. The Queen's three most recent press secretaries have all been women and were previously Civil Service high-fliers all previously worked in government. Both the new incumbent, Ailsa Anderson, and her predecessor, Samantha Cohen, were originally journalists. But unlike most of the public relations industry – whether in politics or in the commercial sector – they inhabit a unique space in which it is almost impossible to use the conventional tools of the trade. They cannot counter a criticism by pointing up a deficiency in a rival because there are no rivals. Spin and the darker arts of the publicist's trade are out of the question. They are routinely challenged on what their clients regard as 'private' matters – by news organisations which view those clients as public property. Yet, compared to the Queen, there isn't a PR client on the planet who has remained so durable for so long. Brand awareness is never an issue.

Most people have an entrenched view of most members of the Royal Family, for better or worse, because they have been aware of them for so long. Much of the job is on a loop. The engagements are often the same, year in year out (the only thing which varies at the annual gathering of the Knights of the Garter, for example, is the seating plan for lunch – arranged so that no one sits next to the same person more than once a decade). But familiarity must not be allowed to breed contempt. After the nonchalance of the sunlit eighties led on to the hellish media storms of the nineties, there is now a fear bordering on paranoia about complacency. And it is certainly easy to be complacent. Since commissioning a private MORI poll in 1999, Palace officials have tracked British public opinion on the fundamental issue of a monarchy versus an alternative constitutional settlement. The figures have barely budged in more than a decade, aside from a minor increase in support during 2002, the year in which the Queen lost her sister and then her mother shortly before the Golden Jubilee. Through good and bad spells, the overall figure remains stubbornly at 70 per cent in favour, 20 per cent against and 10 per cent unsure. MORI has even tried substituting the word 'monarchy' for 'Royal Family' to see if the institution commands more or less support than its representatives. But it has made no discernible difference to the answers.

What the pollsters have determined, however, is that the monarchy's 'key driver' (marketing speak for vital ingredient) is 'relevance'. It is when people feel that the institution is not relevant to them, that it does not engage with them, that support drops away. And that is why the Master of the Household, Air Vice-Marshal Sir David Walker, and his team of chefs, footmen and doorkeepers are preparing to welcome 350 guests from the clothing industry to Buckingham Palace. The Queen is hosting one of her twice-yearly receptions for a particular strand of national life. On this occasion, it is the turn of the rag trade in all its forms – from haute couture to the Sweaty Betty fitness label to J&M Sewing Service, a Tyneside manufacturer of church garments. The idea is to 'showcase' excellence at every level. A team drawn from the Private Secretary's Office, the Master's Department and the Press Office have spent months consulting trade bodies, industry pressure groups, industry charities and government departments to ensure an even spread of guests from all over the country. Also here will be both the mainstream and the fashion media. Events like this, if not designed for television, are increasingly organised with the media in mind. BBC News 24 has been broadcasting from inside the Palace all day and will cover the event live. As a former communications director for the RAF, Walker understands the importance of media coverage at every level: 'You don't want to do these things and not get noticed. It's not a case of "Haven't we done well?" but of making an impact. The fact we've held a reception is then picked up by people far and wide who weren't able to come but say: "At least the Queen has recognised what I do."'

While Walker's team have been sorting out the logistics – invitations, champagne, name badges, etc. – the Queen's Press Secretary and her team have been combing the guest list for interesting case studies to pass on to the press. Sandra Hunt runs Clothing Solutions, a shoestring charity based in an old Yorkshire cotton mill where her team adapt modern clothes for disabled customers. It was an emotional moment when the thick white card arrived with security instructions. 'When I got the invitation I read it three times and then rang the Palace to check it was real,' says Hunt. Her two children were so excited that they have insisted on travelling down with her and spending the night in her hotel. The *Bradford Telegraph & Argus* has already carried a lengthy article about the plucky local charity organiser heading for the Queen's party. The Palace takes the regional press very seriously. If the Queen spends a day in, say, Bedfordshire, it is unlikely to be covered in the national press. In the Bedfordshire press, there is unlikely to be any other story.

Given the professional rivalries between all the designers in the Palace state apartments tonight, it is just as well that the Queen has decided to wear an in-house design made by her dresser, Angela Kelly. At the start, there is a reception line so that the Queen and the Duke of Edinburgh ensure that they have met everyone. She knows quite a few of the guests already. The Duke receives a running commentary. 'He does my hats,' the Queen explains as one of her milliners, Philip Somerville, is introduced. Her eyes light up as Marie O'Regan is announced. 'She used to make my hats,' says the Queen. 'She's retired.' Along comes Stewart Parvin, one of the current crop of royal dressmakers. 'Another one of my designers . . .' the Queen announces. The Duke is particularly struck by Steve Cochrane, a Middlesbrough fashion retailer, who is still wearing his coat, a nylon mac. 'Are you expecting it to rain in here?' asks the Duke. Cochrane roars with laughter and explains it's from one of his own ranges. It is an odd choice of clothing for a reception at the Palace, perhaps, but no stranger than some other outfits. Nabil El-Nayal, twenty-four, has been invited because he is an award-winning student at the Royal College of Art. He is dressed in a black and white highwayman's outfit which he describes as his 'ethereal Elizabeth the First' look. 'I only wear black and white,' he says later. 'I think there is too much colour in the world.'

The last person in the greeting line is in jeans, a hoodie and a crumpled tweed jacket. It is the photographer David Bailey. The Queen does not bat an eyelid, welcomes him to the party and moves through to mingle with her guests. 'I don't know what I'm doing here,' Bailey tells a couple of reporters. 'I'm not much of a royalist and I haven't taken a fashion photograph since 1980. So I'm here under false pretences.' He says he has been to the Palace before, not to take photographs – 'I'm too risky' – but to receive a CBE from Prince Charles. 'I said to him: "I want to get something straight, Prince Charles. I'm not joining. I'm infiltrating."' He laughed a lot.'

For all the studied indifference, Bailey is thoroughly enjoying himself. And it all makes good copy for the journalists. So, too, does the presence of Elizabeth Emanuel, best known as co-designer of Lady Diana Spencer's wedding dress in 1981. Even for a former Palace pro, a night like this has been nerve-wracking. 'I spent all week making something for tonight and then decided an hour before that I wasn't going to wear any of it,' says Emanuel. She has gone instead for a favourite black and duck-egg blue jacket and a black dress. The photographers are busy tonight. Many of the guests are used to the camera, including models Sophie Dahl and Yasmin Le Bon. Both describe themselves as 'massive' fans of the Queen. 'I love her style. She's timeless,' says Dahl. 'She wears her outfits, her outfits don't wear her,' says Le Bon. 'She's comfortable in what she does and she does it in such an elegant way.' Some guests go even further. 'You know the Queen doesn't even have a style,' declares the Spanish-born, London-based shoe designer Manolo Blahnik. 'She is just *her*. She is perfect.'

Many guests are from old family businesses with royal warrants – including Margaret Barbour of Barbour jackets and Douglas and Deirdre Anderson of the fifth-generation royal kiltmakers, Kinloch Anderson. It's usually Douglas's brother who gets the big invitations (Sir Eric Anderson, now a Knight of the Thistle, has the distinction of having taught the Prince of Wales at Gordonstoun, Tony Blair at Fettes and David Cameron at Eton). But tonight it is Douglas and Deirdre who find themselves chatting to the Queen about Deirdre's new national register of tartans, for which she has been awarded the OBE. Needless to say they are both in kilts. 'Are you advertising?' jokes the Duke of Edinburgh. Someone who is uncharacteristically nervous tonight is the *Daily Telegraph*'s vivacious fashion editor, Hilary Alexander. She is a great admirer of the Queen but she is also a respected writer who tells it straight. When she didn't like the Queen's ball gown – another Angela Kelly design – at a recent state banquet, she said so in print. If it irked the Queen, there is no sign of it as writer and monarch cheerfully talk fashion. Alexander congratulates the Queen on tonight's Kelly outfit, a pale gold and soft turquoise silk brocade jacket and matching dress. 'One doesn't want to look like everybody else,' says the Queen. 'Certainly not,' replies Alexander. 'You're not wearing black!' The Queen laughs out loud. Eventually, she makes a discreet departure, leaving everyone to carry on enjoying the party until the Household team think it is time to deploy their subtle technique of steering people towards the door without giving the impression that they want them to leave. Sandra Hunt makes the most of her last minutes at the Palace, taking it all in. She will return to Yorkshire, happy in the knowledge that she has received the same royal treatment as, say, Jasper Conran and Bruce Oldfield.

The following day, there is good coverage in the national and regional press. Most people will simply absorb the message that the Queen has honoured a lot of fashion icons by inviting them for drinks. It will make no difference to their view on the monarchy but it's another brushstroke on that broad impressionist canvas of royal relevance. There were no head-line-grabbing moments – good ones or bad ones – at the reception. But pictures of famous faces having a nice time with the Queen always brighten up a news page. Hilary Alexander writes that the Queen's dress 'was perfectly in tune, both with her own regal signature and with the fashion swing-shift away from the safe LBD [little black dress], as the omnipresent solution to serious dressing-up'. She goes on: 'A dazzling "sunburst" diamond brooch sparkled on her left shoulder. Up close, her skin is just as luminous. As fashion moments go, this one could not be beaten.'

'Really, there wasn't a person there last night who wasn't thrilled to be in Buckingham Palace to meet the Queen,' *Vogue* editor, Alexandra Shulman, reports on her website. And, of course, there is the Palace's own report about the evening. Until a couple of years ago, the Queen's Press Office was entirely dependent on outside media to cover the monarchy's movements. Now it's up with the best of them. While it's not (yet) in the business of scoops and spoilers and some of the other tricks of the journalist's trade, the Palace happily embraces the latest media technology to produce its own reports and mini-films. It's been a steep learning curve. Here was an essentially reactive organisation which, until 2002, still banned emails on security grounds. Back then, the Press Office organised logistics, made very occasional announcements and waited for the phone to ring. Now it is as proactive as any government department, running its own Royal Channel on YouTube and monarchy sites on Facebook, Twitter and Flickr. Its weak point, by its own admission, is working out a satisfactory email system with the public. People who write a letter will always get a reply whereas an email address can swiftly be flooded by spam, timewasters and trouble. But the Palace knows it cannot afford to ignore an important chunk of society. No one must forget the 'key driver' relevance. 'We need to have some system for young people when all their correspondence is electronic and they don't write letters,' says website editor Emma Goodey. 'But it has to be thought through.' For now, public emails to the Palace come via Goodey. She used to run the website for London's Barbican Arts Centre and never imagined that she would end up as the public's online go-between with the Sovereign. If she spots a trend – like a sudden rush of questions about garden party hats or a royal anniversary – she will post a page about it on the website. Among the most frequent topics for questions are the Queen's corgis (they have their own page). But the website also provides some useful feedback on who is interested in the monarchy and why. Of the 2.3 million people from 226 countries who visited the royal website in the first six months of 2010, the British (766,000) were only narrowly ahead of people from the United States (662,000). There was then a marked drop to the Canadians (132,000) and the Germans (103,000) followed by the French (72,000), Australians (65,000) and Italians (42,000). Nearly 70 per cent of them were new visitors, the average time spent on the site was 3.3 minutes and the most popular pages were the traditional ones – those about the Queen, her family and the history of the Palace.

Although the website traffic provides useful data on what interests people, there is still no substitute for the postbag when it comes to finding out what is pleasing or perplexing them enough to write to the Queen. Within hours of the clothing reception, the thank-you messages start arriving. A Fleet Street fashion editor is among the first to get in touch, sending an email via the Press Office: 'Thank you so much for a wonderful evening. To have the Queen endorse the British fashion and clothing industry is immeasurably valuable.' Another email arrives from a Yorkshire textile executive: 'To receive so much time and attention from Her Majesty the Queen was very, very generous. None of the guests I spoke to realised we would have such open access to our hosts.' He also wants to thank the footmen who had kept him 'very nicely supplied' with venison mini-cottage pies.

Most people prefer to express their gratitude in the traditional way – on paper. Over the next few days, traditional thank-you letters pour in. Some are formal and typed, some chatty and handwritten. Several are rather touching, remarking how proud a grandfather or a great-grandmother or a founding father of a particular business would have been to see today's inheritors invited to drinks with the Sovereign. A surprising number pay tribute to the venison mini-cottage pies (who would have thought that meat pies would prove such a hit with a gathering of fashionistas?). One lady guest wants to thank the Duchess of Grafton, the Queen's senior Lady-in-Waiting, for befriending her as she stood looking at paintings on her own. The boss of Lancashire fashion house Sunday Best wants to thank the Duchess of Gloucester 'who was lovely company and made us all feel welcome'. It is often said that the advent of the email has killed off the old art of letter-writing, but not as far as the Palace is concerned.

'The letters go up in number every year,' says Sonia Bonici, the senior correspondence officer in charge of the Queen's post. In 2010, the Queen received almost 50,000 letters and cards (a third of them from overseas) and the Diamond Jubilee will multiply that figure many times. Many are messages of goodwill or thanks for a particular event. In 2010, she received more than 2,000 birthday cards and 4,000 Christmas cards from ordinary people. But many more are seeking some sort of help or satisfaction. The internet-fuelled rise in amateur genealogy has prompted a marked increase in letters about family trees. 'People ask: "Could you find out if my Uncle Jim was related to Queen Victoria?"' says Bonici. It's not the Palace's job to confirm or deny but the team (two full-time, two part-time) will offer advice on researching the internet and the National Archives. 'We really do try to help,' says Bonici. 'We can't do very much but we try.'

It's not an exact science but the Palace has learned that letters to the Queen are a good barometer of the broader concerns of society. The Queen herself takes them very seriously. 'One feels the buck stops here so to speak,' she remarked in the 1992 documentary *Elizabeth R.* 'I had a letter this morning about something. He said: "I've been going round and round in circles but you are the only person who can stop the circle." I thought that was rather nice.'

People who might once have baulked at troubling the Sovereign over a personal issue now seem more inclined than ever to pour their hearts out to her. 'In the old days,' says Bonici, 'they might write about one thing: "My roof is leaking" or "Nobody cares". Now, it's three or four issues. And the tone has changed.'

There was a sudden rise in correspondence immediately after the inconclusive 2010 general election result, just as there was after the MPs' expenses scandal of 2009. 'We had quite a few letters from people who thought that there would be riots in the streets and they wanted the Queen to take over,' says Bonici. 'Following the expenses scandal, people lost their respect for politics and thought: "The Queen doesn't do that sort of thing." So, their view was "Let her sort it out."' Sometimes, the letters are scathing about the Queen herself. None the less, she likes to see a complete cross section, even if they are critical. In any case, until the 9/11 terrorist attacks, she used to open a lot of her own post. Now it is all processed (except for certain private post, identified by specific codes). But the Queen has seen and heard enough over the years to be almost unshockable. 'People are entitled to their opinion, even if they're forceful,' says Bonici's deputy correspondence officer, Jenny Vine. Having previously worked for the manager of a top London hotel, she has experienced most facets of the human character. She has well-established procedures for dealing with crank letters but these are rare. 'Obviously, if they say they're going to blow up Parliament, then that's a threat. But if someone writes in and says: "I despair. The Prime Minister's a plonker," then that's an opinion and we would send that up to the Queen.'

Receiving and sorting the post is done first thing. The next issue is responding. In a few cases, the Queen may suggest a reply herself. Bonici gives the example of a man who recently wrote in asking why the Queen was using a State Bentley to attend a private church service. The Queen returned the letter with a note saying that the service was an official engagement and a suitable reply was promptly drafted. But that sort of micro-management is impossible as a rule. Letters from children and people offering kind remarks are usually passed on to the Queen's ladies-in-waiting who will draft replies on her behalf. More technical matters will be handled in the Correspondence Office. Everyone gets a reply, usually within a week, but that can depend on the issue. Nothing will stay unanswered for more than a month. 'People now have a greater expectation of what the Queen can do for them,' says Bonici. 'They didn't used to be so demanding but they often see the Queen as a last resort. So they write in saying: "We've tried everywhere. Can we try you because you're the head of state?" They might have a social services problem or a childcare problem and we always steer them towards the right government department because it is the *Queen's* government. We do get lots of letters back saying, "Thanks, it's been sorted out."'

If it looks as though the writer has simply been ignored by a government department, the Palace will sometimes forward the letter on to the relevant office. A royal letterhead can sometimes have a miraculous effect on a Civil Service blockage. But, ultimately, there is little direct action the Palace can take. 'I've only been here since 1998 but I think people's expectations have changed over the years,' says Bonici, who ran a gym before joining the Palace.

She holds up a letter, just in, from a girl who is a fan of the Queen's granddaughter Zara Phillips and wants the Queen to sponsor her riding lessons. It begins 'Dear Elizabeth' and includes a photograph of the girl's pony. 'She's gone to a lot of trouble with that letter. It's got a nice picture,' says Bonici. 'We'd say "Thank you, but the Queen gives her support to a number of charities and cannot support individual projects."'

The correspondence team are well aware that whatever they write may end up framed on a wall – or in the local paper. London's Sherlock Holmes Museum proudly steers visitors to a 'royal letter' which turns out to be little more than an official acknowledgement of a letter sent to the Prince of Wales. Jenny Vine has a simple rule: 'I always try to think: "How would I feel if this ended up on the front page of the *Daily Mail*?" But people will often read into a reply what they want to read. We might say that it's not a matter on which we can intervene and they will still write back and say: "Thank you, Your Majesty, for taking such a personal interest in helping me with this case" or something like that.'

It's almost a modern variant on 'touching for the King's Evil', the medieval belief that touching the Monarch would cure sufferers of scrofula. But even if writing to the Queen is not going to solve your dispute with your neighbour or the Inland Revenue, it can be reassuring to know that someone has actually taken an interest. 'We read it all. It's very important to read it all,' says Bonici. 'It might say: "My roof is leaking and the council won't do anything" and then, right at the end, it might say: "I'm very sad because my husband has just died." And if you haven't read that bit you don't know the full story. And it's very important to know that otherwise the Queen can't send her condolences.'

So how has the Queen become this blend of agony aunt and Citizens Advice Bureau? George V was not badgered about street lighting. George VI did not receive letters complaining about his choice of church-going vehicle – and nor, presumably, would he have replied to them if he had. Through the ages, 'good' monarchs have been seen as God-given champions of the people, the ultimate ally of the ordinary against the over-mighty, listeners to petitioners and so on. But modern Britain is not supposed to believe in all that; it was fine in the days of Elizabeth I but surely it's not relevant in the reign of Elizabeth II? The modern Briton has more democratic, professional representation than ever – Scots, for example, have their own representatives in three parliaments (Scottish, UK and European) plus their district and community councils. If the Sovereign is so marginalised these days, why are we increasingly keen to make contact with her? Are all these politicians failing to pull their weight? And if the monarchy is just a soap opera, why are the public more vocal than ever in their opinions on the cost, conduct, appearance, importance and performance of the Royal Family? It's yet another variation on the royal paradox: 'I don't care about the monarchy. But here's what I think . . .'

Just as the Court has changed profoundly in every way under this monarch, so, too, has the court of public opinion. But at least there is a very clear dividing line when it comes to public relations. In that regard, the reign of Elizabeth II falls, very simply, into two parts: the Colville years and the post-Colville years.

Commander Richard Colville remains a fascinating choice as Press Secretary to the Monarch for two reasons. First, he regarded the press as little better than a communicable disease. Second, he remained in the job for more than twenty years. The fact that he lasted so long – only stepping down at retirement age – makes it clear that the Colville approach enjoyed the full endorsement of the Royal Family at the time. The Harrow-educated son of an admiral, his entire career had been in the Royal Navy prior to his arrival at the Palace in 1947. The old joke of the day was that George VI had confused the Fleet with Fleet Street. It is more likely that the King was impressed by Colville's Distinguished Service Cross (the Royal Navy's equivalent decoration to the Military Cross), awarded in 1943. 'He had a heart of gold but he was extremely rude [to the press] and was the last person who should have been Press Secretary,' says a member of the Royal Household from those years. 'He was much liked by the rest of the Household. But his relations with the press – well, that's a book on its own.'

'He did the administrative side with terrific efficiency and won the respect of all those he had to deal with in that way,' says Sir William Heseltine, the man who would succeed him and go on to become the Queen's Private Secretary. 'I was very attached to him but his approach to public relations was certainly a very negative one.'

In Colville's eyes, all publicity was bad publicity. As he famously declared on one royal tour: 'I am not what you North Americans would call a public relations officer.' His basic rule was that any royal activity not specifically described in the Court Circular was not to be filmed, photographed or even discussed. This was an era of respectful, pliant media coverage. But Colville contrived to irritate the most supportive commentators. When the King, Queen and Princess Margaret were due to tour Australia in 1949 (a trip that would be cancelled due to the King's health), the Australian Consolidated Press submitted a list of harmless questions about royal likes and dislikes. Amid all the excitement, these were entirely understandable and legitimate questions. After all, had the tour gone ahead it would have been Australia's first sighting of a reigning monarch. The Palace's terse response? 'No information.' Colville did, however, permit his deputy, Diana Lyttleton, to answer a question about Princess Margaret's favourite dance tempos. 'All kinds of dances, waltzes, reels and modern steps,' came the reply. Even by the standards of the day, it was mind-numbing stuff.

This sort of grudging, nose-holding approach to the media was acceptable during the last years of George VI. Post-war Fleet Street could be relied on to censor itself on most royal matters. The nearest thing to a royal scandal were the jottings of the former royal governess, Marion Crawford. Having entered royal service in 1932, 'Crawfie' was devoted to Princess Elizabeth and Princess Margaret for eighteen years, once tracking down a runaway Margaret during an air raid. She believed in opening their eyes to the wider world with rigorous, modern lessons and even trips on public transport. But after marrying Major George Buthlay a couple of months before the marriage of Princess Elizabeth in 1947, Crawfie decided to retire. The Royal Family provided her with a charming grace and favour home at Kensington Palace but Buthlay was a financial chancer. He kept urging his wife to seek more royal favours and belittled her for not securing a damehood or being appointed as a Lady-in-Waiting. Eventually, Crawfie was persuaded to write a lucrative memoir for an American publisher, at which point the Royal Family severed all contacts.

Her sugary observations bordered on adoration – 'Lilibet', she revealed, was 'an enchanting child with the loveliest hair and skin'. Nor was she the first inside the inner circle to write about it. Even Queen Mary's Lady-in-Waiting, Lady Airlie, had written a memoir. But Crawfie's disclosures of life in the royal nursery were seen as a betrayal. Her short-lived career as a royal commentator collapsed after she wrote a gushing account of the Queen at the 1955 Trooping the Colour for *Woman's Own* magazine. The article had gone to print before the parade was cancelled due to a rail strike. Crawfie's credibility was blown. She moved to Aberdeen with her husband and died, a widow, in 1988. There were reports of an earlier suicide attempt. No royal flowers were sent to her funeral.

But 'doing a Crawfie' remains part of the royal vocabulary. Perhaps it was the neuralgic royal reaction to the harmless blabberings of the tragic ex-governess which shaped Commander Colville's outlook on royal reporting. He was adamant that no event, however innocuous, should be treated as a public matter unless it was clearly defined for public consumption. If the media had hoped for a lighter touch and a fresh outlook (perhaps, even a fresh Press Secretary) after the accession of the Queen, they were in for a disappointment. In this area, the Queen was at one with her late father. The dispute over television coverage of the Coronation was a case in point. The Queen, her Press Secretary and the Prime Minister were opposed to letting the cameras in. The organising committee, chaired by Prince Philip, duly vetoed the idea, citing various technical problems without actually bothering to consult the BBC. A press campaign on behalf of the great excluded masses, backed by a large number of MPs, forced a rethink. But there was no change in royal attitudes to the media. A BBC controller was reprimanded by Colville for daring to suggest that the Royal Family had been pleased with the coverage of George VI's funeral. The Director General of the BBC, Sir William Hayley, promptly issued an edict banning the *Radio Times* from even speculating about royal opinions on broadcasting.

As the Queen was preparing to embark on her great 1953–4 world tour, Colville was laying down the law around the world. The Government of New Zealand was briskly informed that there would be no prospect of an official state photograph of the Queen being taken during the tour. No matter that she was their Queen, too, and that it would be the Queen's first visit to New Zealand. No matter that she would be there for several weeks. 'I am sure that the Queen will not wish to have such a photograph taken,' Colville wrote to officials in Wellington. 'Since Her Majesty will have been subjected to quite sufficient photography daily, I do not think we should add further sessions.' Australia's state broadcaster, ABC, was given the bizarre instruction that it was not to broadcast any of the Queen's speeches to non-Australian ears. So, while the rest of the world would read the Queen's speeches in the papers, they would be not be allowed to see or hear them. 'It is not Her Majesty's or His Royal Highness's wish that any of their speeches should be beamed to such places as North America, Europe, etc.,' Colville wrote to Oliver Hogue, the Australian government official in charge of the media.

'Richard Colville had an old-fashioned aristocratic way of dealing with people,' recalls Sir William Heseltine. 'He insisted on calling people by their surnames but reporters in Fleet Street were not really very enamoured of being called "Smith" or "Jones" in authoritarian tones. One of the things that started Bellisario [Ray Bellisario was the original royal paparazzo] down the road to his deep antipathy to the organisation was Richard's handling of him.'

Colville's attitude during the good times made it harder to control things during the bad. During Princess Margaret's doomed romance with Group Captain Peter Townsend, Palace requests for media calm were ignored. Indeed, upsetting Colville sometimes seemed to be the only way to elicit a response. During the Duke of Edinburgh's long world tour of 1956–7, the American papers were so full of rumours that Colville took the extraordinary step of issuing a formal Palace denial of a 'rift' in the royal marriage. This was a mistake on a number of fronts. The British papers, which had ignored the story, were suddenly forced to explain what it was that they had been ignoring. Their restraint had done them no favours and, worse, had made them look stupid. And it did nothing to dampen speculation.

During the first fifteen years of the Queen's marriage, the French press alone carried seventy-three reports that she and the Duke were to divorce. There was, however, one news organisation which could be relied upon to ignore all disobliging stories about 'rifts' or anything else. But, in time, even the super-loyal BBC would have to move with the times. Through the fifties, it did as it was told. When it was told not to depict Edward VII in a television drama, it obeyed. When it was told that it could not film the Royal Train for children's television in 1958, it concurred. When the writer Lord Altrincham and the broadcaster Malcolm Muggeridge both made disparaging remarks about the Queen in print, the BBC banned them from discussing royal matters on air. It was not a simple matter of deference. There were corporate motives, too. The BBC was keen to prevent the new upstarts of independent television (ITV began broadcasting in 1955) from muscling in on the royal scene.

But the BBC could not ignore the sense of social upheaval as the sixties progressed. By 1963, the monarchy was deemed fair game for the new iconoclasts of television satire. In one famous sketch, a young David Frost ridiculed the fawning tone of royal coverage with a mock commentary of the Royal Barge sinking. Although it appeared on the BBC show *That Was The Week That Was*, the sketch was still deemed too risqué for the London stage. (This was in the days when all theatrical productions still required the approval of Commander Colville's colleagues in the Lord Chamberlain's Office.) As far as the Palace was concerned, if the press were unhappy about the level of access and information they were getting, tough luck. If the monarchy was failing to keep up with the times, so be it. There were no great royal crises. In any case, the marriage of Princess Margaret and the birth of her children had introduced a popular new strand to the royal story. Why bother changing things?

Some people attempted to warn the Palace of the dangers of Colville's complacency. Kenneth Rose recalls: 'I was so dismayed by this blank-wall approach that I wrote to Michael Adeane [the Queen's Private Secretary] whom I knew as a friend and said: "Do you know the effect this has on public opinion and the press?" And he wrote back and said: "You may or may not be right but I'm afraid I can't interfere. It's not my department."' It was, in fact, his department. The Press Office is part of the Private Secretary's Office. But as long as Colville was enjoying the support of his ultimate bosses, nothing was going to change. Colville was even criticised by the Press Council for his obstructive approach but it did him no harm with his employers. In 1965, he became Sir Richard after the Queen appointed him a Knight Commander of the Royal Victorian Order. And she had much to be grateful for. Royal coverage remained, for the most part, worthy and respectful. Amid all the noisy demands for a new world order, there was no overt hostility towards the monarchy. As far as the radicals of the sixties protest movements were concerned, the Windsors were a drearily bourgeois bunch to be placed somewhere between irrelevance and light comedy.

Ron Allison, who would go on to become Press Secretary himself, worked in television throughout the sixties. He once invoked the wrath of Colville simply by speaking to him. 'I was a BBC correspondent in Southampton and Prince Philip was doing something on the Isle of Wight. I called Colville to check something and he was very courteous but not at all expansive. About five minutes later, my phone went. It was Godfrey Talbot [the BBC's royal correspondent] and he said Colville had been on to him complaining and saying: "What's this all about, Talbot? You're the only person I talk to." He saw the press as an enemy.' Yet Allison understands why the Royal Family was happy to stick with Colville for so long. 'The Queen and the Duke were getting a terrific press in those early years. I mean, if you audited Richard Colville, he was doing a great job in terms of column inches and photo spreads and so on.'

Towards the end of Colville's tenure, there were signs of a fresh approach to public presentation. When the yachtsman Francis Chichester returned to Britain in 1967 after his solo circumnavigation of the globe, it was decided he should receive a knighthood. Instead of the usual Palace investiture, there was an unexpected dash of romance and swashed buckle. The Queen gave the accolade* next to the Thames at Greenwich using the same sword with which Elizabeth I had knighted Francis Drake. The public loved it.

And then, it seemed, everything changed – if not quite overnight then over a matter of months. Against a global backdrop of assassinations (Martin Luther King, Bobby Kennedy), conflict (Vietnam, Czechoslovakia) and civic unrest, few in the media paid much attention to an upheaval in relations between the Palace and the press. Yet 1968 was not only the year when the Lord Chamberlain's Office relinquished its historic role as theatrical censor; it was the one in which Sir Richard Colville uttered his last 'no comment' before retiring. His replacement was a young star from the Australian Civil Service called William Heseltine. A new *modus operandi* developed in no time.

Suddenly, the cameras were no longer an irritant on the sidelines. They were to be exploited. The Queen's Christmas broadcast was filmed in colour for the first time. The cameras were allowed inside the Palace to film a state banquet for the President of Italy. But Heseltine envisaged a far more ambitious project. Prince Charles was about to come of age and be invested as Prince of Wales. Princess Anne was about to commence public duties, too. A new royal generation was embarking on what might be called active service. Society was changing. Might it not be time for the first television documentary on the monarchy itself?

'As soon as I became Press Secretary,' says Heseltine, 'the investiture was on the horizon and everyone started suggesting things, including a biography of the Prince of Wales which seemed to me to be fairly stupid because there wasn't much you could say about a twenty-year-old. I had the notion of showing what was in store for him rather than an uneventful

---

* The act of placing the sword on the shoulders is known as the accolade – from the Latin *ad collum* (to the neck). Officially, a knight is not 'Sir' until the accolade is given. Because of the accolade's military connotations and battlefield origins, clergymen cannot receive the accolade because they are 'men of God'. If they become knights, they do not become 'Sir X'– and their wives do not become 'Lady X'. The exclusion only applies to Anglican ministers – a curious example of the Supreme Governor of the Church of England discriminating against her own Church.

programme about his childhood.' Heseltine also believed that a programme would help to revive the waning public interest in the monarchy.

'The young ones had been kept far away from publicity while they were at school. And there was a feeling about them at the time that they were pretty dull. At the same time, the Queen and Prince Philip, approaching middle age, were less newsworthy than they had been in the excitement of the early years of the reign. I had a feeling that something between the stilted accounts you found in the Court Circular and the nastiness of the gossip columns would be a corrective – and a help in launching the young ones on the world. It would demonstrate that, very far from being abnormal, they were a bright and attractive couple.'

Two men, he says, would be pivotal to the project. One was Lord [John] Brabourne who was married to the Duke of Edinburgh's cousin, Lady Patricia Mountbatten. A well-known film producer, he was a trusted royal confidant on media matters and was adamant that the monarchy's flagging reputation would be restored with some public awareness. He also suggested the right man for the project, an experienced BBC director and producer called Richard Cawston. 'That was a critical decision,' says Heseltine, who put the idea to the Queen. Her response was one of cautious enthusiasm: 'Do it and let's see.'

By today's documentary standards, the level of Palace interference would be regarded as intolerable. Once the project had been given the go-ahead, all filming had to be pre-agreed by a committee chaired by the Duke of Edinburgh. However, the leading lady soon warmed to the idea. 'From the word go, the Queen was totally cooperative,' says Heseltine. When watched today, more than forty years later, *Royal Family* is still a remarkable piece of work. There is a certain innocence about the central players as they make salad dressing, waterski, entertain the British Olympic team to drinks or welcome President Richard Nixon to lunch. Until then, their only experience of microphones and cameras had been when launching or opening things. The Queen clearly becomes more comfortable with the camera as the twelve-month filming period progresses. It is when she is being a mother rather than a head of state that she is most relaxed – positively enjoying herself as she takes Prince Edward to buy an ice cream at Balmoral or as she drives him around the Sandringham Estate with a boisterous Prince Andrew.

World leaders come and go in a collage of grand entrances. We see how royalty can reduce the most distinguished to gibberish as the Queen asks newly installed American ambassador Walter Annenberg how he is finding his new post. 'We are in the embassy residence, subject of course to some of the discomfiture as a result of the need for elements of refurbishing and rehabilitation . . .' The Queen later admitted to Tony Benn that she felt that this sequence should have been edited to spare Annenberg's blushes. For the first time, viewers see a Prime Minister (Harold Wilson) attending the weekly audience with the Queen. 'It is the moment when democracy and monarchy meet,' declares the solemn commentator. The programme was narrated by Michael Flanders (of Flanders and Swann theatrical fame – and father of the present BBC economics editor, Stephanie Flanders). But his commentary was written by the man who would make an important contribution to the royal story two decades later, former BBC producer Antony Jay. He delivered a sparing but authoritative script, carefully draping important constitutional themes over 'ordinary' scenes which left the nation agog. 'The Queen represents not the arguments that divide governments but the sentiments that unite peoples,' declares Flanders as the Commonwealth leaders come to town. The 110-minute film draws to a close with a piece of non-triumphal Jay analysis: 'While the Queen occupies the highest office of state, no one else can. While she is head of the law, no politician can take over the courts. While she is head of the state, no generals can take over the government. While she is head of the Services, no would-be dictator can turn the Army against the people. The strength of the monarchy does not lie in the power it gives the Sovereign – but in the power it denies to anyone else.'

Most of those old enough to watch it remember it, simply, for the family barbecue – Prince Charles mixing the dressing, the Queen tasting it ('oily', she grimaces), Prince Philip flipping steaks and Princess Anne predicting 'an absolute total guaranteed failure'. The programme was a broadcasting phenomenon. Aside from setting new viewing records around the world – some 350 million saw it – it had also forced the BBC to work in tandem with its rivals at ITV. The film was shown on both networks, on separate nights, and in Britain alone accumulated a total audience of thirty-eight million. It was not without its critics. Some thought it was all stage-managed – just as there were those, that same summer, who doubted that man really had landed on the moon. 'A lot of people were very sceptical about whether they'd ever had a barbecue before,' recalls Sir William Heseltine, pointing out that Prince Philip's *tour de force* at the grill had been a ritual for years.* Others scoffed at the sight of the Queen paying for an ice cream in a shop – mindful of the myth that she never carries money. 'I don't think she was a very

---

* The barbecue has been a royal staple ever since the Duke saw his first one in Finland. 'It was a great way of bringing the family together and that has developed as time goes on,' says the Duke of York. 'We all have to do it now. If the Duke of Edinburgh isn't there or he doesn't want to do it, he says: "You do it."'

frequent visitor to the shop,' says Heseltine. 'But it was she herself who suggested it on the basis that she had done it before.' The *Evening Standard*'s Milton Shulman (whose daughter, Alexandra, would be the Vogue editor at that aforementioned fashion reception forty-one years later) argued that irreparable damage had been done. 'It is fortunate at this moment in time that we have a royal family that fits in so splendidly with a public relations man's dream,' he wrote. 'Yet, is it, in the long term, wise for the Queen's advisers to set as a precedent this right of the television camera to act as an image-making apparatus for the monarchy? Every institution that has so far attempted to use TV to popularise or aggrandise itself has been trivialised by it.'

David Attenborough, television presenter and nature-watching chum of the Duke of Edinburgh, warned that the programme was 'killing the monarchy' by breaking a great anthropological taboo. 'The whole institution depends on mystique and the tribal chief in his hut,' he said at the time. 'If any member of the tribe ever sees inside the hut, then the whole system of tribal chiefdom is damaged and the tribe eventually disintegrates.' Heseltine remains unrepentant to this day: 'It was a fantastic success. There were one or two voices raised in disapproval. Milton Shulman and one or two of the stuffier Lord-Lieutenants thought this was not a good idea. In later years, when "lack of deference" became a major issue, then a lot of people were prepared to point the finger and say this was "all Heseltine's fault" and that we shouldn't have shown *Royal Family*. I thought then and I think now that was a nonsensical argument because you couldn't go on into the seventies ignoring television as they'd done in the fifties and sixties.'

The film has since become a broadcasting yeti, world-famous yet unseen on television screens since a repeat during the 1970s. It is in no video libraries. A trawl for a VHS or DVD edition will draw a blank. Today, television researchers are only allowed to access it under close supervision. Copyright is controlled by the Queen's Private Secretary and successive private secretaries have kept it under lock and key. The occasional clip has been authorised to form part of another documentary but the film itself remains out of bounds to the public. The official reason is that this was a programme of its time and for its time. 'We put very heavy restrictions on it because we realised it was a huge shift in attitude,' says Sir William Heseltine. 'And we thought it was not something which should be quarried for other programmes or be shown every few months.' Like any home video more than forty years old, it contains scenes which some members of the family would rather keep private – a broken cello string hitting Prince Edward in the face; Prince Charles as a painfully

earnest undergraduate; the Queen joking about a diplomat with arms like
'a gorilla'. To repeat it now would be to invite a degree of ridicule, a lot
of nostalgia and many false comparisons with the present day. On the
other hand, it would also highlight an interesting royal trend. As the
Queen grows older, her staff grow younger. Almost everyone in *Royal
Family*, from pantry to Private Secretary's Office, seems ready for retirement. Compared to these elderly gents, today's Royal Household is run
by a bunch of teenagers. But is it really so anachronistic? Its central
theme has hardly changed: monarchs are born into a contract with the
people – and this is how it works.

*Royal Family* marked a shift not just in the Palace's relations with the
press but in the dynamic between the monarchy and the people. New
ideas were no longer career-threatening. They were actively considered.
A year later, the Queen's tour of New Zealand saw the introduction of
a minor adjustment to a transport schedule which would redefine the
way members of the Royal Family – and, indeed, politicians – would
engage with the public thereafter. All of a sudden, the walkabout was
born. 'It didn't happen by accident,' says Sir William Heseltine. Following
the triumphal tour of 1953–4, the Queen's follow-up tour of Australia
and New Zealand in 1963 was something of a let down. Lower than
expected crowds might have been inevitable but there was still a sense
of anti-climax. The Palace wanted to breathe fresh life into the 1970 tour.
'We were thinking, "How can we make this a bit different so it's not a
repeat of the rather anti-climactic visit in 1963?"' says Heseltine. 'Out
of our deliberations came the idea of closer contact with the public at
large – who'd mostly been the recipients of little more than a wave or a
smile – rather than just mayors, councillors and politicians.' But how?

Monarchs had never gone marching up to people for a chat – certainly
not without an introduction. Patrick O'Dea, the head of New Zealand's
Department of Internal Affairs, had a solution. 'Out of those discussions,'
says Heseltine, 'came the idea that, instead of stopping at the door of a
town hall, the car might stop fifty or sixty feet down the road from the
town hall and the Queen might get out and walk that stretch, stopping
occasionally to say hello along the way.' The police were not keen. But
O'Dea and Heseltine put the idea to the Queen and the Duke who were
happy to give it a go as they arrived in Wellington. It was an instant
success – not just with the people but, crucially, with the press. 'The
most important thing of all was that it got a name – "the walkabout",'
says Heseltine. 'The person who gets the credit for that is Vincent
Mulchrone, who was there for the *Daily Mail*. He was a delightful, cynical
old boy and he completely misunderstood the significance of the word

"walkabout". It's an Australian aboriginal phenomenon which involves not walking and chatting among crowds but getting off on your own in the bush and not having anything to do with anybody. But it had a romantic aura and it became universally acknowledged as the term!' Back home, the Queen undertook her first walkabout in Coventry – a media triumph – and the politicians were soon aping her on the 1970 general election trail. It has been a part of public life ever since.

To his credit, the retired Sir Richard Colville was supportive throughout. 'I saw quite a bit of him in the years afterwards,' says Heseltine. 'He had a lot of ill health but he was always very complimentary and never offered a word of criticism. I think he had the feeling the time was right for a change.'

Heseltine was soon moving onwards and upwards, promoted to the post of Assistant Private Secretary, from where he would eventually progress to the very top of the Royal Household. The Queen's choice of a replacement Press Secretary marked another substantial break with the Colville era. Ron Allison was the first professional journalist to become a member of the royal team, hired straight from the BBC where he had spent the previous four years as royal correspondent. He remembers the BBC reporting his own appointment on the evening bulletin with the words: '. . . and so Allison will become the first member of the Royal Household to live in a three-bedroomed semi-detached house in Twickenham'. It remained the case as he preferred to commute to the Palace rather than move into grace-and-favour royal digs. Allison says that the switch from poacher to gamekeeper was a relatively easy one as he already knew the Palace and its people. There was, he says, no compromise in terms of his approach to the job. He had played a straight bat in his reporting at the BBC and was now expected to do the same in return. 'During my time as Press Secretary, I retained my professional integrity,' he says. 'And I never knowingly told a lie. In Fleet Street and elsewhere, they welcomed the appointment. The only people who were wary were a few people in the Household and ITN.' Independent Television News could hardly be pleased that their old opposition from the BBC was now installed at the Palace, but Allison soon had a chance to prove his worth, both to his new boss and to the media. No sooner had he been appointed than wedding preparations were under way for the marriage of Princess Anne to Captain Mark Phillips. 'I was immediately chucked in at the deep end but it enabled me to demonstrate that I would be totally even-handed.'

Allison's arrival also coincided with a more important change at the Palace, the retirement of the Queen's Private Secretary, Sir Michael Adeane, to be succeeded by the charismatic Martin Charteris. Like

Colville, Adeane had been a trusted member of George VI's inner
sanctum. And, like Colville, he was replaced by a natural innovator. Taken
in the context of the whole reign, this brief period, bridging the end of
the sixties and the early seventies, was unquestionably a watershed. The
royal biographer Sarah Bradford has described it as a deliberate 'relaunch'
on the part of the Queen. Sir William Heseltine insists that there was
nothing on quite such a grand, strategic scale: 'I don't think there
was any idea of relaunching – but a lot of things came together.' The
newly invested Prince of Wales and his sister were becoming part of
the mainstream royal team. The outside world was undergoing social and
technological revolution – from the Beatles to the American civil rights
movement. Man could land on the moon and mankind could watch it
all in the comfort of a living room.

The Queen and Prince Philip had now been around long enough to
have lost their novelty value, as illustrated by the poor turnout during
their 'second time around' tours of the world. It was time, very gently,
to break the George VI mould of monarchy and create a new one. It is,
therefore, unfair to attribute the monarchy's outdated media image
entirely to Richard Colville. The monarchy was not stuck in a fifties
mindset just because Richard Colville was. He was a symptom rather
than a cause. But the media's relationship with the monarchy is the most
obvious litmus test of the monarchy's relationship with the public, and
that relationship continued to develop and improve through the seventies
until it reached a plateau which would stretch from the bunting-festooned
renaissance of the 1977 Silver Jubilee until ten years later when the cloud
of *It's a Royal Knockout* gradually darkened into the gathering storm of
the nineties.

During those happy years of royal engagements, weddings and births,
the only serious hiatus between the Palace and the press was in 1986
when the *Sunday Times* published those stories of a royal rift with
Downing Street. According to supposedly impeccable sources, the Queen
regarded Margaret Thatcher's policies as 'uncaring, confrontational and
socially divisive'. The story was hugely embarrassing for the monarchy
– since it appeared to break every rule on constitutional neutrality – and
equally awkward for the Prime Minister. The *Sunday Times* refused to
name its 'sources' who later turned out to be one source. After several
days of denials and confusion, it emerged that the Queen's Press Secretary,
Michael Shea – who had succeeded Allison in 1978 – had indeed spoken
to the *Sunday Times*. But Shea was adamant that his remarks had been
completely misinterpreted. The debate over who said what continues to
this day and will never be fully resolved since Shea died in 2009. But

what is beyond doubt is that Shea was not speaking with the authority of anyone, let alone the Queen. Furthermore, not a single member of the Royal Household of the period can recall – or even imagine – the Queen saying anything so indiscreet to a member of staff. Charles Anson, who would take up the post of Press Secretary soon afterwards, is emphatic: 'Never in a month of Sundays would the Queen show to anybody, not even to her Private Secretary, that she thought anything bad of Mrs Thatcher or, indeed, any of her prime ministers.'

Shea's former colleagues recall an outgoing figure who liked the company of journalists (they, in turn, liked him). One senior courtier conjectures that Shea was probably 'trespassing over-confidently on political ground' and being pressed into making some anodyne remark about the Queen being 'in the middle' on any given political issue. As the courtier puts it: 'They managed to write it up in a way that suggested she'd probably be voting Liberal if she had a chance.' 'The poor chap's dead,' says another Household colleague, 'but I know that after he'd had the conversation with this journalist, over the telephone, Michael came to a meeting and said to me: "I've just had a rather good chat to so and so and I think there might be quite a good story in the *Sunday Times*." So he was under no feeling that the axe was coming down.'

The axe did not come down immediately. Some months later, Shea left for a senior position in commercial public relations, always insisting that his departure had nothing to do with the Thatcher row. Once again, this was not entirely accurate. 'In the end, we had to encourage him to move on,' says Sir William Heseltine, Shea's boss at the time. 'It was hubris on Michael's part. He just went further than he should have done in attributing attitudes and notions to the Queen and then realised he'd gone too far and denied having done so.'

By now, the glamorous younger members of the family, especially the Princess of Wales, were dominating the media schedules. Most news organisations had appointed designated 'royal' teams to cope with the rising demand for royal stories. And the ever-expanding ranks of the 'royal rat pack' were not particularly interested in what the Queen and Prince Philip were doing. This was of no great concern to the Queen who is not, by nature, competitive about such matters, nor in any doubt about her position in the royal scheme of things. But, ahead of her fortieth anniversary as sovereign in 1992, it was decided that another *Royal Family*-type project would be a useful reminder of what the monarchy was all about.

'At the Palace, I think there was a sense of: "How do we justify all this royal expenditure if the Queen is out of sight?"' says Edward Mirzoeff, the director charged with doing what Richard Cawston had done twenty-three years earlier. 'She was doing tours and visits and yet no one was reporting it. The younger royals were all over the papers. It was partly a question of: "How do we pull this back?"' adds Mirzoeff.

On this occasion, there would be no joint BBC/ITV production. The BBC wanted to keep the project very much to itself, although ITV would be given the finished product to transmit at a time of its own choosing. The BBC's relationship with the Palace had shifted significantly in the intervening years. The Palace might still control the access but there would be no committee chaired by the Duke of Edinburgh this time (indeed, the Duke had little to do with the project). 'The Palace could have no editorial control but they could have negative rights over any material gained through special access – and considering that most of the programme was special access, that was quite a lot of material,' Mirzoeff recalls. There were plenty of teething problems early on. 'There was a constant refrain of "The Queen won't like it." Even if I said, "Did you ask her?" it was still the same response.'

He deliberately hired a few veterans from the 1969 documentary crew. 'I assembled a team who I thought would be familiar, including Peter Edwards who had done the sound on the original. All the royals are far more worried about sound than pictures and Peter was totally trusted. So, we got these amazing conversations.' One of them takes place at the Palace banquet during the 1991 G7 Summit. Sir Edward Heath chides US Secretary of State James Baker for not following his example and meeting Saddam Hussein in person before the outbreak of the first Gulf War. 'He couldn't go to Baghdad like you could,' says the Queen. 'Why not, Ma'am?' says Heath briskly. 'I went to Baghdad.' 'I know you did,' says the Queen with an impish grin, 'but you're expendable now!' It has been suggested that the Queen may later have regretted the remark. Mirzoeff still regards it as a very endearing moment and recalls that Heath got off lightly in the film. 'I remember him at that banquet at the Palace. He kicked up the most awful fuss about where he was seated, grumbling that as a former Prime Minister he should be in a much more senior position. I think in the end they actually reseated him!' Before long, Mirzoeff and the crew had realised that different parts of the Royal Household could work in very different ways.

'I always found that the Court divided into two parts – the male private secretaries who worried all the time and the ladies-in-waiting who were much warmer. I went for months thinking: "This film can't be made." But the mood changed when the ladies-in-waiting warmed to us.' Mirzoeff developed a new filming strategy to get round over-cautious Palace officials. 'A press officer would always say, "Two minutes only!" or "Three minutes left!" and it was incredibly annoying because these things always get better as you go on. So I brought along attractive young women – a researcher, an assistant producer – and their job was to ask questions all the time and create a diversion. All the men seemed to like these pretty girls – with the one exception of Prince Philip who did not seem to respond to any of this.'

The Royal Household's nervousness was understandable. Charles Anson, a new arrival as Press Secretary, had just inherited the project. He was hardly going to let Edward Mirzoeff and the BBC roam the Palace at will. 'Once cameras have rolled and there's some ghastly incident, you're badly stuck if it's on film,' he explains. 'It was hard for Eddie to get what he wanted but he was right to press for it. We became friends but it was blood, sweat and tears for the first six months.' As with *Royal Family*, the Queen seemed to take the view that if she was going to do this television programme then she was going to do it properly. 'There is nothing she doesn't notice,' says Mirzoeff, as if reminiscing about a Hollywood great. 'There were times when she could see that we were not getting the right angle because we were being kept in a corner by officials. So she would gradually slide around and get in shot. She was totally aware of what was needed and what we needed and you'd be thinking, "You're wonderful! You're wonderful!" On *Britannia*, she once came over and said: "Why weren't you filming? That was an interesting conversation." I had to explain that we weren't allowed.'

The result was a beautifully observed, award-winning film. It covers an eventful twelve-month spell spanning the first Gulf War, a G7 summit and the Queen's first meeting with Nelson Mandela plus intimate footage of all the Monarch's regular fixtures, from the Derby to a Dine and Sleep dinner at Windsor Castle. But it also contains what remains to this day the nearest the Queen has ever come to granting an interview. 'We filmed from mid-1990 to late 1991 but when we got to the cutting room, we were still trying to find a shape to the programme,' says Mirzoeff. 'So I said to Charles Anson: "You don't know how much this would be improved by a personal voice." Charles, to his credit, went away and thought about it and then the Queen agreed to do it. And the conditions were wonderful. It was getting dark. There were just me, the sound recordist and Charles. I said to the Queen: "I just want to elaborate on a few things that we have been filming." And she was just terrific. There was no camera there, just her talking. We went away thinking: "Magic!"' Anson felt much the same. 'The final chat was so relaxed and full of insights into how the Queen sees her role,' he says. 'It was the closest ever to an interview – in fact, it was better than an interview because the Queen was so relaxed.' Her remarks are fond, reflective, modest, self-aware, homely. On Balmoral: 'It's rather nice to hibernate.' On Red Boxes: 'Most people have a job and then they go home. In this existence the job and the life go on together. The boxes and the communications just keep on coming. Luckily I am a quick reader . . . though I do rather begrudge some of the hours I have to do instead of being outdoors.' On the honours system: 'I think people need pats on backs sometimes. It's a very dingy world otherwise.'

It is surprising to hear these remarks yet they do not surprise us. They reinforce rather than readjust our perception. Of her meetings with her prime ministers, the Queen says: 'They unburden themselves . . . I think it's rather nice to feel that one's a sort of sponge and everybody can come and tell one things. Occasionally, one is able to put one's point of view. They may not have seen it from that angle . . .'

Mirzoeff says that he was spared any clumsy attempts at censorship and happily acquiesced to just two personal requests from the royal camp – one to edit out an unflattering shot of the Queen Mother's hair and one to lose an ambiguous aside about an animal charity. Harder editing issues presented themselves elsewhere, not least the question of what to do with the Princess of Wales. The Princess was still very much part of the family during the filming but, unwittingly, had a tendency to draw the attention away from the leading lady. 'We took quite a difficult decision,' Mirzoeff admits. 'We had loads of wonderful dialogue with her [Diana] but we cut it out. The film editor just found that when she appeared, she drew the eye away and we didn't want that. At the Diplomatic Reception, she tells the ambassador of Myanmar how she likes to drive round the city at night. It's wonderful stuff. But, in the end, we just cut it.'

As the film was being completed, the Queen decided that she would like a preview. Even for a fearless, veteran filmmaker, it was a nervous prospect as the Monarch, the Duke and the uppermost tiers of the Royal Household and the BBC trooped into a tiny BAFTA screening room. Before the viewing started, Mirzoeff had asked the Queen's Private Secretary, Sir Robert Fellowes, how to decipher the Queen's reaction. Back came the reply: 'You'll just know.' 'She didn't react at all but, early on, there was this great roar of laughter from the Duke of Edinburgh,' Mirzoeff remembers. 'And from that moment, they all started laughing. Then, at the end, I said: "We've got some tea. Would you like some?" And the Queen said: "Yes, that would be very nice." Just as Robert Fellowes had said, that was the moment we knew.'

The documentary attracted a vast British audience of almost thirty million – half the population – across both networks.

Whereas *Royal Family* had been a genuine eye-opener, *Elizabeth R* had been more of a refresher. Yet it marked the high-water mark of the Queen's engagement with the media. It did so with the timing of a Greek tragedy. At the very moment of this landmark in royal communications, lawyers acting for the Duke and Duchess of York were arranging a separation which would mark the start of the infamous *annus horribilis*.

Never again would the Monarch allow the cameras and microphones so close. For the next five years, as we have seen, the Palace and the media would retreat to entrenched positions. Royal correspondents such as Richard Kay of the *Daily Mail* and James Whitaker of the *Daily Mirror* became celebrated mainstays of their respective publications. Their television equivalents, Jennie Bond of the BBC and Nick Owen of ITN, acquired their own celebrity status. Both the Prince and Princess of Wales would use television to present their respective positions to the wider world. At the Palace, Charles Anson and his team simply had to get on with the job. There were all the usual fixtures in the royal schedule – including some historic state visits and anniversaries – and there was nothing officials could do about the private lives of the Queen's children. 'It was like being a sailor in a massive storm where you had to batten down everything and then come up, finally, when the sun appeared to see what needed repairing,' Anson recalls. 'But the Queen was steady, never short; never irritable. Completely steady. That must have been down to experience, going right back to Suez and so on. But it must also be down to temperament.'

Having maintained a dignified silence through the most lurid tales in the media, the Queen and her staff finally ran out of patience. It followed Diana, Princess of Wales's interview with the BBC's *Panorama* in which she cast doubts on her husband's fitness to reign. Not only did the Queen decide that the time had come to urge the Prince and Princess to divorce but the BBC was promptly relieved of its automatic right to produce the Queen's Christmas broadcast. In future, the honour would rotate with ITV (and, latterly, with Sky, too). It might have seemed a small gesture, but in the executive echelons of the BBC and the broadcasting industry it was a very significant moment. The decision was not wholly unwelcome in parts of the BBC. The Corporation's relationship with the monarchy was no longer 'special'. And, for many inside the BBC and beyond, that was to be regarded as a good thing.

In the furore surrounding *Panorama*, the media had overlooked the Queen Mother's own plucky attempt at media management.

She had been due to have a hip operation at some point but, on hearing about the forthcoming *Panorama* programme, she took some spirited pre-emptive action. Knowing that there was a risk attached to invasive surgery on a lady of ninety-five, Queen Elizabeth brought forward her operation to the same week as the broadcast. On that basis, if the operation was not a success, then at least she would have the (posthumous) satisfaction of kicking *Panorama* off the front pages. After a lively lunch at the Ritz with her ladies-in-waiting, she departed for hospital in high spirits – and re-emerged in equally robust form eighteen days later.

The shocking death of Diana, Princess of Wales two years later was followed by a public reaction which surprised the media as much as it did the Royal Household. It was uncharted territory for both, the first royal event of the global twenty-four-hour television news era. Despite some of the rabble-rousing headlines in the run-up to the funeral – 'SHOW US YOU CARE' and so on – the experience had a cathartic effect on relations between the Prince of Wales and the press. When he travelled around southern Africa a few months later, with Prince Harry on board, he allowed a large media posse to accompany him in his plane. Harsher critics began to give him the benefit of the doubt, to focus more on his qualities as a father than as an ex-husband. But it was a slow process. The Queen's press team were less keen on rapprochement. All that royal pain accumulated through the nineties would still take time to disappear. The Queen and Prince Philip were in no hurry to mend fences either. When the Queen came to celebrate her Golden Wedding anniversary in November 1997, the media was kept outside, barring a solitary seat – among the two thousand available – for the Press Association. 'Lack of space,' explained the Queen's new Press Secretary, Geoffrey Crawford. Two months earlier, the media had been assigned several rows of the same abbey for the Princess's funeral. On some occasions, press arrangements harked back to the age of Colville. When the Queen went to open Sydney's new 90,000-capacity Olympic Stadium in 2000, the stadium was empty but only a handful of cameras and reporters were admitted – to widespread guffaws. 'Lack of space' came the official explanation once again.

Meanwhile, relations between the Palace and the BBC suffered another setback when the BBC announced that it would not be broadcasting the pageant for the Queen Mother's one hundredth birthday, having originally indicated that it would. This gloriously chaotic carnival featuring all her three hundred patronages, from the Black Watch and the Special Forces Club to the Poultry Club and the Royal School of Needlework, was to be the highlight of her centenary celebrations and had long been planned for July 2000. The organiser of the event, Major Michael Parker, architect of the Royal Tournament and the great VE Day and VJ Day fiftieth anniversaries, had been happy to fit the event around the BBC1 schedules. The Palace hoped that live coverage would ensure that the event was enjoyed by more than the 12,000 people who could safely be accommodated on Horse Guards Parade. With two months to go, the BBC pulled the plug completely. It was a baffling decision which surprised many within the BBC itself. It then became a political issue when the Conservative leadership accused Corporation executives of being 'out of touch'. Officially, the BBC explained that it was covering a Service of Thanksgiving for the Queen Mother's one hundred years and, besides, the pageant would clash with its popular soap opera *Neighbours*. Major Parker offered to reschedule his event to suit *Neighbours* but the BBC held firm. Publicly, the Palace described the decision as 'an internal matter for the BBC'. Privately, they were dismayed. It looked like yet another case of the monarchy being sidelined by the prevailing 'Cool Britannia' orthodoxy within the new political and media establishments. The new BBC Director General, Greg Dyke, a card-carrying Labour supporter, had just arrived and was keen to make his mark. It was only a few months since the excruciating Millennium Eve opening of the Dome. 'Old Britain' had never felt older. But the matter was not quite dead. A young executive at Carlton Television, London's independent station, spotted an opportunity to trounce the BBC. Carlton's track record with royal programming had not been a great one. In January 1997, the station had screened a shambolic nationwide debate on the monarchy which had left everyone involved faintly embarrassed. One Government Minister had been so appalled by the bearpit atmosphere that he walked out before the start. Here was an opportunity for redemption.

That quick-thinking executive was David Cameron, then Carlton's head of corporate affairs (he would enter Parliament the following year). And during the weekend following the BBC's decision, several ITV bosses received a call from the thirty-three-year-old future Prime Minister. Would they think about tearing up their schedules and reminding the nation that the BBC did not have a God-given right to screen all royal landmarks? They were all ears, as was Major Parker. More than a decade later, the Prime Minister is modest about his role in saving *The Queen Mother at 100*. 'I think I just got the ball rolling, making a couple of calls and getting the interest of the boss and everything followed,' recalls Cameron happily. 'It was an opportunity for us. There were a lot of events like that where ITV just thought: "The BBC's got it so we never will."'

It was utter chaos on the day. Bomb scares at several London railway stations meant that a morning rehearsal had to be cancelled and Major Parker had no choice but to send 8,000 civilians and 2,500 soldiers on parade in front of live television cameras with his fingers crossed. 'It all came out quite fresh,' he admits. But the results were astonishing. The two-hour live production gave ITV its highest early evening audience in seven years. More than seven million viewers tuned in followed by a further five million who watched the evening highlights. Over on the BBC, the allegedly untouchable *Neighbours* drew just 3.5 million viewers. Major Parker became Sir Michael before the year was out (his knighthood was not from the government but a KCVO – a personal gift from the Queen). It was all highly embarrassing for the BBC and a timely reminder of the true extent of grassroots affection for the monarchy.

There was a similar misjudgement on Easter Saturday two years later when the news came through that the Queen Mother had died. The BBC newsroom had been rehearsing the event for years, and kept a stock of dark suits and black ties for precisely this sort of occasion. But, come the moment, as with the pageant, the senior management made the mistake of assuming that mainstream Britain thought as they did. 'Don't go overboard,' the duty editor told newsreader Peter Sissons as he prepared to inform the nation. 'She's a very old woman who had to go some time.' As Sissons recalls in his memoirs, he was also told to wear a burgundy tie rather than a black one. It was the wrong call. But the BBC was not alone. The following day, many papers and the twenty-four-hour news channels were comparing public reactions to the Queen Mother's death with the scenes which followed the loss of Diana, Princess of Wales. The inference was that Britain cared more for the Princess than the last Empress. Aside from the obvious differences between the accidental death of a woman in her thirties and the departure of a centenarian, they had neglected to observe that the days immediately after the Princess's death had been subdued, too. A week later, as people queued for miles through the night to file past the Queen Mother's coffin, the comparisons disappeared.

But there was an upside to all this. The broadcasters and the Palace were finalising their plans for the Golden Jubilee celebrations two months later. Sure enough, the BBC would not make the same mistake again. Greg Dyke and his managers gave producers the freedom to 'go overboard' as the big jubilee weekend approached. This was not a job for the more politically sensitive news operation but for BBC Events, the department which has produced all the big national and global set-piece occasions from Live Aid to Prince William's wedding. It duly rose to the occasion, winning awards and acclaim for its well-judged blend of affection and professional detachment. The scenes were momentous and the BBC's stirring footage would go on to serve as the main video content of London's bid to secure the 2012 Olympics. The underlying message was simple: 'Any city that can lay on a party like this can certainly stage an Olympics.' When the winning name came out of the envelope, it was obvious that the International Olympic Committee had agreed.

The Palace's relations with the media were picking up. But there were still internal issues to be resolved. It had become an open secret that the Buckingham Palace press team were at odds with the Prince of Wales's own operation across the road at St James's Palace, particularly the Prince's Deputy Private Secretary and *de facto* lobbyist Mark Bolland. Many inside Buckingham Palace felt that Bolland was sometimes promoting his master – and the future Duchess of Cornwall – at the expense of other members of the family. But even Bolland's critics had to concede that his work had paid off as widespread goodwill greeted the Prince's marriage to the Duchess in 2005. By then, however, Bolland had left to start his own consultancy and the tensions between the two palaces subsided. Today, the old rivalries have gone. The Queen's staff might use Red Boxes while the Prince's are green. Her household might write menus in French whereas his are in English. But when it comes to communications (as Commander Colville would never have described his job) the prime strategy is a collegiate and uncomplicated one. It's that 'Mon United' idea again.

As for the relationship with the press, it is now workmanlike and, arguably, as stable as it has been at any time since the mid-eighties. The Palace is not taking anything for granted. There is no complacency about happy headlines lasting for ever. Ever since former royal butler Paul Burrell made substantial sums selling his story, the Palace lawyers have tightened up their confidentiality clauses. Not only can staff be sued for indiscretion but they can be liable for indiscretions by others. If a chance remark to a gossipy aunt ends up in the papers, there will be trouble.

The British media is now adjusting to a new royal landscape with a glamorous addition to the regular royal narrative. The hyperbole of yester-year has given way to more measured coverage at home but the level of global interest in the new Duke and Duchess of Cambridge has shown that the world's appetite for a major royal production like a royal wedding is undiminished. Given the media circus which surrounded his mother and the paparazzi car chase which led to her death, Prince William, quite understandably, has a visceral antipathy to all forms of media intrusion. His engagement, stag night and wedding preparations were conducted with all the stealth tactics of a covert military operation. Yet he has endured less harassment than his father experienced during his own youth. And he has managed to maintain a largely satisfactory trade-off with the mainstream media, offering occasional photo-opportunities in return for relative peace. Whether that equilibrium can be maintained now that the Cambridges are a fresh global media phenomenon remains to be seen. What is beyond doubt is that the Duke of Cambridge will be in no mood for compromise, particularly when it comes to the privacy of the Duchess.

There are, on the other hand, some media executives and editors who choose to assume that the monarchy has ceased to be of any great interest or relevance to the general public. It can be a dangerous assumption. In 2007, the BBC produced a publicity trailer for the five-part *A Year with the Queen*, the most extensive royal documentary series ever made. The trailer was a brief collage of highlights, one of which appeared to feature the extraordinary sight of an angry Queen marching out of a photo-shoot with the American photographer Annie Leibovitz. In fact, the Queen had been expressing irritation *before* the photography had started because Leibovitz had asked her to wear the cumbersome regalia of the Order of the Garter. Having struggled into her robes and ribbons, and after voicing her irritation, the Queen then soldiered on with the shoot like a true professional.

So how did the trailer get it all wrong? It turned out that the scene had been re-edited by the production company for internal use. The result had somehow ended up in a selection of promotional clips sent to the BBC. This seemingly momentous royal explosion should have set alarm bells ringing, yet it was never checked with anyone who actually knew what had happened. Instead, the scene was simply unveiled at a press conference.

The blunder cost two senior BBC executives their jobs, nearly sank the production company and forced the entire broadcasting industry to undergo a prolonged spell of therapy. In truth, there had been no intention to deceive. This was cock-up, not conspiracy, but it showed the folly of thinking that the monarchy can be handled as casually as any other reality show. Some members of the media like to describe the Royal Family as a soap opera. The mistake is to treat it as one.

The Queen will never allow another director to get as close as Cawston or Mirzoeff, but she and her staff know that the monarchy must continue 'to be seen to be believed', that the 'key driver' of relevance is an ongoing process. The trade-off, as ever, is access. The result is the occasional high-profile quality documentary series such as *Queen and Country*, *The Queen at 80* and *Monarchy: The Royal Family at Work*.* None of these more recent films has managed to record a family barbecue or a cosy chat with the Queen about her postbag. But it doesn't matter. People do not expect to be surprised by her. They have a very firm idea of the sort of person the Queen is and they are very comfortable with it. For a society in thrall to the makeover and the relentless pursuit for the 'new', the Queen is comfortingly identical to the Sovereign whom millions saw tasting her son's salad dressing back in 1969. Hers is a world which continues to change while the central figure remains resolutely the same. It is what we expect of our Queen. However, should she ever decide to throw another pair of tennis shoes at Prince Philip on camera, it is unlikely that today's cameraman will cheerfully surrender the tape.

* Despite the disastrous trailer, *A Year with the Queen* was completed and successfully broadcast as *Monarchy: The Royal Family at Work*. Here the author must declare an interest. He wrote it.

# 7

## *Her and Us*

*'Happy people are why you are in the Happy People Business.'*

Lieutenant Colonel Gordon Birdwood and his little team are 'hunter-gathering' in the Palace garden. So far, they have snared a pretty good bag – a trio of commissioners from the Girl Guides and a young Royal Naval officer and his wife for the Queen. As for the Duke of Edinburgh, they have a couple of Water Rats and four ladies from the Air League. But they will need to keep on hunting. It's going to be a long afternoon and the Queen and the Duke will expect to meet several hundred people between the moment they arrive on the Palace lawn and the moment they enter the Royal Tent for a cup of tea. From a distance, any monarch since Queen Victoria would instantly recognise this gathering. The royal garden party has been a staple of the summer season for more than a century. Aside from the clothes – fewer morning coats, fewer hats, shorter skirts – it looks much as it did when the Queen was a little girl. It sounds much the same, too – the clink of teaspoon on porcelain over a medley of popular tunes from the Band of the Irish Guards in one corner of the garden, alternating with the RAF Squadronaires in the other. Like everything else around here, of course, the way the Queen interacts with the rest of us is reassuringly familiar – except that it is completely different. From the way she draws up her guest lists to the way she sends her invitations, serves her food, hands out her honours, tours her countries, chooses her representatives and opens up her property, the relationship between our Queen and us has changed with no one noticing. No one, that is, except the Queen.

At the start of her reign, this lawn would have been covered with debutantes, members of the county set and people wearing uniforms or mayoral chains. Today, it is just the uniforms and the mayoral chains which survive, although the latter are unlikely to get a royal introduction. 'I'm not looking for people who have already met members of the Royal Family,' says Birdwood. 'So I don't want Lord-Lieutenants, High Sheriffs or commanding officers. We're after troopers and senior ratings and people who might be backward in coming forward rather than people who are forward in coming forward.'

Birdwood is one of the Queen's Gentlemen Ushers, that utterly dependable band of retired senior officers who, on occasions such as this, help things along and steer people in and out of the royal trajectory as effortlessly as possible. Today they must select suitable guests for the Queen and her family to meet. And by 'suitable' they are not referring to their rank or the shine of their shoes. 'Clothes are immaterial. You get some fantastic people who are really scruffily dressed,' says Birdwood who will soon be promoted to Senior Gentleman Usher. He simply wants people who will enjoy talking to the Queen and who won't clam up. 'And you don't want her meeting three groups of submariners in a row.'

The garden party is the largest event in the Queen's social repertoire. There are four main ones every summer, three at Buckingham Palace and one at the Palace of Holyroodhouse in Edinburgh. With a few exceptions, guests are never invited more than once, the argument being that it really is a 'once in a lifetime' experience for as many as possible. Roughly 9,000 people will be asked to each one and around 8,000 people will turn up (the numbers are slightly higher for Edinburgh). They don't talk about 'refusals'. The Lord Chamberlain's Office, which sends out garden party invitations, refers to 'declinature'. Inevitably, infirmity and distance keep some people away. But it means that, during the course of her reign, the Queen has had two million people to tea.

The guest list is a sociological work of art which takes a small, part-time team – the Garden Party Ladies – months of planning in a Palace basement. For each party, there will be 1,200–1,500 'sponsors', organisations which have a ration of invitations. These range from charities to government departments which are then supposed to scatter royal recognition as widely as possible in their own sphere. The Scottish Office, for example, receives 1,500 invitations each year whereas a tiny charity might get a quota of two invitations every three years. The Lord-Lieutenants will also feed in their own suggestions.

The idea, simply, is to recognise those who graft away quietly for the greater public good. Only three thousand people can receive an honour like an MBE each year. This is a way of extending that national recognition via a raspberry shortcake and a day to remember. And every invitee can bring a companion. The rule used to be just a spouse plus any unmarried daughters between sixteen and twenty-five. By the nineties, the Queen felt that the rules were unfair on the widowed, the divorced, the gay and the single. No one, she decided, should come to the Palace without a friend with whom to share the day. So the rules were changed to include a companion of whatever complexion – and then unmarried sons were included, too. The Garden Party Ladies gather a bundle of passes and badges for all of them. They must check every name and address very carefully, not least because most invitations (and many envelopes) will end up in a frame in pride of place on someone's wall. Fortunately for the team, though perhaps sadly for the rest of us, modern technology has now crept in to this most Edwardian of summer rituals. The Garden Party Ladies no longer write the invitations themselves. It is all done by a machine with a special handwriting font. Household officials point out that it's more efficient and people now get their invitations more quickly. What's more, they say, no one has complained. No doubt they haven't. It would be a little churlish to be invited for tea with the Queen and then grumble about the writing on the invitation. It's just another little bit of modernisation in a far-flung corner of the Palace.

Technically, all royal invitations are a command issued to a senior member of the Royal Household – 'The Master of the Household is Commanded by Her Majesty to invite Mr and Mrs Andrew Other to a reception' etc. The formal way to reply is laid out in a book called *Debrett's Correct Form*, the definitive guide to all forms of etiquette. In the case of a garden party, the invitation comes from the Lord Chamberlain and so the 'correct' response is: 'Mr and Mrs Andrew Other present their compliments to the Lord Chamberlain and have the honour to obey Her Majesty's Command to attend . . .'

In fact, given the huge numbers at a garden party, there is no requirement to reply if you are coming but a simple notification is requested if you are not. It's a security rather than a catering issue.

For smaller Palace events like a reception or a dinner, the invitation will always say 'RSVP'. Interestingly, only half of today's guest list will respond in the traditional way. The rest will write whatever seems comfortable. 'Dear Master of the Household'/'Dear Lord Chamberlain' is a frequent opener. It is an interesting indicator of social habits in modern Britain. People are no longer so bothered about traditional etiquette or 'the form', yet they retain their innate good manners. They want to reply, but they are happy to do it their own way, regardless of that 'form'.

It is not just the guests who have changed. The Palace has updated the RSVP process. Because some people no longer write letters of any sort, royal invitations are now issued with an email address for replies. It is another tiny change but a giant leap in modern manners. Email has finally achieved social respectability. Hyacinth Buckets of this world, take note. Understandably, there are some people who are not aware of the abbreviation of the courtly French term *Répondez, s'il vous plaît* and therefore do not reply at all. Two weeks before an event, Sarah Townend, Deputy Secretary of the Master's Department, will organise a team to start chasing up non-replies. 'Sometimes people don't know they were supposed to reply, sometimes they have forgotten and you might get around fifty who never got the invitation because it went to an old address,' says Townend. 'Imagine how gutted they would be if they later found out what they had missed.'

Every facet of British public life is crunching across the Quadrangle, through the Palace and out on to the terrace where they look down on one of Britain's largest camomile lawns. The Yeomen of the Guard have already started to 'hold ground' – mark out lanes through the crowds. Lieutenant-Colonel Gordon Birdwood and his team wander among the new arrivals chatting to people at random, gently enquiring what has brought them here, where they are from and whether they have met the Queen before. 'If you feel they're right – any conversation has got to be fruitful – you might say, "Would you care to meet me at that corner of the tent at 3.30?" Then I'll come back and position them inside the lane. Only then do I tell them that they really are going to meet the Queen. You don't want to disappoint people.'

One of today's Gentlemen Ushers has specific instructions – or what is known as a 'drift' – to track down specific guests for the Duke of Edinburgh, among them a ninety-six-year-old war veteran from Nottinghamshire. At 4 p.m., the Queen appears on the terrace – she always wears a colourful, visible dress for these events; today it's bright yellow – with the Duke, the Earl and Countess of Wessex and Prince and Princess Michael of Kent. Everything and everyone stops for the National Anthem. Some people suddenly find themselves overwhelmed. Whether it's anticipation, pride, affection, the majesty of the setting or a mixture of all of those, a number of guests start to cry. It happens more and more as the Queen's years advance, particularly since she inherited the mantle of national matriarch from her late mother. It's that sudden acknowledgement of being a personal guest of someone who is not merely famous but exceptional. It can creep up on the most hard-boiled old cynic.

The Gentlemen Ushers are already parking the first fruits of their hunter-gathering in the Queen's lane, explaining that any bowing or curtseying is optional, that it's 'Your Majesty' followed by 'Ma'am as in jam'. They have made brief notes about everyone and hand their crib-sheets to the Lord Chamberlain, Lord Peel, who will introduce guests to the Queen. That way, he can cover the basics in his introduction – 'Ma'am, may I introduce you to Mr John Jones from Leicester who has been a fireman for twenty years' – and there is no need for the usual, 'What do you do?' The Queen gets straight down to conversation.

Jan Butler and her two colleagues from the Girl Guides are still in a mild state of shock. They came here expecting a nice day out. One of Birdwood's team grabbed them on the steps and here they are moments away from a formal introduction to their patron (and founder member of the 1st Buckingham Palace Guide Unit in 1937). Lord Peel does the introductions and suddenly they are chatting away about their big anniversary. 'The Queen knew it was our centenary,' says Butler afterwards as she seeks a badly needed cup of tea. 'And she knew what a lot of work we've been doing. We're thrilled.' The Queen has now moved on to Lieutenant Paul Evans of the Royal Navy and his wife, Annie. At six foot two inches tall, Evans suddenly realises that the Queen is having to look up at him and has the sun in her eyes. 'Would you like me to move to block it out?' he asks her. 'Would you,' the Queen replies. 'You're awfully tall.'

Over in the Duke's lane, there is some lively banter with Derek Martin, the actor who plays cab driver Charlie Slater in the BBC soap *EastEnders*. Martin is King Rat, the head of the show business charity the Grand Order of Water Rats. The Duke is a Companion Rat. 'Where's your emblem?' asks Martin, pointing out that all members are liable to a fine if they are spotted in public without their Water Rat badge. 'It's on the premises!' the Duke pleads.

A less formal crowd has gathered round the Earl and Countess of Wessex. Neena Lall, a primary school teacher from east London, has decided that she is not going home without meeting a member of the Royal Family. So she asks a Gentleman Usher if she can meet the Earl. Moments later, they are discussing education in the East End. 'It's my birthday!' she adds. 'Happy birthday!' the Earl replies. 'It's made it a very special day,' she says afterwards. 'It pays to be pushy.'

Most guests are just happy to gawp and to eat. During the afternoon, the guests will consume gallons of the Queen's own 'Garden Party' tea (a blend of Assam and Darjeeling) and as much food as they can eat from a menu which includes old favourites like scones with clotted cream, coffee éclairs and Wiltshire ham sandwiches plus a few more modern touches such as smoked salmon bagels and passion fruit tarts. There is iced coffee and Sandringham apple juice for those who don't want tea. The whisky in the Dundee cake will be the only alcohol available. The Queen checks it all herself beforehand and makes a few subtle regional variations when in Scotland – shortbread instead of strawberry tart, smoked salmon on oatcakes rather than bagels. For reasons which are not entirely clear, the Scottish guests also devour nearly twice as much – fourteen items per head. Perhaps it is the fact that there is more garden to explore at Buckingham Palace. Snooping is positively encouraged.

'At any formal occasion, it is the touch of informality which makes it enjoyable,' explains Jonathan Spencer of the Lord Chamberlain's Office. 'We want people to go away thinking "Gosh, I enjoyed that" rather than "Phew, I didn't make a mistake".' His colleague Alexander Scully has now produced a new booklet for every guest. It not only contains a map of the garden but also includes walking times so that people can work out how long it will take them to get from, say, the Waterloo Vase to the nearest cup of tea. 'People can go off and explore and kick their shoes off and sit under a tree if they want to,' says Scully.

For the Queen, however, there is no choice. After more than an hour in her lane, she adjourns to the Royal Tent where a group of VIPs are waiting to meet her. Today they include Lady Thatcher, the Archbishop of York and Lord Strathclyde, the Chancellor of the Duchy of Lancaster, who has brought his mother-in-law. Next door, in the Diplomatic Tent, there are thirty-four ambassadors (countries are invited in strict rotation). Guatemala and Jordan have brought their children. In one corner, Birdwood and his perspiring team have a quiet debrief over iced coffee. They are pleased.

Group Captain Hugh Rolfe, in charge of the Queen's lane, reports that the Monarch met a bumper tally of twenty-six different groups, including a bus driver and a lady in a wheelchair clutching a 1946 invitation which she was determined to show to the Queen. The Duke met all fifty of his pre-arranged guests plus another twenty groups besides, although there is a frisson of professional disappointment that the Duke was introduced to three Royal Navy groups in a row. There has obviously been a quiet word to all the disabled guests because, as the Queen and her family return to the Palace, all the wheelchairs have been lined up alongside the path. There is informal chat. One elderly gent is so overcome by the moment that he finds the strength to stand up in his wheelchair as the Queen passes by. It's not quite a miracle. His carer urges him to sit down. Sue Bradshaw, a civil servant from Cornwall, was worried about bringing her seventy-seven-year-old mother, Connie Timmins, all the way from Cornwall in a wheelchair but mother was not missing it for anything. She was supposed to have come to the Palace thirty years before, she explains, but her husband was having his leg amputated that day. Her only complaint is that someone put too much pepper in the cucumber sandwiches. 'We felt like royalty, today, we really did,' says her daughter. 'And, look, I've got a souvenir.' She is clutching a copy of the menu.

It is hard, if not impossible, to think of a British monarch who has witnessed such a revolution in the social diversity, the expectations and the emotional language of the population. The tears and flowers which followed the death of Diana, Princess of Wales, are often cited as an example of Britain's psychological transformation from wartime stoicism to touchy-feely, extrovert emotion. The untold story of the royal hearse is illuminating. After it had carried the Princess's coffin to her final resting place at Althorp, it had to be rebuilt. So desperate were the crowds to ensure that their bouquets landed on the roof of the vehicle that many had loaded them with stones to make them fly further. According to one member of the funeral cortege, the hearse was 'corrugated' by the end of the journey.

As in the wider world, so within the Royal Family itself, some social boundaries have not merely shifted but disappeared. At the start of the reign, Princess Margaret was effectively barred from marrying a divorcee. By the late sixties, the Queen still sought the government's approval before permitting her divorced cousin the Earl of Harewood to remarry (he had to do so in America). By 1992, her own daughter was divorced and remarrying in a Scottish church without a word to the Cabinet. Reflecting but also embracing the changing attitudes of society is a challenge for any monarch. George V understood this well, hence the royal turmoil in the summer of 1917. As the Great War was bleeding Britain of a generation, the Royal Family not only abandoned its German names and titles and became the House of Windsor but the King also introduced the Order of the British Empire. It would be one of the great legacies of his reign. The Order of the British Empire suddenly opened up the prospect of national recognition to millions of ordinary people. Until then, the only orders of chivalry were for grandees (the Orders of the Garter in England and Thistle in Scotland), diplomats (St Michael and St George), commanders (Bath) and royal officials and staff (the Royal Victorian Order). The Order of the British Empire was universal – and unisex. The King created the first knighthood for women, the damehood. Everyone could aspire to one of the Order's five ranks: Member (MBE), Officer (OBE), Commander (CBE), Knight or Dame (KBE/DBE) and, most exalted of all, Knight or Dame Grand Cross (GBE). Today, the Order is thought to number 120,000 living recipients, all of whom have the right to hold services in the Order's chapel in St Paul's Cathedral. By contrast, the Order of the Bath has 1,800 living members. Most exclusive, with just sixteen, is the Order of the Thistle.

George VI sought to bridge the social divide in other ways with his factory tours, his groundbreaking meetings with trade unionists and his boys' camps for pupils from both private and state sectors. Like his father, he also extended the honours franchise further. During the Second World War, he wanted decorations to reflect acts of great courage which had not occurred in combat. To this day, the George Cross ranks alongside the Victoria Cross as recognition of the highest bravery.

With the exception of Edward VIII, modern British monarchs have been careful to respect the great royal paradox, namely that we want our monarchs to be just like 'us' but also completely different from 'us'. What they must never do – and it is a lesson which so many defunct European royal houses failed to learn – is appear superior to 'us'. It helps that they marry 'us', too. When Prince Charles was born, the press made much of his direct descent from Robert the Bruce and Owen Glendower but also rejoiced in the fact that he is descended (via the late Queen Mother) from a clergyman and a plumber called John Walsh. The new Duchess of Cambridge, whose own antecedents include mill owners, solicitors and carpenters, is by no means the first to bring a splash of fresh genealogical colour to the royal family tree.

However arcane the rituals of the early twentieth-century Court may seem to modern minds, the British Royal Family was way ahead of their European cousins in social terms. In 1913, at the wedding of Prince Ernst August of Hanover to Princess Victoria of Prussia, there was royal apartheid when the orchestra struck up a waltz which could only be danced by those listed in Part I of the *Almanach de Gotha* (the old studbook of European royalty). The minor royalty listed in Part II were obliged to leave the dance floor. Queen Mary, deeply conscious of her relatively minor German royal ancestry, studied it to the point of obsession. Our Queen's own interest in pedigree is limited to horseflesh and dogs.

The most successful monarchs have often been those condemned for their ordinariness. European princes, with gold braid and uniforms for every occasion, would mock George V for wearing plain clothes or for raising his family at York Cottage, Sandringham, in a house full of department store furniture.* The same continental cousins would scoff at photographs of the King Emperor perched uncomfortably on a miniature railway or digging potatoes during the Great War. They were less quick to sneer when their own thrones started collapsing. As King Farouk of Egypt would note some years later, as his own throne was about to fall: 'There will soon be only five kings left – the Kings of Diamonds, Heart, Spades and Clubs, and the King of England.'

---

* European royalty were not the only ones sneering. Sir Harold Nicolson, the biographer of George V, observed that the furnishings in the 'glum little villa' were 'indistinguishable from those of any Surbiton or Upper Norwood home'. Nicolson later complained that receiving a knighthood for his literary efforts had been a rather 'middle-class' honour. He reflected that he would have preferred a case of champagne or a carriage clock.

The British Royal Family, like the British public, sees something richly comic about Ruritanian princelings standing on too much ceremony and lineage. It's no laughing matter among some European royalty, however. 'It's junior foreign royalty like Princess Michael of Kent who tend to be the most *protocolaire*, worrying about people bowing and curtseying to them,' says one royal intimate. 'It's usually the ones who've lost their thrones who are the most serious about it because they have nothing else to think about. It's always more important to bow to someone like King Constantine of Greece because he's lost his throne so he'll be more sensitive about it.' That is not to say that there hasn't been some crashing home-grown snobbery around – and about – the monarchy. The original champagne socialist, Beatrice Webb, described Edward VII as a 'well-oiled automaton . . . unutterably commonplace' and George VI and Queen Elizabeth as 'ideal robots'. H. G. Wells attacked George V for his 'alien and uninspiring' Court – 'I may be uninspiring but I'm damned if I'm an alien,' he is said to have retorted. Some of the most withering remarks about the Royal Family often come from ancestor-worshipping aristocrats. As Malcolm Muggeridge wrote in 1957: 'Duchesses find the Queen dowdy, frumpish and banal.' Harold Macmillan's wife, Lady Dorothy, the daughter of a duke, was heard to exclaim on being informed that her husband had been summoned to the Palace: 'What do *they* want?' Her sentiment was no different from that of a grand Norfolk neighbour of the Royal Family. When his wife suggested inviting George V and Queen Mary to dinner, the Earl of Leicester is said to have replied: 'No, don't encourage them.'

Prince Philip's supposed Greekness is a source of jokes to this day. Soon after the Queen came to the throne, he became infuriated by people asking him how he was coping with life at Windsor Castle, the implication being that it must all have been a bit overwhelming for a rootless pauper born in Corfu. He had a ready response: 'Well, my mother was born here and my grandmother was born here and my great-great-grandmother lived here so I know the place quite well.'

Another new arrival into the royal fold, Tony Armstrong-Jones, also resented any 'Cinderella' treatment – almost as much as he had disliked being steered towards the tradesman's entrance during his days as a photographer. His subsequent marriage to Princess Margaret and elevation to an Earldom was a source of eternal embarrassment to his former boss, the society writer Betty Kenward, author of Jennifer's Diary in *Harpers & Queen* magazine. She had once reprimanded him in public, declaring: 'My photographers *never* speak to me at parties.'

The Sovereign can never be 'one of us', not least because sixty million people will all have different ideas about what 'us' means. Just as the Queen is expected to be above politics, so she is expected to be above that most sensitive, inflammable and confusing issue – class. 'The Queen is class-blind. If you're grand enough, it's much easier to be completely oblivious of the class structure below you,' observes a former Private Secretary. Whatever one's analysis of the class structure, monarchs are unquestionably in a class of their own. The Queen's own accent has changed – less clipped, lower in tone than at the start of the reign – and she has remarked that her own grandchildren speak 'Estuary' English (a view supported by the famously plummy critic and aesthete Brian Sewell). Some purists even argue that she has picked up the odd populist habit herself, including her pronunciation of 'Jubilee'.* Yet it would be absurd to describe the monarchy as 'classless'. It is an organisation entirely based on hierarchy. It has its own internal honours system, the Royal Victoria Order, with strict gradations. A footman, for example, will never get a knighthood any more than a Lord Chamberlain will get the Royal Victorian Medal. The Queen draws her closest female confidantes, her ladies-in-waiting, from the traditional aristocracy and most of her circle of personal friends are from the same stratum of society, too. But that does not make the modern monarchy class-ridden or, in modern parlance, snobbish. Like most people, the Queen and her family have friends of similar age, background and interests. The institution she runs is, by definition, traditional. But, crucially, what it does not seek to do is represent or lean in favour of a particular order or class, however much others may think it does. And that has been one of the fundamental changes of this reign.

Many commentators continue to follow Malcolm Muggeridge's argument that the monarchy is the source of class consciousness, that 'the impulses out of which snobbishness is born descend from the Queen at the apex of the social pyramid, right down to the base'. This neglects the fact that several countries routinely held up as progressive, egalitarian democracies – Holland, Sweden, Norway – are also monarchies. It also neglects the ocean-going snobbery to be found in every non-royal society, from Ivy League America to the Crillon Ball crowd in Paris. But Muggeridge was on stronger ground in 1957 than he would be today. Because, as in so much else, the social landscape around the Queen has been transformed during this reign. While Muggeridge was damning the monarchy as 'obsolete and disadvantageous in the contemporary world', the Conservative peer Lord Altrincham was attacking the 'tweedy courtiers'

* Like most people, the Queen says 'Jubil-eee', as opposed to the supposedly smarter 'Jooobly'. Neither can be said to be 'correct'. It's a matter of choice.

around the Queen and her 'priggish' personality. In November 1957, the Palace announced that the Queen would be scrapping presentations at Court at the end of the following 'Season'. The idea of eligible young women 'coming out' into 'society' and being 'presented' to the Monarch as some sort of imprimatur of marriageability was over. The Queen never liked it much anyway. As Harold Macmillan observed in his memoirs: 'She does not enjoy "society".' The debutante gatherings would be replaced by an extra garden party for eight thousand people. There were few protests, beyond the Chester Herald at the College of Arms who warned that the Queen would be 'stranded' socially – and the private grumbles of a number of socially ambitious mothers. But it was a crucial change in that it severed a key link between the monarchy and the old social hierarchy. It was a precursor to that rather more profound rear-rangement of the class system by Tony Blair more than forty years later. The removal of the hereditary element from the House of Lords, as we have seen, has not left the monarchy exposed as some had feared. Instead, as both Blair and the Queen's officials have pointed out, it has served to 'de-link' the monarchy from the old aristocratic cadre. Titles have not been abolished, any more than Cowes Week disappeared with the end of presentations at Court. But just as the old 'Season' has faded from view, so, too, will the significance of the old aristocracy.

At the Queen's Coronation it was the hereditary members of the House of Lords who played a central role, paid formal homage, brought their wives along and were allowed to buy their Coronation chairs afterwards. Members of the elected House of Commons hardly featured in comparison. Here was a glorious display of the most exotic specimens in the aristocratic aviary. The Earl of Shrewsbury, holder of the obsolete but hereditary office of Lord High Steward of Ireland, was given a place in the procession and a special dispensation to carry a white wand. It is likely that, come future Coronations, future Earls of Shrewsbury, along with almost all the hereditary peerage, will be watching on television. The present Duke of Devonshire has already signalled his intention to stop using his title once the last hereditary peers are removed from the House of Lords on the grounds that the aristocracy will have lost its *raison d'etre*. When the previous Garter King of Arms rejected a request from a senior Palace footman for a coat of arms because it was felt that the man was not suffi-ciently 'eminent', the Queen's officials overruled the decision.*

Today the Queen and her family may number old, titled families among

---

* Garter King of Arms is the senior herald at the College of Arms, the governing body for all English, Welsh and Northern Irish coats of arms and family pedigrees. In Scotland, the same role is performed by the Court of the Lord Lyon.

their closest friends. In some cases, she grew up with them. Many have a long family history of royal service and, like her, are racing enthusiasts and substantial landowners. But the connection is now entirely personal. She may be like them, but she is not of them.

While much has been said and written about the political defenestration of the old peerage from Parliament, a less audible little social revolution has been taking place out in the shires. It has involved the quiet transformation of the Queen's ancient network of representatives who serve as her eyes and ears. Every county has a Lord-Lieutenant. Indeed, some counties only continue to exist through their Lord-Lieutenant. You won't find Banffshire on a map these days because the old county council has been abolished. One chunk is now part of Aberdeenshire and the other has been placed in the new administrative area of Moray. But counties have always been a human as well as a geographic entity. The people still regard themselves as part of Banffshire and the Lord-Lieutenant of Banffshire, Clare Russell, is very much alive and rooting for all things Banffshire from the ramparts of her home at Ballindalloch Castle.

Even an entity as famous as the Royal County of Berkshire no longer exists as far as local government is concerned. The county council has been abolished and replaced by a series of district councils, many of which overlap with other counties. The Post Office no longer uses the county name and the old county road signs are in disrepair because no one owns them any more. The old county regiment has disappeared altogether. Ask anyone in Berkshire where they live and the reply will almost certainly be 'Berkshire'. Yet the only official remnant of this ancient shire – the Queen's home county – is its Lord-Lieutenant, Mary Bayliss. When the county council was abolished, the previous Lord-Lieutenant asked Downing Street: 'Where is Berkshire now?' Back came the reply: '*You* are Berkshire now.'

Whenever you see the Queen or a member of her family out and about in the United Kingdom, look for a man in late middle age with spurs and a sword and the uniform of a major general or a lady with a large brooch on a white panel. This is your local mini-monarch – unpaid, non-political and with a direct line to Buckingham Palace. Once, the post of Lord-Lieutenant simply went to the most prominent local landowner, regardless of whether he was suitable for the task. As a result, he would be virtually unsackable. In 1944, the Duke of Argyll was found guilty of assaulting the town clerk of Inveraray but remained in office. Nor was diplomacy regarded as a precondition. When Sir Guy Shaw-Stewart, then Lord-Lieutenant of Renfrewshire, was introduced to Nikita Khrushchev in

Scotland in 1956, he expressed deep sympathy with the Soviet leader: 'I suppose you have to deal with all those communists and socialists.'

Today, many Lord-Lieutenants are still substantial landowners, some of them titled. But many are not. The position has undergone more changes over the last forty years than in the previous four hundred since Henry VIII first created Lieutenants to raise militias and uphold the law in his counties. The Queen has been the first monarch to appoint women as Lord-Lieutenants (the title is not feminised), many of whom have made a great impact on their counties. She has also appointed the first non-white and the first openly gay Lord-Lieutenants in history. She does so on the Prime Minister's advice, although the Palace is closely involved in the selection process. It was John Major who first decided to broaden the social base of this ancient office to beef it up. 'I was very conscious that the Lord-Lieutenants were doing a very good job around the UK, but no one was taking much notice,' he says. 'Although the role is largely ceremonial, it is a really significant one. They are an important part of the social glue, particularly in county areas. I had a series of receptions at Number Ten so that I could meet them all personally. And after that, more trouble was taken in getting a proper balance with regard to their role in the wider community.'

The Queen keeps a keen eye on her Lord-Lieutenants. As well as meeting them on her travels, she invites them to the Palace, holds conferences for them at Windsor and usually confers a CVO, a knighthood or a damehood on the longer serving ones. Like her, they have to be above politics – at every level. When one Lord-Lieutenant learned that a major road project was due to run through his own garden, he did not even complain. He feared it might be misconstrued as an abuse of office.

The first duty of all Lord-Lieutenants is to be dressed up and on duty whenever there is a royal visit to the county, although that is only a tiny part of their work. They must attend official events on behalf of the Queen, hand out medals and prizes and generally lend a sense of official recognition to county life. Their annual meeting in London used to be arranged alongside the Eton v Harrow cricket match for everyone's convenience. That's all changed. But there remains something otherworldly about their gatherings where they often introduce each other by county rather than name: 'Hello, Suffolk. I'm Gwent. Have you met Kincardineshire?' They can also appoint a Vice-Lieutenant to help them plus a quota of Deputy Lieutenants (around fifty DLs in an average county) to spread the load at a more local level. The old joke is that DLs spend most of their time attending the funerals of other DLs. Again, this post has been completely revised during the Queen's reign. It used to be little more than a local badge of honour, a sort of shires MBE, conferring the right to place the letters 'DL' after one's name. Until 1966, all DLs had to be ex-Forces and ex-officer class. When the Lord-Lieutenant of Hampshire attempted to appoint the supremely distinguished lawyer Lord Denning as a DL, the proposal was blocked by the Ministry of Defence on the grounds that Denning's military career had been in the ranks. If those were the rules, it was time to change the rules. Since the seventies, the MoD has no longer had any say and today's DLs are drawn from every level of society. Today, most Lord-Lieutenants expect their DLs to earn their keep. This nationwide diaspora of unpaid local worthies is actually a cheap intelligence service which provides the Queen with a direct line of access from county hall right down to village hall. When the Palace wants nominations for garden party guests or interesting ideas for a royal awayday, it is the Lord-Lieutenant and his emissaries who find them. What all ninety-eight Lord-Lieutenants have in common, aside from enforced neutrality and no pay, is that they must actually work for their counties. The days of grand symbolism are over. Just like the monarchy itself, it is no longer enough simply to 'be'. One has to 'do'.

William Tucker had been enjoying a well-earned retirement when he was suddenly called upon to be the Queen's man in Derbyshire. A thoroughly modern Lord-Lieutenant, he was born in Scotland, left school at fifteen, joined the Co-Operative Movement and rose to the top. He was living in Derbyshire, running all the Co-op's Midlands activities as well as chairing its insurance arm, when a previous Lord-Lieutenant rang him up one day. The Queen's representative knew Tucker and reckoned that a man with a £1 billion turnover and eight thousand staff could help him with a particular task. 'He rang me to say he was retiring and wanted his legacy to be a lifeboat. He said to me: "I want you to help me raise half a million pounds to buy it." I thought: "I don't know how to do it and we're landlocked." But we raised the money, the *Spirit of Derbyshire* is now stationed at Ilfracombe and then he asked me if I would be a DL.' Eighteen years later and four years after retiring from the Co-op, Tucker picked up his post one morning to find a letter from Downing Street. The Prime Minister was asking if he would be happy for his name to go forward as the next Lord-Lieutenant of Derbyshire. Tucker had known the hunt was on because, as a Deputy Lieutenant, his views had been canvassed by the man from the Cabinet Office. But it had never occurred to him that he was in the frame. 'I was shaking,' he says. 'I needed time to talk to my wife and consider it. I was four years into retirement and I would be doing this for twelve years.'

It is, indeed, a very serious undertaking for both the Lord-Lieutenant and the family – years and years of dressing up to attend formal events when you might prefer to be doing something else (or nothing at all). It certainly gives Lord-Lieutenants an extra insight into what it is like to be royal. People do refuse the post and it emerges that they are almost always women. 'They are worried about the impact it will have on their families,' says one Cabinet Office insider. 'It doesn't seem to bother the men so much.' William Tucker discussed it with his family and realised that he could not turn it down. 'The moment I agreed, I suddenly became patron or president of thirty organisations. But I'd never worn a uniform since I left the Boy Scouts.' All new mini-monarchs join the Association of Lord-Lieutenants and receive a thick file of official documents.* Male ones also receive a list of gents' outfitters. Tucker found a former Savile Row tailor in St Albans who produced an immaculate uniform in four weeks (he prefers not to discuss the price but the going rate is somewhere around £4,000). His next task was to find a sword with the appropriate Mameluke hilt. 'I bet you don't know what this is. I had to look it up.' Fortunately, a local DL – a retired major general – had one he could borrow. Tucker found that he had actually inherited thirty-six Deputy Lieutenants from his predecessor, including the Duke and Duchess of Devonshire at nearby Chatsworth House. The Dukes of Devonshire are Derbyshire's very own royalty, obvious Lord-Lieutenant material in the old days. As well as being the most famous landmark in the county, Chatsworth is a major employer, too. But today's Duke is very happy to play a supporting role. 'He's very helpful and always introduces himself as "Stoker",' says Tucker. 'He always says: "Don't hesitate to pick up the phone if there's anything you need." I do hesitate, of course, but they have been very supportive.'

Since taking up the post in 2009, Tucker has been busy most days of most weeks and has not looked back. 'You have to be quite careful what you accept or you could be out every day and night of the year.' He has been particularly proud to be involved in the homecoming parades for the local regiment, the Mercians, who have recently been in Afghanistan. 'We did seven parades across the county recently and they were all marvellous. Even at eleven on a Monday morning, the streets were packed. Part of my job is to present campaign medals to local lads which is a very nice ceremony.'

The military dimension can be a serious challenge for male Lord-Lieutenants who did not enjoy a spell in the Forces, so much so that the

---

* The plural of Lord-Lieutenant is not, as is often supposed, 'Lords-Lieutenant'. They were county lieutenants before the 'lord' prefix was added. The plural of Governor-General, on the other hand, is 'Governors-General'.

Association of Lord-Lieutenants has now produced a DVD for new boys. It features one of the most revered men in the British Army, Garrison Sergeant Major Billy Mott (the man who supervises all the Queen's parades) and it explains how a Lord-Lieutenant should wear his uniform, carry his sword and look like the major general that he isn't. 'It's quite complicated knowing when to salute, especially if, like me, you haven't been in uniform since the school cadet force,' says Lord Shuttleworth, the Queen's man in Lancashire and the chairman of the association. 'If the Queen steps off a plane, I salute her but then I'm not supposed to salute her for the rest of the day. And that can take a lot of nerve if you're standing next to her, the National Anthem is playing and there are a thousand soldiers all saluting.' Lord Shuttleworth's top tip to all newcomers is a simple one: 'Lord-Lieutenants walk. They don't march.' He also advises a spot of sword practice – not in combat but in getting in and out of cars. 'If you use an ordinary car and you're in uniform, it can be very difficult getting out of the back,' he recalls. 'I was sitting in the back with the Prince of Wales who's as fit as a flea, the car stopped and he leapt out. My sword was stuck under the seat, I gave it a tug and the bottom half of the scabbard came off.' He pressed on, hoping no one would notice, until a policeman appeared halfway through the Prince's speech to present him with the missing half of his scabbard.

The uniform presents other occupational hazards, as Miles Jebb records in his excellent history of the office. The Duke of Wellington was once mistaken for a postman and attacked by a dog, while Sir Thomas Dunne, a Lord-Lieutenant for more than thirty years and a Knight of the Garter, was greeted at one event with the words: 'Hey, you're not allowed in here. The band have their tea downstairs.' But beyond the uniform – or the brooch – is a quietly energetic extension of the royal machine. There are not enough members of the Royal Family to cover every new citizenship ceremony or Territorial Army parade or memorial service but the Lord-Lieutenants ensure that these occasions do not go unrecognised by the Sovereign.

Just like the royalty whom they represent, the Lord-Lieutenants must confront their own version of the royal paradox. We want them to be 'ordinary' and to do more and more. But we don't want to fund them. The pool of 'ordinary' people with the private means to support an unpaid, semi-professional, quasi-royal existence for a decade is somewhat limited. It's much more time-consuming than it used to be. 'The working Lieutenancy is a fairly new concept which has come about in the last twenty years,' says Lord Shuttleworth. 'My predecessor would say that he would very rarely expect his Deputy Lieutenants to do anything whereas

I expect mine to do a great deal. If you go to some counties, they're run like a squadron of community volunteers. They're very hot in Kent.'

Most Lord-Lieutenants have a part-time clerk and some secretarial support from a local council. But it can be tricky when the government suddenly has a bright idea and turns to the Queen's team for help. A classic example was the recent decision to honour the wartime service of the women's Land Army. The Queen and the Prime Minister would host a big event in London but that could only absorb a fraction of the old girls who wanted to take part. So the Ministry of Defence asked the Lord-Lieutenants to look after everyone else at county level. They were delighted to do so, but a little perplexed when the government had no budget. Eventually, Ministers discovered £50,000 to cover the entire country. 'It worked out at £1.10 per Land Army girl,' Lord Shuttleworth recalls. 'By the time you've booked a cathedral, got a choir, and done the flowers that's gone before you've arranged tea. So, in my county, I spoke to some people and we got a couple of sponsors to pay for the teas and a local college did the flower arranging. It was all fine but it's not really sustainable. There's this contrast between the expectation that we do something yet no one has the faintest idea of how we pay for it.'

Lord Shuttleworth is not complaining. A genial chartered surveyor and custodian of a small agricultural estate north of Lancaster, he polishes his own boots, adores his job and says that it has changed dramatically in the recent past. 'I'm rather a throwback, a hereditary peer. But the significance today is we are getting people who are in or have been in work whereas, historically, Lord-Lieutenants were people who were military or landowners. I'm not saying they didn't work but people who are "in work" is now the thing and I fit my duties around my own efforts to earn a living. You want people with a very good ability to get on with other people and good contacts in business, charities and the services. And it may be that some remote titled person is not the best person to do that.' On the other hand, some of the most diligent modern Lord-Lieutenants still happen to be peers and landowners. And, unlike the late Marquess of Aberdeen, they are sufficiently switched on that they are unlikely to ask the Queen: 'What are you up to these days?' (according to Miles Jebb, she replied: 'Still Queen.')

The royal awayday is part of the bedrock of modern monarchy. It seldom makes national headlines but is always hugely appreciated at local level. As the Queen has said simply: 'A lot of people don't come to London so we travel to them instead.' That is why a furtive posse of smartly dressed men and women are wandering amid the manure and shavings of a Cheshire equestrian centre on a chilly spring morning. Ten weeks from now, the Queen will be in the county to visit Reaseheath College, a 7,000-strong centre of agricultural and countryside studies near Nantwich. It has received several royal visits over the years, starting with the previous Prince of Wales in 1926. He arrived on a cold day and in a bad mood. Official records show that his temper worsened when there was cream but not milk for the royal tea (Miss Wallis, the matron, kept his cup unwashed for years).

The present Prince of Wales spent an afternoon learning the art of cheese-making here in 2005 and enjoyed it so much that the Duchess of Cornwall visited a year later. The college has attracted £35 million of investment and its hyperactive, OBE-winning principal, Meredydd David, has long been determined that the Queen should come and see some of the new facilities, not least a shiny new equestrian centre and a dairy unit. It was finally arranged after some patient but persuasive advocacy by the Lord-Lieutenant of Cheshire, Sir Bill Bromley-Davenport. He would be welcoming the Queen here except for the fact that he has reached the mandatory Lord-Lieutenant's retirement age of seventy-five so the honour will fall to his successor. That's just the way it goes.

The new Lord-Lieutenant of Cheshire, David Briggs, is the first not to be drawn from the landed gentry or, indeed, from Cheshire's most famous family, the Grosvenors, Dukes of Westminster. Nor is he retired. He runs a family confectionery business and a business selling musical instruments. But Cheshire is a county of many parts. As well as a large rural rump, it has its old industrial sectors and some famously expensive celebrity/footballer enclaves on Manchester's southern fringe. Briggs's talents as a bridge-builder between these various walks of life were spotted during his year as High Sheriff of Cheshire when he made great efforts to get the emergency services and local charities working together on youth projects.*

Now, in his first months as Lord-Lieutenant, Briggs has the honour of welcoming the Queen. A Buckingham Palace team have come to Cheshire to check all the arrangements. They start at Crewe railway station where the Royal Train will drop the Queen after a slow overnight

---

* All English and Welsh counties have a High Sheriff, a ceremonial position with links to the judiciary and a strong charitable aspect. High Sheriffs serve one year only. Like Lord-Lieutenants, they are unpaid, although some may claim a tiny ancient allowance, called a 'craving'. Nominated by a cosy panel of predecessors and likely successors, they are formally appointed by the Queen in a ceremony called the 'pricking of the Sheriffs', unchanged since Elizabeth I. The Queen pierces the parchment next to each name with an ancient spike called a bodkin. Recently, the government has attempted to broaden the social base with an unofficial 'house number' policy – an attempt to recruit more High Sheriffs from houses with numbers rather than names.

trundle from London. It's not just a matter of deciding at which platform the Queen will stop. They must decide where the royal door will open, where the local cadets will be standing to greet the Queen, how many of them will be on parade, where the royal car will be parked and so on. At Reaseheath College, Meredydd David, his trustees and the police are the only ones aware of what is going on. The seven thousand pupils haven't a clue. Security means that this visit is classified until a few days before-hand. There is palpable nervousness among those in the know. The hosts are waiting for the head of the Palace delegation, the Queen's Assistant Private Secretary, Doug King, to tell them what to do. He keeps reminding them that it is up to them to decide what they want to gain from the visit. The occasion is for *their* benefit, not the Queen's. His priority is to ensure that the Queen and the Duke have a clear idea of what is expected of them.

As ever, protocol is an anxiety, almost a millstone. People always assume that the Royal Family need protocol much as the rest of us need oxygen, that the Queen or the Duke of Edinburgh will be mortally offended if someone leaves the room before them or a mayor is in the wrong greeting line. In fact, protocol exists to ensure that everyone else knows exactly what he or she is supposed to be doing and therefore feels comfortable. Jonathan Spencer, Deputy Comptroller and the Palace's man in charge of protocol, is regarded as an almost biblical authority on the matter. As he points out, it's largely common sense: 'We don't even have a book on it because no two situations are the same. We just give practical guidance if we're asked for it.' He is often being grilled by his own colleagues. 'Last week I had a call from Clarence House. The Prince of Wales was going to Cornwall as Duke of Cornwall to the Royal Cornwall Show. Should he fly the Duke of Cornwall's flag? I just told them: "If they want to and you want to and the flagpole's high enough, why not? He's the Duke of Cornwall and it's the Royal Cornwall Show." In other words, common sense.'

In the earlier years of the reign, the Queen was always confronted by long lines of civic worthies. The Palace position is that it is a matter for the hosts to decide these things. But the hosts always want to do what the Queen prefers and, these days, the Queen prefers less formality. So, lines have shrunk. It's the same at her own events. Except for the annual white-tie Palace reception for the protocol-obsessed Diplomatic Corps, the Queen discourages long lines at home. Like the Prince of Wales, she asks her staff to arrange guests into small horseshoe-shaped clusters.

The students at the Reaseheath equestrian centre are too polite to ask why all these strange men in suits are pacing the distance from an

imaginary Bentley to an imaginary handshake. The Palace team are
delighted to learn that a former groom from the Royal Mews is now
working here on the staff. They need to work out a cunning way for him
to be introduced to the Queen. He can't be in the greeting line because
it will upset the civic worthies. Instead, Philip Warren, twenty-four, will
be strategically positioned holding open a gate through which the Queen
will pass. There's always a solution if you think hard enough.

For much of the reign, these awaydays simply happened on a loop. A big
county or city might expect to see the Queen every three or four years.
A tiny, remote one might see her every eight or ten years. Someone would
keep a list and say: 'Right, it's been a while. We'd better go to Liverpool
again.' Wherever the Queen went, the visits would be pretty similar – a
series of ribbon-cuttings interrupted by a civic lunch. That all changed
during the process of internal Palace reforms during the nineties with
the creation of the Co-Ordination and Research Unit (CRU). The idea
was to focus on what sort of contemporary issues the Queen and the
Royal Family should be highlighting and to find places that were being
overlooked. Central London, for example, was always getting royal engagements, for obvious reasons. But outer London was more neglected than
the Outer Hebrides. More recently, the CRU has gone, to be replaced
by the Secretariat, a team of young, sharp-eyed, lateral thinkers whose
basic job is to see what the Royal Family should be doing – and how it
should be interacting with the rest of us.

An important part of the job is scrutinising new legislation for royal
implications. It's not a question of one law for them, one law for us.
Rather it's about safeguards. If a new Bill gives gas inspectors automatic
rights of access to any house in Britain, then, in theory, they might turn
up at a royal residence, flash a pass and snoop around because they can.
So a royal exemption may be required.

Freedom of Information requests – whereby anyone can ask for information held by a public authority – now occupy a good deal of the
Secretariat's time. The Royal Household is not classed as a public authority
and the Royal Archives are not public records. The Queen and her family
have certain exemptions from the Freedom of Information Act because
they work to a different timescale from ministers and civil servants. Many
(if not most) of the politicians the Queen has encountered during her
reign are either retired or dead. But she is still doing the same job. A
controversial issue involving, say, a state visit in the sixties may no longer
embarrass the deceased Foreign Secretary of the day but it could still be
awkward for the Queen.

Royal exemptions only go so far. They do not cover all royal information sitting somewhere in a government office. Ask the Department of Transport something about trains and the resulting information may involve the Royal Train. It is then down to the Secretariat, led by Doug Precey, to establish whether that information should be kept confidential. If he thinks it should remain so, he will have to argue his case. Precey insists that he is not trying to conceal the truth. 'The spirit of the Act is one of transparency,' he says. 'If we can't justify to a civil servant, in the course of a robust conversation, why something is sensitive, then we can't expect them to justify to anyone else why it's sensitive.'

The monarchy's exemptions chiefly concern royal communications. Until recently, any correspondence between public bodies and the Royal Family or their staff – however confidential – could still be revealed, subject to a public interest test. Shortly before the 2010 election, the Labour Justice Secretary, Jack Straw, decided to tighten things up to protect the unique constitutional position of the Queen and all future monarchs. As a result, all communications involving the Sovereign, the heir to the throne and the second-in-line are now automatically exempt from the Act. As Mr Straw points out, the new rules were at his own behest, not the Palace's.

'I managed to get all-party agreement on much better protection for the Royal Family,' he says. 'I felt that they're in a completely different position because they're in it for life. And the whole relationship between the constitutional monarchy, including the heirs to the throne, and the government and Opposition would break down if records of private conversations were disclosed. It would just wreck the process. So I made sure they got an absolute exemption.'

Some newspapers and pressure groups are unhappy with the new rules. They point out that these new exemptions would have prevented the 2009 disclosure that eight government departments had been in discussions with the Prince of Wales's office regarding a property development which the Prince opposed. On the other hand, it would have set a sorry precedent if future Kings could not speak to their future Ministers in complete confidence.

The Secretariat is also a research unit, writing briefing papers for the Press Office or digging up precedents for the private secretaries. Today, for example, Precey and his team are trying to find out what happened the last time one of the Monarch's prime ministers was ousted by a colleague (it has just happened in Australia) and what the Monarch should do if Britain's Andy Murray wins the men's tennis at Wimbledon (it's a case of dusting off the Virginia Wade file from 1977). The Secretariat will cast a watchful eye over all the Queen's patronages. Is a lesser-known charity for ancient mariners still going? Does it still need a royal patron? They must monitor upcoming anniversaries and suggest ideas. What should the monarchy be doing for the thirtieth anniversary of the Falklands conflict, the 200th anniversary of Charles Dickens, Apprentice Week . . . ?

But a major part of the Secretariat's work is just that ordinary day-to-day interaction between the monarchy and us – days like this in Cheshire. 'The Private Secretary's Office might say: "The Queen is going to x or y. Now come up with a plan!"' says Precey. 'So we produce a number of ideas and the day might take shape around that. It's good fun.'

But all good plans need an alternative. Sometimes, things just don't follow the script. And David Briggs, Lord-Lieutenant of Cheshire, has to think fast with just hours before the Queen is due at Crewe railway station. Disaster has struck. The Duke of Edinburgh has had to have a minor operation on his hand and will not be coming. There is now a huge hole in the schedule as the Duke was supposed to be opening the new dairy unit – and it's his birthday to boot (urgent memo to chef: remove candles from cake). When the staff in the dairy unit hear the news, they are so disappointed that they stop hosing down the floor and adjourn for a cup of tea. The Lord-Lieutenant needs an emergency Duke. He cannot perform the role himself as he will be accompanying the Queen all morning. He discusses the matter with the Reaseheath College governors. They all think that the Vice-Lieutenant, Viscount Ashbrook, would be an excellent choice. A self-effacing Manchester solicitor and popular local landowner, Lord Ashbrook could certainly do the job but he wonders if there might not be a better solution. So the honour goes to Steven Broomhead, the chief executive of the Northwest Regional Development Agency. It's a sensible move since the college receives millions of pounds in grants via the agency. It will do no harm to treat its boss, quite literally, like royalty. But as everyone admits: 'It's not quite the same.' And the royal plaque will have to replaced with an unroyal one. The dairy staff are not the only unhappy ones. The managers at the Rolls-Royce factory in Crewe were planning to send a new Bentley prototype to transport the Duke for the day. Now they will not.

Having arrived a day ahead of the Queen, Colette Saunders from the Palace Press Office is checking the entire route all over again. For the first time in its history, the equestrian centre smells of flowers rather than horses. Reaseheath teaches floristry – one pupil apparently came fifth at the world flower-arranging Olympics in Japan – and the faculty of flowers has been busy. Saunders checks that all is ready for the Queen's grand unveiling of a chainsaw-carved statue of two horses. She talks to Philip Warren, the staff member who once worked at the Royal Mews. He is thrilled to be meeting his former employer. He doubts that the Queen will recognise him – 'I did meet her at Christmas drinks but there were a lot of people there' – yet he will always be grateful for his years at the Palace and always likes to tell his students about the 5.55 a. m. starts in the Royal Mews. 'I learned about pride in your work and perfection. Mind you, I don't miss those postilion jackets with a hundred buttons on them.'

The clouds are darkening overhead but Peter Wilkinson, the Queen's official television cameraman, who will provide footage for all the networks, is not worried. During fourteen years of filming the Queen, he has only seen her rained on eleven times. 'She has pretty good contacts,' he explains. There is a sudden flap in another part of the college. Colette Saunders is summoned to advise. It turns out that some of the governors are worried about a flower arrangement which may be obscuring the plaque which the Queen will unveil. It is a footling, hilarious panic but Saunders takes it in her stride. As the royal advance party, her main job is simply to calm everybody down and remind them that they are supposed to enjoy the day. The Queen will not give two hoots about the position of a flower arrangement.

Another problem presents itself. A local radio reporter is at the royal arrival point and broadcasting live, with breathless excitement '. . . The Queen will be seeing the best of Cheshire. Everyone is *so* excited . . .' That's all good. But, for some reason, the lady reporter is wearing a T-shirt several sizes too small, jeans and flip-flops. The Queen has seen it all before but some of the locals are unhappy. The reporter is dressed for the beach, not the Queen. They sense a lack of respect. As the media minder for the day, Saunders has a quiet word. 'We don't see a lot of flip-flops at royal engagements,' she says gently. 'Have you got any other shoes?' The girl shakes her head. She seems genuinely surprised that anyone is bothered. 'I'm sure she would dress properly if someone *important* was coming,' comes a sarcastic stage whisper from one of the crowd. By now, the Queen has arrived at Crewe. Regular trains can do the journey in ninety minutes. The Royal Train has taken a leisurely overnight stroll up the back routes, avoiding all the main lines, and has taken eleven hours and ten minutes. But it arrives at 10.10 a.m., bang on time to the nearest second. David Briggs, the Lord-Lieutenant, does the introductions but keeps the line short. There are royal handshakes for his wife, Lord Ashbrook, the High Sheriff, a trio from the local council, the local MP and the Chief Constable. Cheshire's *de facto* monarch, the Duke of Westminster – a Knight of the Garter and a friend of the Queen – will not be seen at all. Once he would have been at her side all day. These days, everything has changed.

The Queen is clearly delighted to be at an equestrian centre as she steps out of the State Bentley in a pink coat and dress by Stewart Parvin and a Philip Somerville hat. This greeting line has been restricted to three. The Queen walks straight up to a demonstration of equine physiotherapy. A teacher is pointing out the muscles on a mare called Mo who is so overwhelmed by all the attention that she relieves herself just as the Queen is alongside. Unperturbed, the Queen follows the lesson for a few minutes and moves on to a display of equine massage. A few stalls further along, a couple of elderly horses are half asleep as they undergo a course of equine reikí therapy. Mature student Kim McMuldrow explains that her charge, a twenty-year-old mare called Emma, has had cancer. 'Reikí helps horses heal themselves,' explains McMuldrow, her fingers hovering above Emma's back. 'Is it just your hand?' asks the Queen. 'It's very good for making the horses feel very, very calm,' McMuldrow whispers. The Queen is captivated. She stops, as planned, for a few words with Philip Warren as he holds open his gate and asks him how he is getting on. Just fine, he says. He's still not sure if she recognises him from the old days.

Inside the indoor arena, a display is under way with the captain of the British Olympic dressage team, Richard Davison, and his son, Joe, riding the Countess of Derby's prize horse, Artemis. The students have been asked not to greet the Queen with a wall of mobile phones but to pretend to be glued to the display. Once it's over, though, and the Queen is in the ring to unveil the chainsaw sculpture, everyone starts greedily snapping away. Meanwhile, the staff and students at the dairy unit are loyally pretending that Steven Broomhead, the chief executive of the Northwest Regional Development Agency, is the Duke of Edinburgh. But nobody bows.

At the campus headquarters, star pupil Katherine Smith presents the Queen with a bouquet of cream roses, astrantias and hostas. She has been informed that they are the Monarch's 'favourite summer colours'. Meredydd David invites the Queen to unveil a plaque commemorating the opening of the building by the Sovereign 'and HRH The Duke of Edinburgh'. Some of the staff are a little worried that it's wrong. But the Queen laughs and so everyone else laughs, too. David Briggs is looking at his watch. The Lord-Lieutenant has to escort the Queen to her next engagement. This day has had its nerve-wracking moments but he is enjoying himself. Even a sudden disaster like a missing Duke is not insurmountable when you have a visitor as experienced as the Queen. Anyway, as he himself admits, he is rather more nervous about another

event a few weeks hence. He will not only be representing the Queen.
He will be presenting the awards which bear her name.

George V and George VI created their own brands of chivalry to reflect
the ages in which they lived. The Queen has done the same. But the
Elizabeth Cross is very different in tone. Whereas the primary purposes
of George V's Order of the British Empire and George VI's George Cross
are, respectively, to recognise excellence and gallantry, the Elizabeth Cross
is to recognise sacrifice. Very simply, it is awarded to the families of
members of the Armed Forces who die in the service of the country.
Inevitably, it is widows and mothers who tend to wear it. And it is entirely
in keeping with the style of the Monarch who has created it. The columnist
and former *Daily Telegraph* editor Charles Moore has written that Britain
is the most matriarchal society in the modern world, in that the four
most famous public figures since the Second World War have been women
– the Queen, the Queen Mother, Diana, Princess of Wales, and Margaret
Thatcher. It seems fitting that the Queen's personal legacy to the way
Britain salutes its own should strike a feminine – though not a feminist
– chord. It is not another hierarchy of medals for use only on formal
occasions. There is a silver badge, along with a pin-on miniature for
everyday use. It has no Class 1, 2 or 3; no Gold, Silver or Bronze. Just
like every Commonwealth War Cemetery, it knows no rank. It comes
with no protocols on where it is worn or how it sits in relation to other
medals – though it is in no way an alternative to them. It is complementary. By definition, it can only be conferred on those who lived and died
in uniform. It is both a brooch and an emblem, suitable for men and
women; it is classless, different and, simply, very her. Just as the Victoria
Cross captured the mood of the new imperial age, so the Elizabeth Cross
is of its time.

    When presented, there is none of the pomp and suppressed party
atmosphere of a normal investiture. It has to be done with solemnity and
a degree of intimacy and flexibility. And because it is available to the
families of every man or woman who has died in the Forces since 1948
– all 16,000 of them – it is impossible for the Queen to present all the
Crosses which bear her name. So this sombre task is another duty for
the Lord-Lieutenants. 'The fact it has the Queen's name attached to it
– I can't tell you what an effect that has,' says Lord Shuttleworth. 'It's
that thing of personal recognition. It's not the Great British Cross or
whatever. It has her name and the reaction is really touching.' He has
found that presentations need to be small affairs – never more than ten
at once – and has learned not to be surprised by anything.

'These are very emotional occasions. Every single Lord-Lieutenant will tell you of distressing moments during the presentation. There's a lot of bursting into tears and a lot of people are still quite angry. But you want to bring the whole family together in a lovely setting and make sure there is tea and a slice of cake, too.'

Traditional royal investitures are much larger affairs. The Queen has been doing them since she was a Princess and, when she cannot be present, the Prince of Wales or Princess Royal stands in for her. This is one of the great rewards of being royal. The Monarch is the 'Fount of Honour' and there can be few engagements more rewarding than recognising exceptional people on behalf of the whole nation. It's pure Lady Bountiful. Here, too, things have changed a great deal. In the last twenty years, the number of investitures has shot up by 50 per cent to nearly thirty every year. This is not because there has been a rise in heroism or good deeds. It is partly because of a change of policy by John Major's government. He decided that the British Empire Medal, previously the lowest rung on the honours ladder, was demeaning. Henceforth, everyone who would once have got a BEM now receives the MBE instead. The BEM had always been presented by Lord-Lieutenants whereas the MBE has always been presented by the Sovereign. This new MBE boom has added another six investitures to the Queen's annual schedule.

While it might sound laudably egalitarian, it has not pleased everybody. As Kenneth Rose points out: 'The BEM was very useful to give to someone like the barman in the officers' mess who'd been there for thirty years. Now he either gets nothing or an MBE which is what the Regimental Sergeant Major gets. So, all of a sudden, the Regimental Sergeant Major is diminished.' The government is now looking at ways of resurrecting the BEM but creating the perfect honours system has always been impossible. Someone will always feel neglected or hard done by. Kenneth Rose is fond of quoting Winston Churchill on the subject: 'A medal glistens. But it also casts a shadow.'

Because so many troops are now on active service overseas, there has also been a rise in decorations for gallantry, adding another couple of ceremonies each year. Bumping up the numbers of investitures even more has been the Queen herself. At the start of the reign, she might present 250 medals and honours at a time. As the years have progressed, her capacity to stand in the same spot shaking hands and making fruitful conversation has, inevitably, reduced. She doesn't want to spend any less time with recipients so it has simply been a case of shrinking the average investiture down to a hundred awards. 'It's the feet not the head which dictate it's an hour,' says Sir Malcolm Ross, the former Comptroller, who was involved with investitures for twenty years (he is now the Lord-Lieutenant of Kirkcudbrightshire). 'And so it means a few more investitures each year. The Queen understands that.' In any case, a smaller crowd means that there is room for the recipients to bring the family, too. At the start of the reign, they could bring just one guest to the Palace. Today, they can bring three. What's more, the Queen has authorised another improvement which would have been unthinkable just twenty years ago. Every investiture is filmed – from arrival to departure – and the footage then edited to produce a customised DVD. Some find that as gratifying as the gong itself.

Each investiture is a major production for the Royal Household but there is nothing like a table covered in metal and ribbons to give the place a buzz. 'Looking at it from the worm's eye view, I used to love investitures,' says Ross, 'because you are able to help people enjoy one of the great days of their lives. When someone gets a medal from the Queen, you come out thrilled, too. Here are all these happy people – and happy people are why you are in the Happy People Business.'

This arm of the business is run jointly by the government and the Monarch. The government decides who gets which honours, via a network of civil servants and committees. Then the Queen delivers, assisted by the grandly named Central Chancery of the Orders of Knighthood. It is actually a small team based in the lower half of a Georgian house inside St James's Palace. The atmosphere is part Dickensian, part National Lottery. Most people who come into contact with this place will have just received one of the most memorable surprises of their life – an invitation to receive an honour from the Queen. But they may also be confused by the fact that they are joining a club with old and complicated codes and privileges. A medal is not the same as a badge, a decoration is not the same as an honour, a ribbon is not the same as a collar. Everyone joining an Order of Chivalry, from MBE upwards, will receive both a badge and a signed Royal Warrant of Appointment – effectively a proof of ownership. Understandably, people have questions and Rachel Wells, the Central Chancery's Assistant Secretary for more than thirty years, has heard most of them before. As ever, there are worries about what to wear for an investiture. This place may be the last link with the age of chivalry but it must still move with the times. So, ladies' trouser suits have finally been accepted (without great enthusiasm, it must be said). Fancy dress, however, is actively discouraged. Palace staff did not conceal their dismay in 2010 when a Leicestershire milkman arrived to receive an MBE – for community services – dressed in a 'cow suit'. Several gallantry decorations were being presented on the same morning, including a posthumous George Medal. It was a crass and insensitive stunt, but it could have been worse. 'We did persuade him to remove his tail,' says the Secretary of the Central Chancery, Lieutenant-Colonel Alexander Matheson. His staff have come to expect the unexpected, including people who fail to turn up at all. 'We recently had a chap coming from Kent and his sat nav sent him to Croydon,' says Rachel Wells. 'He rang up in quite a state saying, "I'm lost in Croydon." We got him another date.'

Then there are those who accept an award only to send it back again. The Insignia Clerk, Jeremy Bagwell-Purefoy, has a strongroom full of every conceivable medal from across the royal spectrum. He has shelves of OBEs, Garter regalia worth hundreds of thousands of pounds, a handful of Imperial Service Orders (an old colonial honour which the Queen still awards in Papua New Guinea) and the last two examples of the long-dormant Order of St Patrick. He also has an entire cabinet full of insignia returned to the Queen in protest throughout her reign. There are hundreds of medals from Second World War veterans who wanted to register their disgust at the 1971 state visit accorded to the wartime Emperor of Japan. Also here is the MBE given to the late John Lennon in 1965. The musician handed it back in 1969 in protest at British foreign policy. But he never stopped being John Lennon MBE. Similarly, the vault contains the MBE given to the journalist Yasmin Alibhai-Brown in 2001. Two years later, she made a very public show of sending it back in protest against both the Iraq War and the monarchy. She also remains an MBE. Once appointed, you enter the register and there you remain. 'You can't resign, I'm afraid,' says Matheson. 'But you can change your mind about the insignia and we always say: "If you want it back, just let us know."'

That is the last thing on anyone's mind as four hundred people in their finest dresses, suits and uniforms ascend the Grand Staircase at Windsor Castle. There is an atmosphere of gleeful nervousness. It is a sign of the times that most of the men are in lounge suits rather than morning dress. Major Alan Denman, the Castle Superintendent, has a team of staff to steer people through the labyrinth that is the castle. Beneath the soaring displays of spotless armour, chambers full of ancient weaponry, medieval coats of arms and even the bullet which killed Lord Nelson, they feel part of a ritual stretching back down the centuries. It is not the moment to point out that this ceremony dates back as far as 2008 when the Queen finally decided to introduce investitures at Windsor. Before then, they had always been in London, with the occasional ceremony in Edinburgh and Cardiff. Here, once more, is an innovation which has just been introduced with so little fuss that everyone imagines it stretches back to the Normans. It is actually a subtle way of making life easier for the Queen without scaling back her duties. Now in her mid-eighties, the Queen is keen to spend a little longer 'at home' in Windsor, so the occasional investiture is shifted from Buckingham Palace to the castle. 'The private secretaries are being very clever in lightening the workload without it becoming too apparent,' explains Sir Malcolm Ross. 'The Queen is still going to do as many investitures as she can – but why make her come to London on a Tuesday morning when she could be at Windsor? It's just as much fun for the guests – more fun, perhaps – and it means that the Queen doesn't have to slog up to London with everything that goes with it.'

The Queen's Gentlemen Ushers are out in force again, discreetly breaking up the arrivals into different groups. The guests are steered to the Waterloo Chamber to take their seats in front of the royal dais and look at the paintings for half an hour. The recipients are led off to the side for a rehearsal and a calming glass of Sandringham apple juice. The King's Dining Room has some of the most famous pictures in the world on the wall, including Van Dyck's triple-portrait of Charles I. But no one is admiring the art. They are all listening to Lieutenant-Colonel Andrew Ford, the Comptroller – the Royal Household's Master of Ceremonies. And they are rapidly discovering why the Queen employs ex-Forces people for this sort of job. A crack team of retired accountants would not be quite the same. It is all very warm and welcoming but it is also done with crisp military precision. Ford places his key staff around the room to replicate their positions in the Waterloo Chamber and runs through the process as if addressing his troops on the eve of battle: 'Jonathan Spencer, here, will check your name. Ahead of him, at an angle, is Group Captain Hugh Rolfe, here, who is your last safe port of call . . . Jonathan will ask you to go forward and forward you go until you come alongside Hugh. Get nice and close in, your shoulder against his chest so that he can whisper words of encouragement . . .' The banter produces a few smiles but most people are too busy paying attention. One man takes notes. Ford continues: 'When you hear your surname announced, it is the trigger to move. And forward you go three or four paces and turn and face the Queen. Gentlemen, a neck bow, not from the waist, just the neck. Ladies, a little curtsey. It doesn't matter which leg it comes off . . .' At which point, this six foot four bear of a man, a Guards officer for twenty-five years and fully dressed in ceremonial kit and spurs, proceeds to give a demonstration curtsey. By now, everyone is chuckling. 'Forward you go to the point that your toes are almost at the edge of the platform on which the Queen is standing. Please do *not* climb on to the platform . . .'

He offers specific instructions to today's two new knights – 'Down on your right knee, the Queen will touch your right shoulder, then your left shoulder; there's no "Arise, Sir Hero" or anything like that' – and explains how everyone knows when their time is up. 'It comes to an end when the Queen offers you her hand. Take it, shake it, remember to give it back and then walk backwards three or four paces to where you started. Gentlemen, make a bow, ladies, give a curtsey. Turn right and Commodore Lawrie Hopkins, here, will be marking your exit route . . .'

The Gentlemen Ushers are not just signposts. 'We also try to stop runaways,' explains Group Captain Rolfe. 'You do get people who are so overcome that they go the wrong way or try to walk out before they have received their award.' The recipients form a queue, divided up by decoration and sex. Men and women receive different versions of the same award; a man's CBE, for example, goes over the neck on a ribbon while a lady's comes as a badge. In the Waterloo Chamber, all stand as the Queen arrives, accompanied by two Gurkha orderlies, a tradition established by Queen Victoria. The band up in the balcony plays the National Anthem after which the Queen utters her only public pronouncement of the entire morning: 'Ladies and Gentlemen, please be seated.'

First up are the knights. Lieutenant General Sir William Rollo has no problems with the drill and has found the investiture far less stressful than the journey getting here – 'stuck in traffic with bits falling off my uniform'. The orchestra – all from the Bands of the Household Cavalry – immediately start playing a selection of Handel and Schubert plus a spot of 'Edelweiss' to lighten the atmosphere. There will no clapping or cheering, though. The guests have been gently requested to desist. It's fine clapping the first few recipients but how does Number 99 in the queue feel when the audience runs out of applause?

And then begins a rhythmic pageantry so seamless that no one notices it. Before each name is announced, the Insignia Clerk, Jeremy Bagwell-Purefoy, passes the requisite gong on a tray to his boss, Lieutenant Colonel Alexander Matheson, who checks it and places it on a cushion held by the Queen's Deputy Master of the Household, Lieutenant Colonel Charles Richards, who presents it to the Queen. The Lord Steward, the Earl of Dalhousie, reads out the name and, as the recipient steps forward, the Queen's equerry, Wing Commander Andrew Calame, whispers a quick reminder in the Queen's ear. She has already read today's full list along with a summary of every citation. 'She underlines the bit she wants the equerry to repeat in her ear,' explains Sir Malcolm Ross. 'That triggers her memory so there isn't a wasted question, no "Where have you come from?"' So Calame whispers away like a theatrical prompt: '. . . father of three . . . dentist for thirty years . . . met Prince of Wales in 1983 . . .' These are not all conversation points. But the Queen genuinely likes to put faces to names and stories. Sometimes, it can be quite a story. In March 2010, Marion Andrews came to London from Australia to collect an MBE on behalf of her late father. He had been awarded it in 1946 for wartime service in Burma but, amid the post-war chaos, the letter went astray. When his daughter discovered the oversight sixty-four years later, the Queen was delighted to make amends.

The same thing might have happened to Helen Dent who is here to be made a CBE. As she explains in the queue: 'To be honest, I thought it was just another letter from the Tax Office so I shoved it on a pile and then they rang me two weeks later to see if I was "minded to accept". I thought it was a joke.' It's no joke now as she steps forward to receive her award for her work with her charity, Family Action. 'Well done,' says the Queen. 'You deserve it.'

Some conversations flow more easily than others. 'What do you do in the rail industry?' the Queen asks Adrian Shooter as she presents him with his CBE. 'I'm chairman of Chiltern Railways,' he replies. The Queen: 'I suppose that goes through the Chilterns, does it?'

It is all second nature to her, though. As she waits for each CBE to step forward, the Queen instinctively straightens out the pink ribbon, drawing it between her fingers as if untangling a dog lead. There is roughly forty seconds between the announcement of each name. But some recipients seem to get longer. Warrant Officer Class One Barry Dawe of the Royal Marines gets a full one minute and twenty seconds. It is interesting that, afterwards, most recipients imagine that they spoke to the Queen for several minutes. Yet many of them struggle to remember a single word. That's something which never changes.

Some of today's guests certainly stand out. An elderly gent called Alan Beavis has dressed in his Scout uniform to receive the OBE for services to the Scouts. Architect George Ferguson, receiving a CBE, is in red tartan trousers. There are all ages here. Fresh-faced Christopher Kealey looks a little young to be receiving the MBE 'for services to the Foreign and Commonwealth Office'. 'He must be a future Foreign Secretary,' whispers one lady in the audience. The thirty-year-old is in fact being honoured for his two years as political officer at the British Embassy in Kabul. For some people, it is all quite a challenge. When Nora Schneider comes forward in a wheelchair to receive her MBE for services to the community in Berkshire, the Queen steps down from her dais to pin on her MBE. Not that there is actual pinning taking place. Recipients wear a hook on their clothes so that the Queen can attach honours quickly – and painlessly (unlike Queen Victoria who famously drew blood pinning the first VCs; no one flinched). Mary Tame arrives on the arm of the Queen's Senior Page, Sergeant Footman Philip Rhodes, to receive her MBE for services to the community in Oxfordshire. Michael Hopper MBE (services to Jobcentre Plus) is assisted by both a stick and the Page of the Chambers, Ray Wheaton. Derek Bartley, seventy-seven, arrives to a wonderfully incongruous double-billing: 'For services to the Midland Association of Mountaineering and Rhyl Music Club . . .' 'That's an unusual combination,' the Queen remarks. 'Which of the two do you prefer?' Bartley replies: 'They're both wonderful.'

Once the final Queen's Volunteer Reserves Medal has been dispensed, the National Anthem is played and the Queen walks out through the audience. She is actually going in the opposite direction to her part of the castle but she wants to give all the audience a good view of her after sitting there for so long. Detail is all. Suddenly, the mood changes to the boisterous aftermath of a school prize-giving and graduation rolled into one as the newly honoured are reunited with their families. Queues form to have official photographs taken in the Grand Reception Room. The sense of pride is infectious. One or two wives and mothers are dabbing their eyes, happily cursing their ruined make-up. It has been another great day for the Happy People Business.

There will, though, be one division of the modern monarchy which is, perhaps, not quite so pleased about investitures like this. Because every time Windsor Castle closes its state apartments for a royal event, the Royal Collection is deprived of potential income. Much as the Queen discourages a 'corporate' approach to other areas of the monarchy, the Royal Collection has an obligation to be commercial. And Windsor Castle – with a million visitors a year – is its top earner.

Here is a particularly colourful illustration of that shift in balance between 'her' and 'us'. Less than twenty-five years ago, this magnificent accumulation of great art and much else besides was in the hands of a tiny Palace office. In 1987, it was turned into a free-standing department within the Royal Household and is now the largest of the lot, with 320 full-time and 300 part-time staff every summer. It is the Royal Collection Department which brings the public through the royal doors, sells the souvenirs and uses all the proceeds to keep the treasures in one piece. Its mandate is not only to preserve its contents but to ensure that they are seen and enjoyed by as many people as possible. The modern Royal Collection will be one of the Queen's great legacies – a treasure chest of incalculable value which is now a charitable trust generating £38 million a year, all of which is ploughed back into the collection. Without a penny of subsidy, it must support itself. Although the Queen has always held it 'in trust' for the nation, it was often added to estimates of her personal wealth. The creation of the Royal Collection Trust in 1993 put that myth to bed. It underlined the fact that no monarch could sell a Rembrandt any more than he or she could sell Hyde Park or HM Prison Dartmoor.

That same year, the Royal Collection Department was charged with opening Buckingham Palace to the paying public for the summer to finance the restoration of Windsor Castle following the fire of 1992. There may have been opposition within the Palace but the Queen could see the financial and political point. Now it goes unquestioned, a hugely popular summer ritual. Between them, Windsor Castle and the Palace attract 1.4 million people and generate two-thirds of the Royal Collection's income – £17 million in admissions and £5 million in retail. The Prince of Wales is a diligent chairman of the whole operation. Not long ago, he admitted that, if he was given a sabbatical from being royal, he would like to spend his days researching the Royal Collection. It is unlikely the Queen would go that far. Her passions lie elsewhere. But she is proud and rightly concerned about every last teaspoon. 'In terms of access and conserva-tion, this reign has been a high point in the history of the collection,' says Jonathan Marsden, Director of the Royal Collection. 'It will be seen as significant as that of Queen Victoria.'

If she goes down in history as the 'Curator Monarch' – and it is, perhaps, preferable to being lumped in with that old rake George IV, arguably the greatest of the 'Connoisseur Monarchs' – then she will be happy. She is kept informed of all exhibition plans and personally authorises every loan of every work to every institution. Marsden has just sent up a list of items which the Canadian National Gallery wants to borrow. She will consider each one. It's no rubber-stamping exercise, either. Once or twice, her cur-ators have advised against a loan if there is the slightest chance that the work of art might not come back. But the Queen has not always shared their pessimism and has, on occasions, been happy to overrule them.

The Royal Collection is so huge that it rivals – and, in several areas, outshines – the world's greatest collections. No other monarchy has anything like it. As for former monarchies, their treasures have all been dispersed or absorbed into national collections like the Louvre and the Hermitage. The Royal Collection would have a great deal more today had Oliver Cromwell's republican cohorts not sold off great chunks of it – including the Crown Jewels – after the execution of Charles I in

1649. 'Many of the most famous paintings in the Prado, in Vienna and in the Louvre, belonged to Charles I,' says Jonathan Marsden. 'We had to start all over again.'

There are, in fact, somewhere between 750,000 and a million items in the collection. 'It depends whether or not you count the cup and the saucer separately,' says Marsden. It includes mighty collections within a collection – of drawings by Leonardo da Vinci and Holbein, of Sèvres porcelain, of Van Dycks and Canalettos. And it is unique in many ways. 'There is no other collection of this sort which is what I would call "in the wild",' says Marsden. 'By that I mean that many works are used for their original purpose – to provide a setting for the business of monarchy.' There can, surely, be no comparable collection of antiques and treasures which are still used for their original purpose – for eating, for drinking, for sitting on or for putting things on.

What also distinguishes the Royal Collection from the collections in most national museums are the glaring oddities and gaps. It represents the amalgamated personal tastes of British monarchs and has never had a public duty to be comprehensive. It has the best collection of Canalettos in the world, for example, yet it does not include a single work by Turner or Constable.

'Any museum curator would be pacing up and down and agonising about that because acquisitions are the first thing most curators think about when they get up in the morning. But we don't because that is not our principal mission,' Marsden explains. 'The collection reflects the enthusiasms of monarchs, not the collecting interests of curators. So we don't say, "Oh no, the Umbrian School is under-represented."'

Nothing is sold but from time to time there is some careful buying. Marsden points to the 1998 purchase of a little stand for Bonnie Prince Charlie's broth basin as an example of the type of acquisition made by the Queen. These have often been items with strong royal connections. Unlike George IV, though, the Queen has never been accused of being a shopaholic.

Another unique aspect of the Royal Collection is that lack of public subsidy. Unlike so many of Britain's other great galleries and museums, the Royal Collection has to depend on footfall, marketing and commercial activities to survive. It's another royal paradox. We want royal enterprises like the Royal Collection to pay their own way but heaven forbid that they should trade on their royal connections. They have to tread carefully. Marsden points to the example of two books written to accompany an exhibition on Victoria and Albert in the Queen's Gallery. One is a beautifully illustrated, dense academic work with a price tag of £35. The other is a slimmer £9.95 book aimed at the general visitor. Marsden holds up the academic book. 'It's new research and an important piece of scholarship but the only way we can do this book is by getting sponsorship for the production costs and selling 10,000 copies of the other one.' He has to do a lot more than balance the books of his books. The Royal Collection now has a vigorous retail arm selling 1,500 items ranging from cards, DVDs and biscuit tins to mock bearskins for toddlers, illuminated yo-yos and soap, all under the management of Nuala McGourty.

An experienced retail executive, formerly with Marks & Spencer and La Senza, she is keen to push into every section of the market. 'Fine bone china and anything with a royal coat of arms works very well and we're launching a range of ties with some of the architectural features of Buckingham Palace on them,' she explains. 'But we always try to have something a bit light-hearted, so we've got a dog range – liver-flavoured organic dog biscuits. We tried dog T-shirts with [the words] Prince and Princess on them, too. We want to appeal to everyone.' What about cats? 'No! We do corgis here.' McGourty always makes sure the shops are showing a royal documentary on a screen. 'It's good for the atmosphere.'

Her latest project has been a café in the Buckingham Palace garden during the summer opening to cater for those at the end of their tour of the State Rooms. It's not about making money – although it has to break even – but about improving the 'visitor experience'. Every self-respecting stately home has a café, usually in an old stable block or orangery. But the Palace has no empty buildings so the Royal Collection has to build a temporary café on the West Terrace, overlooking the garden. Tea and scones are the predictable bestsellers. But McGourty has found that even some of the rubbish is popular. 'We haven't got the space for washing-up machines so everything is disposable,' she explains. 'But it's amazing how many people want to take the cups away with them. They all have royal branding and people love them.'

It's always a juggling act between financial imperatives and the bounds of royal good taste. McGourty, more than anyone, understands the importance of not devaluing the brand. In any case, there are plenty of opinions to be canvassed before, say, a remote-controlled corgi or an EIIR soap-on-a-rope could ever see the light of day. As Vice-Chairman of the Royal Collection Trust, Lord Peel, the Lord Chamberlain, always keeps a wary eye out for any ideas which might backfire. 'Sometimes, I might suggest looking at something in a slightly less corporate way – a softer approach,' he says. 'But it's been an amazing achievement. They've borrowed millions to build a new gallery in Edinburgh, all without public finance at all, and they've almost paid it all back.'

Without all this commercial activity, of course, there would be no pot to pay for new galleries, education programmes, travelling exhibitions and fresh investments. Marsden's next project is to improve the online side of things, including a significant increase in the number of pieces on the Royal Collection's website. Public appreciation is all part of its *raison d'être* and, if that happens to be via the internet, so much the better. There are even plans for online debates about the attribution of a particular work of art.

Indeed, since becoming a fully fledged department, the Royal Collection has started discovering works it never knew it had.

In recent years, Marsden's distinguished predecessor, Sir Hugh Roberts, had the happy task of visiting the Monarch on several occasions with very great news. The Queen had acquired two Caravaggios and, in 2003, a priceless bronze satyr by Benvenuto Cellini. What's more, it had all happened without going near an auction house or opening a cheque-book. It was simply down to her curators and conservators. These master-pieces had always been somewhere in the collection but no one had identified them correctly before.

The most popular royal treasures of the lot are inside the Tower of London. The Crown Jewels also belong to the Queen 'in right of Crown' so, of course, she can never sell them. The Tower itself is run by a sepa-rate operation, Historic Royal Palaces, a charity which manages all the old royal residences no longer lived in by the Royal Family, such as Hampton Court Palace. It also runs the non-residential part of Kensington Palace. Its most famous attraction, by far, is the Tower which receives nearly 2.5 million visitors each year, more than double the figure for Windsor Castle. Like the Royal Collection, Historic Royal Palaces does not receive a penny of public money and must fend for itself. It's that paradox again: it is *ours* – but do not expect us to pay for it. When the Coalition Government was planning to slash public subsidies for heritage organisations, attention turned to Historic Royal Palaces – until it was pointed out that it had never received a subsidy. Some of the Queen's senior officials sit on the board of trustees but, being detached from the Royal Household, Historic Royal Palaces can afford to be a little more 'corporate'. So the public can hire the Kensington Palace Orangery or the Hampton Court Garden Room for weddings and civil partnerships. Similarly, the whole tone of the organisation is a little less deferential, the atmosphere different from that of the Royal Collection. The organisa-tion's 2010 annual report featured a photograph of an enormous pair of pants belonging to Queen Victoria. It's unlikely that the Royal Collection would illustrate its publications with royal underwear. From blood and guts at the Tower to macabre courtiers at Kensington Palace, Historic Royal Palaces celebrates every aspect of royal heritage, good or bad.

The adventurous young team of curators, led by the historian and documentary maker Dr Lucy Worsley, are keen to broaden the appeal beyond the traditional coach parties to include the 'cool rejector' market. 'They are the fifteen to thirty crowd who don't normally come to places like this,' she says. Hence the recent 'Enchanted Palace' tour of the Kensington Palace state apartments. Exploring the turbulent lives of seven Princesses who had lived there, its underlying message was: 'It's not easy being a Princess' (it is not known whether Catherine Middleton did the tour). Among those included in the exhibition were two of the most famous former occupants of Kensington's residential wing next door – Diana, Princess of Wales, and Princess Margaret. With its arm's-length status, Kensington Palace is ideally suited to handle more sensitive tasks like honouring the memory of Diana. It would feel contrived and uncomfortable if she was put on a plinth at somewhere like Windsor. But Princess Margaret's old Kensington Palace home, Apartment 1A, has now been handed over to Historic Royal Palaces (the title is misleading: Princess Margaret's 'flat' was actually a terraced house with more than twenty rooms, including a dog-washing room, an orchid room, a lift and a garden with a gazebo rescued from Ascot Racecourse). As part of the multimillion-pound transformation of Kensington Palace, it is being turned into a space which can properly reflect the lives of the Queen's sister and former daughter-in law. The Queen follows it all closely. She knows that this is yet another subtle judgement call in getting the right balance between 'her' and 'us'. And she is often less cautious than most people expect. This reign can be characterised in many ways, not least by the number of closed doors which are now open. It's not been some great altruistic gesture. Nor has it been forced on her. It's simply a case of being in the Happy People Business.

# 8

## Her Strength and Stay

*'Not a rebel, no — an innovator!'*

It's not the most promising name for a royal property. But as far as the Duke of Edinburgh is concerned right now, there is nothing quite like Sheep Dip. On this particular morning, it doesn't look very promising either. It has no doors and no windows and a North Sea breeze is tearing right through the middle of it as the builders lay another layer of concrete on the floor. But it is one of the Duke's pet projects and he loves dropping in unannounced with questions and fresh ideas. And he will be back when Sheep Dip is finished to check that this three-bedroom house in the wilds of Norfolk has been finished exactly as he wants it. Because this is his domain. Round here, he is the boss.

For sixty years, this restless, quizzical paterfamilias has had to tread carefully through the constitutional minefield which surrounds the throne. With no rulebook to work from, no precedents beyond some ill-fitting comparisons with Prince Albert, the Duke has carved out a role for himself which has always followed two parallel imperatives – supporting the Queen and being busy.

Much of his life has been spent doing things in spite of rather than because of who he is. From the day he moved into Buckingham Palace, he has had people telling him what is not allowed – things he cannot do, papers he cannot read and so on. Yet he has used his position and his considerable energy to make a mark on the world which has touched millions. He is now the only remaining major figure on the world stage who saw active service in the Second World War. And there are three places where the courtiers' diktats do not hold sway, places where he can exercise his own judgement and try out the inexhaustible supply of ideas rattling through his head. One is Balmoral in Scotland, one is Windsor and the one where he has, perhaps, his greatest freedom is Sandringham in Norfolk. It's not immediately clear where its 20,350 acres begin and end. The easiest way to tell that you are on royal acres is to look at the houses. If the external woodwork and the front door is painted in a gentle white and a pale blue – a shade known as 'Sea Rover' – then you have arrived. It's the estate colour scheme. 'We try to have as few signs as possible,' explains Marcus O'Lone, the manager of the Sandringham Estate. 'The Queen and the Duke like us to be tidy and signposts need maintenance.' Tidiness is certainly a priority round here. There can be few farms which keep their equipment so clean. That is in part because the Duke has installed a tractor-washing machine which recycles its own water. In one area of the estate, a long-legged monster on wheels patrols the hundred-acre blackcurrant crop, almost all of it destined for Ribena. When this machine is not spraying the blackcurrants, it can pick them, too. The Duke is very proud of it. In the organic zone, a tiny plantation of baby hazels and oaks is taking shape. It's the Duke's truffle farm. There has been no sign of a truffle yet but it's early days. This has only been going seven years and, like the monarchy itself, truffle farming is a long game. The Duke is prepared to wait for as long as it takes. The truffle spores have come far and take time to work their magic. The world truffle maestros are the Italians and the French, but they declined to help so the Duke turned to the Kiwis. And, in any case, the Queen is Queen of New Zealand.

Rare game birds abound here because everything is kept as wild as possible. There are no plump pheasant populations emerging from commercial hatcheries as happens on many shoots. Edward VII bought this place as an old-fashioned sporting estate and shooting remains the principal royal recreation here; it is conducted as traditionally as possible. Ditto the delightful and unapologetically old-fashioned Sandringham Museum with its vintage cars, invalid carriages and exotic menagerie of stuffed hunting trophies from another age. Yet, over in the estate work-shops, chief engineer Danny Harvey is never happier than when he and the Duke are inventing some new gismo. One of his proudest creations is the royal picnic trailer. The Duke sketched the original concept and Harvey built it, complete with spice rack, drinks cabinet, rubbish compart-ment, barbecue and drawers for hot and cold food.

The Duke has been in charge here since George VI died on the premises in February 1952. Sandringham, like Balmoral, is private royal property and the Queen inherited the lot. But she had a substantial part of the world to reign over and also wanted to give the Duke some autonomy. So she put him in charge of the Sandringham and Balmoral estates and also appointed him Ranger of Windsor Great Park. The Duke has super-vised the planting of thousands of trees on Windsor's five thousand acres. The castle's main garden, on its eastern front, is his handiwork and he has even introduced a flock of Windsor budgerigars. The latest innovation is a 7.4-acre vineyard which could be producing Windsor wine by 2015.

Anyone travelling through the park will probably wonder why on earth the traffic signs dictate a speed limit of 38mph. It was the Duke's idea. 'See!' he says. 'If it said 40 you wouldn't notice it. But you notice 38mph!' It wasn't an entirely random figure either. It equates precisely to sixty kilometres per hour. Not only is the Duke completely fluent in French and German but he is entirely at home in imperial and metric, too. Sandringham is equally versatile. 'I think imperially myself,' says O'Lone. 'But at a meeting five years ago, the Duke noticed that all the young managers were talking in hectares so he said: "We'd better face up to this. In future please provide everything in hectares." So we do.'

The Duke cannot interfere with Red Boxes or summon Ministers or sign legislation. The Palace of Westminster didn't even give him a proper seat at the State Opening of Parliament for the first fifteen years of the Queen's reign. But on the royal estates he is master of all he surveys, more so at Sandringham than anywhere else. Whereas Windsor Great Park is still part of the Crown Estate and Balmoral's 50,000 acres are constrained by assorted regional and environmental authorities, the Duke has more freedom to do what he wants at Sandringham. Hence Sheep Dip. The Queen and the Duke will not live in it. It is for one of their gamekeepers. Even with 150 existing estate properties to think about, the Duke has always regarded this remote, derelict farmhouse as a wasted opportunity. He likes a spot of property developing. Many years ago, he decided to renovate Wood Farm and it is now a much-loved family retreat. Sheep Dip is a more modest project but he is equally enthusiastic. 'Six years ago, the Duke said, "I'd like to see a keeper here," says O'Lone (whose own office, at York Cottage, is the room in which George V's children were born). 'Back then, it was too expensive because it would have cost £150,000 just to link it to the mains.' Then technology improved and the Duke is now confident that Sheep Dip can thrive with a biodiesel generator and clever insulation. It will certainly be the only gamekeeper's cottage in the area with a sea view and underfloor heating.

Sandringham is more than just a place for shooting and interesting experiments. On the Duke's watch, it has gone from a loss to a surplus (ploughed back into the estate) without a single redundancy. He has opened up six hundred acres of woodland to the public plus a lucrative caravan park and the most intimate tour available in any royal residence. The dining room is not just interesting for its Goya tapestries and Queen Alexandra's collection of illustrated *cartes des visites* from the great and good of her day. This is where the Queen actually has all her meals. Look closely at the table mats and you will see pictures of her racehorses. Next door, in the Small Drawing Room, you can see the pretty bronze ptarmigan which the Duke gave her on their fiftieth wedding anniversary. It's also a reminder that the Prince of Wales is not the only eco-minded member of the family. Knowing the Prince's enthusiasm for organic farming, the Duke has already made a chunk of the estate organic so that Sandringham is ready for the next generation. All important decisions about all the royal estates are taken in tandem with the Prince anyway. The Duke has installed a huge accelerated composter to regurgitate all the leftovers from the visitor restaurant as plant food. The restaurant itself monitors the 'food miles' of all its ingredients. But the Duke knows where to draw the line. He is always very careful not to intrude on the Queen's own personal territory like the Royal Kennels (she breeds and trains gun dogs at Sandringham), the Royal Pigeon Loft (she still races pigeons) or the Royal Stud. When the Queen decided to turn Sandringham's magnificent walled garden into very elegant stallion paddocks, the Duke was certainly not going to quarrel. As he observed in 2010: 'The secret of a happy marriage is not to have the same interests. It's one thing not to argue about.'

Ask any member of the Royal Household past or present to explain the Queen's phenomenal success as a monarch and the Duke will be at or near the top of any list. No study of her and her reign is complete without an appraisal of the man at her side. As she herself declared on their Golden Wedding anniversary: 'He is someone who doesn't take easily to compliments but he has, quite simply, been my strength and stay all these years.'

And, as Prince William acknowledges, it cannot have been an easy transition in 1952. 'In the world that they were in, it was almost back to front,' he says. 'The Queen was taking on her role in a man's world. The Duke of Edinburgh was taking on the role of consort as a very successful naval commander – and would have been an even bigger one. Yet both of them carved their own paths and have done that ever since, to brilliant standards. Together, they're a very good team.'

'He's always been there for all of us,' says the Duke of York. He believes the key to his father's success as consort has been about knowing when to stand back and when to make a well-judged intervention: 'The Duke of Edinburgh has been a constant source of advice, help, teamwork, leadership – taking some things away from the Queen but with that ability to be able to know when to come in.' It has also been about knowing when *not* to come in.

The Queen's middle son points to the potential row over his own service as a Royal Navy helicopter pilot in the Falklands War of 1982. Prince Andrew (as he was then) was determined to serve alongside his comrades, but there were some within the Ministry of Defence who feared that the Number Two in the line of succession would make a prime enemy propaganda target and, thus, increase the threat to those around him. The Duke of Edinburgh, as a former officer, had very strong views on the matter. 'He knew what I was going through and that it was absolutely essential that I went,' says his son. 'As a professional, you couldn't not go. It would have destroyed any credibility as a professional that I'd had. And the Queen knew that.' Yet, this was a Forces, not a family matter. The Duke of Edinburgh managed to restrain himself until the authorities had come to the right conclusion.

'In a sense, his life is very simple. It is 100 per cent support for the Queen,' says his recently retired Private Secretary, Brigadier Sir Miles Hunt-Davis. 'The organisation of his life is based entirely on the Queen's programme. So he will not look at his programme until the Queen's programme has been decided. Only then does he decide what to do.' At any royal occasion, the Duke is not simply there to share the handshakes and the small talk but to offer reassurance. The Queen is always surrounded by able and reliable people but it is still a comfort to know that, a few feet away, there is the man who made a Coronation vow to be her 'liege man of life and limb'. 'He'll be the one lifting children over the barrier to meet the Queen,' says Sir Hunt-Davis, 'or directing her attention to someone in the crowd or showing something of interest which he knows she will enjoy.'

Behind the veneer of the brisk, unsentimental reactionary there lies the same romantic soul who wrote, in 1947: 'Lilibet is the only "thing" in this world which is absolutely real to me'; who turned his hand to jewellery design to mark his wedding anniversary.

One of the prettiest items in the Queen's jewellery collection is the intricate bracelet devised and sketched by the Duke in 1952. Made of diamonds, sapphires and rubies, it features the intertwined letters 'E' and 'P', white roses of the House of York (the Queen was born Princess Elizabeth of York) and an anchor.* It was the Duke who took the fairy-tale Princess out of her gilded cage. 'He's been a tremendous support to her throughout their marriage, especially early on because she had had a sheltered life,' says Sir William Heseltine. 'He was able to open windows on the world to her before television had taken over that role. It was very important.'

Today, the Duke remains as romantic as ever. In June 2010, bidders at Christie's in King Street in London may not have paid much attention to a pretty little double study of the Queen by the artist Edward Seago. In this £6 million sale of Victorian and Impressionist paintings, the star

---

* The Duke's creative streak is reflected in the prestigious Prince Philip Designer's Prize, now going for more than fifty years. Previous winners include James Dyson and Terence Conran. He is not slow to offer opinions on all forms of design. Introduced to a member of the Chartered Society of Designers recently, he remarked: 'Well, you didn't design your beard very well.'

turns were works by Sir Lawrence Alma-Tadema and Sir Alfred Munnings. Seago's fifteen-by nine-inch painting, with an estimate of between £4,000 and £6,000, was of passing interest. Yet someone seemed keen to get it. Indeed, the bidding agent for an anonymous buyer was quite insistent, driving the price up to just short of £10,000. Despite paying well over the odds, the mystery buyer was very happy. Unknown to everyone, it was the Duke. He already had Seago's finished portrait of the Queen in his study and has always loved it. When he learned that the artist's preliminary sketch was coming up for sale, he could not resist it. The two works now hang, reunited, above the Duke's desk.

'There are some people who don't need many friends,' says a close friend of the family. 'And those two, they're just a real love story – taking tea together every day, talking about everything. He might take out a letter and read it to her or crack a joke. They just adore each other.' Both eat sensibly (one aide puts it down to 'iron self-discipline'). The Duke avoids wine – he prefers beer and the occasional dry martini – and tries not to mix protein with carbohydrate. Back in 2000, as the Queen Mother was celebrating her centenary, the Duke told Gyles Brandreth: 'God, I don't want to live to be a hundred. I can't imagine anything worse.' Yet, shrugging off the alarm which followed his Christmas heart scare in 2011 he continues to view old age as another country, in his nineties. In 2010, he undertook more than three hundred public engagements. One of them, shortly before Christmas, was a lunch to mark the retirement of the academic and historian Sir Christopher Frayling from the Royal Mint Advisory Committee. It is worth noting for the simple fact that Frayling was actually at university with the Prince of Wales. The Duke has thus reached the stage in life where he is celebrating the retirement of his children's contemporaries. He can but look on and wonder what it feels like. To adapt a famous wartime royal phrase, the Duke cannot retire without the Queen. And the Queen won't retire.

They have had their disagreements, like every other couple. As the late Lord Charteris pointed out, Prince Philip is the only person on earth who can tell the Queen to 'shut up' and vice versa. On one occasion, he threatened to 'put her out' of the car. On another, she locked herself away in *Britannia*, declaring: 'I'm simply not going to appear until Philip is in a better temper.' As we have learned, there have even been flying objects. The fact that all these anecdotes are somewhere between thirty-five and sixty years old speaks for itself.

Those who know the couple well talk of the way they complement each other. The Duke's biographer Tim Heald has contrasted her famous negative judgement – an innate sense of when to say 'No' – with his inclination to take a risk. If in doubt, she will hold back. He prefers to get to the point. The former Labour Cabinet Minister Barbara Castle always spoke highly of the Queen's professionalism but was less positive about the Duke. At the opening of the Severn Bridge in 1966, the then Transport Secretary was attempting to stand to attention during the National Anthem when a familiar voice muttered in her direction: 'When are you going to finish the M4? You've been a long time at it.' Now that the Queen has overtaken Queen Victoria in age and is fast approaching her sixty-three-year reigning record, historians will increasingly be tempted to compare the two. 'There is one big, big difference between the Queen and Victoria,' says a family friend, 'and it is that Victoria was a confrontational character. The Queen is most definitely not confrontational. And that is where Prince Philip is so important. He helps her make up for that. And I think, sometimes, he gives her the impetus to take a stand.'

Ever since his wedding in 1947, the Duke has inevitably been likened to Prince Albert, husband of Queen Victoria (and the Duke's great-great-grandfather). Perhaps, in time, the words 'Elizabeth and Philip' will just become part of the language, like 'Victoria and Albert'; perhaps, indeed, there will one day be a building called the 'E&P' to rival the 'V&A'. Yet Albert was in a very different situation, not least since he acted as Victoria's Private Secretary, his own desk parked next to hers. From the outset, the Duke has been kept firmly on the other side of the constitutional door. In fact, he has had a good deal less access than his immediate predecessor as consort – Queen Elizabeth. When George VI turned his wartime audiences with Winston Churchill into lunches – or 'picnics' as the Royal Family called them – he would include his Queen. As William Shawcross has pointed out, she was included in some of the greatest secrets of the twentieth century including Ultra, the crucial wartime intelligence gathered at Bletchley Park, Buckinghamshire. In retrospect, it was an act of enormous constitutional audacity by both the Monarch and the Prime Minister. During the current reign, no Prime Minister has found Prince Philip in the audience room. Nor have his fingerprints been found on state papers. He has voiced forthright views on everything from birth control to welfare but only ever in a general context. 'In all the time I've been here, he's stayed well out of anything to do with politics – well, well away,' says his former Private Secretary, Sir Miles Hunt-Davis. 'The fact is I've never heard him make any party political comment at all and that's the way it's got to be as consort to the head of state.' As one of the Queen's former private secretaries puts it: 'I can give him an absolute clean bill of health constitutionally. I've never heard a Minister complain that he interfered.'

At the same time, the government has been very happy to use him as a diplomatic tool.

The Duke is the most widely travelled member of the Royal Family in history. No monarch has been to more places than the Queen. The Duke has not only been with her on all her travels but he has also circumnavigated the globe many more times on his own account. Sir Miles Hunt-Davis points out that whenever his former boss flew to a foreign country on charity business, the leader of that country would often want to see him. World leaders were not remotely bothered by the Duke's lack of constitutional power. He was the Queen's husband. Would he care to stop by for dinner? If he could, he usually would – to the delight of the local British ambassador.

It is sometimes asked why the Queen has never given the Duke the title of Prince Consort. No official answer has been given but the general feeling is that he never wanted it. 'I don't think he ever saw himself as Prince Albert and he resisted the idea of being declared Prince Consort because he did not want it thought he was modelling himself on Prince Albert,' says one former Private Secretary. The late Lord Charteris described the Prince Consort title as 'meaningless'. 'Pretty early on, he decided he was going to do his own things and so he didn't want the title,' says a member of the Duke's team. 'But I think he quite likes coincidences with Albert – like the fact that they both became Chancellor of Cambridge University, that sort of thing.' There may be another reason why he has never been Prince Consort. The Queen had some of the happiest years of her life as Duchess of Edinburgh – the only time she was known by her married name. During those four years and two months between the wedding (when Prince Philip was granted the Dukedom) and her accession, she came as close as she ever has to leading a 'normal' life. As the wife of a Royal Navy officer stationed in Malta, she could drive her little MG sports car around the island and forget protocol or official duties. If the couple suddenly decided they wanted to go out for a picnic or a night's dancing, they could. Back in London, the Duchess could turn Clarence House into a family home. That all changed in February 1952. But at least her husband would carry on being known as the Duke of Edinburgh. Had he been renamed 'Prince Consort', that title and all its happy associations would have vanished into obscurity, just like the Duke's courtesy titles – Earl of Merioneth and Baron Greenwich. As the Palace explained when the Queen changed the family surname from Windsor to Mountbatten-Windsor in 1960, she was keen that her husband's name should 'enjoy perpetuation'. His ducal title has 'enjoyed perpetuation' too.

So when should the Duke be called Prince Philip and when is he the Duke of Edinburgh? He was Prince Philip of Greece until 1947 when he became a British citizen, was made Duke of Edinburgh and dropped his Hellenic title. Ten years later, he was made a Prince of the United Kingdom and so became Prince Philip again. He is now 'HRH The Prince Philip, Duke of Edinburgh'. 'Prince' or 'Duke' are interchangeable – if there are a lot of other Princes around, it can be simpler to use 'Duke' – but the Palace observes a subtle distinction. 'I say "Prince Philip" at the Palace in conversation and, outside, I usually say "The Duke of Edinburgh",' says Sir Miles Hunt-Davis. 'I'd never write to someone saying "Prince Philip has asked me to write" unless it was a very close relationship.'

As with the royal estates, so the Queen also defers to the Duke in certain family matters. 'She may be the Monarch but, in terms of her children, she takes the traditional view that a husband is head of the family,' says one senior ex-member of her Household.

It was the Duke who took the lead in shaping the children's educations and careers; in steering their sons through the more muscular educational system of Gordonstoun in Scotland; in encouraging their daughter to be her own woman – and even, occasionally, man. When the Princess Royal was appointed a Lady of the Order of the Garter and, later, a Lady of the Order of the Thistle, she decided that she did not want to be a 'Lady', with LG and LT after her name. She wanted to be a 'Knight', like her brothers. She is thus the first (and probably last) woman in history to have the initials KG and KT after her name. The heralds at the College of Arms must have had an armorial fit. The Queen does not like any meddling with her personal Orders either. But the Princess must have had some influential backing to push it through. 'She's her father's daughter,' laughs one courtier by way of explanation.

At the Royal Family's Way Ahead Group conferences (now discontinued), it would be the Duke who took control. 'The Queen would sit on one side and the Duke on the other and the idea was that they were jointly chairing,' recalls one of those present. 'But it was always the Duke who took charge while the Queen might gossip with the Lord Chamberlain.'

It is a lazy media shorthand to describe the Royal Family as 'dysfunctional', which is to presuppose that they could ever be an 'ordinary' family in the first place. But the fact that much of their communication is via memos or letters or private secretaries does not make them 'dysfunctional'. As the Queen has explained to one royal guest, she is not one for long chats on the telephone. 'They can come and see me if they want,' she has said.

'There are certain things that we do differently that we find perfectly normal which everyone else thinks is completely mad,' the Duke of York acknowledges. 'For instance, if you ring one of your siblings, you just pick up the phone and ring. But actually we're all quite busy so we have a mechanism with which to find the time to be able to speak to each other. It's *how* we do things – not the fact that we do them or don't do them.'

Even after (or perhaps because of) more than fifty years of being asked 'what it's like' to be royal, there is a note of exasperation as the Duke explains that there was nothing odd about growing up in his world. After all, to a child always surrounded by world leaders, photographers, footmen, deference or Van Dycks, what was so abnormal about it? 'To me, my life is entirely normal and entirely real,' he says sternly. 'To you, your life and your experience is entirely normal and real. I would have some difficulty understanding your reality in the same that you would have some difficulty understanding my reality. The constant issue is that there are more people speculating and trying to find out about our normality and reality than is sometimes healthy. The family life that we have had has been as much a family life as your family life. It's had its ups, it's had its downs. It's had its good times, its bad times. That's the nature of the beast. And we make the most of family time that we can.'

He likens family reunions to some of the organisations he would encounter on his trade missions: 'It's rather like having a business which has a number of diversified subsidiaries. We do our own thing and we conduct our lives but occasionally we come back and talk to the boss of the parent company.' Even then, he says, some people find the royal way of doing things peculiar. 'We're all off doings things and then there are moments when we get together in an environment where there are lots of other people and they suddenly notice that all of us are having a conversation because we haven't actually been together for three months, four months. But that's not because we're not a family. It's entirely because we are performing roles in support of the Monarch.'

Sometimes, those roles also need to reviewed, reassigned or else quietly abandoned. The Duke recalls the 'upheavals' involving hundreds of patronages following the deaths, in quick succession, of Princess Margaret and the Queen Mother in 2002. 'Now that was a case where everybody sat round a table and lists of organisations were produced and you started thinking: "How do we cope with this particular change and who is going to do what, where and when? How many of these organisations are we going to hang on to? How many are going to be relevant in the future?" They created a huge organisational vacuum.' Here was another aspect of 'ordinary' royal life alien to the outside world.

Modish commentators who would not dream of criticising the most complicated or unorthodox modern living arrangements for fear of being thought judgemental are, none the less, still happy to scoff at a family whose members bow and curtsey to each other. It is not 'normal', of course, but nor is it 'normal' to be followed by cameras from cradle to grave or to be prevented from visiting a family burial plot without permission from the Foreign Office.* Royalty *is* different because we want it to be. 'You've got to have a scarcity value if you're a monarch,' former Prime Minister Sir Alec Douglas-Home once said. 'You mustn't make the Queen an ordinary person.'

'How do you describe it? It's a vocational job, it's there,' says the Duke of York. 'None of us can switch off and it's particularly true for the Queen. I mean you can get time away from public life but you're never going to be completely away. Which comes back to reality and normality. You're trying to understand what it is that makes us tick. If you had that experience, you wouldn't think it was odd.' Understandably, the family find the 'dysfunctional' charge rather hurtful, none more so than the Duke of Ediburgh. It was he who expressed the couple's public thanks to their children during their Golden Wedding anniversary: 'Like all families, we went through the full range of the pleasures and tribulations of bringing up children. I am, naturally, somewhat biased, but I think our children have all done rather well under very demanding circumstances and I hope I can be forgiven for feeling proud of them.' Spoken at the nadir of royal fortunes in the nineties, just two months after the funeral of Diana, Princess of Wales, these words had an even deeper resonance.

The Royal Family have their disagreements, like any other. But there is a common perception at large that the Duke and the Prince of Wales are always at loggerheads. Not true say those who know them both well. 'If you see them together, they get on like a house on fire,' says one. 'It's constructive tension. I think in many ways they're on the same routes and it's been helpful to them that they don't always agree. They do approach things from different angles. That's the way life is in families.'

Gyles Brandreth says that the Duke once explained it all to him as follows: 'Prince Charles is a romantic and I'm a pragmatist. And sometimes a romantic thinks that a pragmatist is unfeeling.'

'It's just the classic eldest son and father thing – always seeking approval

---

* Prince Philip's mother, Princess Andrew of Greece, died in Britain in 1969, having left instructions that she wished to be buried at Jerusalem's Church of Mary Magdalene. She was finally interred in 1988 but diplomatic and security considerations prevented the Duke from visiting Israel for another six years. Her children had warned the Princess that her choice of resting place would prove difficult. 'Nonsense,' she replied, 'there's a perfectly good bus service from Istanbul.'

and always wanting to do things differently,' says a member of the Prince of Wales's inner circle. 'He's not like Philip physically,' the Duke's sister, Sophie, Princess George of Hanover, once remarked, 'but very like him in his ways of laughing and his quick way of saying something.'

Others point to the Prince's Trust as an example of shared interests pursued in different ways. The Duke of Edinburgh's Award is a global success, having helped more than six million young people in 120 countries.* Since 1956, it has encouraged young people to set and achieve challenges for themselves. Two decades later, when the Prince of Wales, came to leave the Royal Navy, he used the contents of his pension fund to create the Prince's Trust and give disadvantaged young people help in turning their lives around. It's now one of the giants of the charitable sector. There are many similarities with the Duke's Award but it is neither a copy nor a rival. 'They are complementary,' explains Elizabeth Buchanan, former Private Secretary to the Prince of Wales. 'The Prince's Trust helps a lot of people who might be missed by the awards, people who have been forgotten. So you get the Trust and the Award working very well alongside each other. What the Royal Family don't like to do is bump into each other and operate in the same area. It is not a good use of resources.'

Prince Andrew, the Duke of York, is the one whose professional life has most closely followed that of the Duke – career Royal Navy officer and then globetrotting trade promoter. He gave up the trade role for regular royal duties in 2011. There had been complaints about his robust diplomatic style, his encounters with certain dubious regimes and his friendship with an American financier convicted of sex offences. The Duke of York's supporters have pointed out that he was simply a vigorous champion of British interests and that his meetings with unsavoury regimes were in the line of his (unpaid) duty as a business ambassador, for the British Government. Furthermore, they say, we all have embarrassing friends.

But it is Prince Edward, the Earl of Wessex, who has taken on many of his father's duties, notably the Duke of Edinburgh's Award scheme. These days, it is the Earl and Countess of Wessex who see most of the Queen and the Duke – bringing their young children for tea at Windsor Castle at weekends and hosting the annual private party for the Queen's birthday. It is also the Earl who will ensure that the Duke of Edinburgh title continues to 'enjoy perpetuation'. It goes against all the rules of the hereditary peerage but it is the Monarch who sets the rules and she made this one on Prince Edward's wedding day in 1999. Amid all the excitement, most people overlooked the announcement that, following the

---

* In some countries, the organisers prefer to give the award a different name. In Ireland, for example, it is known as Gaisce, or the President's Award. The Duke's not bothered, as long as it works.

The Sovereign's Parade, Sandhurst, December 2006. Officer Cadet Wales becomes a 2nd Lieutenant.

(*Above left*) The
Grenadier Guards
with their Colonel-in-
Chief.(*Above right*)
Welcoming home the
Royal Welsh
Regiment. Fusilier
Shaun Stocker, 19,
receives his campaign
medal.(*Right*) Flight
Lieutenant Wales of
the RAF welcomes
his 'incredible grand-
mother' to Anglesey.
The most sacred date
in the royal calendar,
(*Left*) Remembrance
Sunday at the
Cenotaph.

(*Above*) 80th birthday greetings outside Windsor Castle.
(*Right*) David Beckham and Kirsty Howard, six, present the Commonwealth Baton to the Queen as she opens the Manchester Commonwealth Games during her 2002 Golden Jubilee.

Garden party crowds are not easily deterred. Those waiting to be introduced forgo their umbrellas.

The new Duke and Duchess of Cambridge

(*Above*) Three generations of the Royal Family gather at Sandhurst for Prince Harry's passing out parade. (*Below*) Family farewells after a Hebridean cruise

(*Clockwise from top*)
Derby Day 2008.

A face in the crowd
at the Royal Windsor
Horse Show.

St Paul's Cathedral,
2006.

3-D glasses are
required at Sheffield
University's Advanced
Manufacturing
Research Centre.

No need for introductions. The Queen meets the Queen on board Cunard's new Queen Elizabeth. She has sat for more than 140 portraits during her reign.

deaths of both Prince Philip and the Queen, the title of Duke of Edinburgh would pass to Prince Edward and his heirs. Otherwise, it would have followed the usual route for a hereditary title and gone to the eldest son, in which case it would simply have disappeared once the Prince of Wales became King.

It is often said that, of all his children, the Duke is closest to the Princess Royal, although the fact that she is an only daughter may have something to do with it. What can be argued with a greater degree of certainty is that it is the Princess who most closely resembles the Duke. Her workaholism, absence of vanity, briskness, coolness under fire (literally, in the case of the 1974 attempted kidnapping), loyalty to staff, contempt for flatterers and ditherers and her love of the sea are all ducal characteristics which seem particularly pronounced in the Princess. Tony Blair was immediately struck by the likeness. In his memoirs he recalls the day his wife met the Princess for the first time at Balmoral. When Mrs Blair attempted some 'Call me Cherie' informality, the Princess replied: 'Actually, I prefer Mrs Blair.' None the less, Mr Blair retains an abiding respect for the Princess: 'I always liked her. I doubt the feeling was mutual. She is a chip right off the old man's block. People think Prince Philip doesn't give a damn about what people think of him and they are right. Anne is exactly the same. She is what she is and if you don't like it, you can clear off. It's not a quality I have but I admire those who do. The unfortunate thing is it stops people seeing the other side of their character.' In fact, in the most trying situations, the Duke can display great sensitivity entirely at odds with his media persona. One of the less predictable disclosures of the six-month inquest into the death of Diana, Princess of Wales, was the correspondence which showed the extent to which the Duke had tried to help and reassure his daughter-in-law during the breakdown of her marriage. Perhaps the Duke's own experience of being up against some of the old Palace hierarchies, of being simultaneously inside and outside the royal loop, help him to identify with others struggling on their royal pedestals.

If there is one concern which even good friends of the family are prepared to voice it is that the Duke's paternal advice to his younger children has pushed the 'be yourself' mantra too far. 'The Duke has encouraged them to be too like him and not enough like her. They do need to be a bit more like the Queen,' says one close ally. 'He has told them to follow their instincts and be their own people and not be bossed around like he was when he arrived at the Palace. While that's admirable, it has led to things like *It's a Royal Knockout*. It's why we get the Duke of York sounding off to a room full of senior businessmen about whatever he thinks.' But the same friends are also quick to point out that what makes the Duke of Edinburgh's attitude entirely understandable – and his achievements so remarkable – is his own extraordinary childhood. His is a story which would today be classified as a borderline case for social services. Yet it produced an uncommonly determined, cheerful, self-starting, intelligent young man who would win the heart of the most eligible young woman on earth. Is it any wonder he has raised his own children to follow their instincts rather than dwell on their frailties?

Prince Philip was born in Corfu on 10 June 1921, the fifth child and only son of Prince Andrew of Greece and Princess Alice of Battenberg (Lord Mountbatten's sister). His father's family were Danish/Russian/German, his mother's German/British, but the baby was sixth in line to the Greek throne. This was not a glittering prize in the Euro-royal scheme of things. Prince Philip's grandfather had been assassinated eight years earlier, his parents had already had one spell in exile and cousin Alexander's reign had come to a sudden end in 1920 courtesy of a fatal monkey bite. Following another military coup, Prince Andrew was made a scapegoat for the disastrous 1919–22 war with Turkey during which he had commanded the 2nd Army Corps. He had fought gallantly but his reward was a death sentence – for 'disobeying orders' – from a kangaroo court in December 1922. Just hours later, a British diplomat managed to negotiate his release for long enough to get him aboard a British warship, dispatched by his cousin George V. Joined by his family, Prince Andrew set sail for a life of exile in France. Prince Philip, still a baby, was famously carried aboard in an orange crate. In Paris, the family lived perfectly comfortably although, by contemporary European royal standards, they were poor. By the age of seven, Prince Philip was sent to Britain to attend Cheam preparatory school and within two years the family had broken up. His four sisters had all married, his parents were separated and his mother was committed to a Swiss sanatorium after a mental breakdown.

When not at school, the young Prince would be passed among Mountbatten relations in Britain or make his own way across Europe to stay with his sisters and his network of royal cousins. It was a life of contrasts not easily comprehensible to modern minds. One week, this ten-year-old child might be alone on a train, heaving a suitcase from Calais to Germany. The next, he might be riding on the shores of the Black Sea with Cousin Michael, the schoolboy King of Romania. As he himself has remarked, it all seemed perfectly normal at the time – though not in hindsight: 'It really is amazing that I was left to cross a continent all by myself – taxis, trains and boats – to get to my sisters.' At school, he was a thoughtful, unstuffy child who neither complained nor bragged about his strange royal existence. Apparently he was known as 'Flop', although he was anything but. Few were aware of his royal links or of the photograph of his cousin George V, which he kept in a suitcase. Yet, come the holidays, he would set off for a kinsman's *schloss*, often to be reunited with his adored father. There would, though, be no contact with his mother until his mid-teens, by which time she had emerged from self-imposed medical exile (mother and son would be much closer in later life). After Cheam, the Prince spent a year at Salem, a German school housed in a brother-in-law's castle and run by the pioneering educationalist Kurt Hahn. Nazism was on the rise. More than sixty years later, the Duke would recall that every new boy was assigned someone called a 'helper' and that his 'helper' was Jewish. One night, a gang of pupils cornered the boy in his bed and cut all his hair off. 'You can imagine what an effect this had on us junior boys,' the Duke recounted. 'Nothing could have given us a clearer indication of the meaning of prejudice and persecution.' Prince Philip gave the boy the cricket cap he had brought with him from Cheam to cover his scalp until his hair grew back. 'It taught me a very important lesson about man's capacity for inhumanity,' the Duke explained. 'And I have never, ever, forgotten it.'

The Nazis drove Hahn (himself the son of a German-Jewish industrialist) into exile and Prince Philip was sent to join his new foundation at Gordonstoun in Scotland. It was a small school, dedicated more to helping every boy achieve his own potential than making him conform to type. Prince Philip flourished and became head boy before signing up for the Royal Navy in 1939. Years later, he said it was probably his maternal uncle, Lord Louis 'Dickie' Mountbatten, who steered him into it. 'He may have persuaded me. I just sort of accepted it,' Prince Philip told Basil Boothroyd in 1970. 'I didn't feel very strongly about it. I really wanted to go into the Air Force. Left to my own devices, I'd have gone into the Air Force without a doubt.' But he flourished at Dartmouth Royal Naval College, emerging as best cadet. It was also during his time there that the King and Queen came to visit with their daughters and Prince Philip was deputed to entertain the two Princesses. If the encounter did not have an enduring impact on him, it left a lasting impression on Princess Elizabeth.

During the Second World War, the Prince was again caught between two worlds. As he later reflected: 'You get swept up into these things. It was tragic.' His three sisters (the beloved Cecile had been killed in a plane crash in 1937) were all married to German officers. His father was marooned in German-controlled Monte Carlo where he would die in 1944. Prince Philip would never see him again.* The Prince's mother, by now recovered, insisted on remaining in occupied Athens. There she organised food and medical supplies for the poor, hid a Jewish family from the Nazis and founded an order of nuns. In short, one way or another, Prince Philip's entire family ended up in enemy territory. His own war took him to the Indian Ocean and then to the Mediterranean. Serving in HMS *Valiant*, he was mentioned in dispatches for his part in the Battle of Cape Matapan. It was his search-light battery which snared two Italian battle cruisers and helped send them to the bottom. With the characteristic modesty of his generation, he now looks back on it as nothing more than 'a bit of activity'.

Promoted rapidly, he became one of the youngest first lieutenants in the Royal Navy, serving as second-in-command of HMS *Wallace* in the North Sea and during the Allied landings in Sicily. He would finish the war in HMS *Whelp*, witnessing the Japanese surrender in Tokyo Bay. During his shore leave in Britain, he would stay with Mountbatten relations and, occasionally, with his distant cousin the King at Windsor Castle. 'I'd call in and have a meal,' he remarked years later, as if recollecting a favourite café. 'I once or twice spent Christmas at Windsor because I'd nowhere particular to go.' But, by now, he had definitely caught the eye of Princess Elizabeth. Despite introductions to a succession of eligible Guards officers on duty at the castle, her heart was set on her sailor Prince. With peace came progress. 'When I got back in '46 and went to Balmoral,' he told his biographer, 'it was probably then that it became, you know, that we began to think about it seriously and even talk about it.'

There was plenty of time to think about it. At the start of 1947, the Princess had to accompany her parents on their four-month tour of southern Africa. She celebrated her twenty-first birthday in Cape Town and returned to find her Prince waiting with a proposal (or, as he later put it: 'it was sort of fixed up when they came back'). The engagement was announced in July and their November wedding brought a much-needed splash of colour to a monochrome, washed-out, ration-book nation. As Duke and Duchess of Edinburgh, life got better and better. Charles and Anne were born in quick succession and the Duke was finally given his own ship, HMS *Magpie*, in 1950. But in 1951 it became clear that the King's health was deteriorating and that the Princess would have to start deputising for her father more and more. The Duke returned

---

*To this day, the Duke reveres his father's memory and recently had Prince Andrew's medals mounted in a special display case at Buckingham Palace. As the Duke has pointed out, his father's role in his life is often overlooked. 'One impression that needs to be corrected,' he once said, 'is that I was brought up by Lord Mountbatten. I don't think anybody thinks I had a father. I grew up very much more with my father's family than I did with my mother's.'

from sea, ostensibly on a temporary basis, to assist his wife until the King and Queen returned from a forthcoming Commonwealth tour. That tour never happened and the Duke never went back to sea. On 6 February 1952, everything changed.

While the apparatus of monarchy was ready and waiting for the new Queen, the Court had no idea what to do with the new, well, . . . what *was* he? The wife of a King is automatically the Queen. But the husband of a Queen, rather like the husband of a Dame or a Baroness, receives no reciprocity. Queen Victoria had complained that no formal role had existed for Prince Albert after their marriage but nothing much was done about it. The Duke was perfectly happy to carry on being the Duke. He was much more concerned about the impact on his young family and, to a lesser extent, on himself. The first of several run-ins with the Prime Minister, Winston Churchill, followed the Duke's suggestion that the family might carry on living at Clarence House. Churchill, primed by the Queen's Private Secretary, Sir Alan Lascelles, was having none of it. Monarchs, the Duke was told firmly, lived at Buckingham Palace. There was even greater tension when the old guard got wind of a house party rumour. Lord Mountbatten, it was said, had been boasting that the 'House of Mountbatten' now reigned. Whether he had or not (Churchill thought it pure Mountbatten), the Prime Minister wasted no time in making it clear that he, the Cabinet and the Queen were adamant that there would be no change of name. It was still the House of Windsor. The Duke had never suggested otherwise but it hurt to be squashed so firmly and so publicly. He was, he said, no more than a 'bloody amoeba'.

Within the Palace, there was a lot of territorial growling from the old guard – the 'men with moustaches' as the Duke's staff would call them. They were determined to keep the new consort in his place in case he got any ideas about being the new master.

Among the dimmer patrician elements it was a case of plain snobbery, even bigotry. The chap was an impoverished outsider from a third-rate, clapped-out foreign monarchy and had a lot of dubious German relations. According to Kenneth Rose, the Duke received an extraordinary snub following the Queen's accession and automatic promotion to Colonel-in-Chief of all the Foot Guards. She suggested that he might take her old appointment as Colonel of the Grenadier Guards. But the idea was sniffily rejected by a cabal of senior officers.* It is a measure of the man that when the same idea was proposed again many years later, the Duke did

---

* The Duke, instead, became Colonel of the Welsh Guards, informing them that they were 'the only regiment in which the Colonel is legally married to the Colonel-in-Chief'. He stepped down in 1975 to make way for the Prince of Wales.

not tell the regiment where it could stick its offer. Instead, he accepted, went on to be a devoted Colonel – and still is. He even spent the evening of his ninetieth birthday – Friday 10 June 2011– chairing the Household Division's Senior Colonels' Conference.

The Duke could live with the snobbery. He had never felt the slightest need to prove his dynastic credentials to anyone. He was neither marrying 'up' nor 'out' of his social position. As one Mountbatten cousin has pointed out, he was 'more royal than the Queen', with lineal connections to almost every throne in Christendom, past and present. It was a family joke that, when in London, his Aunt Louise would always carry a note in her handbag just in case she should fall under a bus. It stated (quite correctly): 'I am the Queen of Sweden.' Lord Mountbatten, never one to underplay pedigree, had traced his nephew's lineage back to Charlemagne, the Holy Roman Emperor. Years later, when a fantasist would claim to be the true Romanov heir to the Russian imperial throne, it was the Duke of Edinburgh who provided a DNA sample and stopped the claim in its tracks. He is even in the line of succession to the British throne himself, although it would take a pretty apocalyptic scenario to get him there. He currently hovers somewhere around the five hundred mark. Breeding was not his problem as far as the Duke's more cerebral opponents were concerned. Their fear was that a headstrong young blade, fresh from a naval command, might put silly, new-fangled ideas in the head of the pretty young Monarch. What it all boiled down to was a simple issue of control. Lord Brabourne later recalled the Household hostility towards the Duke: 'Lascelles was impossible. They were absolutely bloody to him. They patronised him. They treated him as an outsider. It wasn't much fun. He laughed it off but it must have hurt.'

As the late Lord Charteris pointed out, the courtiers even kept the Duke at arm's length during the Coronation itself. George VI had been crowned with his Queen at his side. The Queen was crowned alone. Even today, some members of staff are mindful of what happened to the Duke. 'He was slightly bruised by all that, quite frankly, and he was pretty shoddily treated,' says one. 'If Courts want to gang up on someone, they can do it all right, I can tell you.'

The Duke, however, remains phlegmatic about it all. 'I was told "Keep out" and that was that,' he told Gyles Brandreth a decade ago. 'I tried to find useful things to do. I introduced a Footman Training Programme. The old boys here hadn't had anything like it before. We had an Organisation and Methods Review. I tried to make improvements – without unhinging things. Some of the old guard weren't too happy. We met with a fair bit of resistance. But I think we made a few improvements, dragged some of them into the twentieth century.' It would be another forty years before Michael Peat and his team of management consultants dragged the rest of the Household into the twentieth century. The Duke had long given up by then. If the Palace didn't want his help, then he would carve his own role in the wider world. His office gained a reputation as the exciting place to be in the Palace, the only department where lady clerks were known as 'the girls' and called by their first names. 'There was always lots of laughter,' says one of them, recalling the gales of mirth when the Duke succumbed to jaundice and a lady wrote to him advising a daily diet of twenty-four grapefruit. 'He has always had a wonderful team around him. And if he thinks you know the answer, he'll always come to you. It's great fun to work for someone like that.'

His office staff were a small, devoted crew led by Lieutenant General Sir Frederick 'Boy' Browning, dashing war hero and errant husband of the writer Daphne du Maurier. A single office contained the four 'girls' – 'none over forty; no one got institutionalised' – while the Duke had two equerries next door. One was ex-RAF and one was the Duke's old Royal Navy chum Mike Parker, a quick-witted, rumbustious Australian. 'Boy Browning was an absolutely charming man,' recalls one of the team. 'But he had suffered in the war. He always talked about "me tum" – he'd had amoebic dysentery – and he had trouble with his nerves. Mike Parker could be exasperating at times but he was great fun and fitted the bill very nicely.'

It was Parker who would often bear the brunt of Establishment complaints about the Duke. On one occasion, he was summoned before Winston Churchill to receive a reprimand for allowing the Duke to travel by helicopter. 'Is it your intention,' Churchill asked him, 'to wipe out the Royal Family in the shortest possible time?' 'Churchill was even against Prince Philip learning to fly. The thing you have to remember is that all those old men absolutely adored the Queen and couldn't bear to think of anything happening which would upset her,' says one of the team. The Prime Minister did not win that one. The Duke went on to master fifty-nine types of aircraft, including nine different helicopters, and logged 5,986 flying hours over forty-four years before retiring in 1997 with a last blast, from Carlisle to Islay, at the controls of a BAe 146.

All the sniping merely made him even more determined to do his own thing. When not accompanying the Queen on her travels, he expanded the range of his patronages enormously and created new ones. The Duke of Edinburgh's Award was born in 1956, despite the grumbles of some reactionary elements who warned that it smacked of the Hitler Youth and would kill off the Boy Scouts. Under his leadership – he was always a leader rather than a figurehead – organisations like the National Playing

Fields Association, the Outward Bound Trust, the Automobile Association or the Industrial Society all found themselves propelled in fresh directions.

The Duke was part of the World Wildlife Fund (WWF) from the moment it was founded around a dining-room table in Switzerland in 1961. President of the British arm for twenty years, he became International President for another fifteen and, by the time he left in 1996, it was among the most influential environmental voices in the world. He had paved the way for his eldest son's environmental crusades a generation later – even if he occasionally despairs of some of today's 'tree-huggers' (as he calls the more ethereal eco-warriors). His Commonwealth Study Conferences were ground-breaking assemblies of business and union leaders from all over the world, an international, industrial version of George VI's boys' clubs from a previous generation. Nor had the Duke entirely given up on innovation at the Palace. He knew that the 'men with moustaches' would never let him near state banquets, of course, but he introduced 'Luncheons'. Interesting figures from random areas of national life would suddenly get a call to see if they might like to join the Queen and the Duke for lunch (then, as now, many assume it is a practical joke). They proved so successful that, in 1972, he introduced dinners on the same lines. In private, the Duke was sympathetic to those calling for a more modern monarchy. It is widely accepted that the Duke was instrumental in persuading the Queen to sever links with the annual debutante circus (which she duly did). He wrote books – fourteen in total – and forewords to other people's books. He delivered lectures, to both lay and academic audiences, presented television programmes, visited parts of the world that had never seen a member of the Royal Family. And, over time, his willingness to embrace change started to rub off on the rest of the institution.

Throughout the reign, he has taken a hands-on, troubleshooting role in resolving issues which do not have a political or constitutional dimension but which have been of great sensitivity to the Queen – the organisation of the Coronation, the design of her coins, the filming of the first royal documentary, the restoration of Windsor Castle after the fire, the funeral plans for Diana, Princess of Wales, and so on. During the fifties, it was the Duke who suggested converting the ruins of the bombed-out Palace chapel into a public exhibition space for the Royal Collection. He was greeted by the usual shuffling of papers and courteous inertia, but he persisted. Since 1962, the Queen's Gallery has been visited by millions. It proved so successful that, forty years later, another Queen's Gallery was opened at the Palace of Holyroodhouse.

Typically, the Duke prefers to downplay his role as a catalyst for change.

Asked by the author in 2004 if he saw himself as a royal rebel, he smiled and replied: 'Not a rebel, no – an innovator!' As the Duke told Gyles Brandreth, any changes he made were 'not for the sake of modernising, not for the sake of b\*\*\*ering about with things. I'm anxious to get things done. That's all. I'm interested in the efficient use of resources.'

There is no doubt, though, that the Duke also played a critical role in encouraging the Queen during the great royal reforms of the eighties and nineties. Having learned from long and unhappy experience, he knew that there was no point trying to get involved directly. But that did not stop him helping from the wings. Lord Airlie, the Lord Chamberlain who supervised the overhaul of the monarchy and its finances, remains very conscious of the Duke's contribution. 'Prince Philip played a very important part,' he says. 'The Queen quite often deferred to him on matters where he could make a meaningful contribution. He came up with all sorts of ideas. Some of them were extremely helpful and, if you didn't think they were, you had quite a job arguing him out of it. He could be quite argumentative sometimes. But you do need somebody to challenge you. He made you think.'

'Prince Philip is the unsung hero of the reign,' says a very senior ex-courtier firmly. 'People underestimate the help the Queen has had from him, especially when times were hard. Like all really great men, he's not always easy. But if he was always easy, he wouldn't be the chap he is.' One former Private Secretary remembers being pilloried in a Channel Four television documentary to the point that he could no longer watch the programme and left the Palace for a long walk. On his return he found a letter from the Duke already waiting for him. 'I thought, "I'd better not open this tonight" but then I did. And the Duke had written: "Fear not the taunts of men. The moth shall eat them up like a garment – Isaiah". And I thought that was very good. It wasn't a case of patting you on the back and saying, "Come on, cheer up, old chap." It was just what you wanted at a particular moment. It was very typical of the way he helped the private secretaries.' That has not always been the case. One of those who worked in the Private Secretary's Office during the seventies found that the Duke had not forgotten some of the treatment he received in the fifties.

Retirement, as we have seen, is out of the question. But, since turning ninety, the Duke has made a few concessions to age, stepping down from twenty of his more time-consuming patronages, such as the Chancellorships of Cambridge and Edinburgh universities and the City and Guilds Institute. It follows the quiet internal transfer of a few favourite charities in recent years. Just as the Earl of Wessex has taken on the Duke of Edinburgh's

Award, so the Duke of York now chairs the trustees of the Outward Bound Trust and the Princess Royal looks after the Commonwealth Study Conferences. The Duke does not like long goodbyes and is appalled by the idea of hanging around old haunts. 'If you are the boss and you're handing on, you do not want to be sitting on someone's shoulder,' says Sir Miles Hunt-Davis. 'He's the last person to sit on anybody's shoulder.' Despite his long years of close partnership with some of these organisations, despite all that lobbying and fundraising and head scratching and plaque-unveiling, the Duke wants no part in choosing his successors. If organisations want a younger royal patron and the candidate is happy, all well and good. But some want a change. Some want no patron at all. Hunt-Davis points to the Duke's involvement with the WWF. For many years, the Duke was its dynamic, table-thumping global leader and ambassador. When the time came, he made a discreet exit and then a clean break. Reflecting on the Duke's retirement from the charity, Sir Miles explains: 'It was almost without a ripple. It was painless. It just happened very gradually and very sensibly. He'll still see the annual report but that's it.'

It is the same with the Duke's sporting pursuits. During his life, he has competed internationally at both polo and carriage driving. He founded the world-famous Guards Polo Club and wrote the international rule book for carriage driving. For twenty-four years he was President of the International Equestrian Federation, a full-time job and a lifetime's ambition in itself. He was also a reasonably talented cricketer, holding his own against international opposition on the charity circuit and once bowling England's Tom Graveney. On the water, he was sailing competitively (very competitively at times) well into his seventies. He is entitled to wear the tie and blazer of more clubs than, surely, any man alive, being a member of more than 250 of them, from the Royal Gibraltar Yacht Club to the Singapore Polo Club. But he does not. Once he stops doing something, he likes to move on. It's that lack of sentimentality again. He is, by his own admission, a terrible spectator: 'I've never been a dedicated watcher of anything. I'd much rather be taking part.'

He still enjoys shooting, fishing and recreational carriage-driving (plus the occasional stint as a judge at competitive events). As for all the other sports which once claimed him as their own, he simply has better things to do than sit around watching and reminiscing.

But even if some charities and sporting bodies see less of him these days, it is largely business as usual for the 800 organisations which are still on the Duke's list of patronages. He will remain on their letterheads, attend the occasional event, follow their progress. It will all be stored in the Duke's bespoke filing monster, a rotating vault which hoards tons of paperwork in the bowels of the Palace and then grinds and creaks and serves it up as required.

The Duke's office remains much the same. The unflappable Sir Miles Hunt-Davis retired at the end of 2010 (with the ultimate accolade of a GCVO from a grateful Monarch) to be replaced by another retired brigadier, Archie Miller-Bakewell, late of the Scots Guards. But the Duke continues to be served by a handful of devoted, long-serving staff including his librarian and archivist, Dame Anne Griffiths, who joined the Palace before the Coronation. And today's quartet of young ladies, like the other 'girls' before them, must still handle sackloads of correspondence and feed them into the monster. It remains high on the list of fun postings at the Palace. 'He's always pushing the boundaries,' says one of his team. 'He's got quite a low boredom threshold.' In 2008, Prince Philip took all his staff – plus spouses and partners – for a Christmas treat at Heston Blumenthal's restaurant The Fat Duck, in Bray, Berkshire. Instead of another turkey lunch, the Edinburgh team were served all Blumenthal's famous eccentricities – egg and bacon ice cream, 'foie gras benzaldehyde' and so on. The Duke enjoyed it so much that he subsequently invited Blumenthal to Windsor to cook for the Queen during Royal Ascot. Her own thoughts on snail porridge and 'nitro-green tea' have not been disclosed.

His example has certainly not been lost on the younger royal generations. 'He's been a stalwart of the Queen but let's not forget how much he's done himself independently,' says Prince William, reeling off a list of his grandfather's great causes from climate change – 'he's been at the forefront of that' – to the Duke of Edinburgh's Award. 'There are some fantastic things he's been in front of,' says the young Prince. 'He's always been thinking ahead.'

The Duke's gradual slowdown has no bearing on his military role. He has no intention of cutting back on the dozens of formal ties he enjoys with the Armed Forces, be it as Colonel-in-Chief of the Queen's Royal Hussars or Admiral of the Canadian Sea Cadets. If any member of one of his units is killed, the Duke writes a personal letter to the next of kin. If it is typed, it will have been typed by the Duke himself. 'He types quite a lot of his own letters and memos,' says Hunt-Davis. 'He's thoroughly computer literate.' The Duke has always enjoyed being at the forefront of modern technology. He was very gratified to become the President of the British Association for the Advancement of Science in 1951 and spent months working on his inaugural address, despite commanding a frigate in the Mediterranean at the time. Few members of the Royal Family have done more to promote technology and trade since Prince Albert. George VI, as both Duke of York and King, worked hard to promote industrial relations, so much so that the rest of the family nicknamed him 'The Foreman'. His emphasis was on output rather than commerce. As Frank Prochaska notes in *Royal Bounty*, a single wartime visit by the King and Queen to an Accrington aircraft factory boosted production by 12 per cent in the following week (according to the chairman of the Globe Works, 'Their Majesties sent two extra Lancaster Bombers over Germany'). But the idea of promoting a brand and a balance sheet still remained faintly unroyal as far as the Palace old guard was concerned. The Duke changed all that. Not only did he make a point of visiting the technological front line – he was seldom happier than when stomping through a research lab or testing station in a white coat and goggles – but he took an aggressively proactive stance in trade promotion at home and abroad. In 1962, he led a delegation of British aviation industry executives on an eleven-nation tour of South America. In 1965, he set up a committee which would go one further and slap royal branding all over commercial products. Under the Duke's chairmanship, the Queen's Award to Industry was formally instituted by Royal Warrant. Over the years, it has been reborn as the Queen's Awards for Export and, latterly, as the Queen's Awards for Enterprise but the idea is exactly the same. It's a separate honours system for businesses and business people. And every year, hundreds of winners come to the Palace to receive their prizes in person. The Queen and the Duke shake the hand of every single one. Afterwards, they can look forward to a full grilling from the founder. He likes to pick up new ideas and his staff are well used to being pioneers – guinea pigs, perhaps – for new technology.

It was the Duke who installed some of Britain's first solar panels on the Sandringham Estate. He bought the first royal barbecue after an outdoor lunch at the 1952 Helsinki Olympics and has been grilling ever since. He also acquired one of Britain's earliest personal computers – at the age of sixty-four. 'We had to buy British and so we got this huge thing with a tiny screen called an Apricot,' a member of staff recalls. 'It would be carried around the world with him in a large canvas bag with a little printer. He got the hang of it very quickly.' These days, he happily surfs the internet, often at the behest of the Queen. Although she does not use a computer, she frequently turns to the Duke after learning something new and says: 'You'd better Google that.' He retains an enthusiasm not just for inventing things – be it his barbecue trailer or a shooting brake known as the 'Jumbo' – but mending them, too. Sir Miles Hunt-Davis recalls a no-frills trip to north-eastern Russia on WWF business. 'We were put up in a "guest house" – I think it was a former gulag – and I came in to find Prince Philip standing on the bowl of the lavatory, fiddling with the cistern and saying: "There's no water."' Gadgets continue to enthral him, as long as they have a practical use. Late on a sunny May afternoon, the Royal Family arrives en masse at the Chelsea Flower Show. The various royal groups are so large that they come in a succession of minibuses. For the Queen, this remains one of the highlights of the old summer 'Season'. She might not bother with the rowing at Henley or the sailing at Cowes any more but she never misses Chelsea. There is an Edwardian flavour to the occasion, despite the transport arrangements. The Duchess of Gloucester arrives in a minibus with the Dowager Duchess of Bedford and half a dozen lords and ladies. Princess Alexandra's bus contains an archduchess and a pair of earls. The Queen and the Duke have invited a coachload of cousins and senior Royal Household staff. Once inside, the Queen heads for an urban garden created by prisoners and homeless people – 'very therapeutic, gardening', she concurs with them – and a spectacular display by W. Robinson & Son, fourth-generation Lancashire growers of giant fruit and veg.

But the Duke is off in another direction. He knows that the Queen will want to do her own thing here and he is not interested in pretty flowers. He comes to Chelsea for inspiration and for gadgets. And he doesn't like to stand still. It was here that he picked up the idea for his Sandringham truffle farm a few years ago and he likes to cover as much ground as he possibly can. He drops in on Hunter Boot Ltd – its wellington boots have earned it a royal warrant – and is baffled by some of the funky new designs. 'You've gone into patterns!' he exclaims in mock horror, examining a special edition in floral pink. He stops to inspect the latest in garden shed chic from tool manufacturers Fiskars. There is a long discussion about shears. Over on the Bosch stand, the staff have high hopes. The previous year, the Duke passed by and bought a Ciso, cordless secateurs which can prune almost anything at the click of a button. But he's not in a buying mood tonight. He's just checking what's new on the market. The Queen and the rest of the royal party adjourn to the President's Marquee for drinks but the Duke is still at large. 'Would you like to see our garden, sir?' asks the editor of the *Daily Telegraph*, Tony Gallagher. The Duke takes one look and replies: 'No.' He hasn't the time. But he quickly regales Gallagher with the story of a previous Chelsea Flower Show when an over-zealous exhibitor showered the press with water and the Duke got the blame. With that, he is off. 'I was impressed by his agility,' says Gallagher afterwards. 'He was striding and I mean *striding*.' The Duke's escorts are quick-stepping to keep up as their man heads off down another avenue of exhibition stands. Just as they think they have got him safely to the President's Marquee, he darts off again. His eye has been caught by a display of botanical artists and he starts chatting at length to Barbara Oozeerally. 'He was interested in my painting, my name and my accent,' she says afterwards. 'I am Polish, my husband's Mauritian and I've been a botanical artist for fifteen years.' The Duke looks through some of her paintings and is off. If he doesn't get a move on, the Queen will leave without him.

But Oozeerally may get a call in the future. The Duke's interest in botanical art is not a cursory one. In 1963, he received a letter from Molly Martin, a woman desperate to find a publisher for a lifetime's work by her father-in-law. The retired clergyman had spent sixty years painting and drawing the wild flowers of Britain but no publishing house could see a market for his 1,400 pictures. The Duke was captivated and got his equerry on the case. It was an uphill struggle but eventually they found a publisher. In 1965, *A Concise British Flora* was printed with a foreword by the Duke. It was an instant bestseller, hitting six figures in no time and was still in print more than twenty years later. At the age of eighty-eight, the Revd William Keble Martin was the toast of the book world, picked up an honorary degree, had four of his paintings turned into stamps and lived long enough to publish his autobiography.

The Duke's credentials as a patron of the arts are considerable. Despite marrying into one of the world's finest art collections, he has been an assiduous collector in his own right, assembling more than two thousand pieces. Contrary to the old seadog of popular perception (who would, presumably, cover his walls in maritime prints and sea battles), Prince Philip has a keen eye for landscapes, wildlife and post-war Scottish art. The results are spread around the royal residences. It all began in Edinburgh. As one of his staff explains: 'In the early days, when they started using Holyroodhouse, it was full of these awful *Monarch of the Glen* prints and very depressing. So Prince Philip started going to the Royal Scottish Academy's summer exhibition and buying eight or nine pieces a year. Now the place is transformed.'

During early Commonwealth tours, the Duke developed a taste for Australian art and has bought paintings by William Dobell and Sidney Nolan as well as a number of Aboriginal works. He became a keen painter himself – and still is. His 1956 tour of Antarctica – in the company of Edward Seago – was something of an epiphany, sparking not only his life-long passion for conservation but also for oil painting (he signs his work with a Greek 'P'). It seems to be hereditary. The Duke's father, Prince Andrew of Greece, was a keen amateur artist (a pretty scene, *Tower and Trees*, hangs at Sandringham). The Duke, who prefers oils, believes that Prince Charles has inherited his grandfather's love of watercolour. The Duke and the Queen share a fondness for paintings of birds. The ornithologist Emma Faull is a current favourite. And throughout the reign, the Duke has commissioned pieces from a cross section of artists. Some, like Feliks Topolski, were already famous. Others, like the watercolourist Alan Carr Linford, were barely out of art school when the Duke commissioned a series of Windsor sketches. Today, as the Prince of Wales tours the world with a succession of travelling artists, he is not being old-fashioned or eccentric, as some have suggested. He is simply following in his father's footsteps.

The Duke is also a great collector of books. His personal library at Buckingham Palace now numbers some 13,000 books and is so large that it occupies two rooms, floor to ceiling, on the north side of the Palace. New arrivals are piling up all the time. Favourite subjects of the moment include cookery books (*The Complete Licence to Grill* is just in), anything on carriage-driving, books on religion and any contribution to the 'Who was Shakespeare?' debate. He enjoys poetry – at the recent state banquet in Dublin, he was delighted to find himself seated next to the great Irish poet and Nobel Laureate Seamus Heaney – but fiction does not feature prominently in his collection. Apart from a few detective stories, the Duke does not enjoy novels. In a random week of 2010, the deliveries were as follows: *A History of the Board of Deputies of British Jews*, *England's Last War Against France*, *The Woman Who Shot Mussolini*, *The Mastery of Money*, *Winston Churchill's Toy Shop*, *The Shakespeare Handbook: The Bard In Brief*, two books on Archbishop Gregorios of the Greek Orthodox Church and *The Alpine Journal*.

Nearly nine hundred books occupy a section devoted to birds and there are 1,200 more given over to animals and fish. A random end of a random shelf in the general section throws up Hugh Johnson's *World Atlas of Wine*, *The Nuclear Age* by Jack Le Clerc, *Anglo-Saxon Chronicles* by Emma Savage, *Monuments of Another Age* by Malcolm and Esther Quantril and *The Drawn Blank Series* by Bob Dylan. Who would have had the Duke down as a Dylan fan? A neighbouring shelf is devoted entirely to the works of the lateral thinking guru Edward de Bono. It comes as no surprise to staff at the Palace. 'Prince Philip has a phenomenal enquiring mind,' says Hunt-Davis. 'He's always the one who's looking behind the door. A closed door is always an invitation to be opened – mentally and physically. Make a statement about something and he will come back with: "Why? When? Really? How do you do it?"'

It is that same tendency to come back with a swift retort which, from time to time, has landed the Duke in trouble. He once coined his own word – 'dontopedalogy' – for the science of putting one's foot in one's mouth.

He's always had a quick sense of humour, ranging from pithy four-line clerihews to earthier gags. Working his way down a greeting line at a film premiere early in the reign, the Duke's eye was unavoidably drawn to the low-cut dress doing battle with Elizabeth Taylor's cleavage. Turning to his Comptroller, the dashing 'Boy' Browning, the Duke whispered: 'Hop in.'

In the past, his asides and wisecracks were seen in the broader context of the man and his character. Today, they are simply known as gaffes. What upsets those who know him is that younger generations, less familiar with his achievements, have come to know him solely for his quips. Indeed, for some people, the Duke's public role might as well have begun in October 1986 during the state visit to China. Meeting a group of Edinburgh University students in a crowd, the Duke joked to Simon Kirby that if he stayed in China much longer, he would go home 'slit-eyed'. Kirby innocently repeated the encounter to a journalist from Edinburgh, the phrase was reported as 'slitty eyes' and a gaffe was born. Kirby would later write a letter of apology to the Palace (the Duke thanked him and told him not to worry), the Chinese took no offence ('round-eyed' being common Chinese slang for Westerners) and the Foreign Secretary, Geoffrey Howe, described the visit as a triumph. Yet, a quarter of a century later, 'slitty eyes' is routinely trotted out to reinforce the gaffe credentials of any remotely risqué royal remark.

Many papers keep a gaffe list on standby with the China remark at the top followed by the same old favourites – 'You can't have been here that long; you haven't got a pot belly' (Hungary 1993); 'Aren't most of you descended from pirates?' (Cayman Islands 1994) . . . During an uneventful day of state visiting, such remarks are a godsend for royal reporters although, more often than not, the problem is finding someone who is genuinely offended. The remark then joins the Fleet Street Anthology of Gaffes, much to the irritation of both the Duke and the hosts whose event will have been entirely ignored in the faux furore. Like all good folklore, the gaffe narrative is easily grasped and based on truth. But it is only part of the picture. The Duke does not go out of his way to say something offensive. His default mode when introduced to a group of strangers is to break the ice with a jolly remark. Sometimes it goes wrong. As he himself concedes, the problem with ice-breaking is that you may fall through. Very often, his remark is second- or third-hand by the time it has reached the media. But the context must never get in the way of a good story. In 1999, the Duke was on an engagement in Scotland when he saw a fuse box sprouting a mass of tangled wires. According to reports, he joked: 'It looks as if it was put in by an Indian.' The press leaped on the implied racial insensitivity, despite the faintly baffling Indian/electricity non sequitur, while a Palace press officer gamely suggested that the Prince had meant to say 'cowboy'. The Duke was unapologetic. He later explained that he had most definitely meant to say 'Indian' as he was alluding to the ongoing electricity crisis and power cut protests in India – as anyone should have known if they were bothering to keep up with world affairs.

Another mistake is to imagine that the Duke's gaffes are anything new. Many newspaper databases and online archives go back no further than the eighties but the Duke has had dontopedalogical moments throughout his life. Sometimes, he was simply trying to be polite. During the 1970 royal tour of New Zealand, he met a woman who reflected that she had not been back to England for thirty years. 'You're missing very little,' he assured her. This tiny, harmless exchange duly appeared on the front page of the *People* in the eternal language of the gaffe story: 'Prince Philip was in the centre of a new storm last night after making a remark which apparently knocked Britain . . .'

On occasions, he has managed to offend his own family. At the height of Princess Margaret's romance with Group Captain Peter Townsend, the Queen Mother sighed that the poor couple would have nowhere to live. When the Duke joked that he had heard it was now possible for people to *buy* a house, his mother-in-law walked out and slammed the door. But the Royal Family – along with most of the world – take the view that it is far better to be tactless now and then than to be humourless all of the time. And some of the Duke's remarks remain priceless more than half a century later. Take, for example, his message to his superiors in 1951 when Princess Elizabeth was visiting Athens in HMS *Surprise* and the Duke was in command of her escort ship, *Magpie*. One day, he received a cheery signal from the royal flagship: 'Princess full of beans.' Quick as a flash, the Duke signalled back: 'Can't you give her something better for breakfast?' During a tour of Australia, he was offered the chance to shear a sheep. He tactfully declined: 'I might nick it and we've had enough mutton on this tour.' The tale of Kenya's 1964 independence ceremony is another example. As the British flag was being lowered and the spotlight descended on founding father Jomo Kenyatta for the moment of destiny, the Duke was heard to whisper: 'I suppose you don't want to change your mind?'

The fact is that the vast majority of people are not bothered whenever a gaffe hits the headlines. Much as he may loathe the idea, the Duke, like the Queen, has achieved the status of 'national treasure', typified by a fond, if occasionally ribald, series of parliamentary tributes from both sides of the Commons to mark his ninetieth birthday in June 2011. Labour MP Chris Bryant even quoted the conversation between the Duke and a colleague at a Palace reception.

> Duke to Labour MP: 'So, what did you do before you got this job?'
> MP: 'I worked in a trade union.'
> Duke: 'Bugger all, then.'
> MP (somewhat offended): 'Well, what did you do before you got this job?'
> Duke: 'Fought in the Second World War.'

A few years earlier, such an exchange might have prompted a chorus of synthetic outrage. On this occasion, both sides of the House roared with laughter. 'There are occasions,' Bryant concluded, 'when a little humility from this House towards His Royal Highness is entirely appropriate.' Even the media's tone has switched from mock outrage to an indulgent rolling of the eyes. But the Royal Family and their staff dislike seeing a man who has made a profound impact on the monarchy, his country and the wider world being presented as little more than an amiable blunderer. What's more, the inference of blinkered insensitivity is completely at odds with the Duke's contribution to modern multicultural society. Long before words like 'interfaith dialogue' were in common parlance, the Duke was organising gatherings of Muslim, Jewish and Christian leaders at St George's House, the residential conference centre-cum-retreat he has built inside Windsor Castle. 'Through his involvement with WWF,' the Archbishop of Canterbury points out, 'he is interested in the religious and theological dimension of environmental questions. He's someone with a very active interest in reading theology.' Indeed, during his WWF days, he made great progress in getting different faiths to unite in the cause of conservation. 'If God is in nature,' he argued, 'nature itself becomes divine.' By 1986, he had persuaded all the main religions to issue their own 'Declarations on Nature'. He even established a WWF/Vatican conservation committee with the Pope. Raised in the Greek Orthodox Church, received into the Church of England, married to its Supreme Governor, revered as a god by a tribe in Vanuatu and the son of a nun, the Duke has plenty of avenues through which to explore the meaning of life. He is extremely proud that his mother was granted the

accolade of 'Righteous Among the Nations' by the authorities at Israel's
Yad Vashem Holocaust Memorial Museum in recognition of her protection of Greek Jews during the war. He is equally proud of his Russian
great-aunt, Grand Duchess Ella (another nun). The Bolsheviks pushed
her down a mineshaft and then threw hand grenades after her. She took
three days to die of her wounds, during which she tended fellow victims
and sang hymns. His family's experiences at both ends of the totalitarian
spectrum have made him a passionate advocate of individual freedoms
versus the collective power of the state. In 1982, he published a series
of essays under the title *A Question of Balance*. In them, he attacked
early Soviet sympathisers like Sidney and Beatrice Webb for their 'obsti-
nate and blind commitment' to communist ideology and their 'remarkable
aversion to reality'. More broadly, he deplored communism for its lack
of compassion: 'The concepts of charity (in the voluntary sense), or of
obligation, or of social conscience, hardly exist in Marxist doctrine but
there are vast numbers of people of all classes in this country who give
money generously to charities.' He has also been happy to question more
orthodox socialist dogma, including certain basic assumptions about the
Welfare State. 'The promise of benefits,' he wrote, 'makes people overlook the loss of choice and responsibility which inevitably follows.' All
of this is far meatier media material and far more thought-provoking
than a gag about pot bellies in Hungary, yet it has all passed beneath
the press radar with barely a murmur. Far from knocking diversity, he
is fascinated by it. When a Mountbatten cousin was recently trying to
prop up an old family story that she was descended from the Native
American princess Pocahontas, the Duke put his staff on the case. Sadly,
the investigation drew a blank. There is no lineal connection between
the House of Mountbatten and the Powhatan tribe of Virginia after all.
But he tried.

   The Duke has written books, essays and lectures on theology, spiritu-
alism and even the nature of friendship. He has devoted a large part of
his life to the promotion of academic excellence and is entirely comfortable pondering deep issues in the company of dons. He likes intellectuals
but does not believe they hold all the answers. Indeed, he regards some
of them as a menace. As he put it (to the author) on the eve of the first
state visit to Russia: 'We got over the development of an urban industrial
intelligentsia reasonably easily . . . because we had a constitutional
monarchy.' He would undoubtedly have thrived had he gone to university,
but he is not remotely chippy about the fact that he did not. As he told
a gathering of eminent university leaders: 'I am not a graduate of any
university. Oddly enough, I don't regret it. I owe my allegiance to another

of the world's few really great fraternities, the fraternity of the sea.'

His lust for innovation has resulted in that bulging file of royal patronages. During the earlier part of the reign he was founding and endowing new organisations and prizes with the same panache as his forebear Prince Albert. From the Royal Agriculture Society of the Commonwealth to the Pakistan Army Bagpiping Trophy, they are all still going strong. Quite apart from his contributions to specific causes, millions of young people around the world have enjoyed the benefits of his Award scheme. His initiatives half a century back – from fighting vehicle emissions to campaigning for natural habitats around the world – gave crucial early respectability to causes which are now received wisdom. So it is not entirely surprising to learn that, a few years ago, when his achievements were fresher in the mind, a group of international admirers began mounting a discreet campaign to propose the Duke for a Nobel Peace Prize. He was not even informed of the idea (and would probably have winced if he had been). This is the man who shunned his own ninetieth birthday exhibition at Windsor Castle on the grounds that it was a lot of fuss about nothing. This is the man who refuses to discuss anything as vulgar as his 'legacy'. 'I'd rather other people decided what legacy I left. I'm not trying to create one,' he told the author a few years ago during an interview at Windsor Castle. 'Life's going to go on after me and if I can make life marginally more tolerable for people [who come] after, I'd be delighted.' For whatever reason – timing, perhaps, or politics – that Nobel campaign was left to drift. Might it be revived? The 2007 award to America's Al Gore for his climate change work could be seen as a precedent. It is not as if the Duke is short of honours but it would put the international dimension of his life's work in perspective. Contemporary commentators might scoff at the idea. History may view it otherwise. As the Queen remarked at the end of that Golden Wedding speech: 'I, and his whole family, and this and many other countries, owe him a debt greater than he would ever claim, or we shall ever know.'

# 9

# *Heads and Tails*

*'No monarch is ever looking for a legacy.'*

Some things haven't changed inside these three-hundred-year-old walls. Marlborough House still retains much of the grandeur of the royal residence which it was until the death of Queen Mary – the chandeliers, the grand staircase, many of the royal portraits. Wander round the enormous garden backing on to the Mall and you will find the graves of Queen Alexandra's dogs and the final resting place of her pet rabbit, Benny.

It is hardly surprising that the Queen feels entirely at home inside the world headquarters of the Commonwealth, even if her grandmother's old bedroom – the room in which Queen Mary died – is now the Secretary-General's office. The Duke of Marlborough's victories still decorate the walls of the Blenheim Saloon, the main entrance hall. But no one is looking at the art in the Blenheim Saloon tonight. Everyone is watching a band of half-naked Rwandan drummers wearing huge straw wigs and thumping out traditional tunes.

Rwanda has officially joined the Commonwealth today and President Paul Kagame has come to the Commonwealth headquarters to meet the Queen. He explains that these drummers were performing in the Marlborough House garden when the Rwandan flag was hoisted aloft earlier. 'Not dressed like that?' replies the Queen, shivering at the thought. It has been freezing all day. 'Yes, just like that!' replies the gangly, softly spoken Kagame proudly. Prince Philip attempts conversation with the drummers. 'Is this your own hair?' he asks, pointing to the straw wigs. Blank looks. He tries again. 'Can you vary the note?' he asks, pointing at the drum. More blank looks. It is not surprising. Until recently, Rwanda's language of government was French, because it spent most of the twentieth century as a Belgian colony. Following genocidal civil war in the nineties, it is rebuilding itself with a new English-speaking identity. Joining the British Commonwealth is a crucial part of the process. The Queen is delighted to welcome Rwanda aboard. It is a sign that her Commonwealth still has a purpose and an appeal. 'Good luck,' she tells Kagame, shaking his hand. Now that his nation is in 'The Club', he will be seeing rather more of her in the future.

Today is Commonwealth Day 2010. Every year, on the second Monday in March, the Queen travels to Westminster Abbey for the most unorthodox event in the Abbey's calendar. For a start, it is not a service. It is the 'Commonwealth Day Observance'. Those officiating include representatives from the Muslim, Hindu and Baha'i communities. This year's theme is science and the sermon is delivered by the fertility professor, Lord Winston. The Queen's Commonwealth Day broadcast is screened. She talks about the power of technology to unite the Commonwealth but makes no mention of the Almighty. 'You'd never get St Paul's Cathedral allowing this,' notes an admiring old hand from the Palace. 'Some of the clergy were pretty horrified in the early days but the Queen wanted it. That's why it happens.' With no bishop to answer to, the Abbey is known as a 'royal peculiar'. Its earthly boss is the Supreme Governor of the Church of England and Defender of the Faith. And the Queen also happens to be Head of the Commonwealth. So if she wants *her* Commonwealth to hold its 'observance' in *her* Abbey, she can. In any case, Christianity is actually in third place in the Commonwealth rankings, outnumbered by both Islam and Hinduism. It would be rather rude to make this an entirely Christian do.

From here, everyone adjourns to Marlborough House for the more informal part of the celebrations. All the Commonwealth diplomats are at the party but there isn't an ambassador in the room. Because Commonwealth countries do not regard each other as 'foreign', all ambassadors from one Commonwealth country to another are called High Commissioners. And the Queen ensures that her High Commissioners enjoy a few subtle perks like the best seats at her Birthday Parade. When new diplomats come to present their credentials at the Palace, the Queen always sends a carriage from the Royal Mews to collect them. Ordinary ambassadors are pulled by two horses, but High Commissioners get four. These are tiny but jealously guarded distinctions among the Diplomatic Corps.

As the Queen progresses through her grandmother's old house, it is easy to sense why she is so fond of this organisation, why it is allowed to live in London's grandest non-royal residence (it's much more palatial than Number Ten Downing Street) for a peppercorn rent. This reception is nothing like the usual run of diplomatic events. She discusses homesickness with a group of students from the Falkland Islands, meets the Speakers of the Namibian and Nova Scotian parliaments and recognises

Gary Flather, a disabled guest who has recently lost a much-loved assistance dog. Flather is married to Baroness Flather, a Commonwealth stalwart who was the first Indian-born Mayor of Windsor. The Queen remembers his golden retriever, Gracie, from civic events in Windsor. 'You've always been with your dog before, haven't you,' she says. 'I had to put her down,' Flather sighs. He gets as long a chat as any High Commissioner. Flather is immensely cheered. 'I suddenly saw that look in her face that said she knew exactly the feelings I went through,' he says (when they next meet, Flather has a new assistance dog with him and the Queen is thrilled).

The Queen moves on to meet Professor Bhupinder Sandhu, the woman with arguably the smallest organisation and the longest title in the room – President of the Commonwealth Association of Paediatric Gastro-Enterologists. It is organisations like hers which are the bedrock of the Commonwealth.

Much as many politicians (especially those from the smaller states) enjoy the summits and the ostentatious motorcades, the Commonwealth is never going to save the planet. It has an annual budget of £90 million which equates to, say, a third of the annual turnover of Manchester United Football Club. The Commonwealth's power, like the Queen's, is all about influence rather than coercion. It brings people together but cannot give them orders. It can embarrass bad regimes, endorse good ones and offer free and invaluable expertise through numerous civic societies just like Sandhu's. That is why the second Monday in March, just like the second Sunday in November – Remembrance Sunday – is an unbreakable fixture in the Queen's diary.

The Queen's devotion to the Commonwealth is partly a sentimental thing. Her father helped create the modern Commonwealth shortly before his death, providing a useful, face-saving way for the United Kingdom to shed the British Empire but keep its ties with the former colonies. But it is also a question of personal pride. When it started, the Commonwealth had eight members. Today it has fifty-four. It has literally grown up with the Queen. The whole thing could have fallen apart on several occasions. It could have become an expensive vanity exercise like France's *Francophonie* (in which one country is top dog and hands out favours to the rest). But the Commonwealth remains a free assembly of equals which covers a third of the world's population, includes all the main religions, speaks English, has a British-style legal system and yet frequently enjoys hitting Britain with a big stick. When it started, it was the only show in town apart from the United Nations. Now governments have international groupings galore. Unlike the newer breed of talking shops with their snappy initials – BRIC, EU, G20 and so on – this one has no initials.*

Some would say that it has no purpose either. Around the Commonwealth, there are those who see it as an irrelevant imperial hangover. Many argue that its failure to take a firm stand on human rights abuses from Gambia to Sri Lanka shows that it is toothless and inept. In Britain, many believe that it gives kudos to dictators and kleptocrats or that it is a nostalgic distraction from the realities of life in the European Union. Some British prime ministers have not always seen the merits of spending several days on the other side of the world arguing technicalities with the leader of a microstate which they would be hard pushed to find on a map. Tony Blair does not even mention the Commonwealth in his memoirs. In person, he insists that it is 'important', adding the caveat: 'I took it, frankly, as seriously as it was justified in being taken.' It has been said that the only reason some British prime ministers have bothered with the Commonwealth at all is because they will be accused of snubbing the Queen if they do not. Other leaders admit that, without the Queen, the turnout might be considerably lower. John Key, Prime Minister of New Zealand, tots up all the summits on today's circuit and says: 'You can see the pressure on leaders' time. I don't think you'd get them turning up if it wasn't for the Queen or, after her reign, the King.'

British Foreign Secretary William Hague has pledged to raise the profile of the 'C' in FCO – the Foreign and *Commonwealth* Office: 'I'm not naive about how difficult it is to breathe meaningful life into it. But it's definitely worth the effort because it is the ultimate network and we are entering a network world.' Unlike NAFTA or OPEC, it was not created by geography or economic interest. It is an historic quirk. Why else would Canada and Tuvalu find themselves around a summit table as equals? Its meetings are the only major world summits with no interpreters. The result is a family feel. It thrives on disagreement – its politicians are usually squabbling about five things at once – but, like a family, it can quarrel without falling apart, reinforced by its rich network of associations. 'There's a huge flotilla of professional organisations and they buzz away the whole time,' says Lord Hurd. 'It's not sensational but it's continuous. You never get the bitterness you often get at the United Nations. The Commonwealth has its own vocabulary.' There is even a very distant hope that Ireland might one day rejoin an organisation it left in 1949. The outstanding success of

---

* Its biannual summits, however, do have one of the ugliest acronyms on the international circuit, CHOGM, the Commonwealth Heads of Government Meeting.

the Queen's state visit in May 2011 – the first since the creation of the Republic of Ireland – has made the idea less far-fetched.

If you were starting a new nation from scratch tomorrow, then the Commonwealth could advise you on everything from building a police force to a dental service. There is a queue of countries with no historic British ties – like Rwanda – which want to join to enjoy the networking potential. And if all its fifty-four governments can be expected to agree on just one thing, it is that they are all very happy to have the Queen as head. 'It would be impossible without her,' says John Key. 'She binds together an eclectic group of countries who often have very little in common.' Former Australian Prime Minister Malcolm Fraser thinks it would be madness to remove the royal connection. 'There's no advantage, only a downside,' he says. 'We'd become just like any other institution.' The Secretary-General of the Commonwealth, Kalamesh Sharma, has no doubt that the Queen is the glue in the organisation: 'The Queen's association makes us like a family, a very special community.'

As her former Private Secretary Sir William Heseltine points out, it's an organisation with long memories. 'From the very beginning, when the Queen made her way round the Commonwealth, she got to know some of those African leaders who were youngsters when she first met them,' he says. 'And they grew up together and had a relationship which was, in some cases, quite affectionate, and certainly respectful. And I think they began to regard her as a mother figure of the Commonwealth. Certainly, in the Thatcher days, she was regarded as very much more sympathetic to the organisation than the Prime Minister – which indeed she was. So they regarded her as a protector of their Commonwealth aspirations.' Long before Nelson Mandela was elected President of South Africa, the Queen was quietly treating him as a head of state. When he appeared at the 1991 Commonwealth summit, the Queen, as ever, was preparing to host her traditional banquet for heads of government. Mandela, recently out of prison, was still nearly three years away from being elected one, so he had not been invited to the party. 'Let's have him,' the Queen told the Secretary-General. And he came. Heseltine has no doubts about the Queen's part in the creation of Zimbabwe: 'That was, in Commonwealth terms, one of her great achievements, even if it didn't turn out as well as it might have done.' Zimbabwe's subsequent descent into poverty and corruption will have aggrieved the Queen as much as anyone. It has since resigned from the Commonwealth – just before it was expelled – but even in his most inflammatory rantings against Britain, President Robert Mugabe has avoided attacking the Monarch. After all, she once had him to stay at Buckingham Palace.

The same sense of the Queen as a benign umpire has rubbed off on the new generation of leaders, some of whom were in primary school during the heyday of Commonwealth quarrels. 'She's so well versed, so comfortable with us,' says Mohamed Nasheed, President of the Maldives, the low-lying Islamic republic in the Indian Ocean. 'She keeps her distance to the necessary extent. But I haven't seen anyone who understands us more.'

He was a recent overnight guest at Windsor Castle where he was astonished by the Queen's knowledge of both the Commonwealth and of his country, which she last visited in 1972. 'There were things she mentioned which she couldn't have been briefed about. She mentioned that on her trip to the Maldives a fishing boat had been missing and that she had sent her ship, *Britannia*, to rescue this boat. And she wanted to know how these people were – if they were still alive. After I got home, I wanted to see if they were around. There was no official record of it, so how did she know? But I found that one of the people was alive and I was also able to let her know that all of the people had put up pictures of her in their homes.'

Those close to the Queen say that another reason for this bond is her sense that she has 'earned' it. Everything else – her throne, her Church, her estates – was inherited, but on her watch the Commonwealth has gone from infancy to maturity as a global institution. It is her equivalent of the Duke of Edinburgh's Award, her Prince's Trust. It will undoubtedly come to be regarded as one of the defining elements of her reign. And it is why, in bright November sunshine, she has crossed an ocean with a heavy cold to preside over another gathering of 'The Club'. The Commonwealth leaders meet every two years and, this time, it is the turn of Port of Spain, the capital of the Caribbean twin-island nation of Trinidad and Tobago. Most of The Club are represented by their prime ministers although a few have sent their foreign ministers instead. Some Commonwealth nations are so unstable that it can be risky for leaders to leave their own shores – as the Prime Minister of Vanuatu is about to find out. By the time this three-day conference ends, he will be the ex-Prime Minister of Vanuatu, having been ousted in his absence. Two countries are missing. Fiji is suspended for refusing to hold a democratic election and tiny Nauru (population: 10,000) has not paid its bills.

Politicians fly in from all over the world and drive straight from the airport to the heavily fortified Hyatt Regency hotel from where they will hardly stir. There aren't enough beds in town, so the thousands of lobbyists, Commonwealth associations, charity workers and the media are all berthed on a pair of large cruise ships. In years gone by, the Queen would have stayed in the Royal Yacht. Since *Britannia* is now a Scottish tourist attraction, she is staying in a newly opened boutique hotel. The Carlton

Savannah is so new that the paint is still drying and some of the light fittings have not been completed. The Queen is staying in an eleventh-floor apartment called the 'Wow Suite' – as its future occupants will, no doubt, remark when they are told who stayed there first.

Unlike the politicians, the Queen will actually be out and about among the ordinary people during her time here. She is not only here as Head of the Commonwealth but as Queen of Great Britain, in which capacity she will also pay a state visit to Trinidad and Tobago. When she became Queen, it was a colony. When she first visited in 1966, it had gained independence but had kept her as Queen. By her second visit in 1981, it had voted to become a republic. Third time around, though, the welcome is just as exuberant. Port of Spain is the city which invented the steel drum and calypso. Its carnival ranks alongside those of Rio and New Orleans and is the model for Notting Hill's. Each spring, half the nation join carnival bands and parade past the other half. Six months on, the champion junior band are back in their costumes to greet the Queen outside the country's old national theatre, the Queen's Hall. More than 150 children are dressed in a riotously imaginative collection of costumes – birds, flowers, fish, phantoms and much else. They are all under fourteen but some stand twelve feet tall, swaying on stilts. One poor boy falls off during the long wait but no damage is done and he is propped back up again. Many are from a local children's home. Their carers explain that being in a prize-winning carnival band – and meeting the Queen – will be defining moments in their lives. Anywhere in the world, organisations like this boil down to a few indefatigable volunteers with big hearts and limitless patience, women like Rosalind Gabriel who spent a year sewing and gluing all these costumes together. She is a 'must' on the list of people for the Queen to meet. More children are inside the theatre, either to welcome or perform for the Queen. Adults are not much in evidence, which is how the Queen likes a lot of her engagements these days. 'She's been almost everywhere in the world and she doesn't like spending every visit talking about "the last time I was here",' explains one of her team. Even so, it's nice to see a few old faces. Among those in the greeting line is Thora Dumbell, eighty-five, a former ballet star who once danced with Fred Astaire and choreographed the rally for the Queen in 1966. She must have made an impact. 'Back then, I was invited to have coffee with her, and Prince Philip said: "I wish I could put you in a little pot and take you back to England." I still think of her as *my* Queen.'

The Monarch is dressed for the occasion in a bright red floral dress and white jacket. Rosalind's carnival band shimmers and dazzles and drums and whistles. It has to be persuaded to shut up so that the Queen can

hear Timel Flament-Rivas, aged nine, sing a new calypso written by local
composer Larry Harewood: 'Welcome to our twin islands, a nation under
the sun/A glimpse of your schedule shows your work is never done. May
God pour his richest blessings, keep you in good health./And may you
remain the Head of the Commonwealth.' Veteran royal watchers can tell
that the Queen is enjoying this because she is tapping her foot. She is
not, as a rule, a great foot-tapper. Timel, it turns out, has several verses.
It all goes on rather longer than the organisers planned. There is nervous
watch-checking among the suits but the Queen is in no hurry. In his little
tuxedo and bow tie, Timel is entirely relaxed, too. His mother, Jeaniffer,
speechless with pride, turns out to be a former ju-jitsu world champion
who once hospitalised two muggers. Nerves of steel run in the family.

Inside the auditorium, the audience – almost all children – scream
hysterically as the Queen walks in. Even though it's a Saturday, they are
all in neat school uniforms. If anyone totted up the hours the Queen has
spent watching 'local cultural entertainments' in her life, it must amount
to months if not years. But she is not merely watching this youth concert.
She is sitting forward in her seat, enthralled.

Afterwards, she walks outside to meet the long-suffering carnival band
which has now been standing in the sun for more than two hours. It
explodes into life, gyrating to the drums and whistles. 'Flap any harder
and you'll take off,' the Duke of Edinburgh tells a golden humming bird.
The Queen is enchanted. She meets Rosalind Gabriel and discusses the
challenge of producing 150 costumes. 'Do you reuse them?' asks the
Duke. 'No, we make them new,' says Rosalind. 'He was blown away by
that,' she says later, a little blown away herself. Thora Dumbell is glowing.
'I think the Queen was looking better today than when I first met her.
She looks fantastic,' she says. 'I reminded her of the rally in 1966 and
she said: "You came to see me afterwards." So she remembered me!'

In the Queen's younger days, a state visit like this might have lasted
a week. As the oldest monarch in history, her schedules have been trimmed
back a little but there's always a state banquet. In Trinidad, it takes place
on the lawn of President's House, the former colonial residence. There
is much excitement that the Queen is wearing an Angela Kelly dress
embroidered with the national birds and flowers of Trinidad and Tobago.
Once the Queen gets home, however, the beads and crystals will be
unthreaded and re-embroidered in a maple leaf pattern for next year's
tour of Canada. Her team call this 'credit crunch couture'.

By way of hospitality in return, she hosts a reception for the great and
good of Trinidad and Tobago in her hotel. Football star Dwight Yorke
gives her a signed football. 'Very nerve-wracking,' he says. Cricket legend

Brian Lara gives her a signed bat. There's another reception on the British High Commissioner's lawn where the Queen meets more West Indies cricketers, including Willie Rodriguez, Daren Ganga and Deryck Murray. Talk turns to the new genre of Twenty20 cricket. It is clear that the Queen is not a fan. 'I have a friend who can't bear it,' she remarks, deploying time-honoured royal shorthand for a personal opinion. 'He says: "I won't watch it!"' This is the sporting corner of the party. Rodriguez ignores the old canard that one should never ask the Queen a question (it all depends on the question) and points out that the Queen's horse, Barber's Shop, has been running in England that very afternoon. How did the horse get on? 'No one's told me it won,' she says in mock despair, 'so I presume it has not.' (It has come seventh.)

The Duke is introduced to a group of Red Cross workers, among them Tanya Wood from Britain. 'I was sent here for my sins,' she says. 'And what were your sins?' asks the Duke. He has his own mini-state visit to perform on this tour. Just to make sure that the people of Tobago do not feel overlooked, he flies to the smaller island for a day. The Queen, however, has a Commonwealth to attend to.

This summit is the organisation's sixtieth birthday party but the arguing starts early. The host, Trinidad's Prime Minister, Patrick Manning, wants to make global warming the big issue of his summit. But many of the lobbyists and activists here want the Commonwealth to 'get real' and focus on issues it can actually do something about, namely human rights abuses by its own members. The President of Gambia has just imprisoned a Scottish missionary for calling Gambia 'hell' and has informed political reformers: 'I will kill you and nothing will come of it.' Swaziland is spending more than half its aid budget on a private jet for the King. And Uganda is passing laws to extend the death penalty to homosexuality (which is already illegal in forty Commonwealth countries).

Manning does not want his moment as saviour of the planet soured by such matters. 'These are domestic issues,' he declares at the opening press conference. 'They need not detain us here.' The human rights campaigners are outraged.

Meanwhile, the Commonwealth is under attack from its own fan club. The Royal Commonwealth Society (Patron: The Queen) has conducted an extensive global survey on what people think about the Commonwealth. The results are not comfortable reading. Most people have no idea what it does, aside from the Commonwealth Games, and most people in countries like Australia, Canada and Britain – which fund it – would not be bothered if it disappeared. It clearly needs to decide what it's *for* – and make itself more relevant instead of engaging in what RCS chairman

Peter Kellner calls 'earnest futility'. It's a dilemma not unfamiliar to the Queen. The Commonwealth Secretary-General and his staff are rather cross about this survey and try to bury it. Privately, though, many delegates agree that it is a 'timely wake-up call'. Certainly, no one is objecting in the royal camp. The monarchy knows what happens to organisations which allow themselves to stagnate.

The Queen takes centre stage at the opening ceremony, a colossal production at the brand-new National Academy for the Performing Arts. It's a very expensive, very shiny new addition to Port of Spain's landscape, a Caribbean answer to the Sydney Opera House. It is so new that the cement mixers only stopped working two hours before the Queen's arrival. There is an air of happy chaos. There are no programmes as they are still being printed. Apparently, they will arrive a few days after the grand event is over. As a result, no one is entirely sure what is happening. Despite the climate change agenda, each delegation from each nation arrives at the grand entrance in an individual motorcade. Every government leader is applauded on to the stage, quiz show-style, by a hand-picked local audience. The hosts put on a dizzying cultural *tour de force* involving 935 actors. It's the indoor equivalent of an Olympic opening ceremony. Everyone is genuinely impressed.

The Queen, her voice croaking from a combination of her cold, the air conditioning and jet lag, delivers a speech which chimes entirely with the environmental mood of the national leaders. She urges them to 'lead' the world in fighting climate change, noting: 'The Commonwealth can be proud of the fact that in each of its six decades, it has shaped the international response to emerging global challenges.' The media are so excited about 'Green Queen' headlines that they miss her thinly veiled support for those who want to give the organisation a big shake-up. 'This diamond anniversary year is an important time for the Commonwealth to look forward,' she says. 'Like any good organisation, we must continue to pay close attention to the things that give it distinctive character.'

The leaders go back to the conference room to carry on arguing. Manning has persuaded President Sarkozy of France to drop in en route from South America and lend his support to the Commonwealth's planet-saving declarations. Not everyone is happy. France is not a member – and it means having to find some interpreters. The Queen keeps her distance. She invites all the new leaders who have never attended a Commonwealth summit to drinks at her hotel. She also meets the organisation's youth wing, the Commonwealth Youth Forum, led by an articulate young Australian lawyer, Matthew Albert, twenty-nine ('youth', in Commonwealth terms, stops at thirty). His briefing to the Queen is more polished than some of the stuff she hears from the heads of governments. She must be impressed because she includes Albert and his colleagues in her Christmas broadcast a few weeks later.

It is also an occasion for the Queen to catch up with some of her own prime ministers. John Key, the Prime Minister of New Zealand, has asked for an audience and is summoned to the 'Wow Suite' for a chat. He is enjoying his first Commonwealth summit and, for some reason, has been seated next to President Kikwete of Tanzania at three consecutive meals. Far from running out of small talk, the two men have become friends and have hatched a plan. Key has agreed to send some Kiwi farmers to help Tanzania set up a new agricultural institute. Kikwete has promised him two cheetahs for a New Zealand zoo in return. You don't get that sort of quickfire diplomacy at the G20. The Queen immediately asks Key about plans for Prince William to open Wellington's new Supreme Court building. 'The first thing she said to me was to make sure I look after William when he comes down to New Zealand,' says Key afterwards. 'She seemed very amused by the fact that we were going to abandon the state dinner for a barbecue with the All Blacks.'*

Talk turns to one of Key's coalition partners, New Zealand's minority Maori Party. The Maori community has always believed that when it signed the original 1840 peace treaty with the first European settlers it was dealing with Queen Victoria, not the settlers. 'There's always been a sense from Maori that their historical relationship is with the Crown,' says Key. 'We're in partnership with them and it's one of the things the Queen asks about every time I've seen her. She always asks how the relationship's going and she was pleased that we did it.' It's a fascinating little constitutional insight. As in Britain, so in New Zealand, the Queen is positively enjoying the latest flourishing of coalition politics.

Everyone will have their moment with the Queen at her traditional Commonwealth banquet. She has even brought the Master of the Household and some of his team with her to give it the Palace gloss. Round tables of ten are laid out for a dinner of cured salmon, roast loin of lamb and chocolate cardammon truffle cake. Every place is laid with a Household eye for detail and every menu card tied up with ribbons in the Commonwealth colours of blue and yellow. The Queen has packed the 'Commonwealth Goblets', a gold cup for the head of each delegation.

The leaders of all fifty-four nations and their spouses line up for a formal introduction to the Queen and Prince Philip. It doesn't take long

---

* The Prince retains fond memories of the party laid on by Key – 'a very nice man'. He not only met the All Blacks but ended up wearing an apron and helping Key cook the sausages. His barbecue-mad grandfather, he remarked, would have been proud.

and everyone then mingles informally over drinks. There is a bit of a glitch, though, when it is time to move through from the reception to the banquet. The Secretary-General, Kalamesh Sharma, has been collared by someone so the Queen walks through unaccompanied. She is left to sit down in her chair alone with no one to talk to. It's a blunder. She looks unamused but unfazed. 'It's sloppy,' murmurs one of her team disapprovingly. 'But she's gripping it.'

As far as the Queen's body clock is concerned, it is midnight and she also has a bad cold. She just wants to 'grip' it and get on with it. Eventually she ends up with the Prime Minister of Singapore on her left and Patrick Manning on her right. The seating plan ensures a mix of continents on every table. The Queen's circle includes the President of Kenya, the Crown Prince of Brunei, and the hapless Edward Natapei, the man who is being toppled as Prime Minister of Vanuatu at this very moment.* The Duke sits next to the only female leader at the summit, Sheikh Hasina Wazed, the Prime Minister of Bangladesh. By popular demand, speeches are early and short. Two new boys, John Key and Jacob Zuma of South Africa, have been chosen to say a few words and raise a toast to the Queen and to the Commonwealth. She hits her gavel and rises to say, simply: 'I wish you every success in your deliberations.' With that, the cured salmon arrives and the Queen will play no further part in the proceedings. The following day she is heading home as the leaders produce their grand declaration – 'The Port of Spain Climate Change Consensus'. This gathering has actually been a modest success. The Queen will be pleased. It's been a good few days for other reasons, too. She might have lost one of her thrones over the weekend. The Prime Minister of St Vincent and the Grenadines, an island constellation which still has the Queen as its head of state, had decided to stage a royal referendum to coincide with her visit to the region. Ralph Gonsalves – known locally as 'Comrade Ralph' – had urged his 100,000-strong electorate to vote for a republic. What's more, he had the support of the main opposition party. Since the Grenadines include the famous royal playground of Mustique, this had the potential to be an awkward story. 'MUSTIQUE KICKS OUT QUEEN' is not a great headline midway through a Caribbean tour. In the event, the people rejected the idea by 57 to 43 per cent. Comrade Ralph – who still turned up for the Queen's banquet and still got a smile and a handshake – will not have his head on the coins just yet.

The Queen's view has always been that constitutional issues like this

* The accident-prone Natapei was later reinstated as Prime Minister but ousted again a year later. He was abroad yet again, this time at a climate summit in Mexico.

are entirely a democratic matter for the people concerned, not some popularity contest. She is happy to remain a constitutional monarch wherever she is wanted. The last thing she wants is to be seen as hanging on. Most realms are former dominions or colonies which have chosen to retain their historic ties with the Crown. With Papua New Guinea, it was a case of deliberately *appointing* the Queen. This was Australian territory until 1975 when it sought independence and a republican constitution was prepared. But with more than eight hundred languages among Papua New Guinea's seven million people, the founding fathers decided that the Queen offered greater prospects for national unity. What's more, she had actually been there. So the Queen was invited to add another realm to her portfolio. She gladly accepted and, to this day, Papua New Guinea is the world's most enthusiastic distributor of old imperial honours.

For now, she remains Queen of a large part of the earth's surface. She is head of state of 16 nations, plus another 14 British overseas territories, including Bermuda, Gibraltar and 660,000 square miles of Antarctica. It is only in Britain that she reigns directly. In her fifteen other realms, she does so through a locally appointed Governor-General who fulfils all her ceremonial functions. But the big decisions have always been approved by her – including a little-known *de facto* abdication.

In 1987, when she was Queen of Fiji, there were two military coups. 'The Governor-General had been sort of pretending to be in charge of Fiji,' recalls Sir William Heseltine. 'But after the second coup happened he really couldn't pretend to go on doing that. So the Queen took the initiative in suggesting to him that the time had come for her to accept that Fiji was now a republic. It was no use pretending any longer that Fiji was still a realm. Mrs Thatcher was quite opposed to the idea of the Queen, as it were, abdicating. But it wasn't up to her because it was as Queen of Fiji that she had come to this conclusion.' And it was as Queen of Fiji that the Monarch's mind was made up. The only government was an undemocratic republican one so the Queen told her Fijian self, namely the Governor-General, to resign. He did.

One of the most famous constitutional crises was in Australia in 1975 when the Governor-General, Sir John Kerr, sacked the Australian Prime Minister, Gough Whitlam. The Queen knew nothing about it in advance but it gave considerable momentum to the rising Australian republican movement. That would come to a head in the nineties with a celebrated referendum. It was Australia's Labour Prime Minister, Paul Keating, who began the process towards a grand vote on whether to replace the Crown with a republic. Demonised in sections of the British press as the 'Lizard of Oz' for apparently touching the Queen (he was steering her through a crowded reception; she was not remotely bothered), Keating came to Britain to explain his plans in person to the Queen. It was a tense occasion which neither side particularly enjoyed. As one member of the Household told author Graham Turner, the Queen emerged with the words: 'I really do need a very large drink.' A very senior retired aide recalls that it could have been a lot worse. 'Keating came to Balmoral and it was absolutely fascinating. I liked him. He was a very intelligent man, a great expert on Regency clocks which was an unexpected revelation. And I mean expert, too – he collected them. He was a republican. He minced no words. He was extremely cour-teous to the Queen – he couldn't have been more so – and there was a picnic. And I remember the Queen talking to him about what Menzies [her first Australian Prime Minister] had said to her. And you did feel that this guy was going for more than just a short-term political trick.'

In the event, Keating lost the 1996 election and it was the monarchist Prime Minister John Howard who delivered the referendum in 1999. The choice was between a president elected by Parliament or the status quo. The political and media establishments were overwhelmingly in favour of change. To worldwide astonishment, Australians voted 55–45 per cent in favour of keeping the Queen. Furthermore, constitutional change would have required a majority in four of the country's six states. It occurred in just one. Even diehard royalists would concede that there had not been a sudden resurgence of 1954-style Queen worship. The determining factor, surely, had been the fact that many Australians did not like the republican model on offer – a cosy system of politicians electing the president themselves. But this, in itself, was a reminder of a central element of constitutional monarchy – it's a politician-free zone.

The republican tide continues to ebb and flow. Some, like the late Ben Pimlott, have suggested that the Queen should jump while the going is good in places like Australia rather than wait to be pushed. All those around the Queen regard the idea as unthinkable. They see it as asking for troubles not yet even contemplated. The Royal Family accepts that, ultimately, all these nations may want their own heads of state but would rather let them do it in their own time, as long as it is done by consent. A very senior courtier sums up Palace thinking on the issue: 'The attitude is: "Just tell us when you want us to go" – unless it's a maverick who is twisting the tail of the vast majority of the population. Then you have got to sit it out. But if it's a democratically elected government, then so be it.'

Malcolm Fraser, former Australian Prime Minister, says he is typical of the large numbers of 'geographical' republicans in Australia – and happy to call himself a monarchist for the duration of the present reign. 'Her Majesty can obviously do things for Britain which she can't do as head of state for a country with our geography,' he says. 'The real stumbling block is finding a model which is workable and we're prepared to accept. And that might take longer than people think. But if I was in Britain, I certainly wouldn't be a republican.' He also believes that '90 per cent' of Australian republicans would want to retain the British Monarch as Head of the Commonwealth. 'Australia may become a republic but her links to Britain could be just as strong as they are now through the bonds of the Commonwealth,' he argues. 'There'd be just as much affection.'

The days of appointing a member of the Royal Family to be a Governor-General are long gone, although the Queen did try to give her sons a taste of the 'old' Commonwealth in their youth. Prince Charles spent part of his education in Australia, Prince Andrew in Canada, Prince Edward in New Zealand. In the late eighties, Australian Prime Minister Bob Hawke gave serious thought to appointing the Prince of Wales as Governor-General. The Prince liked the idea but explained that it could only happen with cross-party support. Hawke had to drop the plan when he could not convince his own Labour party.

For many years, the Palace regarded Canada as the republican hotspot, particularly during the rise of secessionist feeling in Quebec in the sixties. But, over time, Canada began to lose its appetite for republicanism. 'I went to Canada with the Queen a lot in the seventies because all the provinces were having their centenaries,' says Ron Allison. 'And then Watergate happened in America and they peered over the border and thought: "That couldn't happen here . . . our head of state and head of the executive are not the same." And I think that greatly strengthened the monarchy.'

After the failure of the Australian referendum in 1999, eyes turned towards New Zealand. With no federal system there, a straightforward plebiscite could topple the Crown more easily and Labour's Helen Clark was no royalist. But she had other business to attend to. Now the tide has turned there, too. After taking power in 2008, John Key and his conservative coalition made a tiny but important decision. They decided to restore titular honours – knighthoods and damehoods – for Kiwis. 'Sir', 'Lady' and 'Dame' had been scrapped by Clark's administration, seen as evidence of a 'cultural cringe' towards Britain and its old imperial ways. Restoring them would only involve a handful of people every year but it also showed a renewed sense of kinship with the Crown. Even Key has been surprised by the success of a policy which scored an 80 per cent approval rating in opinion polls – only narrowly pipped in popularity by a new national cycleway. 'Nearly three years on from the reintroduction of the honours system in New Zealand, it has gone from strength to strength,' says Key, looking back. The Queen's reaction to the plan? 'She was absolutely thrilled.'

Another obstacle for republicans is that even the most rational arguments can succumb to deep-rooted emotion. Dr Jane Connors, chronicler of the great 1954 royal tour of Australia, describes herself as a republican and a 'person of the left'. She recalls demonstrating outside the new Parliament building in Canberra when the Queen came to open it in 1988. And then something strange happened: 'We were all protesting and chanting. But then the Queen arrived and we fell silent. It was funny but we just couldn't boo the Queen.' She believes that the Australian republican lobby's big mistake has been to mock the royalists. 'You had an elitist republican movement which sneered that anyone who likes the royals believes in medieval mumbo-jumbo. They claimed that the monarchy has a negative impact on our daily lives when it doesn't. It was a mess.' She points to the Australian media establishment's collective amnesia about the 1954 tour, a defining moment in the country's history yet one which has barely warranted a documentary since. 'The story has been completely wiped from the national memory because our history has been written from the left and the left have always been embarrassed by that tour. It was seen as a women's event. We were supposed to be a nation of rebels like Ned Kelly. Media people like to say that the arrival of the Beatles in 1964 was the biggest thing in our popular history because it suits the narrative. They only mention the Queen's 1954 tour in relation to later visits, never in its own right.'

While the Crown is never going to enjoy the almost hypnotic allure it enjoyed in places like Australia and New Zealand back then, its profile and popularity have certainly been boosted by the rise of the younger generation. The start of 2011 saw terrible floods in Australia followed by the greatest post-war disaster in New Zealand's history. On 22 February, an earthquake destroyed much of central Christchurch and killed more than 180 people. Just two weeks later, it was announced that Prince William would tour the region within days. He inspected the devastation in the Australian states of Queensland and Victoria. He saw the carnage in Christchurch and the ruins of George Gilbert Scott's cathedral in a city so quintessentially British that it has a River Avon with punts on it. He also visited the site of New Zealand's 2010 Pike River mining disaster which killed twenty-nine. Along the way, he met and consoled many distraught, bereaved people with great sensitivity and passed on messages to and from the Queen. His visit was high profile, of course; quite apart from his position, he was just weeks away from his wedding. But the style was deliberately low-key with a minimum of protocol. 'I felt so strongly about going down there,' says the Prince. 'Because if it was someone you knew or people you cared about, which I do, you'd want to be down there consoling them. They're a good bunch and they've had a horrendous time. Christchurch got destroyed.' It was backed up by the Prince of Wales, who attended various disaster-related engagements and services back in Britain – and made a memorable speech at the Australian High Commission saluting the fortitude of Australian ladies fighting off a flood-borne invasion of crocodiles and snakes. There was nothing laboured about any of this. The monarchy's response was born of deep, familial affection and received as such, by royalists and republicans alike. 'The country was visibly moved when Prince William, as the Queen's representative, visited New Zealand,' says Prime Minister John Key, adding that the Queen continues to receive many letters from people in Christchurch. They still want to tell her how the city and its people are recovering. These are enduring bonds. They will take some breaking.

What is perhaps most surprising about the continued strength of the Queen's various thrones and her role as Head of the Commonwealth is that the relationships have survived the vagaries of British foreign policy. Obviously, she must answer to, say, her New Zealand Prime Minister on anything to do with New Zealand. And when she is acting as Head of the Commonwealth, she must transcend all national boundaries. Former Zambian President Kenneth Kaunda remembers talking to the Queen at a Commonwealth gathering in 1986 at the height of the quarrels about sanctions against South Africa: 'And then she said: "My friend, you and I should be careful. We are under the scrutiny of the British Prime Minister." I looked up and I saw Mrs Thatcher had her eyes fixed on us.'

But for most of the time, the Queen's dealings with the wider world are at the behest of her British Prime Minister and his government. And British foreign policy has not necessarily been in the best interests of the old imperial cousinhood. The days of the Commonwealth as the larder of Britain died with British entry into the future European Union in 1973. However much the Queen has used her Christmas message to the Commonwealth to convey the idea of a united Commonwealth family, many feel that Britain has turned its back. Gillian Raini of the London-based Afromedia Network likens Europe to a second wife: 'As a young person, I feel terribly neglected because of this second marriage which has overruled our first marriage – the Commonwealth.'

When it comes to the Queen's loyalties, there are, inevitably, grey areas. As she herself has admitted, she finds it hard to know whom to support when England's cricketers are playing, say, Australia or the West Indies (like Australia, half of the West Indies still have her as Queen). No single realm may lay a greater claim to her affections than another. If Barbados were to have a great schism with Belize – or Britain for that matter – then she could not take sides. Indeed, she has been fortunate that she has never had a serious constitutional conflict of interest involving two of her realms, although Kenneth Rose points out that it came close in the run-up to the 1964 tour of Canada: 'They were letting off bombs in Quebec. The Canadian government said: "It's OK, do come" and the British Government said, "Don't go." And she went.' But that was an issue involving her personal safety.

In the early part of the reign, most of the Queen's overseas visits were to realms rather than foreign nations. Latterly, the balance has shifted. All British prime ministers quickly come to realise the benefits of having the most famous woman in the world to promote their own policies and prestige all over the globe. As David Cameron explains: 'In terms of our diplomatic heft, she gives an extra string to the bow – a massive extra string. In fact, she's a whole extra orchestra.'

And no monarch has ever played on the world stage quite like this one. From the First World War to his death eighteen years later, George V spent just eight weeks abroad. George VI travelled widely as Duke of York but for much of his reign his capacity for travel was curtailed by war and ill health. The Queen, who had never left the country until shortly before her twenty-first birthday, has visited 135 separate nations, some of them several times. And yet she had to wait until she was eighty-five to visit the nearest of the lot – the Republic of Ireland – in May 2011.

There have also been some notable non-visits. As Sir Malcolm Rifkind points out, the Queen's absence has often been as important as her presence. During the nineties, he accompanied her on the first state visits ever made to the former Eastern Bloc nations of Poland and the Czech Republic. As he recalls: 'One of the consistent speeches made by her hosts was gratitude not for coming but for *not* having come while they were under communist rule. "We will never forget that you did not give respectability to the communists . . ." and so on. To be fair, that was down to the government and to my predecessors' advice but the Queen was the beneficiary of that. And they came out in their thousands.' Rifkind vividly recalls an episode on that first state visit to the Czech Republic. 'The Queen was being driven through a town packed with people. We were going past the local hospital and suddenly we noticed the surgeons on the balcony in their smocks. Some poor chap on the operating table had been abandoned for a couple of minutes so the surgeon could see the Queen!'

His predecessor, Lord Hurd, was worried about the reception the

Queen would receive in the black townships during her historic 1995 return to South Africa at the invitation of Nelson Mandela. The Commonwealth and Margaret Thatcher's government had been at odds over South Africa during the apartheid era. Would the Queen suffer collateral damage? The first test came in Port Elizabeth. 'Here were all these children, absolutely spotless in their uniforms as they always are, and they ran cheering after the royal car and that was a great relief because it was all about the Queen and they knew all about the Queen. There wasn't any hostility. It was quite different from going with Margaret [Thatcher] because, for all her blessings, she was a divisive character and there were always people around who didn't approve of her. The Queen was quite different.'

Few royal tours have commanded more diplomatic nervousness and obsessive pre-planning than that state visit to Ireland in May 2011. No monarch had set foot in Ireland since its bloody struggle for independence during the reign of George V. His last visit had been in 1911. A century on, there were some who argued that the Queen should test the waters with a private excursion before a full-scale state visit. But both governments saw the need for an emphatic statement, as did the Royal Family. 'It was a great time to say: "Let's move on. Some horrendous things have been done over the years but let's look to the future,"' says Prince William. His own appointment as Colonel of the Irish Guards just a few weeks earlier was part of the diplomatic mood music. He describes his appointment as 'a tiny speck' in the scheme of things, although he points out that the Irish Guards recruit many soldiers from the Republic of Ireland. 'The massive deal was the Queen going and cementing the fact that everyone should look for better things.'

That 'cementing' process was almost instantaneous as the trip surpassed almost all expectations. The Queen's sense of excitement was luminous from the start, despite the largest security operation in Irish history. A combined force of 10,000 military and police ensured that the Sovereign and the public barely met each other. Yet, there was pan-Irish applause for the Queen's state banquet speech (garnished with a little Gaelic) expressing 'deep sympathy' for the 'heartache, turbulence and loss' over all those years. There was even greater appreciation of the Queen's silent gestures – her judicious selection of green dresses, her journey to the spiritual home of Gaelic culture and, above all, her bow at Dublin's nationalist memorial to those killed in the fight for independence. That moment, said Gaelic Affairs Minister Dinny McGinley, was when 'the whole nation lost a heartbeat'. There could be no doubt whatsoever that, in her ninth decade, here was a monarch at the very height of her powers.

'She's had so many people congratulating her on it,' says a proud Prince William. 'And rightly so.'

Every tour demands appreciation and respect for local customs. But the Royal Family must always weigh up the risk of offending the hosts versus the danger of upsetting the public at home. In 1961, the Queen and Prince Philip were paying a state visit to Nepal where King Mahendra had laid on a lavish hunting expedition by elephant. The Queen was not expected to fire a gun but Prince Philip definitely was. Miraculously, the newly appointed patron of the World Wildlife Fund had a 'boil' on his trigger finger that day and could not shoot a thing. It was an ingenious affliction. But diplomacy dictated that someone had to take a potshot at the tigress which crossed the royal path. The task fell to the Foreign Secretary, the Earl of Home, who missed three times before the Queen's Private Secretary, Sir Michael Adeane, helped finish the task. Lord Home was clearly more worried about diplomatic rather than public relations. To make amends for missing the tigress, he went on to shoot a female rhino, inadvertently making an orphan of her calf. As if the British media did not have enough of a story already, the Foreign Secretary turned a public relations disaster into a catastrophe. Asked what he would do with his trophy, he replied that the feet might be useful as waste-paper baskets.

It is another indicator of how far things have changed during this reign. Lord Home – like the tigress, the rhino and, indeed, the Nepalese monarchy – is no longer with us. But the Queen keeps on circling the globe – always with a copy of the *Racing Post*, a full-length mirror and a St Christopher's medallion stowed on board her chartered plane.

One of the first foreign policy decisions by David Cameron's new Coalition Government was to revivify Britain's relations with the Arab nations of the Persian Gulf. The decision was taken well before the 2011 risings in Egypt, Libya and elsewhere, events which have only served to concentrate political minds further on the Middle East.

British diplomats felt that links with the Gulf States had been neglected in recent years. But Britain has a unique advantage over most of its European rivals in the sector: the monarchy. 'Frankly, the previous government rather forgot about these countries except when it wanted favours,' says an old Gulf hand. David Cameron agrees. 'Most of them have got royal heads of state, they feel a great affinity with Britain and they feel they haven't had enough attention in recent years,' says the Prime Minister.

The region matters on many levels. The Gulf States are vitally placed for the fights against terrorism and piracy and Britain would be crippled without their oil and gas. The 200,000 British citizens in the region are by far the largest expatriate Western population and two-way trade is in the tens of billions. Gulf nations now own everything from British football clubs to prime parts of London. Tiny Qatar alone has bought Harrods and the London Stock Exchange and has been the first Middle Eastern nation chosen to host football's World Cup. In the Gulf States, it is the royal families who run everything. They are sophisticated financiers, too. No one is naive enough to believe that an Emir is going to hand a billion-dollar contract to a British company ahead of, say, a French one on the back of a cup of tea with the Prince of Wales. But the connection can certainly give bilateral relations a special warmth, not to mention ease of access. Nor will the British Royal Family talk money or deliver lectures on human rights as politicians tend to do.

Hence, the sight of the Emir of Qatar drawing into the Windsor Castle Quadrangle alongside the Queen on a rainswept October morning in the Australian State Coach (the one with the heating). The Emir is being given the full state-visit treatment, the ultimate sign of a thriving relationship.

Sheikha Mozah, his tall and striking wife (he has three), follows alongside the Duke of Edinburgh in the Scottish State Coach. The Prince of Wales and the Duchess of Cornwall come next, accompanying other members of the Qatari royal family. Bringing up the rear is a man with the splendidly practical title of 'Secretary for Follow-Up Affairs'.

The Emir and his wife chose Windsor over Buckingham Palace as their base for their state visit. Every visitor is given a choice and many would argue that this was the right one. Few sights can match a full state banquet in the medieval grandeur of the magnificently restored St George's Hall with 136 guests seated around the 175-foot table. Nor, for that matter, are there many views to match those from their room, Suite 240 – all the way down the Long Walk to the distant statue of George III. The Queen gives the Emir a sixteenth-century engraving of Windsor (he has a home nearby). He gives her a gold box set with amethysts, diamonds and coral. The Queen has also produced some souvenirs of her 1979 state visit to Qatar. The Duke shows Sheikha Mozah the *Britannia* logbook entry for the trip. 'It's quite a long time ago. You weren't born then!' Much laughter. 'No, I wasn't born then,' chuckles Sheikha Mozah (date of birth: 1959). But it is another reminder of the span of this reign.

And it is why, just a month later, there is such a sense of history as the royal charm offensive continues in the Gulf with a tour of Oman and the United Arab Emirates. The Queen was last here in 1979 when a visit by a female head of state was pioneering stuff. Back then, she arrived by Concorde and stayed aboard the Royal Yacht. Those are both museum pieces now, such is the passage of time. On this trip, she is staying in a hotel which has a gold bullion vending machine in reception. Back in

1979, she visited the tallest building in the Middle East, Dubai's thirty-nine-storey World Trade Centre. Today, it is a bungalow compared to the 2,716-foot Burj Khalifa Tower. Everyone knows about her visit back then because it is still in the school textbooks. In the short history of this hyperactive nation, 1979 is like the Middle Ages. And yet, here is that same monarch with that same handbag returning for another visit. It is a substantial landmark. But, as ever, the Queen is keen not to dwell on the past too much, beyond remarking to Dubai's Sheikh Mohamed: 'It's extraordinary how it's all changed.'

It's a short state visit – less than twenty-four hours – but the Queen manages to meet all seven royal families and do two walkabouts, a state luncheon and an investiture. Maurice Flanagan, the ex-RAF pilot who built the Emirates airline empire, becomes Sir Maurice. Most importantly, perhaps, the Queen pays a solemn visit, head covered, to Abu Dhabi's Sheikh Zayed Mosque, one of the world's largest. It is the burial place of the man who built this nation. He was her host last time. Now his tomb is a national shrine. It's another poignant reminder of how far she goes back in the memory of this young country.

In Oman, the Queen's visit has caused the rearrangement of the biggest party in the state's history. It is the fortieth anniversary of the accession of Sultan Qaboos. He had been planning his Ruby Jubilee celebrations for earlier in the year but rearranged them when he learned that the Queen would come in November. The Sultan is an old friend of Britain after a slightly unusual British education – a Suffolk tutorial college, Sandhurst and an internship at Suffolk County Council. He deposed his father in a reasonably civilised coup in 1970 and began modernising a country which then had ten miles of road, three schools and a medieval justice system. Today, Oman is one of the most progressive states in the region with an increasingly vocal democracy movement pressing for reforms, although the Sultan remains an absolute ruler.

When in London, he always likes to see the Queen. And, in Oman, the seventy-year-old bachelor has twinned his Palace with the Tower of London. He is also the proud owner of the world's only camel-mounted bagpipe band.

His immaculate Royal Cavalry – much like Britain's Household Cavalry – escorts the Queen into the capital, Muscat, past thousands of cheering onlookers. It is spectacular but a little sterile, an unspoken tension in the air. The onlookers have all been vetted and divided into male and female sections wearing colour-coordinated robes. They stand at specific points. Elsewhere, the streets are empty. The Sultan seems wary of his general public.

The Queen is staying at the Al-Alam Palace, newly decorated with half a dozen landscapes from London's Tate Gallery which have been lent to Oman to mark the Sultan's jubilee. Someone has included a landscape by Gainsborough. By happy coincidence, it is of the Sultan's adoptive British county. 'Ah, I know Suffolk very well,' he declares as the two monarchs inspect the pictures together. 'I lived near Bury St Edmunds.' The Queen is more taken by the Stubbs – *Mares and Foals* – and discusses the artist's pioneering technique in animal portraiture. 'He was the first to paint the legs properly,' she says. Horses will be a recurring topic of conversation. Both the Sultan and the Queen adore them. He has arranged an equestrian spectacular for the Queen at the Royal Cavalry's showground where 840 horses and 3,340 riders, singers and musicians are on parade. It is a stunning production with dancing horses, bowing horses – and even bowing goats. Acrobatic riders, some of them straddling two or three horses, jump fences at the same time. One horse gallops past with its rider doing a handstand in the saddle. 'The Queen will be loving this,' whispers one of the entourage. 'The Royal Mews will be getting a long memo as soon as she's home.' The event concludes with a colossal carriage being pulled by a record-breaking team of twenty-nine horses. The Duke of Edinburgh, a veteran carriage driver who is more used to four-in-hand, is glued to his binoculars.

Bizarrely, the Sultan had wanted to restrict the entire event to the Queen, the Duke and himself. Palace officials explained that the Queen likes to share these things so a few hundred expats have been invited to create a semblance of an audience. It's a slightly strange way to mark a jubilee. Apparently, there will be more public events in the days ahead. For now, the Sultan is keen to give his undivided attention to the Queen. Again, there are the mandatory elements of every state visit including a garden party at the British ambassador's clifftop residence. It is the hottest ticket in Oman.

There is also the customary state banquet but the Sultan dispenses with speeches or television cameras – because he can. He has commissioned a gold vase and a Fabergé-style musical egg with dancing horses as a gift for the Queen. She has spent a lifetime being given great treasures but is evidently thrilled. Her gifts to the Sultan are less spectacular but equally appreciated – an eighteenth-century book on clocks, one of the Sultan's great passions, and the Royal Victorian Chain, an exalted honour reserved for selected monarchs and very special courtiers. It goes with the GCB she gave him back in 1979. Every detail is being watched by hawk-like officials on both sides, every note of diplomatic mood music being absorbed and savoured. And there is much to savour. Instead of flying home at the end of her visit, the Queen and the Duke stay an extra night for an extra private dinner with the Sultan – just as Prince William recently dropped in here for a private dinner while returning from Afghanistan. The Sultan does not bid farewell at his palace, as he does with most visitors, but accompanies the Queen to the steps of her plane and waves her off from the runway. It is particularly gratifying for the man a little further back down the plane, the Foreign Secretary, William Hague. The British Government's Gulf charm offensive is coming along nicely. The Palace team are pleased, too, that two back-to-back state visits have passed off successfully without any discernible strain on the oldest state visitors on the international circuit.

As well as having travelled further than any monarch in history geographically, the Queen has crossed more boundaries than all her predecessors in other ways. She has been the first reigning monarch to visit a mosque or a Hindu temple. She has been the first to meet a pope, the first to visit the Vatican and the Sikh holy of holies, the Golden Temple of Amritsar. It is worth noting that, in the first year of the Coalition Government alone, she visited or entertained four fellow heads of state – three of them from Islamic countries plus one pope. Just as the story of the Commonwealth is almost entirely contiguous with her reign, so too is the story of multicultural Britain.

Britain had seen little immigration beyond the arrival of 50,000 French Huguenots during the sixteenth and seventeenth centuries and 300,000 Jewish refugees during the nineteenth and early twentieth. The first Commonwealth migrants to Britain arrived from Jamaica aboard the MV *Empire Windrush* less than four years before the Queen came to the throne. Five years into her reign, Commonwealth immigration still amounted to just 36,000. Since 1963, however, some 2.5 million people have arrived from the Commonwealth, not to mention those from the European Union and other parts of the world.

It is by far the greatest demographic change in the country's history and the importance of the Queen as a force for unity throughout cannot be overstated. 'I think she's had perfect pitch really,' says the Archbishop of Canterbury, Dr Rowan Williams. 'It's partly the Commonwealth experience. The fact that she is head of a multicultural, diverse, worldwide association means that she's never felt any instinct to panic about multiculturalism. That's part of the message her Christmas broadcasts have given almost subliminally over the years: "Britain is changing. It's OK. We can cope. Faith is a good and constructive element in this. You know where I'm coming from. I'm a Christian. But there's room for others." And that's been a steady message.' The former Home and Foreign Secretary Jack Straw says that affection for the Queen runs deep among the large numbers of his Blackburn constituents from Asian backgrounds. He also sits on the board of the Oxford Centre for Islamic Studies, of which the Prince of Wales is patron. 'It's very much Prince Charles's baby and he's been absolutely fantastic on this,' says Straw. 'He's got a much better understanding of Islam in society than a lot of politicians I can think of.'

'People who come to live here have seen symbols of Britishness and they want to feel part of that,' says David Cameron. 'What the Royal Family have done, especially with people from the Commonwealth, is give them a shared bond.' Growing up in the sixties and seventies as the London-born child of Jamaican parents, Wesley Kerr came to regard the Queen as something of a hero figure. 'The Queen has been a revolutionary monarch,' says the writer and broadcaster. 'As a child, she was the only public figure whom I regularly saw in the news with black people. And they were never deferential to her but equals, people like Nyrere [Julius Nyrere, father of Tanzanian independence] and Kenneth Kaunda [former President of Zambia].'

On that 1947 tour of southern Africa, George VI was horrified to be barred from decorating black servicemen in South Africa and made a point of doing so in British-controlled territories elsewhere. Princess Elizabeth and sixteen-year-old Princess Margaret became acutely aware of the privations of the black population of South Africa, 'though [as Princess Margaret wrote home] one mustn't say so too loudly'. One could say so more loudly once South Africa had become a republic. When the Queen danced with President Nkrumah of Ghana in 1961, she was denounced in the South African press for consorting with a 'black pagan' and saluted by Ghana's Marxist media as 'the world's greatest Socialist Monarch'. On the 1954 tour of Australia, during which Aboriginal Australians had little more than a token role, she pointedly referred to 'my peoples' in the plural and there was grumbling when she was deemed to have spent too long talking to a group of Torres Strait Islanders. There were ringside seats, too, for many handicapped children who had never enjoyed any sort of public prominence before. The Queen has only ever been able to deal in gestures. But she has been consistent with them. 'Of all the sovereigns since Queen Victoria,' says a former Private Secretary, 'the Queen has been the most clearly party-blind, colour-blind and race-blind.'

She has proved to be one of the more conscientious Supreme Governors of the Church of England. Monarchs also take a separate oath to preserve the Church of Scotland and it is their duty to send a Lord High Commissioner to its annual General Assembly. The Queen has been the first to send herself. She is an assiduous Sunday churchgoer wherever she is in the world (in 1994, a Sunday visit to a Guyanese rainforest had to include a diversion to a mission church for morning service). Her Christmas broadcasts always contain unashamedly Christian messages. Indeed, the Archbishop of Canterbury has noticed the religious theme becoming more explicit in the last ten years. 'The Queen has a very powerful sense that the Monarch is bound up with the religious heritage of the country,' says Dr Williams. 'That's been thinning out quite a bit in the street in the last twenty years. My guess would be that she's deliberately set out to redress the balance.'

It is striking that a nation which can tie itself in knots over the tiniest religious symbolism in public life – even agonising over the appropriate use of the word 'Christmas' – is entirely comfortable with a national figurehead whose own approach to religion is clear and uncompromising. She does not preach. What she does do is give faith, of all kinds, a certain respectability or, as the Archbishop of Canterbury puts it, a 'canopy'.

'People feel that if the Christian faith is secure in this country, so are they,' says Dr Williams. 'It's not competing for territory which is why some of those assumptions that "Oh, non-Christians will be offended by this" are so completely off-key.'

'She is a person of faith and it matters a lot more to her than people understand,' says Tony Blair, one of the more overtly religious occupants of Number Ten Downing Street in many years. As he discovered in office, the public can be uncomfortable with a Prime Minister who brings religion into his work. Not so with the head of state. Other nations are often struck by the way in which Britain can weave religion into a state occasion without blinking. Lord Hurd was talking to his French opposite number, Alain Juppé, as they accompanied the Queen at the fiftieth anniversary of D-Day in 1994. 'We discussed the different ways we did these things and he said: "The difference is that you British bring religion into it and we don't dare do that. We are a secular country but you have hymns and a blessing." And he's right. There's always a bishop somewhere around.'

'The Queen's religious belief is very important in the way she does her job and sees her role,' says Charles Anson. 'She's got that calmness you find in people who are quite naturally religious. There's an official role but there's a lot she falls back on.' A senior aide was surprised to discover a deep well of Christian charity at a time when others might have been less than forgiving: 'I detected it when I had to go to talk to her about the latest issues with the Princess of Wales. There were moments when she could have become exasperated but she didn't. There was a Christian element, a belief that it's wrong to make too many judgements.'

The Archbishop of Canterbury senses that the Queen is someone with a 'powerful, coherent set of values or ideals . . . a deep sense of vocation . . . a dogged confidence that there is a divinity that shapes our ends'. In short, he says: 'It goes deep.'

The Queen is very open about the existence of her faith but, like most people, very private about its nature. We know that she likes Matins, that she seldom takes Holy Communion in public and that, given the chance, she prefers to worship in a smaller church like All Saints in Windsor Great Park rather than sit above the ancestors in mighty St George's Chapel. She does not like a great fuss. When aboard *Britannia*, she was happy to let the rear admiral take Sunday prayers rather than summon a clergyman. In many ways, she is a no-nonsense, traditional Anglican. She prefers the Book of Common Prayer on Sundays and made much of the 400th anniversary of the King James Bible in her 2010 Christmas broadcast. She follows Church politics closely. Jack Straw, who would join the Queen for the swearing-in of new Bishops in his capacity as both Home Secretary and Lord Chancellor, talks of the 'granular details' of her discussions afterwards. She sees her Archbishops several times each year for what Dr Williams calls 'uncluttered time to talk'. He finds the Supreme Governor 'refreshing, perceptive, warm and deeply supportive'. But she does not seek to mould her Church to her tastes.

Her predecessors were bossier. Queen Victoria was an arch-meddler. 'She was quite capable of writing to the Prime Minister and saying, "I want so and so as Bishop of Gloucester. He's a good chap,"' says Dr Williams. Edward VII instructed one Archbishop of York that his duty was 'to keep the parties in the Church together and to prevent the clergy from wearing moustaches'. George V had similarly robust views. 'Wonderful service,' he remarked after his Silver Jubilee service at St Paul's, 'but too many damn parsons getting in the way.' Prince Philip can be equally forthright when it comes to long sermons. As he once remarked: 'The mind cannot absorb what the backside cannot endure.' The Archbishop of Canterbury knows the form. 'I'm always reminded when I preach in the presence that he prefers eight minutes,' admits Dr Williams. 'I don't always obey. My natural length is twelve minutes for a sermon but, on state occasions, I do try and trim it a bit.'

The Queen's approach is different. She prefers to send out what the Archbishop of Canterbury calls 'visible messages', like inviting the Roman Catholic Cardinal Archbishop of Westminster to preach at Sandringham. Indeed, Dr Williams believes that a recurring message through this reign has been: 'Roman Catholics are not foreign eccentrics.' There has been much talk of amending the Act of Settlement on the grounds that it debars the Royal Family from marrying Roman Catholics – but leaves them free to marry members of any other faith. Understandably, this has led to charges that the institution is inherently sectarian. Labour's Jack Straw, who has explored the possibility of amending the legislation, disagrees: 'They won't thank me for saying it but one of the difficulties is with the Church of Rome because they automatically excommunicate Anglicans. So it's one in which we need the help of the Church of Rome.'

Whatever the answer, it is emphatically one for Parliament, not the Supreme Governor, to resolve. The Queen's clear view is that her own Church should be a broad and inclusive one. She studiously avoids overt opinions on schismatic issues like gay clergy. George V or George VI would probably have had robust views on such matters, but the Queen would appear to be more open-minded. 'I don't think there's any hint of her, say, being uncomfortable with women priests,' says the Archbishop. 'The fact that there are female royal chaplains is not insignificant. I would guess her feeling is: "The world's changing. Never mind what I might feel about this. It's important that these things be affirmed as positive changes."'

It's another example of the Queen leading by gesture rather than command.


One of the most colourful, sacred rituals in the Queen's calendar is one which, to a considerable extent, she has reinvented herself. Royal Maundy attracts less attention than it used to. The BBC gave up regular television and radio broadcasts years ago (although the event did return to the screen in 2011 as a royal wedding warm-up). For many of her staff, though, Royal Maundy remains the most enjoyable ritual of the entire royal year. It dates back at least as far as the thirteenth century when King John is known to have washed the feet of the poor and given them gifts of food and clothing on Maundy Thursday – the day before Good Friday. Through the centuries, sovereigns would take part in this homage to the story of Christ's Last Supper. They gave up foot-washing post-James II and, by the mid-eighteenth century, they had stopped turning up altogether. The task of handing out charity – a token sum of money – was left to whichever bishop happened to hold the title of Lord High Almoner.

By Victorian times, the recipients were not 'the poor' so much as public-spirited members of the local community. It's always been equal numbers of men and women, the numbers rising each year to match the Monarch's age. In 1932, George V revived the practice of attending in person and royal appearances became semi-regular from then on. But it was the Queen who gave the ceremony a vigorous new impetus. Royal Maundy was her first public engagement after the death of her father. She'd cancelled everything else but this event seemed appropriate. Then she had the idea of moving the ceremony out of Westminster Abbey and taking it to the country, choosing a different cathedral every year (it returns to the Abbey every tenth year, as it did in 2011). There are now just a handful of cathedrals which have not had the pleasure. And the event grows larger with each passing year.

'The thing I most enjoyed during my time was the Royal Maundy. It's magical,' says a retired Private Secretary. 'It encapsulates what's best about the monarchy. You are walking through a great cathedral as the choir and congregation are singing and the Queen is performing a ritual which goes back for ever and which is giving a huge amount of pleasure to vast numbers of people. It's about as good an experience as you can get. If you had to sum up what the monarchy's about, that's it.' Even by royal standards, there are few events so laden with symbolism. This is an event which brings out some of the most exotic specimens in the royal firmament, some of whom are only seen at this one occasion each year. They are all paid the unprincely sum of 10p in Maundy coins for their troubles.

They are also expected to assemble a day ahead of the grand ceremony to rehearse. On this occasion, Derby Cathedral has been chosen. It's a pretty sixteenth-century church which only became a cathedral in 1927 but has the oldest bells in the land. It is not large. There are so many officials involved in this ceremony that the procession is actually longer than the cathedral and will have to wind its way up the side aisles. The present Lord High Almoner is the Rt Revd Nigel McCulloch, Bishop of Manchester. His appointment was the usual blend of enigma and lunch: 'In 1997, I got a call from the Queen's Private Secretary saying that the Queen would like to hear me preach. "Would any of these dates be suitable? If not, would some other time be better?" It was a case of "There's no getting out of this one, mate." So I went to preach at All Saints in Windsor Great Park and then we had lunch at Windsor Castle. Nothing was said whatsoever about Almonry. Then the next day I got a call from the Private Secretary saying the Queen would like me to be the next Lord High Almoner.' As a result, he is in charge of the Royal Almonry, one of the most ancient and arcane backwaters of the Royal Household. Pulling it all together is Paul Leddington Wright, Secretary of the Royal Almonry, a conductor by profession but a man devoted to an honorary task which his father performed before him.

The event makes a Gilbert & Sullivan opera look underdressed. Local school children will serve as the Children of the Royal Almonry, draped in ancient linen towels to symbolise the washing of feet. The Yeomen of the Guard will be in attendance carrying the Maundy money in little leather purses piled high on trays of gold. The Clerk of the Cheque and the Keeper of the Closet will be on parade. The Maundy Wands have to be removed from their cupboard at Buckingham Palace for the Wandsmen, half a dozen men in morning coats whose original job was to stop Maundy paupers being mugged for their money. Since this year's Maundy money will be worth £6.34, there are unlikely to be muggings. The Wandsmen are led by Leddington Wright's brother, Andrew, a human resources director. It's a family affair. Paul's wife, Sheila, is in the basement of a nearby hotel helping Rosemary Hughes produce a dozen nosegays, bunches of flowers and herbs traditionally used to ward off bad smells in medieval times. The Queen and the main players will each carry one. Hughes runs a floral design business in Leicester but, once a year, earns her Royal Warrant as 'Her Majesty's Supplier of Nosegays'. There will be no bad smells to offend the royal nostrils in Derby but, even so, each nosegay is a complex blend (Hughes calls it a 'recipe') of seasonal flowers and herbs including thyme, rosemary, hebe and purple statice. Each has a hand-sewn cotton sleeve attached to the base and Hughes is always up at 6 a.m. to add primroses. 'Everything has to be fresh,' she says, stifling a sneeze. It turns out that she is allergic to a key ingredient of her own recipe – daffodils.

Inside Derby Cathedral, Lieutenant Colonel Andrew Ford, the Comptroller, maps out every inch of the Queen's progress. She needs a seat for the signing of the visitors' book so he earmarks a rather fine-looking chair. There is a flap. A cathedral official rushes to intervene. 'Not that one,' says the official. 'The Bishop says Queen Victoria sat on it.' Quite why Queen Elizabeth II shouldn't sit on it, too, is a mystery. But Ford relents. 'I have learned it's never worth arguing with a Bishop at the Royal Maundy.' These are nervous moments for the Crown Jeweller, Harry Collins. He spends most of his life running the family jewellery shop in Tunbridge Wells but, since being appointed Crown Jeweller in 2007, he now attends all events where the Crown Jewels are in use. Unlike, say, the State Opening of Parliament, there are no crowns or sceptres at this event but Royal Maundy still involves some of the 'Regalia', including priceless gold platters like the Maundy Dish. Collins has just made an unpopular decision. For centuries, the Yeomen of the Guard have processed with the Maundy money on their heads, but the dishes get heavier each year because the number of recipients increases to match the Monarch's age. Each recipient is given £5.50 in commemorative coins in a red purse for 'provisions' plus a white purse containing Maundy coins equivalent to the Monarch's years. Collins has decided that the weight of it all has now reached a tipping point. The old soldiers of the Yeomen of the Guard, he has reluctantly concluded, must stop carrying the dishes on their heads and hold them in their hands before someone has an accident. 'It's too much strain for the dishes, for the Yeomen and for their hats,' he says. Some traditionalists will be cross. What is the world coming to if a Yeoman cannot put a gold platter of Maundy money on his head?

A large crowd has gathered outside the cathedral several hours before the Queen's arrival. Margaret Kittle, seventy-five, has flown from Ontario, Canada, to watch. Inside, there are eighty-four men and eighty-four women – all over the age of seventy – waiting to receive alms from the Queen. May Brindley, eighty-seven, a lay Methodist preacher, says she thought it was an early April Fool when she received a letter. 'I'm not a raving royalist but it's such an honour that I can't explain it,' she says. Jennifer Haynes, seventy-five, a stalwart of her parish council, has no idea why she has been chosen. But she has already been invited to address both the local Mothers' Union and the Pensioners' Club about her experiences. By such means do royal ripples spread across a county. And the *Derby Evening Telegraph* is already preparing a sumptuous souvenir issue.

The Queen, in a powder-blue Karl Ludwig coat, is thrilled to receive her nosegay at the West Door, the Duke of Edinburgh less so. This is the one event of the year where he has to walk around holding a bunch of flowers. He grasps his bouquet manfully, as if holding a torch. He reads a lesson, as he always does. The music is much the same, too, from one year to the next. The Queen barely looks at her order of service. As with the Commonwealth Observance, she knows it all backwards. She knows that she will be distributing alms to the sound of Handel's *Zadok the Priest*. Her face lights up as she moves down the lines of recipients, reconnecting with monarchs from eight hundred years ago. Some people are too infirm to stand. No one is obliged to bow or curtsey but most have a go. There are brief chats but the purpose is largely symbolic and religious, the gesture as important to the giver as to the receiver. 'For all its pageantry, Royal Maundy has never failed to come over as an act of worship,' says the Lord High Almoner. 'It's often said that, for the Queen, it's one of the highlights of her year and I believe it is. It's unique because it's an occasion when she goes to the people to give honours. Usually people go to her to receive an honour.'

Another way to glimpse the Queen's true values, Christian and otherwise, is through her own philanthropy. Her patronage of charities and organisations extends to more than six hundred different institutions and her reign has seen a marked renaissance in the charitable sector. Inevitably, as the Sovereign, she must be less hands-on than other members of the Royal Family. But she can still donate. Most of her own giving is done discreetly through two vehicles, the Privy Purse Charitable Trust and the Queen's Silver Jubilee Trust. Both are run by her most senior officials, with close personal input from the Queen herself. With £35 million in the pot, the Silver Jubilee Trust is much the largest and was formed with a mandate to help young people. As such, it gives most of its annual grants – which currently run at around £1.3 million – straight to the Prince's Trust.

Smaller grants are scattered across a range of youth organisations. The royal sense of charity can even extend to the board of trustees. Until 2012, they included Sir Fred Goodwin, former chief executive of the Royal Bank of Scotland. Pilloried by most of the world since the collapse of his bank in 2008, he had previously been a key supporter of several royal charities. He stepped down as chairman of the Prince's Trust Council in 2009 has remained on the board of the Silver Jubilee Trust (although, perhaps for reasons of diplomacy, it was omitted from his entry in *Who's Who*). The Queen knew Goodwin, had received him as a guest and saw no reason why a man who had given long service to royal charities should not continue to do so. It was Goodwin himself who terminated the arrangement, resigning as a trustee shortly before his knighthood was annulled in 2012.

Quirkier and more personal is the Privy Purse Charitable Trust which receives a steady income from visitors to Queen Mary's Dolls House at Windsor. It hands out around £300,000 a year across a very wide range. There might be a £50 cheque to Dersingham Cricket Club on the Sandringham Estate or the Friends of Orkney Boat Museum. On a typical morning in 2010, the Keeper of the Privy Purse received a personal memo from the Queen suggesting a donation to a nursing fund in memory of Florence Nightingale. 'I think this is a very worthwhile cause,' the Queen wrote. 'I think we gave something ten years ago.' Sure enough, she had. 'She's got a phenomenal memory which keeps us all on our toes,' says Sir Alan Reid. Soon afterwards, the nurses received several hundred pounds.

A contribution from the Monarch is not measured solely in financial terms. A charity which can say that it has received a contribution from the Queen will often find it easier to elicit donations from others. As Frank Prochaska has pointed out, a £500 donation by Queen Victoria to the Indian Famine Fund in 1897 kick-started a campaign which yielded the stupendous sum of £2 million. Our Queen will often make one-off payments to urgent causes – a £10,000 donation, say, to victims of the London bombings in 2005. But the overwhelming slice of this particular pie – two-thirds in a normal year – is directed in just one direction. It goes to the maintenance of royal chapels, choirs and cathedrals.

No religious service, however, is as sacred to the Queen as the one which happens in the middle of the road in London on the second Sunday of November. The Queen's involvement at the Cenotaph every Remembrance Sunday is brief, wordless and unchanging. This really is a piece of the monarchy which needs no tinkering or judicious adaptation whatsoever. As the years advance and the Queen stands out as the last head of state to wear uniform in the Second World War – the last to know the fear, the spirit, even the songs of that generation – her position at the head of the nation and the Commonwealth becomes ever more poignant at this event. Through wars and National Service, most families in Britain have some lineal connection with the Forces, quite possibly a name on a war grave, too. But Britain is a civilian land now. Yet the Windsors remain very much a Forces family. Of all her headships, the Head of the Armed Forces has a bond with her men and women which goes way beyond the constitutional to the deeply personal. From the moment the Queen became Colonel of the Grenadier Guards at sixteen, she has been fluent in the culture and mindset of the Services in a way which few politicians can ever hope to be. 'We've managed to get a good balance in this country,' says David Cameron. 'There is political control of the military, and yet, as Prime Minister, you're not Commander-in-Chief. You're somewhere in between and that's not a bad thing.'

Chester Racecourse, Britain's oldest, has drawn a huge midweek crowd yet there isn't a horse to be seen. The Royal Welsh Regiment is just back from Afghanistan and its Colonel-in-Chief is here to meet the troops and their loved ones at a homecoming parade. At times, the emotion spills over in the grandstands as the families watch their men and women receiving campaign medals and marching past the Queen. At the age of nineteen, Fusilier Shaun Stocker has only just made it here today. Two months earlier a hidden bomb cost him his legs and most of his sight as well as other injuries. It was so bad that he needed a special plane home. He is in a wheelchair and a little dazed, having only emerged from hospital two days earlier, his arms still peppered with plasters from all the intra-venous drips. He had refused to miss this day of all days.

The grandstands burst into applause as the Queen presents all the wounded men with their medals. 'We never thought we'd see this day. It's made him determined to get better,' says Stocker's mother, Jenny, afterwards. She and the Queen are showing a good deal more composure than some here today. For hundreds of families, this is scene they feared they might never see. Some are still in tears as everyone meets up for a big regimental family lunch. Anne and Royston Williams are here to welcome two sons who have been serving in Afghanistan together. 'I can honestly say this is one of the best days of my life,' says Anne. Her mother, Myra, can't say anything as her eyes well up and the tissues come out again.

The mood is upbeat but not triumphal. Everyone is conscious that a man is missing. Fusilier Jonathan Burgess never made it home, killed in a gun battle in April 2010. His parents are here, along with his fiancée. She has now given birth to the baby girl Burgess never saw, although they found a well-thumbed photograph of the hospital scan in his breast pocket. The family will be in the Queen's marquee for lunch. Before that, there's a big open-air reception where the Queen meets Fusilier Aaron Gray, twenty-two, who has postponed an operation on his injured shoulder until the following morning in order to meet his Colonel-in-Chief. Regimental Sergeant Major Wayne Roberts has even deferred promotion until after today. He should be Captain Roberts by now and doing something else but that would have meant missing the Queen. There's an added bonus. His four-year-old daughter has been chosen to present a bouquet to the Queen. 'I spent two and a half years as RSM and to miss out on this at the end – well, I wasn't having that. I've spent twenty-four years in the army so when you actually meet her, it's massive.'

Just the day before, the Queen had been presenting the George Cross to one fearless bomb disposal expert and a posthumous George Medal to the family of another. She is well aware of the situation on the front line and the stresses which Service life creates at home. The familial bond with the Forces permeates the entire Household culture. It's not just a question of employing a few equerries and orderlies plucked from the Services. It's the way in which Forces charities enjoy the run of the Palace Ballroom or the use of the garden party marquees when there are gaps in the diary. It's the shrugging of shoulders when the Palace reception for the Victoria Cross and George Cross Association descends into cheerful chaos because several of them are stuck on a coach and delayed by a student demonstration. The Queen has other engagements and the time slot for the official photograph has long passed. If they were part of an official delegation, this lack of punctuality would go down very badly. It might even be a diplomatic incident. But not with these guests. The Queen is happy to be kept waiting by her old soldiers. 'Usually, our events are masterpieces of choreography and fine-tuning,' chuckles the Master of the Household, looking at his watch. 'I prefer to call this one "jazz".'

Prince William, like his father before him, has had spells with all three

Services. He believes that his military training has given him invaluable coaching for the job which lies ahead: 'It's a very good way of understanding the position and what it takes. You know, these guys do the most incredible things the whole time. And what better place to realise pressure and stress than serving in the Forces and taking that experience with you?'

As with the monarchy, so he believes that the Forces are an innate part of the national character. 'They link to the heart of what it is to be British. I think they are essential for any country to be proud of itself, for any country to have any identity,' says a man who joined the army as a cavalry officer, went to sea in a Type 23 frigate and now flies a rescue helicopter with the Royal Air Force. 'They are setting an example.'

It helps to explain why the Monarch always celebrates her birthday not with a cake but with a military parade. The Queen's official birthday is Britain's national day, marked as such in government and diplomatic missions around the world. Other nations might have fireworks or festivals. Holland, for example, has Queen's Day, with parties, concerts and flowers. In the United Kingdom, people converge on the Mall and Horse Guards Parade to watch a drill display by the Household Division – Trooping the Colour. The crowds then gather around the Palace to watch the entire Royal Family observe an RAF flypast. But it's not martial or nationalistic or remotely odd. A random survey of the crowd suggests that half are from overseas. Chuck Hatcher, a theatre engineer from Ohio, loves the pageantry and the uniforms – 'best costumes in the world'. Sherri Whitehead, a political researcher from Vancouver, British Columbia, is here for the second time – 'she's our monarch, too'. This is simply how the world expects to see our Queen: dressed in hat and gloves and leading her family out on to the most famous balcony in the world while men in bearskins stand to attention below her. It is not merely for the benefit of the tourism industry. It is a statement that the monarchy is a team effort, not a solo performance. It is a reminder of the future.

And the future needs no reminding that the past will be quite an act to follow. Already the oldest and furthest travelled monarch in British history, the Queen overtook George III's fifty-nine years on the throne in May 2011 and will surpass Queen Victoria's sixty-three-year all-time reigning record in September 2015. The Queen will probably not even acknowledge the moment (she does not believe in being competitive with the ancestors), but the rest of the world will be more excited. In Britain, which will also be marking the 600th anniversary of the Battle of Agincourt and the 200th of Waterloo in the year 2015, the sense of occasion will be unstoppable.

Within royal circles, though, there is now a whispered concern that the more the Queen goes on crashing through the record books, the greater the perception that she is somehow irreplaceable. This, inevitably, grows harder on the man who will do the replacing. Asked if the Commonwealth would have survived in its current state without the Queen, a very senior former courtier replies: 'Probably not. But one should not say that too often because it's dangerous from the point of view of the next generation.'

The Queen is not the only record-breaker. Prince Charles is now the oldest Prince of Wales in history. And he has not wasted his years as heir apparent. In the same way that the Queen has quietly redefined the nature of her unconstitutional role, so the Prince has done the same. His well-known interventions on almost anything relating to the human condition have earned him criticism. But no Prince of Wales has made an equivalent mark on national and international life, in every field from education to urban regeneration. There has never been a more accomplished king-in-waiting. Unlike his predecessors, his entire life has been a case of doing rather than waiting. At his investiture in 1969, no powers were bestowed on him. But after four decades of public duties, he believes that he has identified one. He calls it his 'convening power' – his capacity to get people round a table. 'It's a very interesting role he's carved out. In my view it *is* the role,' says Tony Blair. 'It's got two aspects. The first is he's able to take an aerial global view of certain trends which, in his case, has marked him out as thinking ahead of his time.' He cites the environment and interfaith dialogue as examples. 'The second is that I found he was a transmitter of messages, particularly with, say, the farming community and the Armed Forces. He picked up things in a different way from a politician. I never objected. I was not merely happy with it. I thought it was entirely within his entitlement to do so.'

Some of the Prince's critics argue that he has a butterfly mind and flits from one cause to another. Others argue that he gets *too* involved, that he is a meddler who has veered into unconstitutional territory. They cite his opposition to genetically modified food, for example, or his personal involvement in the planning dispute over the redevelopment of London's Chelsea Barracks. In his recently published diaries, Tony Blair's former Press Secretary, Alastair Campbell, alleges that the Prince over-stepped the mark on politically sensitive issues like hunting and the foot and mouth epidemic of 2001. He even writes that Blair had to have a 'hard talk' with the Prince to urge restraint. But were these episodes constitutionally questionable or were they, in fact, just the usual passionate princely interventions? After all, it was Blair who said in 2007: 'All this

stuff written about Charles interfering with government or getting political – I never found him the slightest bit like that at all.' Certainly, any
suggestion of inappropriate constitutional conduct infuriates another
former Prime Minister. 'I would see Prince Charles several times a year,'
says Sir John Major. 'He'd express views, well-informed views, but he
did not lobby, nor did he behave in any way that could be criticised. He
has a good social conscience and I'd much rather have an heir to the
throne who took an interest in the lives of others, than one who showed
no interest at all. I actually think the criticism of him on that front is
grotesque.'

Such criticism, familiar to Princes of Wales through the ages, has
diminished in recent years. The Prince's reputation as a passionate champion of both the fashionable and the unfashionable – from rainforests to
the Prayer Book Society – is comfortably entrenched in the public
consciousness. His staff describe him as a 'charitable entrepreneur'. The
core network of twenty trusts and foundations (eighteen of which
he created himself) is now Britain's most extensive multi-cause charitable
network, raising £120 million a year. He is a conscientious patron or
president of another four hundred charities besides. Clarence House has
never been busier. Over the last few years, the Duchess of Cornwall has
quietly taken up a carefully chosen cross section of organisations which
have quickly become very fond of their patron. Despite a lifetime's record
of never giving an interview, the Duchess has emerged as an impressive
public speaker, calmly standing before a conference or a Clarence House
reception to deliver a detailed appraisal of the latest work of the National
Osteoporosis Society or the Literacy Trust. In 2011, she gamely delivered
the address at the annual awards of the London Press Club, applauding
freedom of expression while observing that, in her own case, 'no news is
good news'.

But how will the Prince of Wales adapt to the constraints of Kingship?
Just before his sixtieth birthday in 2008, the author asked him if he would
still be able to champion his favourite themes from the throne. 'I don't
know. Probably not in the same way,' he replied. 'But I like to think
perhaps that, after this, eventually people might realise that some of the
things I have been trying to do are not all that mad – and that I might
still have some convening power that could be put to use.'

The Prince will certainly not be able to mount a campaign like the
one which suddenly hit Sir Malcolm Rifkind during his days as Defence
Secretary. No sooner had Rifkind announced plans to merge a lot of
regimental bands than a funny thing happened. 'I suddenly started getting
very similar letters from various Colonels-in-Chief including the Prince

of Wales, the Queen Mother, Princess Margaret, the Duke of Gloucester, Princess Alexandra – almost everyone, in fact, except the Queen herself. I thought: "This is extraordinary."' Although he persisted with his plan, he remained puzzled by such a concerted assault. Two years later, all was revealed when Jonathan Dimbleby's authorised biography of the Prince appeared. 'It was all there!' Rifkind laughs. 'He was a trade union leader and he'd got all his family to write to me.'

While Prince Charles will have to be less outspoken as monarch, those demanding that he should become a carbon copy of the Queen miss the point. As she has shown more than anyone, strong monarchy is about well-judged adaptation, not being or doing exactly the same as before. And no one can have given it more thought than the man himself. 'Prince Charles will be extremely good at it,' says a very senior courtier. 'He's just going to be different. That's the way it is and the way it should be.'

It is striking how little we know of his plans for the monarchy. His aspiration to be a 'defender of faith' – revealed on television in 1994 – is much-quoted but the remark is now almost twenty years old and we have heard very little on that front since. According to the Archbishop of Canterbury, it would hardly represent a break with the status quo. The Queen, he argues, has been doing much the same for years. 'I think that was a bit of a misunderstanding,' says Dr Williams. 'I don't think the Prince was saying: "I don't want to be Defender of the Faith." He was saying, "I would see my role as defender of faiths," keeping the umbrella inclusive.'

The Prince doesn't like to discuss his plans for two reasons. First, there is no need for him to have any big 'plans' at all. This is an institution which stands for continuity. It does not 'do' instant makeovers. Second, whatever ideas the Prince may have, it would be both bad taste and disrespectful towards the Queen to air them in her lifetime. 'They're discussed over dinner parties rather than round table meetings,' says a long-serving courtier. 'No minutes are taken. No decisions are reached. But opinions are aired.' There is no itching for the levers of power, no impatience to do things differently. Nor, for that matter, is the Queen inclined to leave instructions for the future. She has been closely involved in her own funeral arrangements (all royal funeral plans are reviewed and, to an extent, rehearsed on a semi-regular basis) but it is said that she does not wish to be informed about any Coronation plans.

Some differences in taste and tone are inevitable after any change of reign. Those close to the Prince indicate that a trimming of some of the pageantry is likely. The days of ancient bodyguards like the Yeomen of the Guard or the Royal Company of Archers being wheeled out for every royal occasion may be finite. The Gold State Coach, the ultimate in gilded pumpkins, may have already had its last Coronation excursion. Perhaps there might be something a little stronger than iced coffee at garden parties? When the Prince held a garden party of his own at Holyroodhouse in 2000, the resident staff were as surprised as the guests to find Pimm's on offer. One thing is for certain. There will be no Winston Churchill around this time to tell the new sovereign that he has to move into Buckingham Palace if he would rather stay put at Clarence House. All the indications are that he would. At a deeper level, some of the Prince's friends have suggested that he may be more willing to use his legitimate constitutional powers to ask more questions and demand more answers from his governments; that he may still be prepared to speak out on certain issues; that in any sort of political vacuum his default position would be to do something rather than nothing. Old Westminster hands point out that he will have to be very careful. 'It's a matter of choosing your cause,' says one former Cabinet Minister, warning that the Prince will have to curb his interventions in things like planning disputes or else he might 'pick the wrong fight'.

But if we accept that the Queen has brought a feminine subtlety to the job, we can hardly be surprised if the Prince adopts a more 'masculine' approach, like his grandfather and great-grandfather. It was constitutionally acceptable for George VI to wave his shoes at a Labour Chancellor and declare: 'I really don't see why people should have free false teeth any more than they have shoes free.' So it would surely be acceptable for a future King Charles to ask the occupant of Number Ten a few searching questions on global warming.

The Queen's twelfth Prime Minister certainly has no qualms about the Prince's approach thus far. 'I think people misunderstand the way Prince Charles does this,' says David Cameron. 'Yes, he's fantastically interested in a number of subjects which he's been consistent on. When you see him, he'll want to hear how you're getting on with deforestation, complementary medicine, climate control and so on. But he's extremely deferential to the fact that you're the elected government and he's making suggestions. He does not say: "It's outrageous, you haven't done this." And he's also very grateful for the time you give. He knows exactly how the relationship should be. He doesn't push things too hard. He gives things a bit of a heave but that's fine. In the areas where he does throw his weight around – like Business in the Community* – it is an entirely appropriate thing to do.'

---

* Business in the Community was founded in 1982 to drive corporate involvement in the regeneration of inner-city areas. The Prince became its President in 1985.

There may be some changes to the monarchy which are entirely beyond royal control. It is possible that some of the sixteen existing realms may choose to seek a new constitutional settlement having decided not to do so during the Queen's reign. If so, there will be no rearguard action from the throne. The Prince has no wish to outstay his welcome on any of the various thrones he will inherit. He said exactly that to the Australian people as long ago as 1994. 'Some people will doubtless prefer the stability of a system that has been reasonably well tried and tested over the years, while others will see real advantages in doing things differently,' he told his Australia Day audience in Sydney. 'Personally, I happen to think that it is the sign of a mature and self-confident nation to debate those issues and to use the democratic process to re-examine the way in which you want to face the future.'

The position of Head of the Commonwealth is slightly different. It is not enshrined in the Coronation Oath or somehow attached to the Crown. It was a title given to George VI when the new eight-nation Commonwealth evolved from the London Declaration of 1949 but no one said anything about passing the title on. Within hours of the Queen's accession, though, the Indian Prime Minister, Jawaharlal Nehru, had sent her a telegram welcoming her as Head of the Commonwealth. Everyone else just followed suit. Will the same thing happen again? Or will today's fifty-four Commonwealth nations decide to break with the 'tradition'? Among the heads of government, it is hard to detect the slightest appetite for severing the long and largely happy connection with the Crown. Why should they? The monarchy is one of the few things which actually manages to reverse the organisation's gently declining profile and give it a certain star quality. Besides, post-colonial sensitivities are fading. Mohamed Nasheed, President of the Maldives from 2008 to 2012, has been a new-generation Commonwealth leader. 'Of course future monarchs should carry it [the title] on,' he says. 'You know, I was born in 1967. I don't have a hang-up with colonialism.'

But, ultimately, all of this is little more than speculation. It is pointless to compare the succession to the throne with the succession to a political party or a family business or a great landed estate, as commentators often like to do. The monarchy moves at an entirely different pace. And it can never become a competition. That is why any mention of abdication, of the Crown 'skipping a generation' or any other sort of regal beauty contest, is preposterous. That way lies a republic. It would be like striking a match to find your way out of a munitions factory.

The Duke and Duchess of Cambridge are, unquestionably, a tremendous asset to the monarchy, but they have absolutely no interest in jumping their turn in the queue. Prince William is the first to acknowledge the importance of wise heads in a changing world. 'Without the senior members of the family who've seen and done it all, the junior lot wouldn't be relevant. You need to have the balance and the experience. It's like a rugby team,' says the Vice Royal Patron of the Welsh Rugby Union. 'If you're picking for the World Cup final, you're picking experience with youth. Everything is better off having that balance and that mix. I think that, especially, goes for the monarchy as well.'

If anything, the Duke and Duchess seem determined to make the most of whatever vestiges of a private life they can retain. For now, the Duke seems very happy to forge a conventional career in the Forces rather than ponder any new royal role – let alone the big one.

'I try not to think about it, to be honest,' he says. 'As I am flying along in my helicopter through the mountains of Wales, I try desperately hard not to think about it. That can wait until I'm a bit older.'

Any suggestion of tinkering with the succession also neglects an obvious truth. Britain – like many parts of the world – is not going to know what has hit it when there is a change of reign, particularly a reign which has framed an entire epoch of such titanic social change. At such a time, any country would, surely, be grateful to have the most experienced successor in history to hand. 'You can see, going through history, that it is not unusual for the heir to the throne to have criticism thrown at him,' notes Sir John Major. 'But that will fade away when he becomes monarch.' Major's successor agrees. 'Prince Charles is pretty secure in the affections of people,' says Tony Blair. 'They actually think he is someone who genuinely tries his best and does his best. For me, that's the unspoken contract between monarchy and subject – that they put their duty to the country before everything else. While they do that, the monarchy is secure.'

'The whole history of the monarchy is not a straight line,' says Major. 'It's had quite bumpy times. Queen Victoria was very, very unpopular for a long time during the latter part of her reign. The challenge is to maintain the relevance and the affection of the nation . . . to maintain the distinctiveness of the monarchy in the future. That is going to be its main challenge. Over the past five hundred years, it has shown it can do that. But that will continue to be the challenge.'

Our Queen has known that ever since she listened to stories from 'Grandpa England'.* It is the theme which has run through her life. It

---

* Her paternal grandfather, George V, was known as 'Grandpa England'. Sandringham still houses a charming blotter which Princess Elizabeth made for him and then decorated with 'GE' in huge letters.

is the code she has followed ever since the mournful day in February 1952 when she walked down those aeroplane steps to be greeted by Winston Churchill.

Sixty years on, Prime Minister number twelve is in no doubt about the magnitude of her achievement. 'People think about the monarchy as a long-standing, old-fashioned institution,' says David Cameron. 'But it has changed subtly into something the nation is just as proud of today as it was fifty, a hundred or two hundred years ago. The Queen's a fantastic exemplar of what a constitutional monarch can be. She's probably the finest ever.'

Does she see it that way? Does she ever look back and ponder her own position in the pantheon of great monarchs? Those who know her best say not. Like the Duke of Edinburgh, the Queen regards any question of legacy as irrelevant. 'It's important to remember that no monarch is ever looking for a legacy,' says the Duke of York. 'Legacy is a matter of history. Politicians will look to see what legacy they can leave but this is a different concept of operations.'

That this reign will leave a monumental legacy is beyond doubt. And historians will be reassessing it and debating it for many centuries after the last of the New Elizabethans has gone. The Queen knows that there is no point worrying about it now. But, according to her grandson and the man who will, one day, take the throne, her jubilee year should afford her a moment or two of quiet satisfaction. 'She'd want to keep on going regardless,' says Prince William. 'But it's nice for her to know, after sixty years, that she really has made a huge difference and that people massively look up to her. They see this dedication and this service. And I'd hope that people would want to emulate that sort of sacrifice and dedication in their own lives.'

# 10

# Diamond Days

*'I dedicate myself anew to your service'*

History was made quietly beneath snow-flecked Norfolk skies on February 6, 2012. For only the second time in British history, a monarch had achieved sixty years on the Throne. The Diamond Jubilee had started. Yet, there was no sense of exhilaration, let alone a carnival atmosphere, at Sandringham where the Queen likes to be on this day every year. She has always regarded the anniversary of her accession as an occasion to commemorate her dear father, a day for private worship and reflection.

That is why, traditionally, she has spent it behind closed doors. But she could not stay out of sight on Accession Day 2012, however much she might have wanted to. The world would want to see her on this landmark day, the moment when the longest-lived monarch in British history entered her seventh decade on the Throne.

And so a trip was arranged to Sandringham's local town, King's Lynn, where the Queen would receive a loyal address from the mayor. A media circus of journalists, photographers and camera crews from as far afield as Toronto and the Ukraine had assembled outside the town hall. Jubilee messages from world leaders were arriving by the hour. Gun salutes were ringing out across the land. However, the Queen remained impervious to the hoopla. Understatement was the order of the day. Leaving the State Bentley behind, she and her entourage (all four of them) were driven out of Sandringham in a pair of dark green Range Rovers. This might have been a royal milestone but that was no excuse for a new outfit. Her turquoise grey and white wool dress with matching hat and coat, all by her in-house designer, Angela Kelly, had been seen before, notably on the 2011 state visit to Ireland. Nor was this a day for the Crown Jewels, either. Instead, the Queen wore the pretty shell-shaped diamond brooch which her late mother had loved so much.

From King's Lynn, the Queen travelled to a nursery school in Dersingham, on the edge of the Sandringham estate. At one level, this was a timeless scene, scarcely different from the way it might have looked at the time of her Golden Jubilee, her Silver Jubilee or, indeed, in 1952. The pictures of crowns and corgis on the wall, the specially-composed song, the palpitations of staff and parents as the most famous face on earth enters the room. It is a ritual the Queen has been performing since the grandparents of these children were the ones doing the singing.

Yet, here was another illustration of how society has moved on. Walking in to the nursery class, she was confronted by a sign saying 'Royal Laundry' and a display of underpants. The teachers, it transpired, had been using a book called 'The Queen's Knickers' as a way of helping these three and four-year-olds to learn about the Queen. 'Oh, they're doing the washing,' the royal visitor observed with a laugh, quite unruffled. In the main hall, the whole school lined up for the concert, without which no royal visit to a school could be complete. Not so long ago, this event might have involved a nursery rhyme plus a verse or two of the national anthem. Instead, the Queen was treated to 'The Time Warp', the signature dance tune – famous for its 'pelvic thrust' - from the Rocky Horror Show. 'Well done!' she told them as she left.

The world around her has changed so much, in some cases beyond recognition. Yet she has not. For one who has seen and experienced as much as the Queen, it is perhaps easier to see familiar patterns and recurring themes where others simply sense surprise or bewilderment.

Sixty years on, we tend to look back on her accession and see a dazzling young Princess in a seemingly happier age being embraced as Queen by the entire world. Certainly, the story of her accession has entered the canon of colourful royal legends which will be absorbed by schoolchildren for centuries to come. Just as they learn that King Alfred burned the cakes or that George III was mad, so they are taught that Elizabeth II was the first woman to go up a tree as a princess and come back down a queen.

Unlike many royal legends, this one happens to be true. But it is instructive to look more closely at what actually happened in Kenya in February 1952 and to revisit the scene sixty years later. We soon see that the world was, in fact, just as risky and uncertain back then – for royalty as much as anyone.

It was actually a surprisingly dangerous excursion for Princess Elizabeth and Prince Philip as they set off on an overnight adventure into the bush on February 5th. They were on the first stage of what was to have been a round-the-world Commonwealth tour and had reached Sagana Lodge, north of Nairobi. The house had been given to them as a wedding present by the people of Kenya (post-independence, it would become a 'state house' for the president).

The royal couple had been invited to spend a night at Treetops, a genuine treehouse built in the upper branches of a giant fig tree overlooking a watering hole in the lush hills of Aberdare National Park. This extraordinary Tarzan-style construction had three basic bedrooms and a dining room (plus a tiny staff quarter) alongside a long balcony with a glorious panoramic view of all the animal traffic at the saltlick and the lake. And the only way to get to it was to walk for 600 yards from the nearest track through thick undergrowth and then climb a 30-foot ladder.

The royal party was tiny, just Princess Elizabeth and Prince Philip, her lady in waiting and his equerry and the British couple who owned the place. Because the entire purpose of the visit was to watch the wildlife, a major security operation was out of the question as it would scatter all the animals. So, an additional guest was recruited.

Jim Corbett was something of a British Empire celebrity, a vintage Boy's Own hero. He was the Indian-born big game hunter who had bagged some of the most prolific and infamous predators of his day. Two of them, the 'Maneater of Champawat' and the 'Panar Leopard', had allegedly taken 836 Indian lives between them. He had also trained the British Army in jungle warfare during the Second World War. After Indian independence in 1947, Corbett retired to Kenya. His abiding interest had always been conservation (an Indian national park is named after him) and he only killed animals which posed a direct threat to human life. By the time of the royal visit, he was well into his Seventies. But it would be hard to think of a better companion for a journey into the bush.

And he was not just there to kill any wild animal which might be tempted to eat the future Sovereign. Though very little was made of it at the time, he was also there to ward off any threat to the royal party from the increasingly violent Mau Mau guerrillas who were already establishing themselves in the area. During that evening, Corbett spent the night with his gun in his arms and one foot on the ladder, sensitive to the slightest movement. He was not thinking only of big cats and snakes.

Shortly before his death three years later, he wrote an essay on the 20 hours he spent with the Princess as she became Queen. And what comes through is the element of danger, from both man and beast. Corbett describes the recent rise in terrorist activity and the fact that the local media had suppressed the news. He took it upon himself to travel well ahead of the royal party, even looking for footprints in the sand above a particular ravine where the royal car might be especially prone to ambush. Having reached Treetops, he was dismayed when a herd of 47 elephants came stampeding through the jungle below just half an hour before the Princess was due to walk along the path. With good reason, slats of wood had been nailed into the trunks of several trees along the way to provide an escape route in the event of a charging elephant, buffalo or rhino. But postponement or cancellation seemed inevitable.

A few bull elephants were still charging around the same bit of jungle at 'zero hour' as the royal party arrived. To Corbett's astonishment, the Princess pressed on regardless, even when she rounded a bend and found several elephants in full view. 'In the course of a long lifetime, I have seen some courageous acts but few to compare with what I witnessed on that fifth day of February,' he wrote. Even if this loyal son of Empire was exaggerating, his words chime with examples of the Queen's sangfroid mentioned earlier in this book. It is worth noting that just two days after the Queen's departure, four of the main 'escape' trees along that path were uprooted by elephants.

Having climbed up the ladder to Treetops, the Princess and her party spent a magical afternoon and evening watching the natural spectacle unfolding beneath them. When the staff announced that tea was to be served in the little dining room, the Princess replied that she would rather stay put and have it outside. She was fascinated by the way in which a cow elephant coaxed her calf into the water and how another elephant derived enormous pleasure from spraying dust over a flock of doves. Particularly gripping was the duel between two male waterbuck. After one was dramatically impaled on the horn of the other, the Princess was so intrigued about the fate of the wounded animal that Corbett later descended from the tree to discover its fate. Nature does not do happy endings. The defeated buck had become a leopard's dinner. Only later would the Queen be informed of local Kikuyu legend that the killing of one waterbuck by another presages the death of a great chieftain.

The evening was not without incident in the treehouse, either. An overturned oil lamp almost started a blaze. At one point, Corbett spoke to the Princess about the King. 'I told her how distressed I had been to learn from the BBC that her father had stood hatless in a bitter cold wind to wave to her,' he wrote. 'She said that he was like that; he never thought of himself. The Princess then told me of her father's long illness, their anxieties, their fears, their hopes and their joy when one day he put his walking stick to his shoulder and said: "I believe I could shoot now".'

'I have heard it said,' Corbett continued, 'that when the Princess waved goodbye to His Majesty, she knew she would never see him again on earth. This I do not believe. I am convinced that the young Princess who spoke of her father that night with such great affection and pride, and who expressed the fervent hope that she would find him quite recovered on her return, never had the least suspicion that she would not see him again.'

The following dawn, the Princess was thrilled to capture

two quarrelling rhino on her cine-camera before a hearty breakfast of scrambled eggs. She then climbed down the ladder for the precarious return through the jungle to her car and thence back to Sagana Lodge. Sixty years on, Corbett's words remind us of the scale of the shock which the Queen must have felt a few hours later when the news came through from London*.

But she must also have been somewhat perturbed, just two years later, to learn what had happened to that enchanting setting where she spent her last night as a Princess. For her visit to Treetops had not been over-looked by the Mau Mau insurgents in the region. They waited for their moment and, in 1954, they launched a surprise attack. Having torched the treehouse, they burned down the entire giant fig tree tree. Worse still, they led away four of the five staff. Their remains have never been found. Today, the only survivor, Nahashan Mureithi, has happy memories of the day he carried the Princess's suitcase through the jungle and up the tree. 'The bag was light. She did not have much luggage, she dressed simply and her only jewellery was a gold chain,' recalls the former handyman and porter, who was 24 at the time. He remembers the Princess saying 'hello' to him and that she was 'in love with the elephant, the rhino, all the animals'. He also adds an intriguing detail: the Princess was dictating her thoughts on to a recording device. 'She was commu-nicating into something, saying that there were a lot of elephants and so on,' he says. Might the Queen be the first monarch to have consigned some of her observations to tape as well as to her diary?

Mureithi was used to danger. One of his less enjoyable duties was to run down the Treetops path ahead of the guests to flush out any unwanted four-legged loiterers. So when the Mau Mau came calling that day, he managed to disappear into the bush. But it was a close shave. He rolls up his right sleeve to show the scar from the bullet which hit him in the arm as he escaped.

It is a vivid reminder that Britain and the Empire were far from at ease with each other at the start of the Queen's reign. Her accession was not a cause for universal celebration. And it is interesting to find that, today, the site of the original Treetops is unmarked. There is no 'Queen Elizabeth Slept Here' notice, let alone a memorial to the staff who were subsequently massacred. There is just a young fig tree surrounded by a rather dilapidated

---

* The Princess was among the last to learn that she had become Queen. A coded message had been sent from London to the Governor's residence in Nairobi. But the codebook was locked in a safe and the Governor had left for the coast carrying the only key. The Princess's Private Secretary, Martin Charteris, was finally contacted by a local journalist asking if reports of the King's death were true.

fence to defend it from passing elephants. Instead, visitors stay at the modern Treetops, a more conventional 36-room hotel which was built on stilts on the opposite side of the mudflat three years after the Mau Mau attack. This has a plaque commemorating the original royal visit and continues to draw many visitors as a result. In early 2012, it was given a complete overhaul (and en suite bathrooms) in honour of the Diamond Jubilee.

The owners have noticed a fascinating trend in recent years. The fastest-growing section of the Treetops clientele, by some margin, consists of visitors from China. An African safari is an increasingly popular holiday option among China's newly-affluent middle class. But large numbers of them specifically demand that their itinerary includes the place where the Queen of Great Britain became Queen. It is not so much curiosity as superstition. Treetops, these Chinese visitors believe, has brought the Queen longevity, prosperity and greatness. Perhaps a visit to this place might bring them similar good fortune, too?

You do not need to be superstitious to be struck by the continued inde-fatigability of the oldest Sovereign and the longest-serving consort in British history. Very occasionally, though, there is a reminder that this astonishingly consistent double-act cannot last forever. And one such moment would occur dramatically just weeks before the start of the Diamond Jubilee.

The tail end of 2011 – a year subsequently described as an 'annus mirabilis' following the wedding of the Duke and Duchess of Cambridge and the profusion of great royal moments – saw the most significant Commonwealth tour since the 1995 state visit to Nelson Mandela's post-apartheid South Africa.

The Queen and the Duke of Edinburgh flew to Australia for a coast-to-coast tour culminating in a summit of all 54 member nations of the Commonwealth in Perth. From the outset, however, this trip – the Queen's sixteenth to Australia – had a very different atmosphere when compared to previous Down Under tours. A major factor was the decision, by large parts of the Australian media, to herald this as the Queen's 'farewell tour'. There were certainly no indicators from the Palace contingent to suggest that the Queen and the Duke felt the same way. But many Australians – royalists and even some republicans – suddenly found themselves feeling an emotional pull which surprised them.

Every step of the ten-day tour attracted numbers which exceeded all expectations. In Brisbane, a crowd of 45,000 gathered to glimpse the Queen's arrival on a boat. Some had been waiting since before dawn and required treatment for sunstroke. In Melbourne's Federation Square, the scheduled walkabout took twice as long as planned. Once again, more than half a century on, there were echoes of that euphoric inaugural tour in 1954. The more the public came out in their droves, the more the Queen and the Duke enjoyed themselves and the more a gentle, sentimental glow suffused the entire trip. The authorities had been worried about the disruptive effect of an ongoing 'Occupy Melbourne' protest organised on the same lines as the one which had brought the precincts of London's St Paul's Cathedral to a standstill. Come the day, however, the Melbourne protestors agreed to stop their occupation for the duration of the Queen's visit. The nearest thing to public disorder was when a Brisbane construction worker was arrested for 'mooning' at the royal party. It was not a political statement, either. He did it for a bet.

Just 12 years earlier, Australia had held a referendum on abandoning the Crown altogether. Now, opinion polls were showing that support for a republic was running at around 34 per cent, the lowest level since the mid-Eighties. There was no great enthusiasm for a renewed debate from either side, rather a sense that the issue could be mothballed for the foreseeable future. There was a half-hearted attempt by some of the media to crank up a row about a lack of curtseying from Australia's republican-minded (and British-born) Prime Minister, Julia Gillard. But Gillard's obvious liking and respect for the Queen throughout the tour put paid to any idea of a 'snub'.

One royal official felt that the tour, far from feeling 'valedictory', rather had the feel of a 'revival'. It was not just about affection for the Queen. It illustrated the age-old appeal of stable, solid institutions in times of uncertainty. As in Britain, so in Australia, the Monarchy can help convey a sense of security. One well-known political commentator is fond of quoting his grandmother on the subject. Having arrived in Britain as a Jewish refugee, she would say: 'As long as the Queen is safe in Buckingham Palace, I am safe in Hendon.'

The Australian itinerary ranged from traditional fixtures such as the presentation of military colours and a garden party, to more telegenic royal engagements like a tram ride through Melbourne and a visit to an Aboriginal college where the Queen was presented with a jar of kangaroo stew. The final engagement was at a park in Perth where tens of thousands of people gathered for a mass barbecue; here was a much more informal (and comfortable) successor to those dusty post-Coronation rallies of 1954.

By the end, the 'farewell tour' headlines had faded away. 'The Queen and the Duke were on absolutely top form, unbelievably relaxed and chatty and really lifted by the public reaction,' says one of their Australian hosts. Despite their combined age of 175, the royal couple had no rest days and were in action from the moment they landed. 'They've never liked rest days,' says a former Private Secretary. 'I would often try to work a day off into the middle of an overseas tour but they wouldn't have it. I think they saw it as an extra night in a strange bed.'

For the Australian tour, Palace officials had designed a programme which included a major encounter with the public every day but, equally, gave the Queen some time to rest. Yet, the schedule was not quite busy enough for the Duke. 'We had to include some extra engagements – a university visit, a Commonwealth Study Conference reception and so on – so he wouldn't get bored,' says one of the entourage.

The Duke's restlessness was no great surprise. A few months earlier, as staff past and present travelled to Windsor Castle for a chapel service and a party to celebrate his 90th birthday, one coachload from Buckingham Palace were most amused as the bus turned into the castle. 'It was pouring with rain and we were coming in past the stables about half an hour before the service,' says one. 'We looked out of the window and there was the Duke with his ponies, soaking wet and still carriage-driving.'

Just a day after arriving back in Britain from Australia, the Duke had been due to fly off to Italy – on the budget airline, Easyjet – for a multi-faith conference on environmentally-friendly pilgrimages. Only a sore throat and some firm words from his doctors persuaded him to cancel. As ever, his steadfast determination to press on with his public engagements met with indulgent smiles and rolling of eyes. Two days later, he was attending a Trinity House dinner in his honour and, the following morning, he was receiving a delegation from the British Sub-Aqua Club before an engagement at Westminster Abbey. The next week, his schedule was back to normal — receptions for his Duke of Edinburgh Award scheme and the Diplomatic Corps, a day-trip to Margate and so on. But there were no indulgent smiles a few weeks later when the Duke's health suddenly became a subject of worldwide alarm. Two days before Christmas, he was airlifted from Sandringham to Papworth Hospital in Cambridgeshire after suffering chest pains. While Palace and hospital staff talked about 'precuationary tests', there was no concealing the level of concern. In 2008, the Duke had spent three nights in hospital with a chest infection and had refused all visitors except staff bearing office paperwork. This time it was very different. The day after his arrival at Papworth, the Queen and the couple's three younger children flew in by helicopter to see him while the Prince of Wales came by road. On Christmas Day itself, the grandchildren drove across from Sandringham.

'This was a real wake-up call, a real scare,' says one member of staff. 'It's all very well people saying 'how amazing' it is that the Queen and the Duke are still going strong at their age. Here was proof that they can't always go on like this, that we need to be more careful with them.'

In the event, the Duke returned to Sandringham four days later after a 'minimally invasive' remedial procedure known as 'coronary stenting'. And having been forced to miss the ritual of the Boxing Day shoot, he pointedly attended church the following Sunday, making the journey – more than quarter of a mile – on foot. Afterwards, he walked back at the same brisk pace.

Just like his 90th birthday earlier in the year, this episode was a reminder of the Duke's pivotal role in Britain's modern royal story. Prince Harry had an endearing way of putting it during a conversation with the BBC's Andrew Marr shortly before the scare: 'Regardless of whether my grand-father seems to be doing his own thing, sort of wandering off like a fish down the river, the fact that he's there – personally, I don't think that she could do it without him, especially when they're both at this age.' That a naturally shy and reserved woman could have led Britain's foremost institution with such confidence and style for so long is due, to a very great extent, to the man at her side.

Because the Queen has evidently enjoyed robust good health, we tend to overlook the stress of the job. That has, very occasionally, proved too much, notably during that chaotic summer of 1969 when, as we discovered earlier, the Queen suddenly withdrew from public duties. These days, commentators would have talked about a royal 'nervous breakdown' and analysed the intolerable 'pressures of the job'. Back then, little was said. It is certainly noteworthy that it was the only year of the Queen's entire reign when she did not make a Christmas broadcast. A written message was released instead*. But on the rare occasions when the Queen has been out of action, she has never been absent for long. Just days after her recu-peration in 1969, she was back in full head of state mode, presiding over a full state visit for President Urho Kekkonen of Finland. As long as Prince Philip has been at her side, nothing has really seemed insurmountable during this reign. So the prospect of the Duke playing a reduced role in the Queen's Diamond Jubilee celebrations did not bear thinking about.

Yet, there was an upside of sorts. A note of caution had been inserted into the hitherto unruffled arrangements for the Jubilee. The Queen's Golden Jubilee, ten years earlier, had been preceded by gloomy media predictions and then great sadness following the deaths of Princess Margaret and the Queen Mother. The eventual, tumultuous success of the anniversary stemmed, in part, from that sense of jeopardy at the outset. As the Diamond Jubilee approached, some within the Palace had

---

* Palace officials explained that the absence of a Christmas broadcast in 1969 was simply to avoid over-exposure. This had been the year of the first modern royal documentary, Royal Family, and the televised investiture of the Prince of Wales.

feared that everything in the royal garden was looking a little too wonderful and near-perfect to be true. It was.

Just days after Prince Philip's chest pains, the lead-up to the Diamond Jubilee received another jolt when the newly re-elected Prime Minister of Jamaica, Portia Simpson Miller, suddenly announced that the time had come to remove the Queen as head of state. Since 2012 would mark the fiftieth anniversary of Jamaica's independence, some sort of debate might have been expected. However, Simpson Miller had neglected to give the Queen any notice of her intentions. It would certainly add to the diplomatic challenge facing the Queen's Diamond Jubilee emissary to Jamaica – Prince Harry.

More worryingly, the once unthinkable prospect of a dis-United Kingdom was beginning to become a possibility. With a majority in the Scottish Parliament, the Scottish National Party leader, Alex Salmond, began 2012 by announcing his plans to dissolve Great Britain. He proposed to use 2014 – the 700th anniversary of Scotland's victory over the English at the Battle of Bannockburn – to stage a referendum on Scottish independence*. Despite his insistence that an independent Scotland would retain the Sovereign as head of state, the very suggestion places the Queen in an extremely awkward position. The first pledge of her Coronation Oath was 'to govern the Peoples of the United Kingdom of Great Britain and Northern Ireland'. Remove Scotland from the equation and Great Britain ceases to exist. Yet she is constitutionally obliged to remain above party politics. Even this famously inscrutable Sovereign may find it hard to conceal her feelings on an issue of such magnitude†.

These, though, remained issues entirely beyond the Queen's control. The early preparations for the Jubilee itself could hardly have gone more smoothly. While the organisers of the 2012 Olympics were beset with rows about finances, security and ticketing, not to mention the contents of the opening ceremony, the quarrels surrounding the Jubilee seldom progressed beyond light entertainment. When the Duchess of Cornwall launched a 'Cook for the Queen' competition for schools, the anti-monarchy pressure group, Republic, decided to take a stand. It is hard to envisage an issue less likely to start the tumbrils rolling than a children's contest to create

---

* He also chose Burns Night 2012 – the annual feast in honour of Scotland's national poet – to announce his proposals.

† Scottish devolution was a live issue during the Queen's Silver Jubilee in 1977. Such was her concern at the time that she allowed herself an extraordinary foray into party political territory. Addressing both Houses of Parliament, she said: 'I cannot forget that I was crowned Queen of the United Kingdom of Great Britain and Northern Ireland. Perhaps this Jubilee is a time to remind ourselves of the benefits which union has conferred'

a 21st Century alternative to Coronation Chicken. However, Republic's chief executive, Graham Smith, was adamant that schools would be in breach of the Education Act if they encouraged children to take part in 'uncritical celebrations' of the Jubilee without also discussing republicanism. The Secretary of State for Education (and ardent monarchist), Michael Gove, thought otherwise. Few arrests were expected.

There was also some mild huffing and puffing over the Jubilee pop concert planned for a giant stage in front of the Palace. In 2011, the Queen's officials and the BBC had convened a cross-section of great minds from the world of entertainment to develop an appropriate line-up. After all, one of the great successes of the Queen's Golden Jubilee had been the BBC concerts – one classical, one pop – in the Palace garden. The original Diamond Jubilee panel included the theatre producer, Sir Cameron Mackintosh, the Oscar-winning screenwriter, Lord [Julian] Fellowes and Gary Barlow, the Take That singer and X-Factor judge along with various record producers. Great ideas proved abundant but, with so many creative egos at work, compromise was harder to find. 'We couldn't get much agreement on anything,' says one who took part. The panel shrank until, eventually, it was agreed that Barlow would organise the event in tandem with the BBC. He set about approaching an international cross-section of artistic talent spanning the reign. Few turned down a formal invitation from the Palace. Britain's pop grandees – including Sir Elton John, Dame Shirley Bassey, Sir Paul McCartney, Sir Tom Jones, Sir Cliff Richard – would be joined by younger acts like Jessie J and Ed Sheeran. According to Barlow, the younger members of the Royal Family had given him plenty of suggestions.

The public response was instant, electric and overwhelming. An online lottery for the 10,000 seats would be bombarded for weeks. When the 2002 pop concert took place, a million people turned up just to listen over the Palace walls and watch the fireworks. Would central London be able to cope if the crowds were even bigger?

Throughout it all, the star turn was informed of everything. 'The Queen will probably go off when I start playing and come back on for Cliff Richard,' joked Barlow. In fact, not only did she approve the entire running order for the concert but she even wanted to see – and approve – the contents of the complimentary Waitrose picnic box for each ticketholder. No detail can be too trivial. Royal staff still talk of the unfortunate technician who was preparing the Palace gardens for the televised celebration of children's literature which the Queen hosted in the summer of 2006. The man was just about to hack off part of an inconvenient tree when a window flew open on the first floor of the Palace. Out popped a very angry Sovereign with a very clear order to desist.

'As she grows older, it actually becomes more and more important to ensure that she is not shielded from the decision process,' says one of her staff, explaining that well-intentioned officials sometimes imagine that they must lighten the Queen's load. She will not thank those that try.

Her attitude to the Jubilee celebrations was one of practicality. She would lend her support to the big set-piece events and campaigns – from the great equestrian pageant at Windsor Castle to the Woodland Trust's plan to plant six million Jubilee trees. But she would do so by turning up. The Palace, it was emphasised, would not get involved in the management or the financing of these projects. Nor was public money to be involved. The Queen was acutely aware of public concern over the billions being spent on the London Olympics (while she was happy to open the Games, she would leave the closing ceremony to others). She did not want her 60th anniversary soured by similar complaints. Hence that Palace budget of just £1 million for the entire Diamond Jubilee (most of it for administrative costs). When it came to the cost of staging all the big Jubilee events, the organisers would have to find their own funding elsewhere.

Corporate Britain was happy to offer discreet support with companies like Sainsbury's providing sponsorship while not overdoing the branding. Various movers, shakers and philanthropists got on quietly with their moving, shaking and donating. They included figures like NCP founder, Sir Donald Gosling, a benefactor of many royal causes, and Lord Sterling, former head of P&O and architect of previous jubilees. He commissioned a new £500,000 royal rowbarge for the Thames river pageant, an event supervised by the Marquess of Salisbury (whose own great, great grandfather had been the Prime Minister in charge of the previous Diamond Jubilee for the Queen's great, great grandmother). During the Nineties, while serving in John Major's Cabinet, Lord Salisbury had managed the fiftieth anniversaries of D-Day, VE Day and VJ Day, royal high points during a grim decade. John Major himself then resurfaced on the eve of the Jubilee celebrations as chairman of the official Jubilee charity appeal. And so it went on as this low-profile, supremely well-connected, pro bono publico network of canny old royalists spread their influence and their powers of persuasion far and wide.

The Royal Household, meanwhile, concentrated on the logistics of enabling the oldest monarch in history to meet and be seen by as many people as possible. At the same time, the Queen was happy to try out new ideas. One of the most eye-catching innovations was also one of the simplest – sharing engagements with younger members of the family. So, when the Queen was planning a Jubilee trip to the famous London store, Fortnum & Mason, she decided to invite the Duchess of Cornwall and the Duchess of Cambridge to come with her. This was much more than a trip to a favourite royal haunt*. The prospect of three generations of leading royal ladies – a Queen and two future Queens - all sharing an outing like this was, in protocol terms, just as extraordinary as, say, the Queen's first walkabout in 1970. Evidently, the Sovereign considered that it was time, once again, to rewrite protocol. Here was another vivid example of 'Mon United' in action. Household officials even had a new word for these multi-royal outings – 'jointery'.

This sort of event was calculated to transmit several important messages. First, the plan suggested a blueprint for future royal engagements as the Queen's years advance. It was a reminder, too, that monarchy is a team game. But it also made the point that new arrivals in the Royal Family are not left to fend for themselves. A criticism sometimes levelled at the monarchy by supporters of Diana, Princess of Wales was the notion that the Princess never received any royal training and was just thrown into official duties. Not so, say those who had tried to offer her help and tuition. It has also been suggested that the Duchess of York might have found it easier to adapt to the pressures of royal life if the Duke had not been away for so much of the time with the Royal Navy. A generation on, the Queen clearly wanted to take the latest royal newcomer under her wing, especially at a time when the Duke of Cambridge was on an overseas posting to the Falkland Islands. As the Duke himself has explained earlier in these pages, the Queen does not like to tell her family how they should go about their royal duties. But it is helpful to see how it is done. She prefers to lead by example rather than instruction. Having absorbed so much about royal duty from her grandmother, Queen Mary, it is clear that the Queen sees herself in a similar role.

A similar example of 'jointery' was scheduled for the following week. The Queen and the Duke of Edinburgh were due to start their Jubilee tour of the United Kingdom in Leicester. So they invited the Duchess of Cambridge along to that, too. It might be imagined that the prospect of sharing such an important occasion with the most experienced duo in the business would be a daunting prospect for a 30-year-old newcomer to royal duties. But the Duchess of Cambridge was delighted. To be invited to join the Queen on Day One of her Diamond Jubilee tour was a pretty clear statement of faith in the Duchess's abilities.

The Duchess has impressed her in-laws – with her enthusiasm and her willingness to learn. She is treading carefully but purposefully into her

* Over 150 years, the owners of Fortnum & Mason have held various Royal Warrants as 'Grocers', 'Oilmen', Furnishers', 'Confectioners' and 'Foreign Warehousemen' to members of the Royal Family ranging from the Queen to Princess Christian of Schleswig-Holstein.

new role, mindful of the primary importance of 'supporting the Queen' while also developing her own range of patronages. Rather than spreading her attentions across all the organisations bombarding her with invitations for support, she has chosen to focus on a handful of charities with an emphasis on youth and the arts. They include a children's hospice and the National Portrait Gallery. She also has an easy and affectionate rapport with the Duchess of Cornwall who is not only her stepmother-in-law but who, six years earlier, was the previous new recruit to the royal frontline.

Around the world, public interest in the sixtieth anniversary dwarfed that for the Silver and Golden Jubilees. But there could be no prospect of sending the Queen and Prince Philip, at their stage in life, on a round of international tours. So plans were drawn up to send members of the Royal Family to every one of the Queen's fifteen other realms, with the Prince of Wales taking on most of the major destinations. Prince Harry was to be despatched to Belize, the Bahamas and Jamaica (notwithstanding its recent republican noises). The Duke and Duchess of Cambridge were allotted the smallest and remotest of the lot, tiny Tuvalu, a Pacific archipelago somewhere between Hawaii and Australia. For a nation with the world's third smallest population, five miles of road and only a handful of hotel rooms to accommodate an international media circus, 2012 was likely to be a year to remember.

There was more of this sort of teamwork at home. When the Queen held a pre-Jubilee party at the Palace for the media, there was an unprecedented royal turnout for an industry reception. The royal front rank – the Queen, Prince Philip, the Prince of Wales, the Duchess of Cornwall and the Duke and Duchess of Cambridge – were all there. It was very much a case of 'duty calls' for the Duke who would much rather have been asleep at his Welsh RAF base having been up all the previous night flying emergency operations in the Irish Sea. His helicopter had saved the lives of two Russian sailors after their ship sank in a gale, an act which prompted an instant message of thanks from the Russian ambassador. At the media reception, he was congratulated by one group of guests for doing more for UK-Russian relations in one night than diplomacy had achieved in years. The Duke joked that it had been nothing. Flying a helicopter into a storm in pitch darkness, he said, was far less scary than walking into a room full of 300 journalists.

Much has been said of the pace of royal change in recent years. There would certainly be no easing off during the happy chaos of 2012. Thanks to the Jubilee and the Olympics, much of the Buckingham Palace calendar was torn up. No sooner had the doors been opened to the summer tourists than they would have to be closed again for VIP events. One garden party was cancelled, another moved to May. Minor alterations, perhaps, but decisions involving tens of thousands of people, none the less. At another level, the more that 2012 grew in scale, the more the Queen sought to insert an element of humility and humanity. Her pre-Jubilee Christmas broadcast was a case in point. Amid all the worries about Prince Philip's heart, few noticed that this was one of the most overtly religious broadcasts she has made in her reign. The difference was striking. Ten years earlier, for example, she had merely observed that 'Christmas marks a moment to pause, to reflect and believe in the possibilities of rebirth and renewal.' A decade later, and the Queen's words had the flavour a sermon. She quoted from the Bible, recited from a Christmas carol and concluded: 'It is my prayer that on this Christmas day we might all find room in our lives for the message of the angels and for the love of God through Christ our Lord.' It is hard to argue with the Archbishop of Canterbury's theory, articulated earlier, that the more society turns away from religion, the more the Queen sees it as her role to try to adjust the balance.

To mark Accession Day, she issued a statement harking all the way back to 1947 and that 21st birthday pledge 'dedicating' her life to her people. Now, 65 years later, she declared: 'In this special year, as I dedicate myself anew to your service, I hope that we will all be reminded of the power of togetherness and the convening strength of family friendship and good neighbourliness'. For all the excitement among the media and the public about her pageants and her pop concert, there was no question of which event mattered most to the Monarch herself. In her view, the centrepiece of the entire anniversary would be the service of thanksgiving at St Paul's Cathedral.

Throughout the build-up to the Jubilee, one crucial player barely featured, preferring to remain quietly on the sidelines, ready to offer help when needed. As we have seen, the dynamic between the Government and the Palace has not always been a smooth one during this reign. Sometimes it has been down to events, sometimes to personalities. But it is clear that an easygoing relationship exists between the Queen and the current occupant of Number Ten Downing Street. He is a visceral, uncomplicated monarchist, one who camped outside the Palace in his teens to watch a royal wedding. David Cameron has certainly not regarded it as his duty simply to defend the royal status quo. He has done more royal tinkering than any of the Queen's prime ministers (with no sign of royal unease).

Aside from replacing the 250-year-old Civil List, he also decided to tackle the inflammatory smallprint in the ancient laws governing eligibility for the Throne. Given the euphoria surrounding the 2011 royal wedding and the natural assumption that another royal generation might be on its way fairly soon, Cameron believed the time had come to tackle the two main strands of discrimination affecting royal succession: the law giving brothers precedence over sisters and the laws preventing monarchs from marrying Roman Catholics. The Prime Minister knew that he would need the consent of the other fifteen realms which have the Sovereign as head of state. Since the prime ministers of all of them were due to attend the 2011 Commonwealth summit in Australia, here was the ideal opportunity to discuss the issue and he convened a mini-summit within the summit. In the event, there was unanimity. The Queen, for her part, could make no comment on what remains a political matter but the signals seemed clear enough. Opening the summit, she declared: 'The theme of this year is "Women as Agents of Change". It reminds us of the potential in our societies that is yet to be fully unlocked, and it encourages us to find ways to allow girls and women to play their full part.' All the realms agreed to prepare their parliaments for the necessary amendments. Britain would need to go first and the rest would follow. Of course, in opening up these ancient laws for revision, there would be the risk that some republican-minded legislators might try to unravel the entire system of constitutional monarchy. But then, if the process was a straightforward one, someone would have done it years before.

Public opinion was favourable towards changing the rules. But it was hardly surprising. The Queen has now been on the Throne so long that many people have come to regard the monarchy as a feminine institution. In a world of male-dominated politics, the fact that the Monarch is female has come to accentuate her otherness from the unloved political class. Few, these days, would argue that a king is somehow preferable to a queen. Many more might now argue the opposite.

The Diamond Jubilee is changing the aura around Elizabeth II once again, just as the Golden Jubilee did so a decade before. Back then she was recast as a grandmotherly figure, a national treasure – someone so reliable that she could safely be taken for granted. Now, on her sixtieth anniversary, we view her differently once more. She is more than a national treasure. She is no longer taken for granted. We sense that we are living in the presence of that elusive royal quality – greatness. Our Queen is being elevated right up there alongside Victoria, whose reigning record she will match in 2015. What on earth will it be like when she overtakes her?

# Sources and Bibliography

Sources have been quoted directly when possible, anonymously when not. In addition to all the research for this book, I have drawn on my coverage of royal matters – in newspaper, book and television form – over the last twenty years.

I have gathered fresh material from internal Buckingham Palace records and the London Metropolitan Archives. I have consulted many publications and official records (Hansard, the *London Gazette*, etc.) but I commend the following list of selected works, all of which make an important contribution to our understanding of the modern monarchy.

Allison, Ronald and Riddell, Sarah, *The Royal Encyclopaedia* (Macmillan, 1991)

Blair, Tony, *A Journey* (Hutchinson, 2010)

Boothroyd, Basil, *Philip: An Informal Biography* (Longman, 1971)

Bradford, Sarah, *Elizabeth: A Biography of Her Majesty the Queen* (William Heinemann, 1996)

Brandreth, Gyles, *Philip and Elizabeth: Portrait of a Marriage* (Century, 2004)

Connors, Jane Holley, *The Glittering Thread* (University of Technology, Sydney, 1996)

Dimbleby, Jonathan, *The Prince of Wales: a Biography* (Little, Brown, 1994)

Heald, Tim, *The Duke: A Portrait of Prince Philip* (Hodder & Stoughton, 1991)

Hoey, Brian, *At Home With the Queen* (HarperCollins, 2002)

Jay, Antony, *Elizabeth R* (BBC Books, 1992)

Jebb, Miles, *The Lord-Lieutenants and Their Deputies* (Phillimore, 2007)

Lacey, Robert, *Royal* (Little, Brown, 2002)

Longford, Elizabeth, *Elizabeth R* (Weidenfield & Nicolson, 1983)

Paxman, Jeremy, *On Royalty* (Viking, 2006)

Prochaska, Dr Frank, *Royal Bounty: The Making of a Welfare Monarchy* (Yale, 1995)

Roberts, Andrew, *The Royal House of Windsor* (Kindle, 2011)

Roberts, Andrew, *The House of Windsor* (Weidenfield & Nicolson, 2000)

Rose, Kenneth, *Kings, Queens and Courtiers* (Weidenfield & Nicolson, 1985)

Shawcross, William, *Queen and Country* (BBC Books, 2002)

Shawcross, William, *Queen Elizabeth, The Queen Mother* (Macmillan, 2009)

Turner, Graham, *Elizabeth –The Woman and the Queen* (Macmillan, 2002)

Vickers, Hugo – *Elizabeth, The Queen Mother* (Hutchinson, 2005)

# Index